Fodor's 2015

LAS VE

D0726024

WELCOME TO LAS VEGAS

Las Vegas knows what everyone wants and delivers it in spades. Megaresorts fund their 45-foot bronze lions, half-size Eiffel Towers, and towering glass pyramids with the collective desires and dollars of more than 30 million annual visitors. From a Wolfgang Puck dinner to a Wolfpack-like adventure on the Strip, you're sure to find your perfect indulgence. Swim up to a blackjack table, chow down at a buffet, or chill out in an ultralounge. A Las Vegas vacation disorients and delights; when you're here, you're all-in, and the "real world" seems far out.

TOP REASONS TO GO

★ **Resorts:** Colossal hotels present exotic themes and over-the-top amenities.

★ **Dining:** Few cities in the world can claim a higher concentration of top restaurants.

★ **Gambling:** Novices and pros alike come to Vegas for legendary casino action.

★ **Shopping:** Lavish malls and bargain outlets provide retail options for every budget.

★ **Nightlife:** Master mixologists serve creative cocktails and famous DJs spin nightly.

★ **Shows:** Cirque du Soleil, international singers, and local stars perform day and night.

Fodor's LAS VEGAS 2015

Publisher: Amanda D'Acierno, *Senior Vice President*

Editorial: Arabella Bowen, *Editor in Chief*; Linda Cabasin, *Editorial Director*

Design: Fabrizio La Rocca, *Vice President, Creative Director*; Tina Malaney, *Associate Art Director*; Chie Ushio, *Senior Designer*; Ann McBride, *Production Designer*

Photography: Melanie Marin, *Associate Director of Photography*; Jessica Parkhill and Jennifer Romains, *Researchers*

Maps: Rebecca Baer, *Senior Map Editor*; Mark Stroud (Moon Street Cartography), David Lindroth, *Cartographers*

Production: Linda Schmidt, *Managing Editor*; Evangelos Vasilakis, *Associate Managing Editor*; Angela L. McLean, *Senior Production Manager*

Sales: Jacqueline Lebow, *Sales Director*

Marketing & Publicity: Heather Dalton, *Marketing Director*; Katherine Punia, *Senior Publicist*

Business & Operations: Susan Livingston, *Vice President, Strategic Business Planning*; Sue Daulton, *Vice President, Operations*

Fodors.com: Megan Bell, *Executive Director, Revenue & Business Development*; Yasmin Marinaro, *Senior Director, Marketing & Partnerships*

Copyright © 2015 by Fodor's Travel, a division of Random House LLC

Writers: Dante Drago, Francesca Drago, Heidi Rinella, Susan Stapleton, Matt Villano, Mike Weatherford

Editor: Eric B. Wechter

Production Editor: Jennifer DePrima

ISBN 978-0-8041-4275-5

ISSN 1542–345X

SPECIAL SALES

This book is available at special discounts for bulk purchases for sales promotions or premiums. For more information, e-mail specialmarkets@randomhouse.com

PRINTED IN THE UNITED STATES OF AMERICA

10 9 8 7 6 5 4 3 2 1

CONTENTS

Fodor's Features

MAPS

ABOUT THIS GUIDE

Fodor's Recommendations

Everything in this guide is worth doing—we don't cover what isn't—but exceptional sights, hotels, and restaurants are recognized with additional accolades. Fodor's Choice ★ indicates our top recommendations; and **Best Bets** call attention to notable hotels and restaurants in various categories. Care to nominate a new place? Visit Fodors.com/contact-us.

Trip Costs

We list prices wherever possible to help you budget well. Hotel and restaurant price categories from $ to $$$$ are noted alongside each recommendation. For hotels, we include the lowest cost of a standard double room in high season. For restaurants, we cite the average price of a main course at dinner or, if dinner isn't served, at lunch. For attractions, we always list adult admission fees; discounts are usually available for children, students, and senior citizens.

Hotels

Our local writers vet every hotel to recommend the best overnights in each price category, from budget to expensive. Unless otherwise specified, you can expect private bath, phone, and TV in your room. For expanded hotel reviews, facilities, and deals visit Fodors.com.

Restaurants

Unless we state otherwise, restaurants are open for lunch and dinner daily. We mention dress code only when there's a specific requirement and reservations only when they're essential or not accepted. To make restaurant reservations, visit Fodors.com.

Credit Cards

The hotels and restaurants in this guide typically accept credit cards. If not, we'll say so.

Top Picks
★ Fodor's Choice

Listings
- ✉ Address
- ✉ Branch address
- ☎ Telephone
- 🖷 Fax
- ⊕ Website
- ✉ E-mail
- 🎟 Admission fee
- ⊙ Open/closed times
- Ⓜ Subway
- ✛ Directions or Map coordinates

Hotels & Restaurants
- 🛏 Hotel
- ⤴ Number of rooms
- ⏽⊙⏽ Meal plans
- ✗ Restaurant
- ⬱ Reservations
- 👔 Dress code
- ⊟ No credit cards
- Ⓢ Price

Other
- ⇨ See also
- ☞ Take note
- 🏌 Golf facilities

EXPERIENCE
LAS VEGAS

LAS VEGAS PLANNER

When to Go

Las Vegas doesn't have a high or low season by the standard definition, but you'll find it least crowded between November and January. Hotels are at their fullest July through October. Specific events—New Year's Eve, Super Bowl weekend, spring break, March Madness, major conventions—draw big crowds, so plan accordingly.

It's well known that summer highs often exceed 100°F, but with low humidity and ever-present air-conditioning, you can stay comfortable as long as you limit your time outside to short intervals. Even in the hottest months (late June through September) you can bear the heat, provided you stay hydrated and don't try to walk too far. And with more than 300 days of sunshine a year, the chances of a rain-out (or snow-out in winter) are slim.

On the other hand, nights can be chilly between late fall and early spring, so bring a sweater or windbreaker for your evening strolls beneath the neon-bathed skies.

Getting Around

Bus Travel. Public bus transportation is available via Regional Transportation Commission of Southern Nevada (RTC). Tourist-friendly double-decker buses (dubbed "The Deuce") run up and down the Strip approximately every 15 minutes 24/7—a 24-hour pass is $8. The fare also includes access to the "Strip and Downtown Express" (STX) and all RTC routes, which serve most of the Las Vegas Valley. Stops are near most resort properties, and are marked with signs or shelters. Visitors also can connect to and from McCarran International Airport via a 10-minute ride to the RTC's South Strip Transfer Terminal on Route 109. Buses from there connect to the Deuce, Strip and Downtown Express, and more. For detailed information about how to get around town using public transit, check out the RTC's special website ⊕ www.ridethestrip.com.

Car Travel. If you're exploring the Strip or Downtown, it's best just to park your car (it's free at most casinos) and walk. If you think you'll be operating beyond the Strip during your stay, get a rental car.

Monorail Travel. The Las Vegas Monorail costs $5 per ride (or $12 for a one-day pass) and runs from the MGM Grand to Harrah's before making a jog out to the Convention Center and terminating at the Sahara Avenue Station near the SLS Las Vegas. It's no sightseeing tour; the train runs along the back sides of the resorts. But it's a fast way to travel the Strip, especially on weekends when even the Strip's backstreets are full of traffic. The trains run 7 am–midnight Monday; 7 am–2 am Tuesday–Thursday; and 7 am–3 am weekends. Discounts are available when you purchase tickets online, ⊕ www.lvmonorail.com.

Taxi Travel. Cabs cost $3.30 initial fare plus $2.60 per mile. They are convenient and worthwhile, especially if you're splitting a fare (no more than five people allowed in a cab). Note: Cab rides originating at McCarran International Airport include a $1.80 surcharge.

Safety Tips

Few places in the world have tighter security than the casino resorts lining the Strip or clustered together Downtown (just ask the fabled "Bellagio Bandit" of early 2011). Outside of these areas, Las Vegas has the same urban ills as any other big city, but on the whole, violent crime is extremely rare among tourists, and even scams and theft are no more likely here than at other major vacation destinations. Observe the same common-sense rituals you might in any city: stick to populated, well-lighted streets, don't wear flashy jewelry or wave around expensive handbags, keep valuables out of sight (and don't leave them in unattended cars), and be vigilant about what's going on around you.

Reservations

Many attractions don't require reservations; some places don't even accept them. But any activity with limited availability—a stage show, a restaurant, a guided tour—deserves a call ahead.

Use common sense. Ask yourself these questions:

■ Am I bringing a big party (six or more people) to this event?

■ Is this a weekend event at a popular time of day (6–9 pm for dinner, 10 am–2 pm for golf)?

■ Is the venue very popular?

■ Will I be disappointed if I arrive to find the venue full?

■ Will the people I'm traveling with hold me personally responsible for ruining their morning/day/evening?

If you answered "yes" to one or more of these questions, then you need to make a reservation, or you need someone to call ahead for you. Who would be willing to do such a thing? Your hotel's concierge, that's who. And don't wait until you check in; call the concierge before you leave home to get a jump on the crowd (just be sure to tip him or her accordingly).

Las Vegas Hours

Hoping for sushi at 4 in the morning, or looking to work out at a gym at midnight? Sounds like you're a night owl, and that means Vegas is your kind of town. There are all kinds of businesses that run 24/7 in this city of sin, from supermarkets to bowling alleys. Oh yeah, and they have casinos, too.

Attractions, such as museums and various casino amusements, tend to keep more typical business hours, but you can almost always find something to keep you entertained no matter the hour.

Visitor Centers

The Las Vegas Convention and Visitors Authority (LVCVA) runs a visitor center (☎ 702/892–0711 ⊕ www.lasvegas.com) at 3150 Paradise Road, open weekdays from 8 to 5. Stop by for brochures and advice on what to see and do in town.

The LVCVA also operates the Las Vegas Hotline (☎ 877/847–4858), with operators who are plugged into every major resort and restaurant in the region. Think of them as a concierge service for all of southern Nevada.

WHAT'S WHERE

1 **South Strip.** Between fight nights at the MGM Grand and concerts at Mandalay Bay, the section of Strip between the sprawling CityCenter and the iconic "Welcome to Las Vegas" sign could be considered the entertainment hub of Vegas. Resorts in this area include the Tropicana, Monte Carlo, New York–New York, Excalibur, MGM Grand, and Luxor. Rooms on this side of town generally are within 15 minutes of the airport and are slightly more affordable than their Center and North Strip counterparts. Between Hershey's Chocolate World, M&Ms World, and the Excalibur, this also is one of the most family-friendly parts of the Strip.

2 **Center Strip.** The heart of the Strip is home to CityCenter and iconic resorts such as Bellagio, the Cosmopolitan, the Flamingo, the Mirage, and Caesars Palace. This section, a 20-minute cab ride from the airport, stretches north from CityCenter to the Venetian. Other draws are the High Roller and the sights

and sounds of the LINQ, as well as the mega-boutique shopping inside CityCenter, Planet Hollywood, and Caesars.

3 **North Strip.** The North Strip is defined by luxury. Wynn Las Vegas, Encore, the Venetian, and the Palazzo have some of the swankiest rooms in town. About a 30-minute ride from the airport, the North Strip clubs and restaurants are some of the best in town.

4 **Downtown.** Experience the old Vegas tradition— dice and drinks. With the exception of the Golden Nugget, D Hotel, Downtown Grand, and the Cabana Suites at the El Cortez, rooms range from shabby to mediocre. Nightlife in this neighborhood has made a comeback with the opening of the Smith Center for the Performing Arts, Commonwealth, and others. The Downtown Project, powered by Zappos.com, has brought new life to old City Hall.

5 **Paradise Road.** Parallel to the Strip, a short drive or 15-minute walk east, is the mellower Paradise Road area, which includes the Convention Center. There's less traffic, and there's monorail service along one stretch. Hotel options include the LVH (formerly known as the Las Vegas Hilton), Hard Rock Hotel, and the Platinum.

6 **West Side.** West of the Strip, on the other side of Interstate 15, are the Palms, Rio, and the Orleans. This isn't a glamorous area, and you'll be cabbing or driving to and from the Strip. Chinatown and the city's largest In-N-Out Burger are short rides (or long walks) away.

7 **Airport.** Within a few miles' radius south of McCarran International Airport is the M Resort, South Point, a bunch of budget motels, economical time-shares (i.e., Tahiti Village), a huge shopping mall, and lots of chain restaurants.

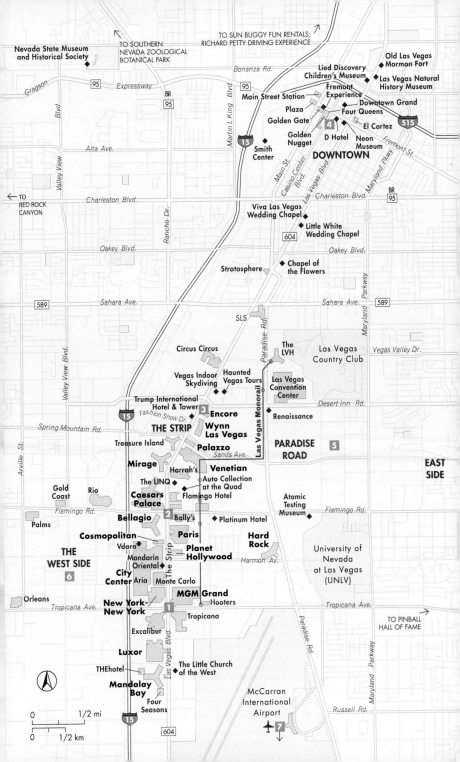

Nevada State Museum
and Historical Society

TO SOUTHERN
NEVADA ZOOLOGICAL
BOTANICAL PARK

TO SUN BUGGY FUN RENTALS;
RICHARD PETTY DRIVING EXPERIENCE

Old Las Vegas
Mormon Fort

Bonanza Rd.

Lied Discovery
Children's Museum

Las Vegas Natural
History Museum

Main Street Station

Fremont
Experience

Downtown Grand

Gragson

95

95

Expressway

BR
95

15

Plaza

Four Queens

Golden Gate

El Cortez

515

Alta Ave.

Smith
Center

Golden
Nugget

4

D Hotel

Neon
Museum

DOWNTOWN

Fremont St.

Valley View

Charleston Blvd.

Rancho Dr.

Main St.

Casino Center Blvd.

Las Vegas Blvd.

Maryland Pkwy.

Charleston Blvd.

BR
95

TO
RED ROCK
CANYON

Viva Las Vegas
Wedding Chapel

Little White
Wedding Chapel

Oakey Blvd.

604

Oakey Blvd.

Stratosphere

Chapel of
the Flowers

Sahara Ave.

589

Sahara Ave.

589

SLS

Circus Circus

The
LVH

Las Vegas
Country Club

Vegas Valley Dr.

Vegas Indoor
Skydiving

Haunted
Vegas Tours

Las Vegas
Convention
Center

Paradise Rd.

Trump International
Hotel & Tower

Fashion Show Dr.

3

Encore

Desert Inn Rd.

15

THE STRIP

Wynn
Las Vegas

Renaissance

Spring Mountain Rd.

Treasure Island

Palazzo

Las Vegas Monorail

Sands Ave.

Mirage

Harrah's

Venetian

PARADISE
ROAD

5

EAST
SIDE

Arville St.

Gold
Coast

Rio

The LINQ

Caesars
Palace

Auto Collection
at the Quad

Flamingo Hotel

Atomic
Testing
Museum

Flamingo Rd.

Bellagio

2

Bally's

Platinum Hotel

Flamingo Rd.

Palms

Cosmopolitan

Paris

Hard
Rock

THE
WEST SIDE

6

Vdara

Mandarin
Oriental

Planet
Hollywood

University of
Nevada
at Las Vegas
(UNLV)

Harmon Av.

City
Center

Aria

Monte Carlo

The Strip

Orleans

Tropicana Ave.

New York-
New York

MGM Grand

Hooters

1

Tropicana

Tropicana Ave.

TO PINBALL
HALL OF FAME

Excalibur

Las Vegas Blvd.

Luxor

The Little Church
of the West

THEhotel

Mandalay
Bay

Four
Seasons

McCarran
International
Airport

Paradise Rd.

Maryland Parkway

Russell Rd.

15

604

7

0   1/2 mi

0   1/2 km

WHAT'S WHERE

8 University District. This neighborhood, part of the East Side, comprises University of Nevada, Las Vegas, and the surrounding blocks. There aren't many noteworthy hotels, but restaurants and museums abound. Also, this area is home to the city's gay-friendly neighborhood, endearingly nicknamed "The Fruit Loop."

9 Boulder Strip. Las Vegas's fastest growing neighborhood comprises development along the Boulder Highway, on the far east and southeast side of the Valley.

10 Lake Las Vegas. This man-made lake southeast of the Strip is a resort area with high-end hotels including Ravella Lake Las Vegas. Check out the shopping at Monte-Lago Village.

11 Summerlin. West of Downtown, this tony neighborhood looks out on the gorgeous Red Rock National Conservation Area. It's home to Red Rock Casino Resort & Spa and the JW Marriott Las Vegas Resort & Spa.

12 Henderson. Southeast of the Strip but west of Lake Las Vegas, this area's perhaps the most stereotypically "suburban" in the Valley. Still, its outlets are popular, and locals come from miles around to gamble at Green Valley Ranch Resort & Spa Casino.

13 North Side. This area, between Summerlin and Nellis Air Force Base (and north of Downtown), encompasses the neighborhood known on maps as North Las Vegas. It's home to the Las Vegas Motor Speedway, the Aliante Station Casino & Hotel, and a host of up-and-coming restaurants.

14 Outskirts. This catchall area includes resorts and eateries to the distant south, far east, and northeast of the greater Las Vegas metropolitan area.

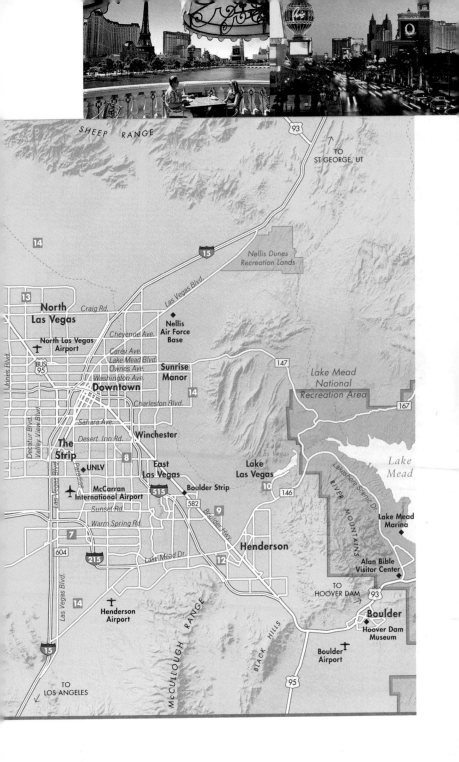

LAS VEGAS TOP ATTRACTIONS

Spectacular Spectaculars

(A) Will it be an acrobatic Cirque du Soleil extravaganza? A standing act by a musical legend? An afternoon comedy show, or Broadway-lite (90-minute cut-downs of the original productions from the Great White Way)? A classic feather revue, or a spooky hypnotist show? Maybe you're just in the mood for a plain old lounge show where the microphones squeal, the singer is slightly out of tune, and a great time is all but guaranteed. It's practically against the law to be bored in Vegas.

World-Class Restaurants

(B) The $2.95 lobster dinner has gone into hiding, but those cheap chow deals of yesteryear are hardly missed; Las Vegas has become a foodie's dream destination. Every major resort offers at least half a dozen fine-dining options in addition to the ubiquitous snack bars and fast-food places. If you stayed in Vegas for a year, you'd never have to eat at the same place twice.

Rolling the Dice

(C) Never mind those buffets, swimming pools, spas, traffic jams, dancing girls (and boys, and water), wedding chapels, and circus acts. It's Vegas, baby, and you're here to roll the bones and go all in.

Natural Wonders

(D) Consider heading out of the casino and taking in one of the many natural wonderlands surrounding Las Vegas. Explore Lake Mead or Red Rock Canyon. During the winter months, hit the ski slopes at Mt. Charleston. There's more to this area than neon.

The High Roller

(E) At 550 feet tall and 520 feet in diameter, this Observation Wheel at the back of the LINQ, off the Center Strip, is the largest in the world—larger than the Singapore Flyer and the London Eye. Full rotations from the swanky wheelhouse

take about 30 minutes. The views are unbeatable.

Shopping at Crystals, CityCenter

(F) This chichi shopping and dining mall designed by Daniel Libeskind has taken the retail and culinary scene in Vegas to an even higher level. In addition to stellar restaurants like Mastro's Ocean Club and Social House, this austere space contains dozens of fine stores, including Gucci, Fendi, and Tom Ford, as well as dozens of pieces of public art.

Legendary Nightlife

Sky-high bars with Valley-wide views. Thumping bass lines and flashing lights. Semi-clothed Adonises and Venuses swinging overhead. Whether you're looking for a wild dance club or a sophisticated lounge scene, Vegas comes alive after dark. So dress to the nines, grab a kamikaze shot, and join the 24-hour party.

Over-the-Top Pools

(G) The tanning booth is now a ubiquitous feature in the Anytown strip mall, but it still can't compare with the old-fashioned poolside sun soak—especially if that soak is in Las Vegas, land of toned bodies, cocktails, cabanas, Euro-style bathing, man-made beaches, and swim-up blackjack.

Hoover Dam and Lake Mead

(H) If you have time for just one trip outside of town, make it to this Depression-era concrete monstrosity, considered one of the seven wonders of the industrial world. You'll understand why when you tour the interior and see the massive turbines that make the lights go on in Pasadena. Combine the trip with a visit to nearby Lake Mead, where you'll enjoy boating, waterskiing, and other watery activities.

FREE THINGS TO DO

Yes, Vegas brims with cash, glitz, and glamour, but that doesn't mean you can't find freebies (or cheapies).

Experience Fremont Street. The Downtown casinos' answer to the spectacle of the Strip is the Fremont Street Experience, played out on a 90-foot-high arced canopy that covers the entire street. Every hour between sunset and midnight it comes alive with an integrated video, graphics, and music show. Several different programs run each night, and contribute to a festive outside-in communal atmosphere that contrasts with the Strip's every-man-for-himself ethic.

Watch a Free Show. You can easily spend $100 or more on seats at a typical Vegas concert or big-name production, but several casinos offer fabulous, eye-catching extravaganzas that won't cost you a penny. There's the erupting volcano at the Mirage, the graceful Fountains of Bellagio, and the Wildlife Habitat (with a flamboyance of flamingoes!) at the Flamingo Las Vegas. Of course, people-watching is a free show of a different kind, too.

See the New Old Downtown. The Downtown casinos don't attempt to compete with the opulence of the Strip, but Fremont and connecting streets have their own charm. PICNIC, the new day-use pool area at the Downtown Grand, offers a grassy knoll for sunbathing or, as the name suggests, picnicking. Also, sip handcrafted cocktails at newer lounges, such as Commonwealth and the Lady Silvia. Stroll through history as you tour old signs at the Neon Museum and check out the art deco–inspired Smith Center for the Performing Arts.

Preview a TV Show. Vegas is home to several preview studios, where you're asked to watch and offer feedback on TV shows. Some studios offer a small cash stipend for your time; for others you'll have to be satisfied with free refreshments, coupons, and the thanks of a grateful nation. We like **CBS Television City research center** (⊠ *3799 Las Vegas Blvd. S, South Strip* ☎ *702/891–5752* ⊙ *Daily 10–8*) at the MGM Grand. ⚠ **No kids under 10.**

Cruise the Strip. You haven't done Vegas until you've been caught—either intentionally or unwittingly—in the slow-mo weekend-night crawl of traffic down the Strip. You can handle the experience like a been-there local, or you can play the delighted tourist: relaxed, windows down, ready to engage in silly banter with the carload of players in the convertible one lane over. We suggest the latter, at least once. Just be mindful of all the pedestrians, who can crowd the crosswalks and are just as dazed as you are by the cacophony.

Seek History. Don't miss out on the opportunity to explore bits and pieces of bygone days. Downtown, drop by **The Mob Museum** (⊠ *300 E. Stewart Ave., Downtown* ⊕ *www.themobmuseum.org*), which examines the city's ties to the mafia, and resides in the formal federal courthouse and U.S. Post Office. Also check out the Neon Museum (⊠ *770 Las Vegas Blvd. N, Downtown* ⊕ *www.neonmuseum. org*), which curates a lot full of neon signs that fronted casinos of yesteryear. Beyond Downtown, Vegas is full of well-preserved examples of fine architecture, midcentury—we like the **Morelli House**—and modern, like the Frank Gehry–designed **Cleveland Center.** Wander through the older hotels on the Strip and Downtown that will, eventually and inevitably, be torn down to make way for new construction. You'll be able to say you were there.

HISTORY, VEGAS-STYLE

by Matt Vilano

Over the last few years, we've all heard the brilliant marketing slogan "What happens in Vegas stays in Vegas." But a whole lot has happened in Vegas in the last few hundred years, and most of the stories *have* made it into the history books.

Archaeologists believe civilization in the area now known as Sin City stretches back almost 2,000 years. This once lush area was home to numerous Native American tribes, including the Kawaiisu, Kitenamuk, and Serrano. In the 1820s, Spaniards traveling from Mexico to northern California on the Old Spanish Trail named the area "Las Vegas" (meaning "The Meadows"). When the area became part of the U.S. in 1855, the name stuck.

The railroad arrived in 1905, and, over the next decades, Las Vegas grew from a rail hub to a leisure destination. The Hoover Dam, built in the 1930s, played a large part in development, but gam-

bling put the city on the map. Since 1940, Las Vegas has seen casinos rise, fall, and rise again—bigger than before. These casinos have launched some of the greatest names in show business, including Frank Sinatra, Dean Martin, and Wayne Newton.

Today, Las Vegas and its environs (population: 2 million) shelter those who make the casinos whir. And nothing here sits for long; the town becomes hipper, bolder, and more sophisticated every year. The city is now home to 18 of the 21 largest hotels in the world. From a place nicknamed Sin City, you'd expect nothing less.

TIMELINE

| 1829: water-rich Las Vegas valley (the Meadow) gets its name. | 1855: Mormons build fort. | 1864: Nevada becomes 36th state. | 1885: State Land attracts farmers. |

Precolonial Era   1800   1850   1900

COL. FREMONT

(left) Detail from poster for John C. Fremont 1856; (above) Las Vegas circa 1895; (right) construction workers working Hoover Dam spillway between 1936 and 1946.

Native Occupation

1500s–1800s

Cultural artifacts indicate that human settlers including the Kawaiisu, Kitanemuk, Serrano, Koso, and Chemehuevi occupied the area as far back as the 100 or 200 A.D. Archaeologists have said the land would have been hospitable—the region's artesian wells would have provided enough water to support small communities, and skeletal remains indicate wildlife was prevalent. It also stands to reason that many of the earliest inhabitants took advantage of the lush meadows after which the region ultimately was named; excavated pieces of detailed weavings and basketry support these theories.

Early Settlers

1820s–90s

Spaniards settled the area in the 1820s, but John Fremont, of the U.S. Army Corps of Engineers, quickly followed on a scouting mission in 1844. After annexation, in 1855, Brigham Young sent a group of missionaries to the Las Vegas Valley to convert a number of modern Native-American groups, including the Anasazi. The missionaries built a fort that served as a stopover for travelers along the "Mormon Corridor" between Salt Lake City and a thriving colony in San Bernardino, California. Dissension among leaders prompted the Mormons to abandon Las Vegas by the 1860s, leaving only a handful of settlers behind.

Industrialization Arrives

1890s–1920s

Everything in Las Vegas changed in the 1900s. Just after the turn of the century, local leaders diverted the spring and resulting creek into the town's water system. The spring dried up and the once-vibrant meadows turned into desert. Then, in 1905, the transcontinental railroad came through on its inexorable push toward the Pacific. The city also began to serve as a staging point for all the area mines; mining companies would shuttle their goods from the mountains into Las Vegas, then onto the trains and out to the rest of the country. With the proliferation of railroads, however, this boom was short-lived.

| 1905: Las Vegas is founded as a city. | 1911: Divorce laws are liberalized in Nevada | 1931: construction begins at Hoover Dam sight. Population booms. Gambling is legalized. | 1941: El Rancho Vegas, first hotel and casino on the Strip. | 1951: First Atomic Bomb is detonated north of Las Vegas. |

1920   **1940**   **1960**

1

IN FOCUS HISTORY, VEGAS-STYLE

(above) The Flamingo Hotel; (below) Bugsy Siegel; (top right) The Rat Pack.

1930s

Early Casinos

— Las Vegans knew they needed something to distinguish their town from the other towns along the rails that crisscrossed the United States. They found it in gambling. The Nevada State Legislature repealed the ban in 1931, opening the proverbial floodgates for a new era and a new economy. Just weeks after the ban was lifted, the now-defunct Pair-O-Dice opened on Highway 91, the stretch of road that would later become known as the Las Vegas Strip. The city celebrated another newcomer—dedicating the Boulder (now Hoover) Dam on the Colorado River in 1935.

1940s–50s

Bugsy Takes Charge

No person had more of an impact on Las Vegas's gambling industry than gangster Ben "Bugsy" Siegel. The Brooklyn, New York native aimed to build and run the classiest resort-casino in the world, recruiting mob investors to back him. The result was the Flamingo Hotel, which opened (millions of dollars over budget) in 1946. Though the hotel was met with historic fanfare, it initially flopped, making Siegel's partners unhappy and suspicious of embezzlement. Within six months, Siegel was "rubbed out," but the Flamingo lived on—a monument to the man who changed Vegas forever.

1950s–60s

Rat Pack Era

Frank Sinatra, Dean Martin, Sammy Davis, Jr., Peter Lawford, and Joey Bishop were a reckless bunch; upon seeing them together, actress Lauren Bacall said, "You look like a goddamn rat pack." The name stuck. The quintet appeared in a number of movies—who can forget the original *Ocean's Eleven?*—and performed live in Las Vegas. Their popularity helped Sin City grow into an entertainment destination. They also played an important role in desegregation—the gang refused to play in establishments that wouldn't give full service to African-American entertainers, forcing many hotels to abandon their racist policies.

TIMELINE

| 1966: Howard Hughes arrives in Las Vegas. | 1971: Hunter S. Thompson writes *Fear and Loathing in Las Vegas.* | 1970s: Elvis Presley and Liberace are Las Vegas's top performers. | 1980: MGM Grand catches fire. It's the worst disaster in the city's history. | 1989: Steve Wynn opens The Mirage |

1970   **1980**   **1990**

(left) Howard Hughes; (center top) Frank Rosenthal interviewing Frank Sinatra; (center bottom) Elvis Presley; (top) Liberace; (right top) Steve Wynn; (right bottom) Siegfried and Roy; (right) Bellagio's dancing fountains.

A Maverick Swoops in

1960s

Multimillionaire Howard Hughes arrived in Vegas in 1966 and began buying up hotels: Desert Inn, Castaways, New Frontier, Landmark Hotel and Casino, Sands, and Silver Slipper, to name a few. He also invested in land—then mostly desert—that today comprises most of the planned-residential and commercial community of Summerlin. Hughes also wielded enormous political and economic influence in Nevada and nearly single-handedly derailed the U.S. Army's plan to test nuclear weapons nearby. His failure in this matter led to a self-imposed exile in Nicaragua until his death in 1976.

Mob Era

1960s–80s

Elvis Presley made his comeback in 1969 at The International (now the Las Vegas Hilton) and played there regularly until the middle of the next decade. In the same era, East Coast mobsters tightened their grip on casinos, prompting a federal crackdown and forcing some to return to the east when gambling was legalized in Atlantic City, New Jersey, in 1976. Frank "Lefty" Rosenthal, largely seen as the inventor of the modern sports book, narrowly survived a car bomb in 1982. Others, such as Tony "The Ant" Spilotro, were not as lucky—Spilotro and his brother, another casino gangster, were beaten and strangled to death in 1986 and buried in a cornfield in Indiana.

Era of Reinvention

Late 1980s–90s

The years immediately following the mob crackdown weren't pretty. The nation was in a recession, and tourism was down. Large fires at major resorts such as MGM Grand, Aladdin, and Monte Carlo killed visitors and devastated the city's economy and image. Gradually, Las Vegas recovered. Big corporations purchased hotels off the scrap heap, and several properties underwent major renovations. With the help of clever marketing campaigns, properties began attracting tourists back to experience the "new" Vegas. In 1989, Steve Wynn opened the city's first new casino in 16 years—the Mirage—and triggered a building boom that persists today.

| 1993: Work begins in Fremont Street Experience. | 1996: Las Vegas Motor Speedway opens. | 2001: Green Valley Ranch Resort and Spa opens. | 2005: The Wynn opens; Las Vegas celebrates its centennial. | 2010: The new Las Vegas CityCenter is completed. |

2000   2010   BEYOND   1

IN FOCUS HISTORY, VEGAS-STYLE

1990s Age of the Mega-Hotel

— In all, more than a dozen new mega-resorts opened in the 1990s. The Mirage, which opened in 1989, started the domino effect of new hotels up and down the Strip. It was followed by the Rio and Excalibur in 1990; Luxor and Treasure Island (now TI) in 1993; the Hard Rock Hotel in 1995; the Stratosphere and the Monte Carlo in 1996; Bellagio in 1998; and Mandalay Bay, the Venetian and Paris Hotel & Casino in 1999. These, coupled with the $72-million, 1,100-acre Las Vegas Motor Speedway, which took the city from exclusively gambling destination to a NASCAR destination, made the city incredibly visitor-friendly. Tourists obliged, arriving in record numbers.

2000s Variations on a Theme

— Never fans of complacency, Vegas hoteliers have continued to innovate. Steve Wynn, of Mirage and Bellagio fame, opened arguably the city's most exquisite resort, Wynn Las Vegas, in 2005. Sheldon Adelson, CEO of Sands Corporation, countered by opening The Palazzo next door to the Venetian, giving the two properties 7,000 rooms combined. Off the strip, multimillion dollar mega-resorts such as the Palms and Red Rock offered more exclusive, intimate experiences. Then, toward the end of this decade, Vegas experienced a new trend: hotels without casinos of any kind, outfitted for nothing but complete relaxation.

2015 & Beyond What's Next

The Park is an open-air plaza connecting New York–New York with Monte Carlo. Parts of the plaza opened during the summer of 2014. Eventually, by 2016, **The Park** will run all the way back to an 18,000-seat arena that will rise from parking lots that currently sit behind the two properties.

On the distant horizon is **Echelon Place**, a mega-project from Boyd Gaming that was postponed in 2008 due to lack of funds. It was purchased in 2013 by Singapore-based Genting, who plans to resume construction and open a new property named **Resorts World Las Vegas** on the site across from Wynn.

LAS VEGAS GOLF

With an average of 315 days of sunshine a year and year-round access, Las Vegas's top sport is golf. The peak season is any nonsummer month; only mad dogs and Englishmen are out in the noonday summer sun. However, most of the courses in Las Vegas offer reduced greens fees during the summer months, sometimes as much as 50% to 70% lower than peak-season fees. If you want to play on a weekend, call before you get into town, as the 8 to 11 am time slots fill up quickly. Starting times for same-day play are possible (especially during the week), but if you're picky about when and where you play, plan ahead. Some of the big Strip resorts have a dedicated golf concierge who can advise you on a course that fits your tastes. In some cases, these people can get you access to private courses.

Best Courses

Bali Hai Golf Club. This island-theme course is dotted with palm trees, volcanic outcroppings, and small lagoons. The entrance is a mere 10-minute walk from Mandalay Bay. The clubhouse includes a pro shop and restaurant. Online specials are available for as low as $125. ⊠ *5160 Las Vegas Blvd. S, South Strip* ☎ *888/427–6678, 702/450–8191* ⊕ *www.balihaigolfclub.com* ✉ *From $199 for nonresidents* ⚑ *18 holes, 7002 yards, par 71.*

★ Fodor's Choice

Bear's Best Las Vegas. Jack Nicklaus created this course by placing replicas of his 18 favorite holes (from the 270 courses he's designed worldwide) into a single course. There's also a short course that measures just over 3,000 yards. If all of these on-greens options don't make you reach for your ugly pants, then consider that the clubhouse has enough Nicklaus memorabilia to fill a small museum. A huge dining area doubles as a banquet hall, and an even bigger pavilion provides beautiful views of the mountains and the Strip. ⊠ *11111 W. Flamingo Rd., Summerlin* ☎ *702/804–8500* ⊕ *www.clubcorp.com/Clubs/Bear-s-Best-Las-Vegas* ✉ *From $149 for nonresidents* ⚑ *18 holes, 7194 yards, par 72.*

Las Vegas National Golf Club. Built in 1961, this historic course has played host to Vegas royalty and golf's superstars over the years. Tiger shot 70 on the final round of his first PGA Tour win during the 1996 Las Vegas Invitational, and Mickey Wright won two of her four LPGA Championships here. You'll find five difficult par-3s and a killer 550-yard par-5 at the 18th. The course is about a $15 cab ride from most properties on the Strip. ⊠ *1911 E. Desert Inn Rd., East Side* ☎ *702/734–1796, 866/695–1961* ⊕ *www.lasvegasnational.com* ✉ *$39–$99 for nonresidents* ⚑ *18 holes, 6815 yards, par 71.*

Las Vegas Paiute Golf Resort. You can play three Pete Dye–designed courses here: Wolf, Snow Mountain, and Sun Mountain. Snow Mountain fits most skill levels and has been ranked by *Golf Digest* as Las Vegas's best public-access course. Sun Mountain is a player-friendly course but its difficult par-4s make it marginally more challenging than Snow. Six of those holes measure longer than 400 yards, but the best is the fourth hole, which is 206 yards over water. Wolf, with its island hole at No. 15, is the toughest of the three and arguably the most difficult in the area. If you want to play last-minute, all courses offer great twilight 9-hole rates. ⊠ *10325 Nu-Wav Kaiv Blvd., Summerlin* ☎ *702/658–1400, 800/711–2833* ⊕ *www.lvpaiutegolf.com* ✉ *$119–$189*

for nonresidents ⛳. *Snow Mountain: 18 holes, 7165 yards, par 72; Sun Mountain: 18 holes, 7112 yards, par 72; Wolf: 18 holes, 7604 yards, par 72.*

Rhodes Ranch Golf Club. One of the better courses in the Las Vegas Valley, the Rhodes Ranch course was designed by renowned architect Ted Robinson to provide enough challenges for any skill level—numerous water hazards, difficult bunkers, and less-than-even fairways. Twilight rates can drop to $55 or lower. ⊠ *20 Rhodes Ranch Pkwy., West Side* ☎ *702/740–4114, 888/311–8337* ⊕ *www.rhodesranchgolf.com* ⊠ *$79–$99 for nonresidents* ⛳. *18 holes, 6909 yards, par 72.*

Royal Links Golf Club. Similar in concept to Bear's Best, Royal Links is a greatest-hits course, replicating popular holes from 11 courses in the British Open rotation. You can play the Road Hole from the famed St. Andrews, and the Postage Stamp from Royal Troon. If you're feeling lonely, sign up to golf with one of the course's "Parmates," a group composed of buxom beauties who are masters with the clubs. Also on-site is Stymie's Pub. Online specials can be as low as $95. ⊠ *5995 E. Vegas Valley Dr., East Side* ☎ *702/450–8181, 888/427–6678* ⊕ *www.royalinksgolfclub.com* ⊠ *$171–$219 for nonresidents* ⛳. *18 holes, 7029 yards, par 72.*

SouthShore Golf Club. Technically, the Jack Nicklaus–designed Signature Course at this Lake Las Vegas golf club is members-only, but a relatively new change in the bylaws allows guests at the Hilton Lake Las Vegas Resort & Spa and the Westin Lake Las Vegas Resort & Spa play with limited access. Hard-core enthusiasts say the layout is challenging; there are nearly 90 bunkers in all. Still, with views of Lake Las Vegas and the surrounding River Mountains, the experience is second to few others in the Las Vegas Valley. ⊠ *100 Strada di Circolo, Lake Las Vegas, Henderson* ☎ *702/856–8402* ⊕ *www.pacificlinks.com/southshore* ⊠ *$150–$175 for nonmembers* ⛳. *18 holes, 6917 yards, par 71.*

TPC Las Vegas. The PGA manages this championship layout next to the JW Marriott. The course features a number of elevation changes, steep ravines, and a lake. It's also one of the venues for the Las Vegas Invitational, a stop on the PGA Tour. ⊠ *9851 Canyon Run Dr., Summerlin* ☎ *702/256–2500, 888/321–5725* ⊕ *www.tpc.com/tpc-las-vegas* ⊠ *$150–$250 for nonresidents* ⛳. *18 holes, 7081 yards, par-71.*

Wynn Golf Course. Tom Fazio's lavish urban golf course is built on the site of the old Desert Inn Golf Course, but bares little resemblance to the original. You're up against significant elevation changes and water hazards are in the mix on 11 of the 18 holes. The 37-foot Wynn waterfall on the 18th hole is a pleasant backdrop for the end of the course. On-site pro shop has clubs and shoes available for rental at all times. Open to hotel guests only. ⊠ *Wynn Las Vegas, 3131 Las Vegas Blvd. S, North Strip* ☎ *702/770–7000, 888/320–7123* ⊕ *www.wynnlasvegas.com* ⊠ *$500* ⛳. *18 holes, 7042 yards, par 70.*

TIE THE KNOT

Vegas wedding chapels: They're flowers and neon and love ever after (or at least until tomorrow's hangover). They're also mighty quick, once you get that marriage license.

Chapel of the Flowers. Enjoy a brief facsimile of a traditional ceremony at this venue, designed to be a turnkey wedding operation, with three chapels and an outdoor garden, as well as on-site flower shop, photography studio, and wedding coordinators. Sure, it's still Las Vegas, so an Elvis impersonator is available for all ceremonies. ⊠ *1717 Las Vegas Blvd. S, North Strip* ☎ *800/843–2410, 702/735–4331* ⊕ *www.littlechapel.com.*

Clark County Marriage License Bureau. A no-wait marriage certificate can be yours if you bring $60 cash ($65.15 credit card), identification (prison IDs are accepted on a case-by-case basis), and your beloved to the Clark County Marriage License Bureau. ⊠ *201 E. Clark Ave., Downtown* ☎ *702/671–0600* ⊕ *www.clarkcountynv.gov* ☉ *Daily 8 am–midnight.*

Little Church of the West. This cedar-and-redwood chapel on the South Strip is one of the city's most famous. The kitsch is kept under control, and the setting borders on picturesque (it's even listed on the National Register of Historic Places—ah, Vegas). Since it opened in 1942, the church has been the site of more celebrity marriages than any other chapel in the world. ⊠ *4617 Las Vegas Blvd. S, South Strip* ☎ *702/739–7971, 800/821–2452* ⊕ *www.littlechurchlv.com.*

A Little White Wedding Chapel. The list of ALWWC alums is impressive: Demi Moore and Bruce Willis, Paul Newman and Joann Woodward, Michael Jordan, Britney Spears, and Frank Sinatra. Patty Duke liked it so much, she got married here twice. Try the Hawaiian theme, where the minister plays a ukulele and blows into a conch shell to close out the ceremony. Or, get hitched in a pink Cadillac while an Elvis impersonator croons. One of the five chapels is a drive-thru, for the ultimate in shotgun weddings. ⊠ *1301 Las Vegas Blvd. S, North Strip* ☎ *800/545–8111, 702/382–5943* ⊕ *www.alittlewhitechapel.com.*

Office of Civil Marriages. At the Office of Civil Marriages a commissioner will do the deed for $75 cash ($81 credit). The catch: You must call ahead to make an appointment. Exact change and at least one witness are required. ⊠ *330 S. 3rd St., Downtown* ☎ *702/671–0577* ⊕ *www.clarkcountynv.gov* ☉ *Sun.–Thurs. 2–6 pm, Fri. 10–9, Sat. 12:30–9.*

Viva Las Vegas Wedding Chapel. An endless variety of wedding themes and add-on shtick is available, ranging from elegant to casual to camp; say your vows in the presence of Elvis, the Blues Brothers, or Liberace. The main chapel features a live webcam on its website that lets you track the nuptials in real time. Of the five other chapels, one has a Doo-Wop Diner theme. ⊠ *1205 Las Vegas Blvd. S, North Strip* ☎ *702/384–0771, 800/574–4450* ⊕ *www.vivalasvegasweddings.com.*

EXPLORING
LAS VEGAS

Updated by
Matt Villano

Easter Island, Machu Picchu, and other celebrated wonders of the world are certainly impressive. But Las Vegas . . . Las Vegas is a land where jungles thrive and fountains dance in the middle of the desert. It's a place that unites medieval England and ancient Egypt with modern-day Venice, Paris, and New York. It's a never-ending source of irony and improbability where you can turn a chip and a chair into a million dollars, or celebrate your shotgun wedding by shooting machine guns. Where else does such a wonderland exist? Nowhere. But. Vegas.

The smallish city (geographically) is larger than life, with a collective energy (and excess) that somehow feels intimate. Maybe it's the agreeable chimes and intermittent cheers from the casino floor that fade to tranquillity when you enter a sumptuous spa. Maybe it's the fish flown in nightly from the Mediterranean that lands on your plate. For each individual, Vegas is an equation where you + more = more of you: more chances to explore aspects of your personality that may be confined by the routine of daily life. It's for this reason alone that the "what happens here stays here" phenomenon is shared by so many visitors.

The city itself has a number of different faces. For a dose of history, head Downtown and explore everything from old casinos to a museum that pays homage to the mobsters who built them. For fun, glitz, and glamour, head to the Strip, which itself has three distinct sections (south, center, north). For outdoor adventure, head west and south, either to the Spring Mountains beyond Summerlin or out to Hoover Dam and Lake Mead—man-made accomplishments of an entirely different sort. Along the way, you can pamper yourself at world-class spas and restaurants, engage in retail therapy at some of the best shopping spots in the world, dance the night away at rocking nightclubs, or—of course—court Lady Luck long enough to strike it rich. With the right itinerary, Vegas even can work for families with young kids.

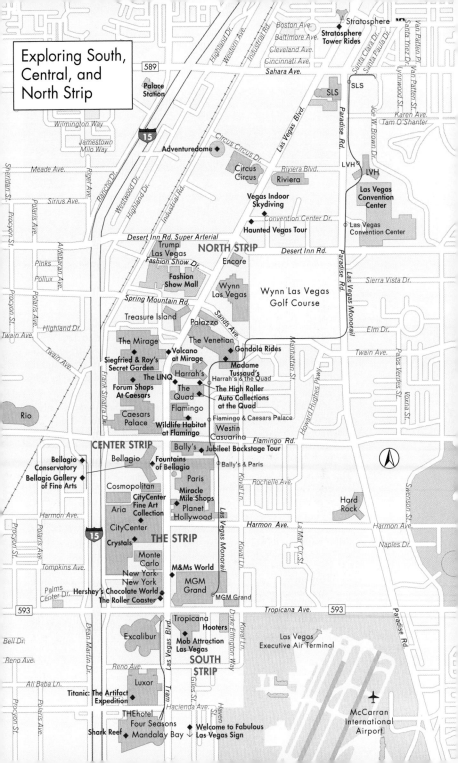

SOUTH STRIP

Dining
★★★★

Sightseeing
★★★★

Shopping
★★★

Nightlife
★★★

Fun and fantasy collide on the South Strip. Whether it's a man-made beach lagoon, a glass pyramid, a medieval castle, or an Oz-like complex, imagination in these parts most certainly runs wild.

A first-time tour should start at the iconic "Welcome to Las Vegas" sign, just west of the runways at McCarran International Airport. From there, swing through the shark habitat at Mandalay Bay, check out the "Sphinx" in front of Luxor, and the circa-1950 stained-glass skylights inside the renovated Tropicana Las Vegas.

The jousting in the Tournament of Kings at Excalibur is topped only by the gravity-defying loops of the roller coaster at New York–New York. Then, of course, there's the MGM Grand—still the largest hotel in the world. And Monte Carlo, with fountains and marble staircases that evoke the style and panache of the European city by the same name.

Dig deeper and you start to appreciate the details of the South Strip resorts. The palm-frond fans inside Mandalay Bay. The South Beach white of the Tropicana. Even New Yorkers say the West Village–inspired food court at New York–New York feels like home. And the giant bronze lion in front of MGM Grand is a throwback to the hotel's affiliation with the movie company, but it's also a veiled reference to the *Wizard of Oz,* which inspired the building's green hue.

Noncasino destinations are worth visiting, too. M&Ms World satisfies chocolate desires of every age. Town Square, an open-air mall, is a great place to spend the day to escape the casino vibe and spend a day shopping. Compared to the rest of the Strip, which is more modern and, at times, stuffy, the South Strip is whimsical and just plain neat. It's also a perfect introduction to the grandeur, luxury, and history quite literally down the road.

GETTING HERE AND AROUND

Everything on the South Strip is relatively close. Most resorts are within a 10- or 15-minute cab ride from the airport, and all are accessible by public transportation. A monorail connects Mandalay Bay with the Luxor and Excalibur. What's more, pedestrian bridges across Las Vegas Boulevard link Excalibur to Tropicana and New York–New York to MGM Grand (other bridges across Tropicana Avenue link Excalibur to New York–New York and the Tropicana to MGM Grand). If it's not July or August, a walking tour of this area is a fun activity (⇨ *see feature boxes*). From ground level, the heft of casinos never gets old.

TAXI!

You're never far from a taxi, but it's downright impossible to hail a cab on the Strip. Hotels welcome you to their taxi stand lines in the hope that you'll come back and play in their casinos.

The Las Vegas Monorail begins (or ends) on this part of the Strip at the MGM Grand station. The RTC (Regional Transportation Commission of Southern Nevada) services this part of the Strip with public buses and double-deckers (⇨ *see also Bus Travel in Travel Smart*).

TOP ATTRACTIONS

FAMILY

Fodor's Choice

★

The Roller Coaster. There are two reasons to ride the Coney Island–style New York–New York roller coaster (aka Manhattan Express): first, with a 144-foot dive and a 360-degree somersault, it's a real scream; and second, it whisks you around the amazing replica of the New York City skyline, giving you fabulous views of the Statue of Liberty, Chrysler building, and, at night, the Las Vegas lights—you climb to peak heights around 200 feet above the Strip. Get ready to go 67 mph over a dizzying succession of high-banked turns and camelback hills, twirl through a "heartline twist" (like a jet doing a barrel roll), and finally rocket along a 540-degree spiral before pulling back into the station. ⊠ *New York–New York, 3790 Las Vegas Blvd. S, South Strip* ☎ *800/689–1797, 702/740–6969* ⊕ *www.newyorknewyork.com/attractions* ⊠ *$14; all day-ride pass $25* ☉ *Sun.–Thurs. 11–11, Fri. and Sat. 10:30 am–midnight, weather permitting.*

FAMILY

Shark Reef. Your journey through Mandalay Bay's long-running Shark Reef attraction begins in the mysterious realm of deep water at the ruins of an old Aztec temple. It's tropical and humid for us bipeds, but quite comfy for the golden crocodiles, endangered green sea turtles, and water monitors. Descend through two glass tunnels, which lead you deeper and deeper under the sea (or about 1.6 million gallons of water), where exotic tropical fish and other sea creatures swim all around you. The tour saves the best for last—from the recesses of a sunken galleon, sharks swim below, above, and around the skeleton ship. Elsewhere you'll find a petting zoo for marine life, a Komodo dragon exhibit, and a special jellyfish habitat. If you plan to visit other MGM Resorts attractions you can save with their three-for-$57 promotion. ⊠ *Mandalay Bay, 3950 Las Vegas Blvd. S, South Strip* ☎ *702/632–4555* ⊕ *www.sharkreef.com* ⊠ *$18 adults, $12 kids 5–12* ☉ *Fri. and Sat. 10–10, Sun.–Thurs. 10–8 pm.*

GREAT WALKS: SOUTH STRIP

Mummies to Big Apple: Inside Luxor's pyramid, follow the enclosed walkways to Excalibur. From there, it's an easy walk across a pedestrian bridge to New York–New York's new gaming floor. Total time: 15 minutes.

All about M's: Inside the MGM Grand, resort guests can explore the grounds—both the MGM Grand and the area surrounding the Signature towers. Then you can join the masses and hit the Strip heading north toward M&Ms World, the town's biggest candy store. Total time: 30–40 minutes.

See an Icon: Head south on Las Vegas Boulevard from Mandalay Bay and you'll spot the famous "Welcome to Las Vegas" sign. If you want to take a picture directly under the sign, be careful crossing the street; the sign sits in the center median and there's no crosswalk. Total time from Mandalay and back: 40 minutes.

WORTH NOTING

Hershey's Chocolate World. Chocoholics rejoiced in spring 2014 when the two-story, West Coast flagship of Hershey's Chocolate opened as part of the streetscape between the New York–New York and Monte Carlo. The attraction includes a retail store, a café, and a tester area where visitors can sample some of Hershey's newest confections. ✉ *3790 Las Vegas Blvd. S, South Strip* ☎ *702/740–6969* ⊕ *www.newyorknewyork. com.*

FAMILY **Titanic: The Artifact Exhibition.** Travel down to the bottom of the North Atlantic where the "ship of dreams" rests after grazing an iceberg in 1912. The 25,000-square-foot exhibit inside Luxor Las Vegas includes a replica of guest compartments, the grand staircase, and a promenade deck that movie fans will recognize from a little film by James Cameron. Among the 250 emotionally arresting artifacts: luggage, clothing, a bottle of unopened champagne, and pieces of the ship including a massive section of the iron hull, complete with bulging rivets and portholes. ✉ *Luxor Las Vegas, 3900 Las Vegas Blvd. S, South Strip* ☎ *702/262– 4000, 800/557–7428* ⊕ *www.luxor.com/entertainment* 💲*$32 adults, $24 kids 4–12* ☉ *Daily 10–10.*

"Welcome to Fabulous Las Vegas" sign. This neon-and-incandescent sign, in a median of Las Vegas Boulevard south of Mandalay Bay, is one of Sin City's most enduring icons. The landmark dates back to 1959, and was approved for listing on the National Register of Historic Places in 2009. Young Electric Sign Company currently leases the sign to Clark County but the design itself was never copyrighted, and currently exists in the public domain. (This, of course, explains why you see so many likenesses all over town.) There is a parking lot in the median just south of the sign. If you prefer to go on foot, expect a 10-minute walk from Mandalay Bay. ✉ *5100 Las Vegas Blvd. S, South Strip.*

CENTER STRIP

Dining
★★★★★

Sightseeing
★★★★★

Shopping
★★★★★

Nightlife
★★★★★

It's fitting that this part of the Strip comprises the heart of today's Las Vegas. Even before the $8.5-billion CityCenter project was completed, this stretch captured the American consciousness like no other. It is, quite literally, where modern Vegas was born.

It began with the Flamingo more than 60 years ago, and then the Mirage ushered in the age of the modern megaresort in the late 1980s. That renaissance gained momentum with Bellagio and snowballed from there. Today the stretch includes other classics such as Caesars Palace and Bally's, as well as thematic wonders such as Paris and Planet Hollywood. The centerpiece is, fittingly, CityCenter, a city-within-the-city that includes everything from public art to apartment-style living and more. Then, of course, there's the relative new kid on the block: the über-hip Cosmopolitan of Las Vegas.

There's no shortage of spectacles in this part of town. From the fountains in front of Aria and Bellagio to the Eiffel Tower at Paris and the volcano in front of the Mirage, the Center Strip truly is a feast for the eyes. Art is on display here as well; CityCenter has a $42-million collection for visitors to enjoy, and the Bellagio has one of the most highly regarded galleries in town. Another popular pastime: shopping. A day of exploration here should include strolls through vast retail destinations such as Crystals, Miracle Mile, and Forum Shops—all of which offer some of the finest boutiques and shops in the United States.

No visit to the Center Strip would be complete without a little pool time. For an intimate vibe, check out the Cosmopolitan's eighth-floor pool deck that looks down on the Strip. To live like royalty, check out the seven-pool Garden of the Gods Pool Oasis at Caesars Palace. Reclining on a lounger, soaking up the sun, you'll be experiencing Vegas the way countless others have over the years. The more things change, apparently, the more they stay the same.

GETTING HERE AND AROUND

CityCenter makes the Center Strip challenging to navigate; at some point, almost all pedestrian traffic along the Strip must go near or through the Crystals Retail & Entertainment Center. Another bottleneck: the fountains at Bellagio, especially on weekend evenings when the most crowds gather. One way to avoid these backups is to take advantage of the Las Vegas Monorail between Monte Carlo and Bellagio. If you're traveling by cab, expect anywhere from 15 to 20 minutes to the airport, and 10 to 15 minutes to get to other parts of town.

Las Vegas Monorail stations here include the Bally's/Paris station, Flamingo/Caesars Palace station, and farthest north, the Harrah's/Quad station. RTC services this part of the Strip with public buses and double-deckers (⇨ *see also Bus Travel in Travel Smart*).

COOLING MIST

Numerous casinos and restaurants have public water misters. Our favorites: outside Diablo's Cantina at the Monte Carlo; at Spanish Steps, the frozen-margarita bar outside Caesars Palace (northwest corner of Flamingo and the Strip); and various shops outside Fashion Show Mall in the North Strip.

TOP ATTRACTIONS

FAMILY
Fodor'sChoice
★

Bellagio Conservatory and Botanical Gardens. The flowers, trees, and other plants in Bellagio's soaring atrium are fresh and alive, grown in a 5-acre greenhouse. The artistic floral arrangements and ornamental landscaping here is breathtaking. Displays change each season, and the lighted holiday displays in December (for Christmas) and January (for Chinese New Year) are particularly dramatic. In 2013, Bellagio added daily live musical performances in the South Garden from 5 to 6 pm. ⊠ *Bellagio, 3600 Las Vegas Blvd. S, Center Strip* ☎ *702/693–7111, 888/987–6667* ⊕ *www.bellagio.com/attractions* ☞ *Free* ☉ *Daily 24 hrs.*

Bellagio Gallery of Fine Art. This gallery—one of the last of its kind inside Strip hotels—originally was curated from Bellagio founder Steve Wynn's private collection. Today, with Wynn long gone, the gallery operates independently, bringing in traveling exhibits from some of the most famous art museums in the world. Recent shows have featured works by Georgia O'Keeffe, Andy Warhol, and Claude Monet. But you're just as likely to see works by Picasso, Hopper, and others. Guides lead a daily tour at 2 pm. Also, on the second Wednesday of each month, the gallery pours select wines from Bellagio's cellar, and patrons can interact with the hotel's director of wine. ⊠ *Bellagio, 3600 Las Vegas Blvd. S, Center Strip* ☎ *702/693–7871, 877/957–9777* ⊕ *www.bellagio. com/attractions* ☞ *$16* ☉ *Daily 10–7.*

CityCenter Fine Art Collection. CityCenter includes $42 million in public art. Pieces range from sculptures to paintings and elaborate fountains. Our favorite: "Big Edge," an amalgam of kayaks and canoes by Nancy Rubins. ⊠ *CityCenter, Las Vegas Blvd. S, Center Strip* ⊕ *www. citycenter.com* ☉ *Daily 24 hrs.*

FAMILY
Fountains of Bellagio. At least once on your visit you should stop in front of the Bellagio to view its spectacular water ballet from start to

2

finish. The dazzling fountains stream from more than 1,000 nozzles, accompanied by 4,500 lights, in 27 million gallons of water. Fountain jets shoot 250 feet in the air, tracing undulations you wouldn't have thought possible, in near-perfect time with music ranging from Bocelli to the Beatles to "Billie Jean." Some of the best views are from the Eiffel Tower's observation deck, directly across the street (unless, you've got a north-facing balcony room at The Cosmopolitan). Paris and Planet Hollywood have restaurants with patios on the Strip that also offer good views. ✉ *Bellagio, 3600 Las Vegas Blvd. S, Center Strip* ☎ *888/987–6667, 702/693–7111* ⊕ *www.bellagio.com/attractions* ⊘ *Weekdays 3–7 every ½ hr, 7–midnight every 15 mins; weekends noon–7 every ½ hr, 7–midnight every 15 mins.*

FAMILY **The High Roller.** Standing more than 100 feet taller than the iconic London Eye, the High Roller opened in March 2014 as the largest observation wheel in the world. The giant Ferris wheel at the east end of the LINQ features 28 glass-enclosed cabins, each of which is equipped to hold up to 40 passengers (yes, the cabins are available to rent). One full rotation takes about 30 minutes; along the way, riders are treated to a dynamic video and music show on TV monitors in the pod, as well as one-of-a-kind views of Sin City and the surrounding Las Vegas Valley. The experience begins and ends in a state-of-the-art wheelhouse, where visitors can read about the engineering behind the project as they wait in line, or buy souvenirs commemorating the spin. The best time to ride the wheel is nighttime, when 2,000 LED lights on the wheel itself create an otherworldly vibe. ✉ *3545 Las Vegas Blvd. S, Center Strip* ☎ *800/223–7277* ⊕ *www.thelinq.com* ✉ *$25–$35, depending on time of day* ⊘ *Daily 10 am–2 am.*

The LINQ. Between the Flamingo and the Quad a huge outdoor entertainment complex offering open-air shopping, restaurants, and attractions has arrived. To lure pedestrians from the Strip, Caesars Entertainment pumped $550 million into the LINQ, creating a new streetscape with everything from restaurants and bars to bakeries, self-serve margarita joints, clothing stores, and a new spin on the old O'Shea's casino. Headlining music play at Brooklyn Bowl, which is part bar, part nightclub, part bowling alley, and part concert hall. The big draw, however, is the **High Roller**, a 550-foot-tall observation wheel with spectacular views of the city. ✉ *3545 Las Vegas Blvd. S, Center Strip* ☎ *800/223–7277* ⊕ *www.thelinq.com.*

FAMILY
Fodor's Choice
★
Siegfried & Roy's Secret Garden & Dolphin Habitat. The palm-shaded sanctuary has a collection of the planet's rarest and most exotic creatures. Animals are rotated regularly, but at any time you're likely to see white tigers, as well as lions, a snow leopard, a panther, and an elephant. (The tiger that mauled Roy in 2003 is not on view.) Atlantic bottle-nosed dolphins swim around in a 2.5-million-gallon saltwater tank at the Dolphin Habitat. Pass through the underwater observation station to the video room, where you can watch tapes of two dolphin births at the habitat. In addition to the regular admission, there are VIP edu-tours as well as a paint-with-the-dolphins experience for $199, and a deluxe trainer-for-a-day program for $500 or so. ✉ *The Mirage, 3400 Las Vegas Blvd. S, Center Strip* ☎ *702/791–7111* ⊕ *www.mirage.com/*

GREAT WALKS: CENTER STRIP

See the Fountains: Catch the dancing fountains outside Bellagio. Showtimes (basically) are every half hour. It's best to go at night, when the fountains are illuminated with spotlights. Total time: 20–30 minutes.

Retail Therapy: Start by circling the stores in Crystals at CityCenter, then hit the Miracle Mile Shops at Planet Hollywood. To wrap things up, cross the street and explore the Forum

Shops at Caesars Palace. Total time: three hours, depending on stops and dressing-room time.

Molten Fun: The Mirage's volcano is worth a gander, but the best views are from the opposite side of the Strip. From Bally's, head north and stop in front of the Casino Royale. It's best to go at night, when the "lava" glows like the real stuff. Total time: 25 minutes.

attractions 🎫 *$19.95 adults; $14.95 kids 4–12* ⊙ *Weekdays 11–5:30, weekends 10–5:30.*

FAMILY **Volcano at Mirage.** This erupting volcano, a 54-foot mountain-fountain surrounded by a lake of miniature fire spouts, is a must-see free attraction on the Strip. Several times an hour the whole area erupts in flames, smoke, and eerily backlit water that looks like lava. The thundering island percussion sound track was created by Grateful Dead drummer Mickey Hart. ■TIP→ **The best vantage point is near the main drive entrance, or on the east side of Las Vegas Boulevard in front of Casino Royale.** ✉ *Mirage, 3400 Las Vegas Blvd. S, Center Strip* ☎ *702/791-7111* ⊕ *www.mirage.com/attractions* 🎫 *Free* ⊙ *Daily 7–11 pm, every hr. on the hr.*

WORTH NOTING

FAMILY **The Auto Collections.** Collectively billed as the "world's largest classic car showroom," the 150 antique, classic, and special-interest vehicles at this attraction on the fifth floor of the self-park garage of The Quad Resort & Casino (formerly the Imperial Palace) will keep gearheads entertained for hours. All the vehicles on the lot are for sale, so the collection is constantly changing. But at any given time you might see "famous" cars, like the Trans Am that acted as the pace car at the 1983 Daytona 500, or cars that once belonged to famous people, like the '39 Chrysler the late Johnny Carson rode in to his senior prom. Many of the cars are just vintage rides: a supercharged '57 T-Bird, or the immaculate '29 Rolls-Royce Springfield Phantom I straight out of *The Great Gatsby*. Free admission coupons are available online. ✉ *The Quad, 3535 Las Vegas Blvd. S, Center Strip* ☎ *702/794-3174* ⊕ *www.autocollections. com* 🎫 *$12.95 adults, $8.95 kids under 12* ⊙ *Daily 10–6.*

Jubilee! Backstage Tour. Admit it—you're just as mesmerized by all the sequins and fancy headpieces of a classic feather show as we are. On this tour, a real showgirl (or male dancer, depending on the day) escorts you backstage to see firsthand the workings behind the curtains for this $50-million stage production. The hour-long tour shows you many of the show's 71 backdrops, the mechanics of the stage, costumes, and dressing rooms. Visitors must be 13 years or older and should be able to move up and down several cases of stairs. ⊠ *Bally's, 3645 Las Vegas Blvd. S, Center Strip* ☎ *702/967–4938* ⊕ *www.ballyslasvegas. com* ⌨ *$19.50; $14.50 with purchase of show ticket* ☉ *Mon., Wed., and Sat. 11 am.*

FAMILY **The Wildlife Habitat.** Just next to the pool area at Flamingo Las Vegas, a flamboyance of live Chilean flamingos lives on islands and in streams surrounded by sparkling waterfalls and lush foliage. Other animals on-site include swans, ducks, koi, goldfish, pelicans, ducks, hummingbirds, and turtles. The small habitat makes for a fun, brief stroll. ⊠ *Flamingo Las Vegas, 3555 Las Vegas Blvd. S, Center Strip* ☎ *702/733–3349* ⊕ *www.flamingolasvegas.com* ⌨ *Free* ☉ *Daily 24 hrs.*

NORTH STRIP

Dining
★★★★★

Sightseeing
★★★★

Shopping
★★★★★

Nightlife
★★★★★

Like the best nights out, the North Strip is the perfect mix of luxury, fun, and debauchery—a blend of the very best that Vegas has to offer in high-end, low-brow, and laugh-out-loud diversion. Wynn, Encore, Palazzo, and Venetian are posh celebrity favorites. Carnival acts at Circus Circus, and thrill rides at the Stratosphere entertain the masses. In between, the Trump International Hotel offers elegant, apartment-style living in a nongaming environment.

Sister properties dominate the landscape in this part of town—resorts that complement each other wonderfully. One pair, the Venetian and Palazzo, whisks visitors to Italy, where they can ride gondolas and marvel at indoor waterfalls. Another pair, Wynn and Encore, offer a different kind of luxury, one that Steve Wynn himself has sharpened after years in the business. Encore in particular is a one-of-a-kind blend of classic (authentic antiques pervade the property) and modern (windows in the casino). Also not to be missed: the Encore Beach Club, a thumping day-lounge experience.

Farther north, this part of the Strip embraces the circus. In the Adventuredome, behind Circus Circus, visitors can participate in an actual carnival, complete with cotton candy and midway games. On top of the Stratosphere tower the attractions aren't for the faint of heart, considering that they suspend you about 900 feet over the ground.

The North Strip has improved on a number of familiar Vegas experiences, too. Circus acts at Circus Circus are as campy as ever. The golf course behind Wynn is a premier experience. And the "sports book" at Palazzo doubles as a casual restaurant from Emeril Lagasse. The North Strip presents a number of familiar sights; it just does them better.

2

GETTING HERE AND AROUND

The North Strip is far enough from the airport (up to 30 minutes) that if a cabby opts to take the Interstate, it's probably not worth arguing for him to change course. A pedestrian bridge between the Palazzo and Wynn makes exploring these two properties easy. The journey from Trump and Encore to Circus Circus and the Stratosphere is deceptively long; on hot days, it pays to take a cab or public transportation. Be warned, on foot from the Stratosphere, it's still 20 to 30 minutes to Downtown.

Las Vegas Monorail stations here include the Harrah's/Quad station, the Las Vegas Convention Center station, the LVH station, and the SLS Vegas station. RTC services this part of the Strip with public buses and double-deckers (⇨ see also Bus Travel in Travel Smart).

TOP ATTRACTIONS

FAMILY

Fodor's Choice
★

Stratosphere Tower Rides. High above the Strip at the tip of the Stratosphere Tower are four major thrill rides that will scare the bejeezus out of you, especially if you have even the slightest fear of heights. Don't even think about heading up here if you have serious vertigo. People have been known to get sick just watching these rides.

The **Big Shot** would be a monster ride on the ground, but starting from the 112th floor—and climaxing at more than 1,000 feet above the Strip—makes it twice as wild. Four riders are strapped into chairs on four sides of the needle, which rises from the Stratosphere's observation pod. With little warning, you're flung 160 feet up the needle at 45 mph, then dropped like a rock. The whole thing is over in less than a minute, but your knees will wobble for the rest of the day.

The **XScream** tips passengers 27 feet over the edge of the tower like a giant seesaw again and again. Sit in the very front to get an unobstructed view of the Strip, more than 800 feet straight down!

Another unobstructed view can be seen by dangling over the edge of the tower off the arm of **Insanity**. The arm pivots and hangs you out 64 feet from the edge of the tower; then it spins you faster and faster, so you're lifted to a 70-degree angle by a centrifugal force that's the equivalent of 3 g-forces.

The newest ride, **SkyJump Las Vegas**, is a controlled free fall that sends you careening off the side of the 108th floor. ⊠ Stratosphere, 2000 Las Vegas Blvd. S, North Strip ☎ 702/380–7777 ⊕ www.stratospherehotel. com/Tower/Rides 🎟 Tower $18 adults, $10 kids; Big Shot, XScream, or Insanity $15; SkyJump $109 and up; unlimited rides and tower day pass $34 ☉ Sun.–Thurs. 10 am–1 am, Fri. and Sat. 10 am–2 am.

Venetian Gondola Rides. Let a gondolier "o sole mio" you down Vegas's rendition of Venice's Canalozzo. We love this attraction because it's done so well—owner Sheldon Adelson was obsessed with getting the canals *just right*: he had them drained and repainted three times before he was satisfied with the hue, and the colossal reproduction of St. Mark's Square at the end of the canal is authentic right down to the colors of the façades. The gondoliers who ply the waterway are professional entertainers and train for two weeks to maneuver the canals. It all makes for a rather entertaining way to while away an hour on the

GREAT WALKS: NORTH STRIP

Viva Italy: The Strip has plenty of Italy to explore. To immerse yourself, stroll the canals around the Venetian's shops, then follow signs toward Barney's New York and Palazzo. All told, you never have to step outside. Total time: 45 minutes.

Wynn Nature: Conservatory gardens in both Wynn Las Vegas and Encore feature seasonal flowers and trees—both rarities in the middle of the Las

Vegas desert. To care for this greenery, Steve Wynn employs more than 50 gardeners. Total time: 40 minutes.

Mall and Trump: On superhot days, avoid the sun with a stroll through Fashion Show Mall, then cross Fashion Show Drive and head into the Trump Hotel Las Vegas for a martini at DJT. Total time: 45 minutes.

Strip. Outdoor gondola rides along the resort's exterior waterway are also available, weather permitting. A gondola carries up to four passengers. ⊠ *The Venetian, 3355 Las Vegas Blvd. S, North Strip* ☎ *702/414–4300* ⊕ *www.venetian.com* ➧ *$18.95 per person (gondolas seat 4) or $75.80 total for a 2-seater* ☉ *Sun.–Thurs. 10 am–11 pm, Fri. and Sat. 10 am–midnight.*

Fodor's Choice   **Vegas Indoor Skydiving.** This attraction, just north of Encore Las Vegas, ★   provides the thrill of skydiving without leaving the ground. After 20 minutes of training you enter a vertical wind tunnel that produces a powerful stream of air. You'll float, hover, and fly, simulating three minutes of freefall. Airspeeds reach 120 mph. You can make reservations a minimum of 48 hours in advance for parties of five or more. The place closes for private parties from time to time, so it's wise to call ahead. ⊠ *200 Convention Center Dr., North Strip* ☎ *702/731–4768, 877/588–2359* ⊕ *www.vegasindoorskydiving.com* ➧ *$75 for 1st flight; $40 per repeat flight* ☉ *Daily 9:45–8.*

WORTH NOTING

FAMILY   **Adventuredome Theme Park.** If the sun is blazing, the kids are antsy, and you need a place to while away a few hours, make for the big pink dome behind Circus Circus. The 5-acre amusement park has more than 25 rides and attractions for all age levels, and is kept at a constant 72°F. The newest roller coaster, El Loco, opened in early 2014 and includes a barrel roll and a number of g-force drops. Also check out the Canyon Blaster, the world's largest indoor double-loop roller coaster, a huge swinging pirate ship, bumper cars, several kiddie rides, a mini-golf course, a laser-tag park, a rock-climbing wall, and much more. There even are attractions with computer-generated iterations of Dora and Diego and SpongeBob SquarePants. ⊠ *Circus Circus, 2880 Las Vegas Blvd. S, North Strip* ☎ *702/794–3939, 866/456–8894* ⊕ *www. adventuredome.com* ➧ *$5–$8 per ride; all-day pass $29.95 (adults) or $16.95 (kids)* ☉ *Hrs vary. Call or look online for hrs.*

FAMILY   **Madame Tussauds Las Vegas.** Audition in front of Simon Cowell or stand toe-to-toe with Muhammad Ali as you explore the open showroom filled with uncanny celebrity wax portraits from the worlds of show

FAMILY FUN

WILDLIFE

This may be Sin City, but there are plenty of great family-oriented activities. There's wildlife galore, starting with exotic birds at **Flamingo** and fish and reptiles at **Shark Reef at Mandalay Bay**. Next, head to the **Mirage** to see the white tigers of the **Secret Garden** and the eponymous mammals of the **Dolphin Habitat**.

FAST TIMES

If your family prefers adrenaline-based bonding, scream your way up the Strip, starting at the **Roller Coaster** at **New York–New York**. Continue north along the Strip (via the Monorail to SLS station), stopping at **Circus Circus**'s indoor theme park **Adventuredome** on your way to the **Stratosphere Tower**. Here the Big Shot, XScream, and Insanity–The Ride fly high above the Strip at 1,149 feet. Can't decide between wild animals and wild rides? Go Downtown for both at the Tank at **Golden Nugget**, where a three-story waterslide includes a ride through a glass tube into the heart of a 200,000-gallon shark tank.

DOWNTIME

For a mellower afternoon, head to the Venetian's **Madame Tussaud's Wax Museum**. After posing next to Denzel and J-Lo, check out the exploding volcano at the **Mirage**. Since you're at the Mirage, grab last-minute tickets for ventriloquist **Terry Fator**'s one-of-a-kind musical puppet act. You can minimize your kids' sinful intake by staying at the **Trump International Hotel Las Vegas**, posh accommodations that are unusual for being smoke- and casino-free.

business, sports, politics, and everywhere in between. Crowd-pleasers include the characters from *The Hangover*, Lady Gaga, Tom Jones, Hugh Hefner, and Abe Lincoln. An interactive segment lets you play golf with Tiger Woods, shoot baskets with Shaquille O'Neill, play celebrity poker with Ben Affleck, dance with Britney Spears, or marry George Clooney. Discount tickets are available online. ⊠ *Next to the Venetian, 3377 Las Vegas Blvd. S, North Strip* ☎ *866/841–3739* ⊕ *www. madametussauds.com/lasvegas* ⊠ *$25.95 adults, $19.95 kids 4–12* ⊙ *Daily 10–9.*

DOWNTOWN

Dining
★★★

Sightseeing
★★★★

Shopping
★★

Nightlife
★★★

With neon lights, single-deck blackjack, and a host of new attractions that spotlight yesteryear, old Vegas is alive and well Downtown.

This neighborhood revolves around Fremont Street, a covered pedestrian walkway through the heart of the Downtown gambling district. Originally, this attraction was nothing more than a place to stroll; today, however, the canopy sparkles with millions of lights, and outfitters have set up everything from zip lines to band shells on street level down beneath. Use Fremont Street to access resorts such as the Golden Nugget (our fave in this neighborhood), Four Queens, the Plaza Hotel & Casino, and others. Just be prepared for sensory overload.

Old is new again all over Downtown. The Mob Museum, which opened in February 2012, pays homage to Las Vegas's mafia years. Also on Third Street, the Downtown Grand has brought back some of the 1950s-era swagger. The Smith Center, a world-class performing arts center that opened in March 2012, was designed to invoke the same art deco style that inspired the Hoover Dam. Then, of course, there's the Neon Museum, where visitors can behold the greatness (and, in a few cases, the glow) of original Las Vegas neon signs.

With the Downtown Container Park and the new Zappos.com headquarters in the (renovated) old City Hall, the Downtown is undergoing a renaissance. A vibrant arts-and-mixology scene is emerging—the "First Friday" walkabout celebrates local art and artists on the first Friday of every month, and a burgeoning Arts District attracts fans of the avant-garde from all over the world.

No visit to Downtown Vegas would be complete without a pilgrimage to one of the neighborhood's most lasting legacies: Luv-It Frozen Custard. Flavors here change regularly, but cinnamon and almond chip are mainstays in the rotation. Try some in a homemade waffle cone with chocolate sauce on top.

2

GETTING HERE AND AROUND

Taxi and public transportation are the easiest ways to get to Downtown from the South, Central, and North strips, but be warned that city buses must stick to Las Vegas Boulevard and often get stuck in terrible traffic around rush hour. Once you're Downtown, everything is walkable. Don't stray from populated areas, and travel in pairs at night. And if you've had too much to drink, it's admirable but not advisable to walk back to the North Strip: It's more than an hour on foot. Best to take a taxi.

TOP ATTRACTIONS

Downtown Arts District. The emergence of the offbeat 18b Arts District (so called because it comprises 18 blocks bounded by South 7th, Main, Bonneville, and Charleston streets on downtown's southeastern corner) continues to generate excitement in the city's arts community and, increasingly, among visitors. With a number of funky, independent art galleries in its confines, the area, officially named in 1998, is a growing, thriving cultural hub—think of it as the Anti-Strip. In addition to the galleries—some of which contain impressive collections of locally known and world-famous artists—you'll find interesting eateries and dive bars to serve the alternative artists, musicians, and writers who have gravitated to the neighborhood. Each month the district hosts a "First Friday" gallery walk from 6 to 10 pm with gallery openings, street performers, and entertainment. It's an excellent time to come check out the still-nascent but steadily improving scene for yourself. ⊠ *Downtown*

Arts Factory. An intriguing concentration of antiques shops and galleries is found on East Charleston Boulevard and Casino Center Drive, anchored by the Arts Factory. This former warehouse houses studios and galleries for art of all types, including painting, photography, and sculpture. There's also a bistro on-site. The Arts Factory comes alive on "First Friday" with gallery openings, exhibits, receptions, and special events. "Preview Thursday," the day before First Friday, offers the same artwork with fewer crowds. Guided tours available upon request (and with reservation). ⊠ *107 E. Charleston Blvd., Downtown* ☎ *702/383–3133* ⊕ *www.theartsfactory.com* ☜ *Free* ☼ *Daily 9–6; First Fridays 6–10 pm.*

Downtown Container Park. It turns out shipping containers—the same kinds you see on cargo ships and tractor trailers—can be pretty versatile. At this open-air mall, for instance, on the outskirts of the Fremont East neighborhood, the structures have been repurposed into food stalls, boutiques, offices, and even a three-story "tree house" complete with grown-up-friendly slides. The place also has an amphitheater stage fronted by real grass. Although the treehouse is fun (especially with young kids), the highlight of the attraction is the large, fire-spewing praying mantis, which was originally constructed for use at the Burning Man festival in Northern Nevada. The whole spot is part of the $350-million Downtown Project. ⊠ *707 Fremont St., Downtown* ☎ *702/637–4244* ⊕ *www.downtowncontainerpark.com* ☼ *Daily 9 am–11 pm.*

Exploring Downtown

FAMILY **Fremont Street Experience.** If you're looking for something a little different, head to this ear-splitting, eye-popping show that takes place on the underside of a 1,450-foot arched canopy 90 feet overhead. The 12.5 million synchronized LED modules, 180 strobes, and eight robotic mirrors per block treat your eyes, while the 208 speakers combine for 550,000 watts of fun for your ears. The shows play five to seven times a night depending on the time of year and the six-minute presentations change regularly. At street-level, "entertainment" includes everything from break-dancers to people in furry mascot costumes. ⊠ *Fremont St. from Main to 4th Sts., Downtown* ⊕ *www.vegasexperience.com* ⊠ *Free* ⊙ *Daily.*

Gold & Silver Pawn Shop. Reality television fans flock to this run-of-the-mill pawn shop for a glimpse of owner Rick Harrison and the rest of the staff, all of whom appear regularly on The History Channel's *Pawn Stars* reality television show. On any given night, the line of people waiting to get in might be 30 or 40 people deep. Inside, dozens of glass cases are chock-full of jewelry, poker chips, and other curios. The merchandise area, which sells everything from G&S T-shirts to G&S shot glasses, is just as spacious. ⊠ *713 Las Vegas Blvd. S, Downtown* ☎ *702/385-7912* ⊕ *www.gspawn.com* ⊙ *Daily 9–9.*

Fodor's Choice
★

Insert Coin(s). Combine one part video arcade with two parts nightclub and lounge and—voila!—you've got this epic anchor of the Downtown scene. On one side, the venue offers a traditional arcade, complete with Ms. Pac-Man, Asteroids, and all of the most popular games of the 1980s. On the other side, the place is a typical Vegas nightclub, with table service, VIP booths, and DJs. In between, the venue offers a bar where patrons can play Xbox and Playstation while downing drinks, and gaming booths that are VIP versions of the same idea. Rumor has it that if you beat owner Chris LaPorte at a game of Street Fighter, drinks are on him. ✉ *512 Fremont St., Downtown* ☎ *702/477-2525* ⊕ *www. insertcoinslv.com.*

The Mob Museum. It's fitting that the $42-million Mob Museum sits in the circa-1933 former federal courthouse and U.S. Post Office downtown; this is where the Kefauver Committee held one of its historic hearings on organized crime in 1950. Today the museum pays homage to Las Vegas' criminal underbelly, explaining to visitors (sometimes with way too much exhibit text) how the mafia worked, who was involved, how the law brought down local mobsters, and what happened to gangsters once they were caught and incarcerated. Museum highlights include bricks from the wall of the St. Valentine's Day Massacre in 1929, and a mock-up of the electric chair that killed a number of mobsters (as well as spies Julius and Ethel Rosenberg). ✉ *300 Stewart Ave., Downtown* ☎ *702/229-2734* ⊕ *www.themobmuseum.org* 🎟 *$19.95 adults, $13.95 kids 11–17* ◷ *Sun.–Thurs. 10–7, Fri. and Sat. 10–8.*

FAMILY
Fodor's Choice
★

Neon Museum. Consider this Downtown museum the afterlife for old neon signs. The facility, which displays more than 150 signs that date back to the 1930s, opened to the public in October 2012 on the site of the old La Concha Motel Downtown. The hotel's iconic lobby was renovated and now serves as the museum's entry point. The sign collection includes the original signs from the Stardust, the Horseshoe, and other properties. To get up close, visitors must take an educatoinal and informative one-hour guided tour. Daytime tours, especially in summer, can be scorching. For an alternative, try one of the nighttime tours, where you can see four of the signs illuminated the way they were intended to be. ✉ *770 Las Vegas Blvd. N, Downtown* ☎ *702/387-6366* ⊕ *www. neonmuseum.org* 🎟 *$18* ◷ *Daily. Tours 10–8:30.*

Slotzilla. It wouldn't be Vegas enough to build the world's largest slot machine and just leave it there. Now thrill-seekers can take off from a platform atop the 12-story slot machine and soar over Fremont Street. There are three options to zip: One that averages 70 feet above the ground ($20), a second line that averages 110 feet ($30), and both lines ($40). If you'd rather just play the big slot machine, you can do that, too. It is Vegas, after all. ✉ *425 Fremont St., Downtown* 🎟 *$20–$40.*

WORTH NOTING

FAMILY **DISCOVERY Children's Museum.** The DISCOVERY Children's Museum is one of the most technologically sophisticated children's museums in the entire country. Formerly known as the Lied Children's Museum, it changed names and moved into new digs next to the Smith Center for the Performing Arts in March 2012. Overall, the new facility comprises nine themed exhibition halls, all of which are designed to inspire visitors—both children and adults—to learn through play. The star of the show: a 12-story exhibit dubbed "The Summit," with education stations on every level and a lookout that peeks through the building's roof. Parents of the smallest visitors also will love "Toddler Town," an area designed for those who are still crawling or just learning how to walk. ⊠ *360 Promenade Pl., Downtown* ☎ *702/382–5437* ⊕ *www.discoverykidslv.org* ⬚ *$12* ☉ *Tues.–Fri. 9–4, Sat. 10–5, Sun. noon–5.*

Gold Spike. Once a (seedy) casino, the Gold Spike has been resuscitated as part of Tony Hsieh's $350-million Downtown Project. In this case, that means gambling is out and free gaming is in. Gaming, as in shuffleboard, giant versions of Connect Four, and, on the back patio, life-size Jenga. Sure, at times (especially on Thursday night) it feels that the former casino floor is now a clubhouse for employees of Zappos.com. But the new hot spot is open to the public and is becoming a popular place for locals, visitors, and hipsters to hang, too. ⊠ *217 Las Vegas Blvd. N, Downtown* ☎ *702/476–4923* ⊕ *www.goldspike.com.*

FAMILY **Las Vegas Natural History Museum.** If your kids are into animals (or taxidermy), they'll love this museum, where every continent and geological age is represented. You're greeted by a 35-foot-tall roaring T-Rex in the dinosaur gallery that features Shonisaurus, Nevada's state fossil. From there, you can enjoy rooms full of sharks (including live ones, swimming in a 3,000-gallon reef tank), birds, cavemen, and scenes from the African savannah. Kids especially enjoy the various hands-on exhibits; the Young Scientist Center offers youngsters the opportunity to investigate fossils and animal tracks up close. After that, tour the Wild Nevada Gallery, where kids can see, smell, and even touch Nevada wildlife. ⊠ *900 Las Vegas Blvd. N, Downtown* ☎ *702/384–3466* ⊕ *www.lvnhm.org* ⬚ *$10, $5 children 3–11* ☉ *Daily 9–4.*

Picnic. The 35,000 square-foot party deck atop the Downtown Grand Las Vegas is two venues in one. By day, it's the hotel pool, complete with a grassy knoll for sunbathing, an outdoor tent with communal tables and open-air blackjack, and upscale picnic grub by Caesars' former Central chef, Todd Harrington. By night, it's an eclectic party space, complete with deejays, life-size games, and more. Perhaps the biggest departure from the ordinary is that the hot spot offers day-use passes to locals and nonguests. Passes are $15 during weekdays and $25 on weekends, and they include a cocktail or beer of your choice. ⊠ *206 N. 3rd St., Downtown* ☎ *855/384–7263* ⊕ *www.downtowngrand.com.*

FAMILY **Springs Preserve.** This 180-acre complex defies traditional categories, combining botanical gardens, hiking trails, live animal exhibits, and an ultramodern interactive museum. The overarching theme of the facility is the rich diversity and delicate balance of nature in southern Nevada's deserts. Kids love the simulations of the flash-flood ravine, the re-created Southern Paiute Indian village (complete with grass huts!) and the green-theme, "Lawn Gobbler" Pac Man-style video game designed to teach the importance of water conservation. The NV Energy Foundation Sustainability Gallery teaches about eco-friendly living, while a 2014 addition, DesertSol, educates visitors about solar-powered homes. There are also a few miles of walking trails that swing you by archaeological sites and may—if you're lucky—bring you face to face with some of the local fauna such as bats, peregrine falcons, and Gila monsters. The Springs Café provides famished eco-explorers with sustainable choices, like ethically raised cheeseburgers and environmentally mindful salads. The **Nevada State Museum**, with its famous fossil ichthyosaur and a number of exhibits on local mining, is on the site (and included with admission), as well. ⊠ *333 S. Valley View Blvd., Downtown* ☎ *702/822–7700* ⊕ *www.springspreserve.org* ✉ *$18.95 adults, $10.95 kids 5–17* ⊙ *Daily 10–6.*

Vegas Vic. The 50-foot-tall neon cowboy outside the Pioneer Club has been waving to Las Vegas visitors since 1947 (though, truth be told, he had a makeover and was replaced by a newer version in 1951). His neon sidekick, Vegas Vicki, went up across the street in 1980. ⊠ *Fremont St. and North 1st St., Downtown.*

PARADISE ROAD AND THE EAST SIDE

Dining
★★★

Sightseeing
★★

Shopping
★

Nightlife
★★★

The East Side of Las Vegas, an area that includes Paradise Road and stretches to the University District, is as eclectic as it is convenient. Much of the area is residential, save for a handful of (older) resorts that rise from the landscape like beacons. There also is a preponderance of restaurants, extensive medical offices, and most of the area's collegiate athletic facilities.

Paradise Road itself is the Strip's sister street. On the southern end the Hard Rock Hotel & Casino is one of the most popular off-Strip resorts in town, and despite the opening of increasingly over-the-top Strip properties, has remained popular over the years. A number of other resorts, such as the Platinum and the Rumor Boutique Hotel, qualify as nongaming, but are still within walking distance of larger casinos. This stretch also comprises the heart of the area affectionately known as "Fruit Loop," Vegas's gay-friendly neighborhood. Especially on Friday and Saturday nights, the parties at Gipsy and the Piranha Nightclub are some of the biggest raves in town.

Though there aren't any resorts in the University District, UNLV (University of Las Vegas) and the Thomas and Mack Center provide plenty of things to see and do, from sporting events to (on-campus) museums and more. As is the case with most college towns, the cost of living in this neck of the woods is considerably lower than it is elsewhere in town. In other words, you can usually get dinner and a beer for less than $6. You don't have to be a freshman to know that's a good deal.

GETTING HERE AND AROUND

Public transportation from the Strip to the East Side is actually pretty reliable, so long as you're not traveling in the middle of the night. Taxis know the area well, too, especially if you're heading from the Strip over to the Hard Rock or into the University District. As is the case with most of the Vegas suburbs, the best bet here is to rent a car.

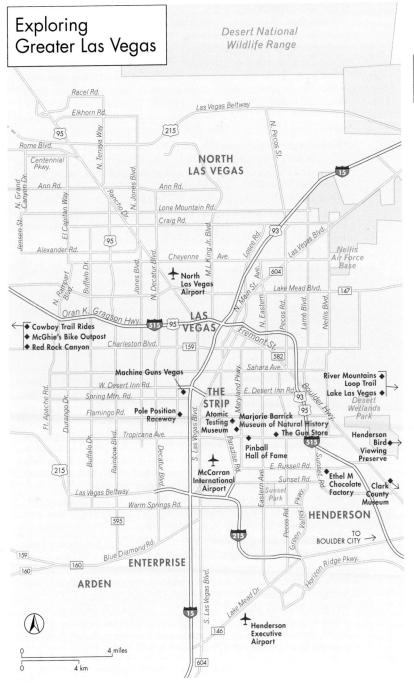

Exploring
Greater Las Vegas

2

Desert National
Wildlife Range

Racel Rd.

Elkhorn Rd.

Las Vegas Beltway

215

95

Rome Blvd.

N. Tenaya Way

N. Pecos St.

Centennial
Pkwy.

NORTH
LAS VEGAS

Ann Rd.

N. Grand Canyon Dr.

N. Jones Blvd.

Rancho Dr.

Ann Rd.

El Capitan Way

Lone Mountain Rd.

Jensen St.

Craig Rd.

95

Alexander Rd.

N. Decatur Blvd.

Cheyenne   Ave.

M.L.King Jr. Blvd.

Losee Rd.

93

Las Vegas Blvd.

Nellis
Air Force
Base

Buffalo Dr.

Jones Blvd.

✈ North
Las Vegas
Airport

N. Main St.

N. Eastern Ave.

Pecos Rd.

Lake Mead Blvd.

Lamb Blvd.

Nellis Blvd.

604

147

N. Rampart Blvd.

Oran K. Gragson Hwy.

515   95

LAS
VEGAS

Fremont St.

◆ Cowboy Trail Rides
◆ McGhie's Bike Outpost
◆ Red Rock Canyon

Charleston Blvd.

159

582

Sahara Ave.

River Mountains ◆
Loop Trail
Lake Las Vegas ◆

◆ Machine Guns Vegas

W. Desert Inn Rd.

Maryland Pkwy.

E. Desert Inn Rd.

Boulder Hwy.

93

95

Desert
Wetlands
Park

Ft. Apache Rd.

Spring Mtn. Rd.

THE
STRIP

Durango Dr.

Flamingo Rd.

Pole Position ◆
Raceway

Atomic
Testing
Museum ◆

Marjorie Barrick
Museum of Natural History

Buffalo Dr.

Rainbow Blvd.

Tropicana Ave.

S. Las Vegas Blvd.

Decatur Blvd.

Paradise Rd.

◆ The Gun Store

515

Henderson
Bird ◆
Viewing
Preserve

Pinball
Hall of Fame

215

✈
McCarran
International
Airport

E. Russell Rd.

Eastern Ave.

Sunset Rd.

Sunset
Park

Pecos Rd.

Sunset Rd.

◆ Ethel M
Chocolate
Factory

Clark ↘
County
Museum

Las Vegas Beltway

Warm Springs Rd.

595

HENDERSON

Green Valley Pkwy.

TO
BOULDER CITY →

15

Blue Diamond Rd.

ENTERPRISE

Horizon Ridge Pkwy.

159

160

160

ARDEN

S. Las Vegas Blvd.

Lake Mead Dr.

15

146

✈
Henderson
Executive
Airport

604

0   4 miles
0   4 km

TOP ATTRACTIONS

The Gun Store. Opened in 1988, The Gun Store puts you on the range with a machine gun of your choice. When you walk in you're greeted with a wall full of weapons, most of which are available to rent. Pick your era; hose the target a steady diet of lead Cagney-style with a Thompson. World War II buffs might go for an MP40 Schmeisser. Have a flair for the international? Grab an Uzi or Sten. They've got handguns, rifles, and shotguns too. ⊠ *2900 E. Tropicana Ave., East Side* ☎ *702/454–1110* ⊕ *www.thegunstorelasvegas.com* ✉ *Machine gun rentals start at $50, handguns $25* ⊙ *Daily 9–6:30.*

Haunted Vegas Tours. As you ride through the streets of Las Vegas on this 2½-hour tour, your guide, dressed as a mortician, tells the tales of Sin City's notorious murders, suicides, and ghosts (including Bugsy Siegel, Elvis, and Tupac Shakur). A 30-minute *Rocky Horror*–like sideshow, called Haunted Vegas, runs prior to the 21-stop tour. Make reservations in advance and note that kids have to be 13 for the Haunted tour and 16 for the Mob tour. ⊠ *Royal Resort, 99 Convention Center Dr.* ☎ *702/677–6499, 866/218–4935* ⊕ *www.hauntedvegastours.com* ✉ *$99.95* ⊙ *Daily 9:30 pm.*

FAMILY **Las Vegas Pinball Hall of Fame.** This fun facility has more than 140 games from 1947–2009, including the old wood-rail models. Though it may sound more like an arcade than a museum, the local club is a nonprofit organization whose goal is to preserve these pieces of Americana and share the joy of the silver ball with as many folks as possible. All quarters get donated to the local Salvation Army. ⊠ *1610 E. Tropicana Ave., East Side* ⊕ *www.pinballmuseum.org* ✉ *Free entry, 25¢ or 50¢ per game* ⊙ *Daily 11–11.*

FAMILY **Marjorie Barrick Museum of Natural History.** This museum, which was renovated in the spring of 2012, sits on the University of Nevada–Las Vegas campus. The museum has an excellent permanent collection of objects that predate the arrival of Europeans in the American Southwest and throughout Mexico. There's also a live reptile exhibit featuring regional lizards and snakes, plus a Xeriscape (they call it "Xeric") garden featuring drought-tolerant flora from the four corners of Earth. For kids, the best experience is the "archaeology dig" in the museum lobby, where youngsters can jump into a (glorified) sandbox and excavate for cultural treasures. ⊠ *4505 S. Maryland Pkwy., University District* ☎ *702/895–3381* ⊕ *barrickmuseum.unlv.edu* ✉ *Suggested contribution $5 adults, $2 kids* ⊙ *Mon.–Wed. and Fri. 9–5, Thurs. 9–8, Sat. noon–5.*

FAMILY **National Atomic Testing Museum.** Today's Las Vegas is lighted by neon and LCD, but during the Cold War, uranium and plutonium illuminated the area from time to time as well in the form of a roiling mushroom cloud in the distance. This museum, in association with the Smithsonian, commemorates southern Nevada's long and fascinating history of nuclear weapons research and testing with film footage and photographs of mushroom clouds; testimonials; and artifacts (including a deactivated bomb, twisted chunks of steel, and bomb-testing machinery from the Nevada Test Site). ⊠ *755 E. Flamingo Rd., Desert Research Institute,*

East Side ☎ *702/794–5151* ⊕ *www.nationaltomictestingmuseum.org* 🎫 *$14 adults, $12 kids 7–17* ⊙ *Mon.–Sat. 10–5, Sun. noon–5*

Nevada National Security Site. Group tours of the 1,375-square-mile Nevada National Security Site—an area that is larger than the state of Rhode Island and used to be the spot in the desert where the government tested atomic bombs—take you onto the terrain for visits to test-site craters and observation points. The site is 65 miles northwest of Downtown, and each tour usually covers a total of 250 miles. Tours leave from the Atomic Testing Museum; to register for a tour, contact the Nevada office of the National Nuclear Security Administration. And be warned: Tours book up to a year in advance. ☎ *702/295–0944* ⊕ *www.nv.doe.gov/outreach/tours.aspx.*

HENDERSON AND LAKE LAS VEGAS

Dining
★★
Sightseeing
★★★★
Shopping
★★
Nightlife
★★

Suburbia spreads quickly to the east and southeast of the Las Vegas Strip, and it continues to spread; Henderson is one of the fastest growing cities in the entire nation. Much of this area is residential, with only a smattering of casinos.

One of those casinos—the M Resort—has commanding views of the Strip. Because the property is uphill from town, it literally looks down on the rest of the Valley. Another casino resort, Green Valley Ranch, is adjacent to one of the best shopping malls in the area. Both are worthwhile destinations for either a weekend or an afternoon.

Out near Lake Las Vegas, the vibe is much more luxurious. Resorts such as the Westin Lake Las Vegas Resort & Spa and the Hilton Lake Las Vegas Resort & Spa dot the shoreline of a man-made lake, providing the perfect backdrop for golf and a variety of other outdoor activities. Bicyclists, joggers, rollerbladers, and walkers will love the River Mountains Trail, a 35-mile loop that links Henderson, Lake Las Vegas, and Boulder City to the south. Pedaling over the sometimes-formidable mountains, it's hard to believe this deserted region is just a dozen miles from a major city.

Farther afield are the main attractions in this part of the Valley: Lake Mead National Recreation Area and Hoover Dam *(⇨ see also Side Trips chapter).* If you've got the time, rent a houseboat for a multiday vacation on the lake; it's the best way to explore the body of water at your own pace. At the dam, take the tour for an inside look (literally) at one of humankind's greatest engineering feats. These icons are packed in summer, so it's best to plan your trip for a shoulder season such as spring or fall.

GETTING HERE AND AROUND
From the Strip, both Interstate 515 and Boulder Highway wind southeast toward Henderson, while Lake Mead Drive cuts due east toward Lake Mead. Public transportation serves this area, but the easiest way to get around is to rent a car. Once you're out by Lake Mead, bicycles actually are a great method of transportation. If you're philosophically

Green Valley Ranch, an elegant resort that rivals many big Strip properties, is a great property to explore in Henderson.

opposed to exercise in Las Vegas, fear not—taxis are always just a phone call away.

WORTH NOTING

FAMILY **Clark County Museum.** Step into the past (quite literally) at this modest museum, a 30-acre site that features a modern exhibit hall with a timeline exhibit about southern Nevada from prehistoric to modern times. The facility also offers a collection of restored historic buildings that depict daily life from different decades in Las Vegas, Boulder City, Henderson, and Goldfield. Other attractions include a replica of a 19th-century frontier print shop, and a 1960s wedding chapel that once stood on the Las Vegas Strip. There are also buildings and machinery dating from the turn of the 20th century, a nature trail, and a small ghost town. If you can't get to the Las Vegas Springs Preserve, on the North Side of town, this is a worthwhile substitute. ✉ *1830 Boulder Hwy. S, Henderson* ☎ *702/455–7955* ⊕ *www.clarkcountynv.gov* 🎫 *Adults $2, seniors and children $1* ⊘ *Daily 9–4:30.*

FAMILY **Ethel M Chocolate Factory.** Watching gourmet chocolates being made will make your mouth water; fortunately the tour is brief and there are free samples at the end. You can buy more of your favorites in the store. This is a self-guided tour, so if your youngsters start to get impatient, pick up the pace (or not). ✉ *1 Sunset Way, Henderson* ☎ *702/458–8864* ⊕ *www.ethelm.com.*

FAMILY **Henderson Bird Viewing Preserve.** More than 200 bird species have been spotted among the system of nine ponds at the 100-acre Henderson Bird Viewing Preserve. The preserve's ponds, located at the Kurt R. Segler Water Reclamation Facility, are a stop along the Pacific flyway

LAS VEGAS BOWLING

Bowling in Vegas incorporates elements of casinos, bars, and nightclubs, with lively crowds to match. Locals take their leagues seriously, so "spare" yourself some heartache and call ahead to make a lane reservation.

The Orleans Bowling Center. Tucked inside the Orleans Resort and Casino, this 70-lane bowling center is located in a working-class neighborhood just off the Strip. Be sure to check out the pro shop, as well as the video arcade, which can get rocking on weekend nights. ⊠ *4500 W. Tropicana Rd., West Side* ☎ *702/365-7400* ⊕ *www. orleanscasino.com* ⊗ *24/7.*

Red Rock Lanes. This 72-lane bowling alley has all the amenities, including Cosmic Bowling—glow-in-the-dark bowling with a deejay—until 2 am on Friday and Saturday nights. Roll on through until morning—it's open 24 hours a day. If you've got the bankroll, you can live the full nightclub-plus-bowling dream with bottle service at your own VIP Lanes. ⊠ *Red Rock Casino Resort Spa, 11011 W. Charleston Blvd., Summerlin* ☎ *702/797-7467, 866/767-7773* ⊕ *www.redrocklanes. com* ⊗ *Mon.-Thurs. 8 am-2 am, Fri.-Sun. 24/7.*

Sam's Town Bowling Center. This is a 56-lane locals' alley where leagues and tournaments are taken seriously. Tourists come for the cocktail lounge, connecting casino, and "Xtreme Bowling Experience" starting at 9 pm on Friday and Saturday nights that will allow you to "strike out" in a nightclub like never before, Present a movie ticket stub or receipt from the on-site T.G.I. Friday's, and the (first game of) bowling is free.

⊠ *5111 Boulder Hwy., Boulder Strip* ☎ *702/456-7777, 800/897-8696* ⊕ *www.samstownlv.com* ⊗ *24/7.*

Santa Fe Station Bowling Center. This 60-lane facility at Santa Fe Station Casino is a traditional bowling center, with video arcade, bar, and the top-of-the-line Brunswick electronic scoring system. Cosmic bowling with a DJ is held every Saturday 7-11 pm. ⊠ *4949 N. Rancho Dr., West Side* ☎ *702/658-4988* ⊕ *www.stationcasinoslanes. com* ⊗ *Sun.-Thurs. 8 am-midnight, Fri. and Sat. 8 am-1 am.*

Silver Nugget Bowling. This alley has 24 lanes and new equipment, a pro shop, and a modern automatic scoring system. Its version of Cosmic Bowling, which includes fancy lights and a booming sound system, goes 7 pm-midnight on Friday and Saturday. Weekday rates are $1.50 per person per game on weekdays and $2.50 on weekends; on weekend days you can rent lanes by the hour, instead of paying per person per game. ⊠ *2140 Las Vegas Blvd. N, North Side* ☎ *702/399-1111* ⊕ *www.silvernuggetcasino.net* ⊗ *Sun.-Thurs. 9 am-10 pm, Fri. and Sat. 9 am-midnight.*

Suncoast Bowling Center. Reflecting its upscale Summerlin neighborhood, the bowling center at the Suncoast, with 64 lanes, is designed to provide every high-tech toy for bowlers. The alley has Cosmic Bowling on Saturday and hosts a number of different leagues throughout the week. ⊠ *9090 Alta Dr., Summerlin* ☎ *702/636-7111, 877/677-7111* ⊕ *www. suncoastcasino.com/entertain/ bowling* ⊗ *Sun.-Thurs. 8 am-2 am, Fri. and Sat. 24/7.*

for migratory waterbirds, and the best viewing times are spring and fall. The earlier you get there the better if you want to fill your bird checklist. The ponds also harbor hummingbirds, raptors, peregrine falcons, tundra swans, cormorants, ducks, hawks, and herons. The office will loan out a pair of binoculars if you ask. Keep the bags of bread crumbs at home; the preserve doesn't allow the feeding of wildlife, and bikes and domestic pets are not allowed. ✉ *350 E. Galleria Dr., Henderson* ☎ *702/267–4180* ⊕ *www.cityofhenderson.com/parks/parks/ bird_preserve.php* 🖃 *Free* ⊙ *Daily, hrs vary according to season.*

Lake Las Vegas. This 320-acre, man-made lake outside of Henderson is regarded for its golf courses, boating, fishing, and hotels. Two resorts sit on the lake shore, including Hilton Lake Las Vegas Resort & Spa and the Westin Lake Las Vegas Resort & Spa. The lake was created by an earthen dam in 1991. ✉ *Henderson* ⊕ *www.lakelasvegas.com.*

FAMILY   **River Mountains Loop Trail.** Stretching 35 miles around the River Mountains, this multi-use paved trail is perfect for hiking, biking, running, jogging, and horseback riding. For a stretch, the trail parallels the shores of Lake Mead, and connects with a historic spur that leads from the Lake Mead National Recreation Area to a parking lot just north of the Hoover Dam. The route runs through Boulder City, Henderson, and Lake Las Vegas. You can rent bikes at **JT's Bicycles** in Henderson (⊕ *www.jtsbicycle.com*) and **All Mountain Cyclery** (⊕ *allmountaincyclery.com*) in Boulder City. The most popular trailheads are at the Alan Bible Visitor Center inside the recreation area and Bootleg Canyon Park, at the north end of Yucca Street in Boulder City. Access is also available at the eastern end of Equestrian Drive in Henderson, and the Railroad Pass Hotel & Casino, also in Henderson. ✉ *Alan Bible Visitor Center trailhead, 8 Lake Shore Rd., Boulder City* ⊕ *www.rivermountainstrail.com.*

WEST SIDE

Dining
★★★

Sightseeing
★★

Shopping
★

Nightlife
★★★

The West Side of Las Vegas technically isn't a suburb (it's actually part of Las Vegas proper), but it sure feels like one. Big-box stores and fast-food chains abound. Housing developments sit on just about every major corner. Sure, resorts such as the Palms and the Rio do double-duty as locals' joints and major tourist draws with vibes just as swanky as Strip properties. But for the most part, malls and tract houses in this stretch give way to a small number of locals' casinos here such as the long-standing Gold Coast.

There are hidden gems in this area, and most of them exist in the industrial section a stone's throw (west) from the Strip. Number one on the list: Machine Guns Vegas, a decidedly upscale shooting range. Kuma Snow Cream, a frozen yogurt–like treat from chef Jet Tila, opened in 2013 and has garnered a cult following since then.

The West Side also has a small but thriving Chinatown. This three-block area has everything from ramen to vegan donuts to world-class Thai food. In particular, restaurants in a stretch of strip malls along Spring Mountain Road are known for their unpretentious and authentic experience. Not surprisingly, this is where many Strip chefs come to eat when they're not on the clock.

GETTING HERE AND AROUND

The Palms and the Rio are within easy taxicab distance from the Strip. The Rio is even walkable from the Center Strip—about 20 minutes west on Flamingo. As you venture beyond the Palms, you approach rental-car territory. Because the West Side is home to thousands of casino employees, public transportation blankets the area.

WORTH NOTING

Machine Guns Vegas. Swanky nightclub meets gun range in this only-in-Vegas addition to the scene. In an industrial neighborhood just west of the Interstate, "MGV" (as it's known) offers 10 shooting lanes, including two in an ultra-exclusive VIP area. Many of the instructors are attractive women. Visitors have dozens of firearms to choose from, everything from "miniguns" and .22-caliber handguns up to an M-60 fully automatic machine gun. Package deals include multiple guns. Guests can select their targets; among the options are evil clowns and Osama bin Laden. ⊠ *3501 Aldebaran Ave., West Side* ☎ *800/757–4668, 702/476–9228* ⊕ *www.machinegunsvegas.com* ⊲ *From $30 for handguns, $50 for machine guns* ☉ *Daily 9–6.*

FAMILY **Pole Position Raceway Las Vegas.** This is no putt-putting lawnmower-engine powered go-kart. These miniature racers are electric (think: souped-up golf carts) and reach up to 45 mph. You and 12 competitors zip around the ¼-mile indoor track full of twists and turns. The Pole Position computers track your overall performance from race to race, and over multiple visits. You'll get a score sheet giving a detailed score breakdown to compare with your friends. A free shuttle service is available from the big Strip hotels, 11–5 daily. ⊠ *4175 S. Arville, West Side* ☎ *702/227–7223* ⊕ *www.polepositionraceway.com/las-vegas* ⊲ *$50 for adults for 2 races, $44 for kids* ☉ *Sun.–Thurs. 11–11, Fri. and Sat. 11–midnight* ☞ *Adults must be 56 inches tall to ride; kids must be 48 inches.*

NEED A BREAK?

Ronald's Donuts. The best donuts in Vegas are sold at this tiny Chinatown storefront tucked in a strip mall along Spring Mountain Road. Locals rave about the apple fritters, but more traditional selections, such as Boston Creme, are addicting, too. Surprisingly, all of the offerings are vegan, a quirk that has put the hole-in-the-wall on the national map in recent years. Whenever you go, expect a line. ⊠ *4600 Spring Mountain Rd., West Side* ☎ *702/873–1032* ☉ *Weekdays 4–4, Sat. 5–4, Sun. 5–2.*

SUMMERLIN AND RED ROCK CANYON

Dining
★★★
Sightseeing
★★★★
Shopping
★★
Nightlife
★★

There's a master plan behind the western suburb of Summerlin, and it shows. The town—which was founded by movie legend Howard Hughes—has been developed and built out according to a written-on-paper strategy, a "planned community" through and through. Today the neighborhood comprises dozens of gated communities, as well as a handful of epic golf courses and casino resorts such as the J.W. Marriott and Red Rock Casino Resort & Spa.

Although the Red Rock Casino is hip and fun, the highlight of the region is the casino's namesake, the Red Rock National Conservation Area. This area, managed by the Bureau of Land Management, is an expansive open space that heads from civilization into the ocher-rock wilderness of the Spring Mountains beyond. Canyon walls boast some of the best rock climbing in the world. There also are petroglyphs, drawings by Native Americans who first inhabited this area more than 1,000 years ago.

One of the best ways to explore the wilderness outside Summerlin is, without question, on horseback. A number of outfitters run half- and full-day guided trips; some even include dinner. Just about every ride brings visitors up-close-and-personal with native flora and fauna, including Joshua trees, jackrabbits, and more. If possible, ask your guide to lead you to the top of the canyon for a one-of-a-kind glimpse of the Strip.

GETTING HERE AND AROUND

Public transportation to Summerlin exists from the Strip, but considering how long it would take you to get out there, the best bet is to rent a car. Interstate 215 winds around the outskirts of the Las Vegas Valley and ends in Summerlin; other options are taking surface roads such as Charleston Boulevard and Spring Mountain Road.

The West Side of Las Vegas is the gateway to the Red Rock Canyon National Conservation Area at the base of the Spring Mountains.

Visitor Info Red Rock Canyon Visitor Center. This modest visitor center, operated by the Red Rock Canyon Interpretive Association, contains an informative history of the region, as well as a number of exhibits on local flora and fauna. ⊠ *1000 Scenic Loop Dr.* ☎ *702/515-5367* ⊕ *www.redrockcanyonlv.org* 💳 *$7 per vehicle ($3 for bikes and pedestrians)* ⊘ *Weekdays 8–4:30; scenic loop open year-round, 6 am–dusk.*

TOP ATTRACTIONS

FAMILY
Fodor's Choice
★

Red Rock Canyon National Conservation Area. Red sandstone cliffs and dramatic desert landscapes await day-trippers and outdoors enthusiasts at Red Rock Canyon National Conservation Area. Operated by the Bureau of Land Management (BLM), the 195,819-acre national conservation area features narrow canyons, fantastic rock formations, seasonal waterfalls, desert wildlife, and rock art sites. The elevated Red Rock Overlook provides a fabulous view of the cream and red sandstone cliffs. For a closer look at the stunning scenery, take the 13-mile, one-way scenic drive through the canyon. The backcountry byway is open from dawn to dusk. Other activities including hiking, mountain biking, rock climbing, canyoneering, picnicking, and wildlife-watching. A developed campground, located 2 miles from the visitor center, has 71 campsites ($15 per night; $40 for group sites), pit toilets, and drinking water for visitors wanting to extend their stay. ⊠ *1000 Scenic Loop Dr., Summerlin* ⊕ *www.blm.gov.*

WORTH NOTING

Cowboy Trail Rides. The best way to explore the mountains of Red Rock National Conservation Area is by horseback, and Cowboy Trail Rides has it covered. The outfitter runs one-hour, half-, and full-day trips from a location just east of the Red Rock Visitor Center. Some of the trips include lunch or dinner. Scenic packages include the Sunset BBQ Ride (1 hour 45 minutes; $169 per person) and the WOW ride (5 hours; $329 per person). Beautiful views of the Strip give way to desert wilderness. Keep your eyes peeled for jackrabbits, Joshua trees, and other notable desert life. The view of the Strip isn't too shabby either. ⊠ *Red Rock Canyon Stables* ☎ *702/387–2457* ⊕ *www.cowboytrailrides.com.*

FAMILY **McGhie's Bike Outpost.** One of the largest outfitters in the Las Vegas Valley, McGhie's rents equipment for skiing, bicycling, and sandboarding. This location, in downtown Blue Diamond (there's another one closer to Summerlin), specializes in bikes; convenient, since it's right on the doorstep of 125 miles of hard-core mountain-biking. The company rents bikes individually, and also offers a host of guided tours around the Red Rock National Conservation Area and beyond. Unlike other outfitters in the area, McGhie's also rents bikes specifically for kids. ⊠ *16 Cottonwood # B, Blue Diamond* ☎ *702/875–4820* ⊕ *www.mcghies.com.*

WHERE TO STAY

TOP LAS VEGAS POOLS

You, a lounge chair, a tropical drink, and a gorgeous pool. Sound like your kind of vacation? Then plant yourself poolside in Sin City. Las Vegas might just be America's coolest landlocked beach resort.

Swimming pools can be just as over-the-top as the Strip sidewalk shows: fringed with lush landscaping and tricked out with wave machines, swim-up bars, ultraquiet misting machines, and wild waterslides. Or they can be snazzy affairs—think private cabanas (satellite TV, Wi-Fi, and private misting machines) that range in price from about $40 a day for a basic one at the Monte Carlo to $500 a day (on weekends) for one of the cabanas at Mandalay Bay's Moorea Beach Club, which offers European-style (read: topless) sunbathing for guests 21 and older.

Alas, unless you're a guest of the resort, many resorts don't allow you to use their pool facilities. If swimming and sunning are important to you then choose from any of the following resorts with pools that are guaranteed to be the perfect oases in the desert.

TOP PICKS

Caesar's Palace. The ancient Romans revered water for its healing powers, and they built sumptuous public baths amid fragrant gardens, exercise areas, and playing fields. Caesars Palace has re-created those glorious havens with its 4½-acre Garden of the Gods Pool Oasis, which is comprised of six pools and two whirlpool spas. Surrounding each pool are 40 posh rental cabanas and ample room for sunbathing. A poolside bar serves up cold treats as well as a full food menu.

Encore. Building off the success of the opulent pool next door at Wynn Las

Vegas, Encore boasts the Encore Beach Club, a two-tier pool and dayclub. The complex is open to hotel guests and the general public (generally beautiful public, that is). Inside, the semicircular spectacle revolves around a main pool with daybed-style cushions that appear to float like lily pads. Twenty-six cabanas ring the perimeter and eight bungalows offer the most indulgent accommodations (private hot tubs and bathrooms and individual air-conditioning). There's a gaming pavilion with craps and blackjack. In summer, premier deejays spin house every Sunday. The dayclub, naturally, becomes a happening nightclub after dark when the pool complex becomes an extension of Surrender Nightclub.

Hard Rock. The Hard Rock throws fabulous pool parties and bears an uncanny resemblance to that Polynesian beach hideaway you've always dreamed about. Its lushly landscaped Beach Club has truckloads of soft, white sand. There's even a high-quality underwater sound system. Grab a colorful cocktail at Palapa Lounge, with its Indonesian vibe and tropical waterfalls. Feeling lucky? Hit the swim-up blackjack bar. The cabanas resemble Tahitian huts, with thatch roofs and rattan chairs. Predictably, the Hard Rock caters to a young-adult crowd of hipsters and bon vivants in their 20s and 30s. If you're

outside this demographic, you may feel a bit like a fish out of water.

Mandalay Bay. The mother of all Vegas pools. The experience includes an 11-acre beach spread with a huge wave pool, a Euro-inspired topless poolclub with plush daybeds, a meandering river, and some of the cushiest cabanas in town. The beach is piled high with a couple thousand tons of California-imported golden sand, which feels just perfect between the toes. You can raft along the river, admiring the verdant foliage. After the sun sets, the beach becomes one of the city's hottest nightspots. There are also two casual restaurants and a casino right by the beach. A huge soundstage overlooks the wave pool, hosting concerts by a wide range of rock and pop acts all summer long.

HONORABLE MENTIONS

The Flamingo. The Flamingo may have lost its luster, but its pool still is one of the best around. Take a dip in Bugsy Siegel's original oval-shape pool, play swim-up blackjack, explore waterfalls in the lagoon pool, or swim beneath stone grottoes not unlike those at the Playboy Mansion (sorry, no naked women here). Throughout the entire pool area, real penguins, swans, and pink flamingoes roam free. Average pool furniture is on the cheap side, but it's Vegas—you can always pay to upgrade.

The Mirage. If you prefer a shaded, tropical spread, check out the verdant pool area at the classy Mirage. The two main pools are connected through a series of dramatic lagoons and waterfalls. The Mirage won't wow you with nonstop activities or goofy gimmicks—it's just a handsome, well-maintained pool that's ideal whether you're a serious aficionado or a toe-dipping dabbler. Lounge chairs are outfitted with comfy mesh sailcloth. The cabanas are chichi here, with teak chairs and high-end entertainment systems.

The Palms. This 3-acre complex at the Palms is open to the public (weekdays 9–6). It has three separate pools, all of which are fed by waterfalls and have colorful underwater lighting. The best feature is the triangular Glass Bar, set cleverly under a glass-bottom pool deck. If you want to go all out, book one of the 27 cabanas or bungalows, which are outfitted with high-end sound systems, plasma TVs, and swank furnishings. A handful of bungalows have their own lap pool, double-sided fireplace, bedroom, and lawn.

WORTH NOTING

Red Rock Resort has a beautiful swimming complex with a giant circular pool. The best of the Downtown pools is at the **Golden Nugget.** Be sure to try the waterslide that tunnels through the middle of the new 200,000-gallon aquarium. At the posh **M Resort** in Henderson, the entire Villagio del Sol pool complex offers sweeping views of desert mountains and the entire Strip.

3

Updated by
Matt Villano

The world of Vegas-area casino hotels changes constantly. In the early 2000s just about every resort was investing heavily in family-friendly accommodations and activities. Today, however, most places have refocused squarely on decadence and indulgence.

Just about every property now has a special pool for topless (they call it "European-style") sunbathing. Many resorts also have expanded their cocktail programs (the fancy word for this is now "mixology").

Some of these efforts have been more successful than others. The posh Encore Beach Club, at Encore, exemplifies the new notion of a "day-club" in that it creates a nightclub vibe during the day. Developments at the Cosmopolitan Las Vegas have had a similar impact; the property has three on-staff mixology gurus and a special kitchen where these cocktail whizzes whip up recipes all day long.

Other properties have established new benchmarks in amenities. When CityCenter opened in 2010, the $8.5-billion complex included Crystals, a new-era shopping mall with flagship stores of Prada, Tiffany & Co, and some of the spendiest boutiques in America. Also in 2010, the Palazzo launched "Prestige Suites," an optional $100 reservation upgrade that grants guests access to a concierge level including daily snack service, drink service, and a business center.

Despite competition from these up-and-comers, the established properties still pack 'em in. Bellagio's rooms still carry cachet, and the Mirage—the hotel that started the megaresort trend more than 20 years ago—continues to sell out. At Wynn Las Vegas and the Venetian, guests rave about everything from comfy beds to exquisite restaurants and great shopping. At Caesars Palace the constantly evolving Qua Baths & Spa might be one of the top spas in town. And for overall experience, the Four Seasons Las Vegas, which occupies top floors of the tower at Mandalay Bay Resort & Casino, is still one of the best.

WHERE SHOULD I STAY?

	Vibe	Pros	Cons
South Strip	Fun! Resorts here are glamorous, but not as serious as Center and North Strip properties. With roller coasters, arcades, shows, and beaches, properties are also the most kid-friendly.	Close to airport; plenty of diversions for the whole family; bargains at top Strip properties can be found here.	Need to take a taxi or monorail to hit Center Strip. Fewer shopping options than Center and North Strip.
Center Strip	Happening, hip section of Strip has the newest resorts with all of the latest and greatest amenities. Shopping in this part of town also is second to none.	Many rooms are new or recently renovated; spas are among the largest and most popular in town.	Traffic congestion, both on sidewalks and off; rooms generally pricier than they are elsewhere in town.
North Strip	Glitz and glamour rule. Rooms are among the largest and most ornate, and on-property amenities are all top-of-the-line.	Most (but not all) rooms are suites; incredible restaurant options; golf course at Wynn Las Vegas.	Highest prices on-site; long (and pricey) cab ride from the airport.
Downtown	Vegas as it used to be—back when rooms were an afterthought and everything was about the casino downstairs.	Affordable lodging; classic casinos; proximity to other diversions in the area.	Rooms are bare-bones; streets aren't entirely safe after dark; expensive taxi ride to big resorts on the Strip.
West Side and Summerlin	Smaller, more amenity-heavy resorts sit west of the Strip, with the most lavish of the bunch offering glamorous pools and golf courses nearby. Many resorts appeal to locals.	Quieter and away from the hustle of the Strip; lower room rates; incredible views of the Spring Mountains and the Strip.	Summerlin is a half hour from the Strip.
East Side and Henderson	Resorts here (and along Paradise Road) are functional. Instead of offering the latest and greatest in amenities, rooms are on the small side.	Lower prices than the Strip; on-site diversions such as bowling; proximity to local services.	Long taxi ride to the Strip (half hour from Henderson); doesn't have the excitement of the Strip.

LAS VEGAS LODGING PLANNER

TIMING YOUR TRIP

Especially on weekends, accommodations in Las Vegas fill up fast. When it's time for a big convention—or a big sporting event—it's not unusual for all of Las Vegas's roughly 150,000 hotel rooms to sell out completely. Combine those with three-day holidays, and you can see why it's wise to make lodging arrangements for busy weekends as far ahead as possible.

Many rooms in the Cosmopolitan have large, comfortable seating areas that make great places to relax with friends.

On the other hand, 2011 and 2012 marked the era of the last-minute deals. Many hotels, eager to fill rooms, were offering rock-bottom prices and tempting packages for as low as $79 per night (most offered these deals on their Twitter accounts). What does this mean for you? If you're not traveling during a busy weekend and have the luxury of waiting until the last minute, you probably can find a room somewhere in town—for dirt cheap. Look around.

GETTING THE BEST ROOM

There's no surefire way to ensure that you'll get the room you want, when you want it, and for the lowest price possible. But here are a few tips for increasing your chances:

Book early. This town's almost always busy, so book as early as possible. Generally, if you book a room for $125 and later find out that the hotel is offering the same category of room for $99, the hotel will match the lower price, so keep checking back to see if the rates have dropped. Of course, this won't work if you prepay for a room on Expedia, Orbitz, Kayak, or Priceline. It also won't work if you buy in for a prepaid package deal. Once you go this route, you either can't get out of the reservation or you may have to pay a hefty cancellation fee.

Getting the room you want. Actual room assignments aren't determined at most Vegas hotels until the day before, or the day of, arrival. If you're hoping for a particular room (for example, a room with a view of the Strip), phone the hotel a day before you arrive and speak with somebody at the front desk. This applies whether you booked originally through the hotel or some other website. Don't be pushy or presumptuous. Just

BEST BETS FOR LAS VEGAS RESORTS

Fodor's offers a selective listing of quality lodging experiences in every price range, from the city's best budget beds to its most sophisticated luxury hotels. Here are our top recommendations by price and experience. The very best properties—those that provide a particularly remarkable experience in their price range—are designated in the listings with the Fodor's Choice logo.

Fodor's Choice ★

Aria, p. 85
Bellagio, p. 87
Cosmopolitan Las Vegas, p. 91
The Delano, p. 110
Encore, p. 103
Four Seasons Hotel Las Vegas, p. 110
Green Valley Ranch Resort & Spa, p. 113
Mandarin Oriental Las Vegas, p. 93
Nobu Hotel, p. 111
The Palazzo, p. 105
The Platinum Hotel and Spa, p. 114
The Venetian, p. 107
Wynn Las Vegas, p. 109

Best By Price

$

Flamingo Las Vegas, p. 111
Green Valley Ranch Resort & Spa, p. 113
Harrah's Las Vegas, p. 111
Las Vegas Hotel & Casino, p. 114
Red Rock Casino Resort & Spa, p. 115
Rio All-Suite Hotel & Casino, p. 115

$$

Hard Rock Hotel & Casino, p. 113
Luxor Las Vegas, p. 75
MGM Grand Hotel & Casino, p. 79
Monte Carlo Resort and Casino, p. 110
New York–New York Resort & Casino, p. 81
Palms Casino Resort, p. 115
Paris Las Vegas, p. 97
Planet Hollywood Resort & Casino, p. 99
The Platinum Hotel and Spa, p. 114
Treasure Island, p. 112
Tropicana Las Vegas, p. 110

Trump International Hotel Las Vegas, p. 112
Vdara, p. 111

$$$

Aria, p. 85
Bellagio, p. 87
Caesars Palace, p. 89
Cosmopolitan Las Vegas, p. 91
The Delano, p. 110
Mandalay Bay, p. 77
The Palazzo, p. 105
The Venetian, p. 107
Wynn Las Vegas, p. 109

$$$$

Encore, p. 103
Four Seasons Hotel Las Vegas, p. 110
Mandarin Oriental, Las Vegas, p. 93

Best By Experience

BEST CONCIERGE

Bellagio, p. 87
Caesars Palace, p. 89
Four Seasons Hotel Las Vegas, p. 110
Mandarin Oriental, Las Vegas, p. 93
Nobu Hotel, p. 111

BEST HOTEL BAR

Aria, p. 85
Bellagio, p. 87
Cosmopolitan Las Vegas, p. 91
Mandarin Oriental, Las Vegas, p. 93
New York–New York Resort & Casino, p. 81
The Venetian, p. 107
Wynn Las Vegas, p. 109

BEST GYM

Aria, p. 85
Caesars Palace, p. 89
Encore, p. 103
Mandarin Oriental, Las Vegas, p. 93
Red Rock Casino Resort & Spa, p. 115
The Venetian, p. 107

BEST FOR ROMANCE

Caesars Palace, p. 89
Encore, p. 103
Mandarin Oriental, Las Vegas, p. 93

3

Paris Las Vegas, p. 97
Red Rock Casino
Resort & Spa, p. 115

BEST FOR BUSINESS

The Delano, p. 110
Four Seasons Hotel
Las Vegas, p. 110
Mandarin Oriental,
Las Vegas, p. 93
MGM Grand Hotel &
Casino, p. 79
The Venetian, p. 107

BEST VIEWS

Cosmopolitan Las
Vegas, p. 91
The M Resort, p. 114
Palms Casino Resort,
p. 115
Paris Las Vegas, p. 97
Red Rock Casino
Resort & Spa, p. 115

HIPPEST HOTELS

Aria, p. 85
Cosmopolitan Las
Vegas, p. 91
Hard Rock Hotel &
Casino, p. 113

Palms Casino Resort,
p. 115
The Platinum Hotel
and Spa, p. 114

BIGGEST (BY ROOM COUNT) HOTELS

Aria, p. 85
Caesars Palace, p. 89
Cosmopolitan Las
Vegas, p. 91
Mandalay Bay, p. 77
MGM Grand Hotel &
Casino, p. 79
Planet Hollywood
Resort & Casino, p. 99
The Venetian, p. 107

BEST LOBBY

Bellagio, p. 87
Caesars Palace, p. 89
Cosmopolitan Las
Vegas, p. 91
Four Seasons Hotel
Las Vegas, p. 110
The Palazzo, p. 105
Wynn Las Vegas, p. 109

BEST POOL

Caesars Palace, p. 89

Encore, p. 103
Flamingo Las Vegas,
p. 111
Hard Rock Hotel &
Casino, p. 113
Mandalay Bay, p. 77
Mirage Las Vegas,
p. 95
Palms Casino Resort,
p. 115
Wynn Las Vegas,
p. 109

BEST SERVICE

Bellagio, p. 87
Caesars Palace, p. 89
Four Seasons Hotel
Las Vegas, p. 110
Mandarin Oriental
Las Vegas, p. 93
Nobu Hotel, p. 111
Trump International
Hotel Las Vegas, p. 112
Wynn Las Vegas,
p. 109

BEST BUILDING ARCHITECTURE

Aria, p. 85
Caesars Palace, p. 89

Luxor Las Vegas, p. 75
Paris Las Vegas, p. 97
Red Rock Casino
Resort & Spa, p. 115
The Venetian, p. 107

BEST LOCATION

Aria, p. 85
Bellagio, p. 87
Caesars Palace, p. 89
Flamingo Las Vegas,
p. 111
Mirage Las Vegas,
p. 95
Paris Las Vegas, p. 97
Planet Hollywood
Resort & Casino, p. 99

BEST-KEPT SECRET

Monte Carlo Resort
and Casino, p. 110
Planet Hollywood
Resort & Casino, p. 99
The Platinum Hotel
and Spa, p. 114
Red Rock Casino
Resort & Spa, p. 115
Rio All-Suite Hotel &
Casino, p. 115

BEST BEDS

Caesars Palace, p. 89
Cosmopolitan Las
Vegas, p. 91
Encore, p. 103
Nobu Hotel, p. 111
The Palazzo, p. 105
Red Rock Casino
Resort & Spa, p. 115
Wynn Las Vegas,
p. 109

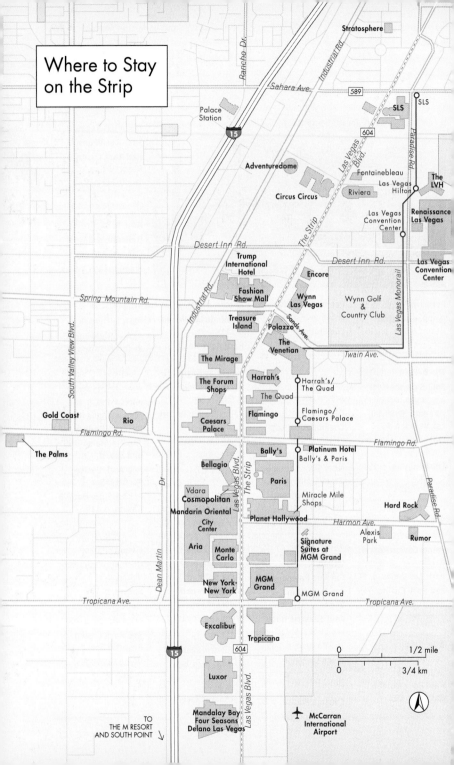

Where to Stay on the Strip

Stratosphere

Rancho Dr.

Industrial Rd.

Sahara Ave.

589

SLS

SLS

Palace Station

15

604

Paradise Rd.

Adventuredome

Fontainebleau

Las Vegas Blvd.

Riviera

Las Vegas Hilton

The LVH

Circus Circus

Las Vegas Convention Center

Renaissance Las Vegas

The Strip

Desert Inn Rd.

Desert Inn Rd.

Las Vegas Convention Center

Trump International Hotel

Encore

Spring Mountain Rd.

Industrial Rd.

Fashion Show Mall

Wynn Las Vegas

Wynn Golf & Country Club

Las Vegas Monorail

Treasure Island

Sands Ave.

Palazzo

The Venetian

Twain Ave.

South Valley View Blvd.

The Mirage

Harrah's

Harrah's/ The Quad

The Forum Shops

The Quad

Flamingo/ Caesars Palace

Gold Coast

Rio

Flamingo

Caesars Palace

The Palms

Flamingo Rd.

Platinum Hotel

Flamingo Rd.

Bally's

Bally's & Paris

Paradise Rd.

Bellagio

Las Vegas Blvd.

Paris

Hard Rock

Vdara

Cosmopolitan

Miracle Mile Shops

Mandarin Oriental

City Center

The Strip

Planet Hollywood

Harmon Ave.

Aria

Alexis Park

Rumor

Dean Martin Dr.

Monte Carlo

Signature Suites at MGM Grand

New York-New York

MGM Grand

Tropicana Ave.

MGM Grand

Tropicana Ave.

15

Excalibur

Tropicana

604

0   1/2 mile

0   3/4 km

Luxor

Las Vegas Blvd.

TO THE M RESORT AND SOUTH POINT ↓

Mandalay Bay
Four Seasons
Delano Las Vegas

McCarran International Airport

explain that although you realize the hotel can't guarantee a specific room, you'd appreciate it if they'd honor your preference.

Your second-best bet. Simply check in as early as possible on the day of arrival—even if no rooms are yet available (and you have to wait in the casino), you're likely to get first preference on the type of room you're seeking when it opens up.

What about upgrades? It's virtually never inappropriate to request a nicer room than the one you've booked. At the same time, it's virtually always inappropriate to expect that you'll receive the upgrade. The front-desk clerk has all the power and discretion when it comes to upgrades, and is unlikely to help you out if you act pushy or haughty. Gracious humility, smiles, and warmth go a long way.

Do I tip for an upgrade? It's not customary to tip hotel clerks for upgrades, especially at nicer properties. If you wave some cash around discreetly, it might not hurt, but it won't necessarily help either.

THE LOWDOWN ON RATES

In general, at an average of about $95 per night, rates for Las Vegas accommodations are lower than those in most other American resort and vacation cities. Still, the situation is changing; though rack rates for fancy properties are higher than ever, many hotels still offer fantastic deals. There are about a hundred variables that impact price, depending on who's selling the rooms (reservations, marketing, casino, conventions, wholesalers, packagers), what rooms you're talking about (standard, deluxe, minisuites, standard suites, deluxe suites, high-roller suites, penthouses, bungalows), and demand (weekday, weekend, holiday, conventions or sporting events in town).

When business is slow, many hotels reduce rates on rooms in their least desirable sections, sometimes with a buffet breakfast or even a show included. Most "sales" occur from early December to mid-February and in July and August, the coldest and hottest times of the year, and you can often find rooms for 50% to 75% less midweek than on weekends. Members of casino players clubs often get offers of discounted or even free rooms, and they can almost always reserve a room even when the rest of the hotel is "sold out."

WHAT IT COSTS				
	$	$$	$$$	$$$$
For two people	Under $140	$140–$220	$221–$320	over $320

Prices in the hotel-resort reviews are the lowest cost of a standard double room in high season, excluding taxes and service charges.

THE SOUTH STRIP

With an Oz-like structure that stretches forever, a pyramid with a light you can see from space, and a replica of the New York City skyline, the southern third of the Strip between CityCenter and the iconic "Welcome to Las Vegas" sign could be considered the entertainment hub of Vegas.

Resorts in this area include the Tropicana, Mandalay Bay, Luxor, Excalibur, MGM Grand, New York–New York, and Monte Carlo. Rooms on this side of town generally are within 10 to 15 minutes of the airport and are slightly more affordable than their Center and North Strip counterparts. After major renovations at the Tropicana and New York–New York in 2010 and 2011, the South Strip is among the most recently updated sections of Sin City's most famous street.

SOUTH STRIP TOP PICKS

Luxor Las Vegas

Mandalay Bay/The Delano

MGM Grand

New York–New York

This part of town has a small claim on Strip history as well; the Tropicana dates back 50 years, and the MGM, Mandalay Bay, and the Luxor were early entrants in the megaresort race of the '90s. And with every fight night at the MGM Grand, concert at Mandalay Bay, and annual event such as the Country Music Awards, entertainment history is written and rewritten from this side of Las Vegas Boulevard.

Another trend here: Ultra-exclusive hotels within the ordinary hotels. Mandalay has Delano Las Vegas and the Four Seasons; MGM has Skylofts; Monte Carlo has Hotel 32. You don't have to splurge to have a great time on the South Strip, but enjoying sumptuous linens, exclusive amenities, and unparalleled service every once in a while sure is special.

DID YOU KNOW?

New York–New York's towers, which include replicas of the Empire State Building, the Chrysler Building, and the CBS Building, are approximately one-third the actual size of the real buildings.

LUXOR LAS VEGAS AT A GLANCE

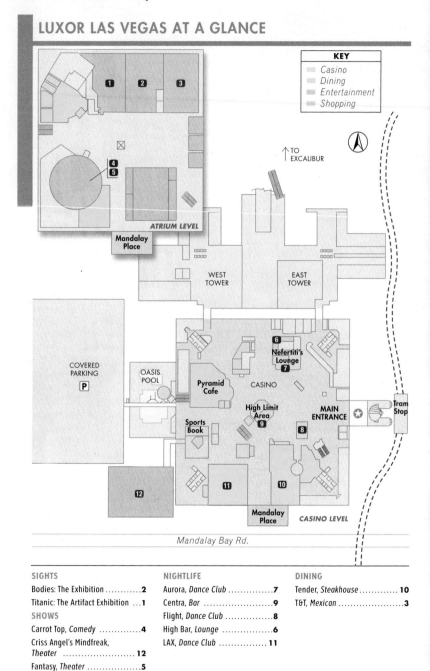

KEY
- Casino
- Dining
- Entertainment
- Shopping

1 **2** **3**

4
5

↑ TO
EXCALIBUR

ATRIUM LEVEL

Mandalay Place

WEST
TOWER

EAST
TOWER

COVERED
PARKING

P

OASIS POOL

Pyramid Cafe

CASINO

6
Nefertiti's Lounge
7

High Limit Area
9

Sports Book

8

MAIN ENTRANCE

Tram Stop

12

11

10

Mandalay Place

CASINO LEVEL

Mandalay Bay Rd.

LUXOR LAS VEGAS

Rooms from: $189 ✉ 3900 Las Vegas Blvd. S, South Strip ☎ 702/262-4000, 877/386-4658 www.luxor.com 3,958 rooms, 442 suites No meals.

AMENITIES

- The Luxor has one of the largest pools on the Strip. For a truly indulgent treat, rent a cabana and receive poolside VIP services such as hand-delivered treats and iced aromatherapy towels, to name a few.
- At Nurture, the resort's spa, enjoy a eucalyptus steam bath, dry sauna, and whirlpools as preparation for any number of rejuvenating massage treatments.
- Women (or couples) eager to take sexy (but tasteful) photos can schedule an in-room boudoir photo session with a local photographer.

Welcome to the land of the Egyptians—Vegas style. This modern-world wonder is topped with a xenon light beam that burns brighter than any other in the world and can be seen from anywhere in the valley at night; for that matter, it's supposedly even visible from space. The exterior is made with 13 acres of black glass. Forget elevators; climbing the slanted walls of the Luxor pyramid requires four "inclinators" to reach guest rooms. On each floor, open-air hallways overlook the world's largest atrium. Pyramid rooms are large but otherwise nondescript. One wall slopes because of the building's design—an interesting effect, but it makes these rooms feel cramped. We prefer the twin 22-story towers next door: they're newer and have brighter rooms with large windows, many that offer killer views of the pyramid. Bathrooms are spacious and have separate showers and tubs. Spa suites in the pyramid have plenty of extra space and deep whirlpool tubs with brilliant views of the skyline. **Pros:** decent value; hip casino; expansive pool. **Cons:** slanted room walls; removed from main Strip action.

HIGHLIGHTS

The Atrium: Inside is the world's largest atrium—you get the full impact of the space from the second floor, where "BODIES . The Exhibition" gives guests an eerie view of the human body.

Fantasy: This seductive adult revue is fun to share with your significant other.

The . . . um . . . archaelology: For something entirely unique, head outside the casino, walk past the porte cochere, and follow the sidewalk inside a replica of the Great Sphinx of Giza. Only in Vegas.

MANDALAY BAY AT A GLANCE

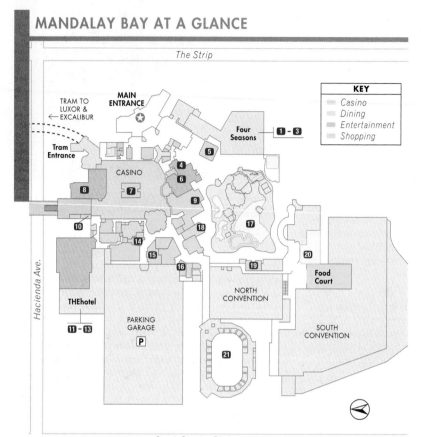

SIGHTS

Shark Reef **20**

SPAS AND POOLS

Four Seasons Pool **5**

Four Seasons Spa **1**

Mandalay Bay Pool **17**

Spa Mandalay **4**

THEbathhouse **11**

ENTERTAINMENT VENUES

House of Blues at Mandalay Bay,
Arts Center **8**

Mandalay Bay Events Center,
Arts Center **21**

NIGHTLIFE

Eyecandy Sound Lounge & Bar,
Lounge **7**

The Lounge at Delano Las Vegas,
Lounge **13**

Mix at Delano Las Vegas,
Lounge **12**

EXPENSIVE DINING

Aureole, Contemporary **18**

Charlie Palmer Steak,
Steakhouse **2**

Fleur, Continental **8**

MIX, Continental **12**

RM Seafood, Seafood **10**

Stripsteak, Steakhouse **16**

Verandah, Contemporary **3**

MODERATE DINING

Border Grill, Southwestern **19**

House of Blues, Cajun–Creole ...**8**

Lupo, Italian **15**

Red Square, Contemporary **14**

INEXPENSIVE DINING

Bay Side Buffet, Buffet **9**

Raffles Cafe, American **6**

MANDALAY BAY

$ *Rooms from: $279* ⊠ *3950 Las Vegas Blvd. S, South Strip* ☎ *702/632-7777, 877/632-7800* ⊕ *www.mandalaybay.com* ⌁ *2,775 rooms, 436 suites* ⏐◯⏐ *No meals.*

3

AMENITIES

■ Mandalay Beach offers guests a wave pool, lazy river, three swimming pools, and 2,700 tons of real sand that's trucked in regularly. The Beach has premium seating and the exclusive Beachside Casino. Moorea Beach Club also offers raft and tube rentals, as well as cabanas, daybeds, and bungalows and villas with personalized service.

■ Two on-site spas–Spa Mandalay (at Mandalay Bay) and Bathhouse (at the Delano)–offer a variety of relaxation chambers and dozens of signature treatments. Men love the gentlemen's facial at Spa Mandalay; women swear by the crème brûlée treatment at Bathhouse.

■ Mandalay Place, a shopping corridor that connects Mandalay Bay to the Luxor next door, offers a number of shops, including Nike Golf, Urban Outfitters, and more.

This resort is actually three hotels in one—the namesake Mandalay Bay, the Delano, and the Four Seasons Hotel Las Vegas. Each brand is distinct, and each has a separate entrance. Mandalay itself is decked out like a South Seas beach resort, complete with the scent of coconut oil drifting through the casino and pagodas rising out of the vast casino floor. It's the most affordable and least fabulous lodging component of the overall resort, but it's still a first-rate property with cavernous rooms. Bathrooms have stone floors and counters, as well as deep soaking tubs with separate showers. Guests also receive full access to the Beach, the Beachside Casino, and the Moorea Beach Club, which offers topless sunbathing. Perhaps the only downside to staying at Mandalay Bay is the spacious layout of the property itself; without a map, it could take you five or six tries to get your bearings when you come and go. **Pros:** large rooms; ample options; the beach. **Cons:** getting used to the sprawling layout takes time.

HIGHLIGHTS

The Sharks: The whales may be at the tables, but the Shark Reef aquarium features a 1.6-million-gallon saltwater tank with more than 2,000 different animals.

The Concerts: Between an outdoor pavilion and the House of Blues inside the casino, there's never a shortage of good live music at this joint.

The Views: Atop Mandalay Bay, The Foundation Room brings in deejays every night of the week. Atop the Delano, MIX Lounge serves up fancy cocktails and some of the most incredible views in town.

The Eats: Celebrity-chef restaurants by Charlie Palmer, Hubert Keller, Rick Moonen, and Mary Sue Milliken offer foodies plenty of options for just about every night of a stay.

MGM GRAND AT A GLANCE

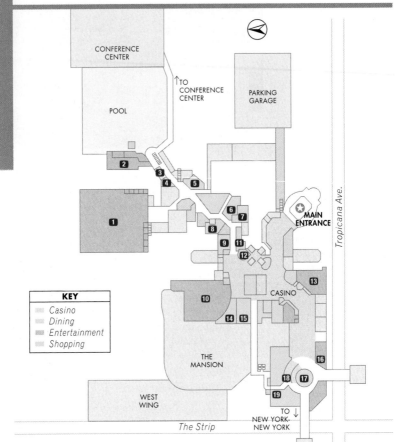

KEY
- Casino
- Dining
- Entertainment
- Shopping

CONFERENCE CENTER

TO CONFERENCE CENTER

PARKING GARAGE

POOL

MAIN ENTRANCE

Tropicana Ave.

CASINO

THE MANSION

WEST WING

TO NEW YORK–NEW YORK

The Strip

MGM GRAND HOTEL & CASINO

$ *Rooms from: $209* ✉ *3799 Las Vegas Blvd. S, South Strip* ☎ *702/891–1111, 877/880–0880* ⊕ *www.mgmgrand.com* ⤶ *4,293 rooms, 751 suites* ⑩ *No meals.*

AMENITIES

■ MGM has one of the largest pool complexes in the world—five separate pools, three separate whirlpools, and a lazy river for meandering in giant inner tubes.

■ Airport check-in from 9 am to 11 pm

■ Rooms in the hotel's "Stay Well" program include air purification systems, as well as vitamin-C showers and dawn simulator alarm clocks.

■ In-room "entertainment hubs" allow guests to connect to the Internet, project presentations on the flat-screen television, charge multiple devices, and play MP3 players.

The four emerald-green, fortress-like towers of the MGM Grand make up one of the largest hotels in the world. Rooms in the 30-story towers come in nine different varieties. Standard accommodations are masculine and modern. Further up the line, the various types of suites are more stylish and striking, and offer many fun perks. The best of the bunch include the 650-square-foot Bungalow suites, which are fitted with black-and-white Italian-marble bathrooms; the corner Premiere suites, which come with four-person dining areas and two TVs; and the two-story Terrace suites, which have 14-foot vaulted ceilings. At the very high end, the super-posh **Skylofts** occupy the hotel's top two floors and include airport transfers via Mercedes limos, separate check-in, butler service, and preferred seating at top restaurants and *KÀ*. There also are 29 villas in the **Mansion at MGM Grand**, the resort's high-roller palace. Overall, few resorts in the world have a bigger pool and sunbathing area—a maze of pedestrian bridges, fountains, river courses, and waterfalls lends a tropical air to these popular grounds. **Pros:** truly grand, great concerts and fights; fantastic restaurants. **Cons:** long schlep to parking (use free valet, but it can take up to 10 minutes to get your car.)

HIGHLIGHTS

Hakkasan: This upscale restaurant and nightclub has amassed a following in London and New York.

The "City of Entertainment": MGM delivers on their self-proclamation with the impressive MGM Grand Garden Arena—which hosts big-name concerts and championship boxing matches.

Family fun: Younger kids enjoy the Rainforest Cafe with its talking robot-animals; older kids love providing feedback on television pilots at CBS Television City.

NEW YORK–NEW YORK AT A GLANCE

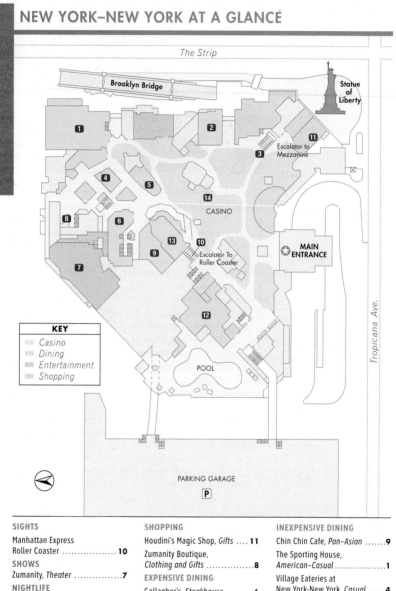

The Strip

Brooklyn Bridge

Statue of Liberty

1

2

3 Escalator to Mezzanine

11

4

5

14

CASINO

8

6

13

10

9 Escalator To Roller Coaster

7

MAIN ENTRANCE

12

KEY
- Casino
- Dining
- Entertainment
- Shopping

Tropicana Ave.

POOL

PARKING GARAGE
P

SIGHTS

Manhattan Express
Roller Coaster **10**

SHOWS

Zumanity, *Theater* **7**

NIGHTLIFE

The Bar at Times Square,
Piano Bar/Lounge **5**

Center Bar, *Lounge* **14**

Coyote Ugly, *Piano Bar/Lounge* .. **3**

SHOPPING

Houdini's Magic Shop, *Gifts* **11**

Zumanity Boutique,
Clothing and Gifts **8**

EXPENSIVE DINING

Gallagher's, *Steakhouse* **6**

MODERATE DINING

America, *American* **12**

Il Fornaio, *Italian* **13**

Nine Fine Irishmen, *Irish* **2**

INEXPENSIVE DINING

Chin Chin Cafe, *Pan–Asian* **9**

The Sporting House,
American-Casual **1**

Village Eateries at
New York-New York, *Casual* **4**

NEW YORK–NEW YORK RESORT & CASINO

$\boxed{\$}$ *Rooms from: $169* ⊠ *3790 Las Vegas Blvd. S, South Strip* ☎ *702/740–6969, 800/689–1797* ⊕ *www. newyorknewyork.com* ⇌ *1,920 rooms, 104 suites* ❢❢ *No meals.*

AMENITIES

■ At the Spa at New York–New York, therapists perform a variety of treatments, including Swedish and deep-tissue massages, hydrotherapy, and facials.

■ The Salon is a great place for haircuts and mani-pedis.

■ The pool is small, but if you splurge $40 or more extra for a VIP pass you get guaranteed seating, two raft rentals, an assortment of nonalcoholic beverages, and a snack basket.

Vegas takes on Manhattan in this fantasy version of the Big Apple. The mini-Manhattan skyline is one of our favorite parts of the Strip—there are third-size to half-size re-creations of the Empire State Building, the Statue of Liberty, and the Chrysler buildings, as well as the New York Public Library, Grand Central Terminal, and the Brooklyn Bridge. Rooms are quite a bit larger than the typically tiny hotel rooms in the *real* NYC. Beyond all the legroom, they're not particularly fancy, but the hotel has made some improvements in recent years. Also, the trek from the front desk to some of the towers can feel longer than the New York City Marathon, and the Manhattan Express roller coaster that loops around the hotel can be intrusively loud if your room is near the tracks. Several grades of room are available, and as you pay more, you get plush amenities such as separate sitting areas with sofas, marble bathroom counters, and separate glass showers. **Pros:** one of the most fun-theme resorts; art deco lobby; casino floor center bar. **Cons:** cramped sports book; mediocre pool.

HIGHLIGHTS

The Roller Coaster: Also known as the "Manhattan Express," this attraction darts between the "buildings" of the hotel's skyline and is hands down the best ride on the Strip.

Big Apple flavor: While you explore, keep your eye out for details such as names on mailboxes and brownstone apartment façades with air-conditioners in the windows.

Chocolate heaven: Hershey's Chocolate World, a two-story wonderland of all things chocolate, has the goods to satisfy the strongest sweet tooths.

3

DID YOU KNOW?

One of the best places to view the Bellagio's famous dancing fountains is from the Eiffel Tower's observation deck, directly across the street.

3

THE CENTER STRIP

Things tend to be larger than life in the heart of the Strip. Consider the scale replica of the Eiffel Tower—half the size of the original. Or wander into CityCenter, the $8.5-billion city-within-a-city.

This part of the Strip stretches from CityCenter and Planet Hollywood to the Mirage, including Mandarin Oriental, the Cosmopolitan, Paris, Bally's, Caesars Palace (and the Nobu Hotel), the Flamingo, and Harrah's along the way. Taken as a group, these properties represent some of the most storied on the Strip (Caesars Palace and the Flamingo) and the newest (the Cosmopolitan).

The Center Strip can be characterized by shopping. Lots and lots of shopping. The highest of the high-end stores are inside Crystals, the gateway to CityCenter. At Planet Hollywood, reputable brands dominate the Miracle Mile. Stores inside the astonishing Forum Shops, next to Caesars, fall somewhere in between. The Center Strip even is home to one of the largest Walgreens in the world. Another commonality among hotels here: great spas. Treatment options at Mandarin Oriental, Aria, the Cosmopolitan, and Caesars Palace could keep visitors busy (or is it relaxed?) for months. Some spas also offer hammams.

Rooms themselves in this area are all over the lot; some, like standard rooms at Bally's, are affordable and bare-bones; others, such as those inside the Cosmopolitan, make all others appear to be so yesterday. It pays to shop around

CENTER STRIP TOP PICKS

Aria

Bellagio

Caesars Palace

The Cosmopolitan

Mandarin Oriental

The Mirage

Paris

Planet Hollywood

ARIA AT A GLANCE

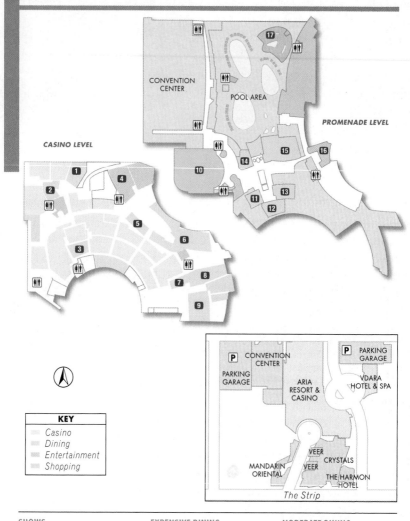

ARIA

$ *Rooms from: $269* ✉ *3730 Las Vegas Blvd. S, Center Strip* ☎ *702/590–7757, 866/359–7757, 877/580–2742 SkySuites* ⊕ *www.aria.com* ⇲ *3,436 rooms, 568 suites* ⑩ *No meals.*

3

AMENITIES

■ Aria's spa is one of the few spas in the country to offer Japanese stone sauna "Ganbanyoku" beds, and boasts three private spa "suites," each of which serves up to eight people at a time.

■ Crystals, the adjacent shopping and entertainment complex, offers some of the most high-end boutiques in the nation, including Gucci, Prada, Mikimoto, Tom Ford, and Harry Winston (to name a few).

■ Aria remains one of the largest buildings in the world to achieve LEED Gold certification from the U.S. Building Council.

★ **Fodor's Choice** Glistening like a futuristic oasis in the heart of the Strip, Aria truly deserves most of the attention it receives. The lobby is a soaring, three-story atrium bathed in natural light (a novel concept in this town). There's even more natural light upstairs, where every guest room boasts floor-to-ceiling windows. Tech-geeks will love the touch-screen control pad that operates everything from curtains to television, music, and lights. Bathrooms are modern and spacious, and nightly turndown service and laptop-size safes are nice touches. The Aria SkySuites are notable; starting at 1,050 square feet and getting larger from there, these upper-floor accommodations are downright palatial and have some of the best views in town. **Pros:** high-tech rooms; natural light; service. **Cons:** confusing technology for Luddites; shower set-up soaks the tub.

HIGHLIGHTS

The art: Aria is home to many of the pieces that comprise CityCenter's $40 million fine art collection—Maya Lin's "Colorado River," an 84-foot sculpture of reclaimed silver that mirrors the route of the eponymous waterway, hangs in the lobby behind the check-in desk.

The show: *Zarkana* offers a Cirque du soleil spin on the traditional variety show.

The pools: Take a dip in (or just people-watch near) one of three ellipse-shape pools on the secluded pool deck. Inquire about deals for cabanas; especially midweek, they can be surprisingly affordable.

The room-service: Most of the on-site restaurants will deliver to your room; all you have to do is ask.

BELLAGIO AT A GLANCE

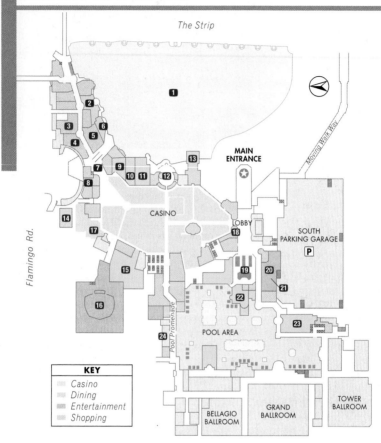

BELLAGIO LAS VEGAS

⑤ *Rooms from: $249* ✉ *3600 Las Vegas Blvd. S, Center Strip* ☏ *702/693–7111, 888/987–6667* ⊕ *www.bellagio.com* 🛏 *3,421 rooms, 512 suites* 🍽 *No meals.*

AMENITIES

■ Marvel at the Mediterranean-infused alfresco pool complex, which comprises five pools, a café, and a pool bar. Book a chair inside one of the ultra-exclusive Cypress Premier Lounges and enjoy chilled towels and smoothie shots throughout the day.

■ Spa Bellagio, where traditional treatments such as Swedish and deep-tissue massages are complemented by innovative hydrotherapy and hot-stone options. The salon, which offers full nail services, also is considered one of Vegas's best.

■ The Via Bellagio shopping corridor contains luxe boutiques, with names like Chanel, Dior, and Gucci.

★ **Fodor's Choice** Bellagio is impressive more for its refined elegance than for gimmicks. If it's pampering you're after, stay in the Spa Tower, which has impressive rooms and suites (with steam showers and soaking tubs), as well as an expanded full-service spa and salon. Rooms in the original hotel tower are snazzy, with Italian marble and luxurious fabrics that were refreshed in 2011. Elegant, faux Italian provincial furniture surrounds either a single king-size bed or two queen-size beds. Bellagio has one of the higher staff-to-guest ratios in town, which results in visibly more solicitous service than you might expect at such an enormous property. This service is best in the Executive Suite Lounge, which opened in January 2009 and offers complimentary business center services. **Pros:** centrally located; posh suites; classy amenities. **Cons:** not kid-friendly; pricey; pretentious attitude among some guests.

HIGHLIGHTS

Top-tier meals: With eateries from Michael Mina, Jean-Gorges Vongerichten, and Julian Serrano, Bellagio (still) has one of the best restaurant-rosters in town.

The Bellagio fountains: More than 1,200 fountains erupt in a choreographed water ballet across the man-made Bellagio lake.

The lobby: Walking into the lobby, you're greeted with a fantastic and colorful glass sculpture called *Fiori di Como*, by famed artist Dale Chihuly.

The Conservatory: A beautiful indoor botanical conservatory. The gardens are particularly stunning during Christmas and Chinese New Year.

CAESARS PALACE AT A GLANCE

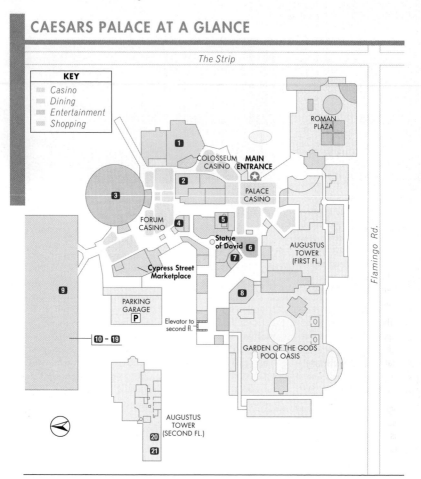

SPAS

Qua Baths & Spa **20**

SHOWS

Celine Dion, *Theater*..............**3**

Colosseum at Caesars Palace,
Arts Center **3**

NIGHTLIFE

Cleopatra's Barge, *Lounge* **5**

PURE, *Dance Club* **1**

Shadow, *Lounge* **4**

SHOPPING

Burberry,
Men and Women's Clothing **19**

Christian Dior, *Men and Women's
Clothing* **18**

Forum Shops at Caesars, *Mall* **9**

Gucci, *Women's Clothing* **12**

Harry Winston, *Jewelry* **11**

Louis Vuitton,
Luggage & Accessories **16**

Michael Kors, *Accessories* **10**

Salvatore Ferragamo,
Men's Clothing **17**

EXPENSIVE DINING

BOA Steakhouse, *Eclectic* **13**

Guy Savoy, *French* **21**

Mesa Grill, *Southwestern* **2**

Payard Patisserie, *Bakery* **6**

Rao's, *Italian* **8**

MODERATE DINING

Beijing Noodle No.9, *Chinese* **7**

Joe's Seafood, Prime Steak &
Stone Crab, *Seafood* **14**

Spago Las Vegas,
Contemporary **15**

CAESARS PALACE

$ *Rooms from: $239* ✉ *3570 Las Vegas Blvd. S, Center Strip* ☎ *702/731–7110, 866/227–5938* ⊕ *www.caesarspalace. com* 🛏 *4,141 rooms and suites* 🍽 *No meals.*

AMENITIES

■ Guests continue to rave about Qua Baths & Spa. For massages, the facility offers 51 treatment rooms, including wet rooms with Vichy showers and an herbal steam room.

■ Hair highlights are the specialty at the on-site salon, Color—a Salon by Michael Boychuck.

■ At The Men's Zone barber Sal Jeppi administers old-school flat-razor shaves with lather from a latherizer machine that's probably older than you are.

■ Dogs that weigh 50 pounds or less are welcome in certain rooms through the hotel's PetStay program.

The opulent entrance, fountains, Roman statuary, bas-reliefs, and roaming centurions all add up to one over-the-top Las Vegas icon. Here you can get your picture taken with Caesar, Cleopatra, and the centurion guard; find the full-size reproduction of Michelangelo's *David*; or amble along Roman streetscapes in the Forum Shops to see replicas of fountains from Italy. Caesars was one of the first Vegas properties to offer lavish rooms; today they're as sumptuous as any on the Strip. Book a Deluxe Room in the Octavius or Augustus towers; these rooms have marble-and-brass bathrooms with oversize whirlpool tubs. **Nobu Hotel**, a Japanese-theme hotel-within-a-hotel, features feng shui spaces and minimalist, natural-hued rooms. The second floor of the Augustus Tower features Qua Baths & Spa and Guy Savoy, the famous French chef's first restaurant outside Paris. **Pros:** Arctic ice rooms at Qua; Garden of the Gods Pool Oasis; storied property. **Cons:** complex floor plan is difficult to get your bearings; small casino; limited on-site parking.

HIGHLIGHTS

The shopping: Caesars has some of the best shopping of any Vegas resort, with more than 160 stores at the Forum and Appian Way shops.

The pools: The lavish Garden of the Gods Pool Oasis, a series of Roman-style gardens, baths, and fitness areas anchored by the Temple pool, is one of the best pool spots in town.

The entertainment: Shows at the Colosseum include Celine Dion, Shania Twain, and Jerry Seinfeld.

The service: Through a program called The Laurel Collection, guests of certain rooms in the Augustus and Octavius towers get personalized check-in and their own entrance to the Garden of the Gods pools.

COSMOPOLITAN LAS VEGAS AT A GLANCE

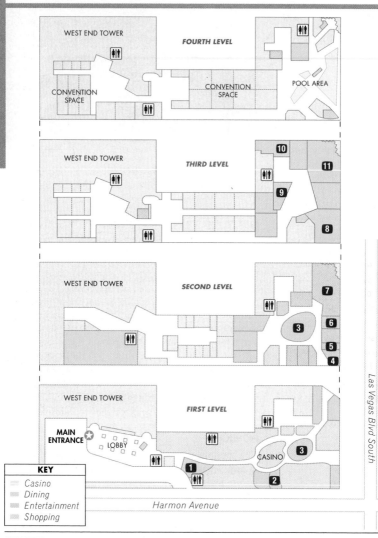

NIGHTLIFE

Book and Stage, *Lounge* **1**

The Chandelier, *Lounge* **3**

Marquee, *Nightclub* **2**

SHOPPING

AllSaints, *Vintage Clothing* **7**

DNA2050, *Women's Clothing* **4**

Molly Brown's,
Women's Clothing **5**

Stitched, *Men's Clothing* **6**

EXPENSIVE DINING

Estiatorio, *Greek* **8**

Jaleo, *Spanish Tapas* **9**

MODERATE DINING

Comme ça,
French Brasserie **11**

Scarpetta, *Italian* **10**

THE COSMOPOLITAN OF LAS VEGAS

$ Rooms from: $289 ⊠ 3708 Las Vegas Blvd. S, Center Strip ☎ 702/698–7000 ⊕ www. cosmopolitanlasvegas.com ⇨ 2,436 rooms, 559 suites ⏊ No meals.

AMENITIES

■ A slate of restaurants that includes offerings from Scott Conant (Scarpetta, D.O.C.G.), Jose Andreas (Jaleo, China Poblano), and Costas Spilidas (Estiatorio Milos) will excite even the most jaded diner.

■ The on-site spa, Sahra, offers dozens of unique skin and body treatments, and boasts one of the few open-to-the-public hammams in town.

■ Violet Hour Salon, the on-site beauty parlor, specializes in hair, nails, and makeup.

■ One-of-a-kind boutiques, including Stitched (men's clothes), Retrospecs & Co. (eyewear), and Kid Robot (toys).

★ Fodor's Choice The Cosmopolitan is truly different Las Vegas resort experience—a blend of arty sophistication and comfortable elegance. Everything about accommodations starts with the open-air private terraces. The vast majority the hotel's 2,995 rooms and suites boast them, and they're the only standard outdoor balconies on the Strip (north-facing terraces are the best, as they look out on the Fountains at Bellagio next door). The other distinguishing characteristic in many Cosmo rooms is the kitchenette; a mini-fridge and microwave are available for guest use. Rooms also feature plush and comfortable couches, coffee-table art books, and a spacious work desk. Bathrooms are enormous, and most feature a soaking tub, stand-alone shower, and ample counter space. All rooms boast state-of-the-art technology that allows guests to preset ambiences including lighting, music, and temperature, and book dining and spa reservations through the TV. **Pros:** terraces; in-room technology; Yoo-Hoo in mini-bar! **Cons:** kitchenette seems random; walls paper-thin.

HIGHLIGHTS

The nightlife: The main attractions are Marquee night-club and The Chandelier—a three-story bar that exists in a giant light fixture. Rose.Rabbit.Lie comprises three bars, a restaurant, and live circus-like entertainment.

The creativity: Consider the vending machine with wood-block paintings from local artists and the limited-edition sneakers at CRSVR Sneaker Boutique.

The Club: The Talon Club is more than just a high-limit gaming salon; it's a speakeasy and a place to unwind from the hubbub of the casino floor.

The pool deck: Three different pools on the mezzanine offer three different daytime experiences.

MANDARIN ORIENTAL LAS VEGAS AT A GLANCE

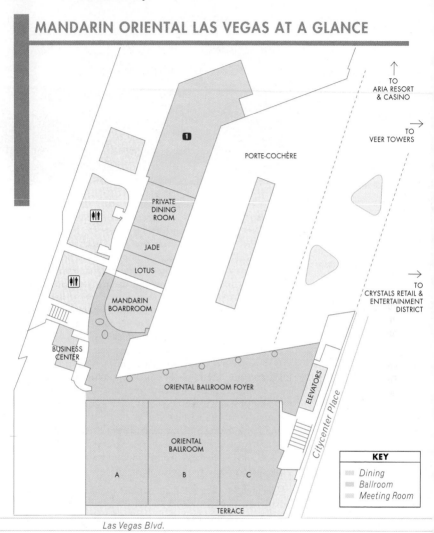

TO
ARIA RESORT
& CASINO

TO
VEER TOWERS

PORTE-COCHÈRE

TO
CRYSTALS RETAIL &
ENTERTAINMENT
DISTRICT

PRIVATE
DINING
ROOM

JADE

LOTUS

MANDARIN
BOARDROOM

BUSINESS
CENTER

ORIENTAL BALLROOM FOYER

ELEVATORS

Citycenter Place

ORIENTAL
BALLROOM

A   B   C

KEY

Dining
Ballroom
Meeting Room

TERRACE

Las Vegas Blvd.

EXPENSIVE DINING
Twist (23rd floor)

MODERATE DINING
Mozen Bistro **1**

MANDARIN ORIENTAL, LAS VEGAS

$ Rooms from: $399 ⊠ 3752 Las Vegas Blvd. S, Center Strip ☎ 702/590–8888, 888/881–9578 ⊕ www.mandarinoriental.com/lasvegas ⤳ 335 rooms, 57 suites ♉ No meals.

AMENITIES

■ The Mandarin's spa is one of the most sophisticated in town, comprising a hammam, laconium, and rhassoul, as well as a full line of reflexology treatments and a special Chinese foot spa.

■ Shoes are shined on-site and returned to guests through special valet closets that provide security and privacy at the same time.

■ Luxurious bed linens, flat irons, Frette robes, and private valet closets in rooms.

As a brand, Mandarin Oriental pledges to provide everything for the business traveler, and the Vegas property certainly delivers on that promise. Rooms are on the small side, though sumptuous sheets and soothing Asian-inspired artwork relieve any closed-in feelings you might have. The in-room desk comes with hardware that can project a laptop screen on the television; a special "valet" closet near the door enables butlers to drop off dry cleaning safely without disturbing guests; and the flat iron is a wonderful amenity in the bathroom. The spa at the Mandarin Oriental, Las Vegas, is only open to hotel guests, so there's never a crowd. In addition to a Chinese foot spa (which quiets even the most loudly barking dogs), guests can experience a hammam, a laconium, an ice fountain, and a ladies' rhassoul (a treatment that revolves around special Moroccan mud). Men will appreciate the face, shoulder, and scalp massage. On the 23rd floor, the Mandarin Bar serves up great cocktails and views alike. **Pros:** efficiency; relative tranquillity; valet closet. **Cons:** smallish rooms; almost overly formal.

HIGHLIGHTS

The tea: Afternoon tea at Mandarin Bar includes finger sandwiches, desserts, and the option of a glass of champagne.

The wellness: Free daily yoga classes are held in a studio overlooking the Strip.

The pool: The Mandarin pool is both intimate and exclusive, the two best qualities in a Las Vegas swimming hole. Sun-worshippers also can order food from the Pool Café.

The eats: Pierre Gagnaire, the father of modern fusion, presents Twist, one of two on-site restaurants. MOzen Bistro serves a top-notch breakfast menu and one of the most eclectic Sunday brunches on the Strip.

MIRAGE AT A GLANCE

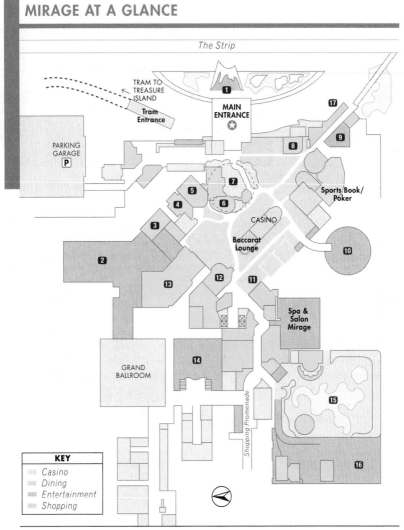

The Strip

TRAM TO TREASURE ISLAND

Tram Entrance

MAIN ENTRANCE ⭐

PARKING GARAGE P

Sports Book/ Poker

CASINO

Baccarat Lounge

Spa & Salon Mirage

GRAND BALLROOM

Shopping Promenade

KEY
- Casino
- Dining
- Entertainment
- Shopping

SIGHTS

Mirage Pool 15

Siegfried & Roy's Secret Garden and Dolphin Habitat 16

Tropical Lobby Rainforest 7

Volcano at Mirage 1

SHOWS

Love, *Cirque du Soleil Theater* 10

The Terry Fator Theater 14

NIGHTLIFE

1 Oak, *Dance Club* 2

REVOLUTION, *Lounge* 11

Rhumbar, *Lounge* 17

EXPENSIVE DINING

Fin, *Seafood* 4

Japonais, *Pan Asian* 6

Onda, *Italian* 3

Samba, *Brazilian* 12

STACK, *Contemporary* 5

INEXPENSIVE DINING

BLT Burger, *Bistro* 9

Carnegie Deli, *Deli* 8

Cravings Buffet, *Buffet* 13

MIRAGE LAS VEGAS

$ *Rooms from: $209* ✉ *3400 Las Vegas Blvd. S, Center Strip* ☎ *702/791–7111, 800/374–9000* ⊕ *www.mirage.com* 🛏 *2,763 rooms, 281 suites* 🍽 *No meals.*

3

AMENITIES

■ No, it's not a mirage—the pools at the Mirage really are as beautiful as they seem. Surrounded by lush tropical landscaping, the pools interconnect through lagoons and link around a magnificent cascading waterfall. At Bare Pool Lounge, the newest addition to the pool complex, DJ-spun music sets a lively mood as guests enjoy European-style sunbathing secluded by towering palms.

■ The on-site salon specializes in hair coloring. If you're seeking a blow-out, be sure to ask about discount packages.

■ The Spa offers challenging (but almost offensively expensive) pool- and dolphin-side yoga classes on weekends.

When Steve Wynn opened the Mirage in 1989, the $630-million property was the most expensive resort-casino in history. The hotel's distinctive gold windows get their color from actual gold used in the tinting process. Once it started to look a little *too* 1989, compared to modern hotel trends, the Mirage's casino and restaurants received an end-to-end makeover, giving the iconic property a cosmopolitan look with blacks, dark browns, and deep reds. Bathrooms have marble accents and sumptuous appointments but tend to be on the smaller side. Rooms with incredible views of the Strip and the volcano cost a bit more, but you can sometimes get a free upgrade if you request one at check-in. Several upscale restaurants, including STACK and BLT Burger, give the Mirage an impressive slate of both high-end and casual eateries. **Pros:** classic Vegas; incredible views; one of the best pools in town. **Cons:** casino floor gets crowded and difficult to navigate on weekends.

HIGHLIGHTS

The Love: The Beatles showcase from Cirque du Soleil is amazing.

The tropics: There's a 20,000-gallon aquarium behind the hotel's front desk, an indoor tropical rain forest, and the wondrous Siegfried & Roy's Secret Garden and Dolphin Habitat.

The volcano: This longtime Strip spectacle features breathtaking fire effects and music composed by Grateful Dead drummer Mickey Hart.

The dolphins: Say hello to Flipper at Siegfried & Roy's Secret Garden & Dolphin Habitat. Guests willing to burn a few c-notes can don a wet suit and act as "trainer" for a day.

PARIS LAS VEGAS AT A GLANCE

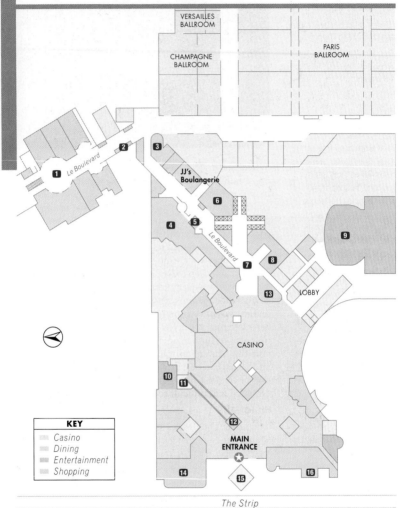

The Strip

KEY
- Casino
- Dining
- Entertainment
- Shopping

SIGHTS

Eiffel Tower Experience ... **11, 15**

SHOWS

Anthony Cools, *Theater* **10**

Jersey Boys, *Theater* **9**

NIGHTLIFE

Chateau, *Nightclub* **16**

Le Central, *Lounge* **13**

Napoleon's, *Lounge* **3**

SHOPPING

Bally's–Paris Promenade**,** *Mall* ... **1**

La Cave, *Food* **5**

Le Boulevard, *Mall* **7**

Les Eléments,
Gifts & Souvenirs **8**

Paris Line,
Women's Clothing **2**

EXPENSIVE DINING

Eiffel Tower Restaurant,
French **12**

Mon Ami Gabi, *French* **14**

MODERATE DINING

Le Provençal, *French* **6**

Le Village Buffet, *Buffet* **4**

PARIS LAS VEGAS

$ *Rooms from: $199* ⊠ *3655 Las Vegas Blvd. S, Center Strip* ☎ *702/946–7000, 877/796–2096* ⊕ *www.parislasvegas. com* ⥱ *2,621 rooms, 295 suites* ⦿ *No meals.*

AMENITIES

■ The resort's 2-acre, octagonal Soleil Pool and exquisitely manicured French gardens are a great place to spend the afternoon.

■ Paris Spa by Mandara offers the latest in body treatments and fitness regimens.

■ Shopping is limited but noteworthy: the shops on Le Boulevard feature boutiques, gift shops, and a gourmet food shop, while the Bally's-Paris Promenade shops sell exclusive French jewelry and women's accessories.

■ Le Rendezvous Lounge, on the 31st floor, provides continental breakfast, afternoon hors d'ouevres, and free drinks. It's well worth the surcharge at check-in.

This homage to the City of Light aims to conjure up all the charm of the French capital, and while it isn't quite as glamorous as the Strip's other Euro-metropolis-theme wonder (the Venetian), it's still good and elegant fun. Paris' standard units have marble baths with separate tubs and showers. Still, some find the heavy-handed decor a little busy. West-facing rooms overlook the magnificent fountains and lagoon across the street at Bellagio. A handful of rooms, dubbed "Red Rooms," have 42-inch plasma TVs and custom-designed furniture with French-inspired decorative elements and artwork. Suites add not only more space, but also considerably more dashing red, beige, and gold furniture and rich fabrics. Downstairs, the fabulous buffet serves dishes from five French regions. Other dining options—including the steak house from Gordon Ramsay—are mediocre, save perhaps for Mon Ami Gabi bistro. A massive octagonal pool sits in the shadows of the Eiffel Tower on the hotel rooftop. Chateau Nightclub and Gardens remains a top nightspot. **Pros:** campy decor; spacious rooms; views. **Cons:** some rooms are tired; lack of standout restaurants.

HIGHLIGHTS

The Faux-tastic: Replicas of The Arc de Triomphe, the Paris Opera House, the Hôtel de Ville, and the Louvre, along with an Around the World in Eighty Days balloon marquee are magnifique!

The Eiffel Tower: The crowning achievement is the 50-story, half-scale replica of the Eiffel Tower where guests are whisked 460 feet to the top for spectacular views of the valley.

The Valley: Tap your feet to the music of *Jersey Boys*, the Broadway hit about Frankie Valley and the Four Seasons.

PLANET HOLLYWOOD AT A GLANCE

CONVENTION AREA

Chapel

CASINO LEVEL

1

2

3

4

5 **6**

7

9

8

THEATRE ENTRANCE →

10

11

12

13

MEZZANINE LEVEL

STORES

MIRACLE MILE

MIRACLE MILE STORES

REGISTRATION

Guest Elavators

Casino Escalators

Bell Desk

Guest Elavators

14

MAIN ENTRANCE

LOBBY

KEY

Casino
Dining
Entertainment
Shopping

The Strip

SHOPPING	NIGHTLIFE	MODERATE DINING
Miracle Mile Stores **13**	Extra Lounge, *Lounge* **7**	P.F. Chang's, *Asian* **9**
ph Stuff, *Gifts* **14**	Heart Bar, *Bar* **8**	Planet Dailies, *Café* **6**
SPAS	The Playing Field, *Lounge* **11**	Yolos, *Mexican* **10**
Mandara **4**	**EXPENSIVE DINING**	**INEXPENSIVE DINING**
SHOWS	Koi, *Asian* **3**	Earl of Sandwich, *Café* **12**
Sin City Comedy **1**	Strip House, *Steakhouse* **2**	Starbucks, *Café* **5**

PLANET HOLLYWOOD RESORT & CASINO

⑤ *Rooms from: $189* ✉ *3667 Las Vegas Blvd. S, Center Strip* ☎ *702/785–5555, 866/919–7472* ⊕ *www. planethollywoodresort.com* ↪ *2,333 rooms, 163 suites* ⦶ *No meals.*

Everything at Planet Hollywood is designed to make ordinary people feel like stars, and the lodging accommodations are no exception. The modern standard rooms are a spacious 450 square feet, and feature a king or queen bed, a 27-inch flat-screen television, iPod docking stations, plush chairs, and warm, fuzzy robes. On higher floors, some of the hotel's pricier suites come with butler service—the "PHabulous" suites feature six plasma televisions, as well as foosball and pool tables, and stripper poles in the showers (of course). Each of these suites also comes with its own private butler. The adjacent Planet Hollywood Towers Westgate offers 1,201 apartment-like rooms and a separate pool. **Pros:** classic Hollywood vibe; incredible views; posh suites. **Cons:** relatively small casino; in-room bath products are nothing special.

AMENITIES

■ The Spa by Mandara still has traces of its original Arabian theme (from when the property was the Aladdin), but female guests rave about the in-house nail salon.

■ The pool deck offers limited bar and food service, and the better-late-than-never Pleasure Pools VIP section is swanky.

■ For a shopping fix, hit the on-site mall, the Miracle Mile Shops, which include an H&M department store and Urban Outfitters, to name a few.

HIGHLIGHTS

The Brit-pop: Planet Hollywood's main attraction has become Piece of Me, a rollicking residency show from one of pop music's biggest names, Britney Spears.

The premieres: Because Planet Hollywood is obsessed with celebrities, the property often hosts world-premiere events that attract stars from all over the world.

The restaurants: At the upscale KOI and Strip House, paparazzi are a common sight. Yolo's is good, too, not as much for celeb-sightings, but more for its fresh Mexican food.

The dancers: On the casino floor, inside "The Pleasure Pit," scantily clad dancers hug the poles while men play blackjack and stare.

THE NORTH STRIP

Luxury reigns supreme in the top third of the Las Vegas Strip. There aren't as many resorts here but spacious rooms, exquisite details, and deep-sleep-inducing beds make four of them among the most luxurious in the world. This part of town is about a 30-minute ride from the airport and at least 20 minutes to the South Strip, so visitors often stay put. But when you're staying at resorts that have just about everything, who wants to leave?

The cluster of hotels that make up this section include the Venetian, Palazzo, Treasure Island, Wynn, Encore, and Trump Hotel Las Vegas. Of particular interest: pools. Swanky, ultra-exclusive day-lounge areas surround the pools at North Strip properties; the Palazzo's Azure Pool is one of the newest and Encore Beach Club is by far the most popular. As with most pools in Vegas, these offer European-style sunbathing sections, too. Bikini tops optional.

NORTH STRIP TOP PICKS

· Encore

Palazzo

Venetian

Wynn

Other amenities are worth raves, as well. Wynn, for instance, houses a master barber. Venetian has one of only two Canyon Ranch spas in the country. Factor in additional amenities such as golf courses, shopping, indoor gardens, and breathtaking design, and it's no wonder the North Strip is seen as the spot where Vegas meets high fashion, year after year.

DID YOU KNOW?

Venetian owner Sheldon Adelson was so obsessed with getting the canals just right that he had them drained and repainted three times before he was satisfied with the hue.

ENCORE LAS VEGAS AT A GLANCE

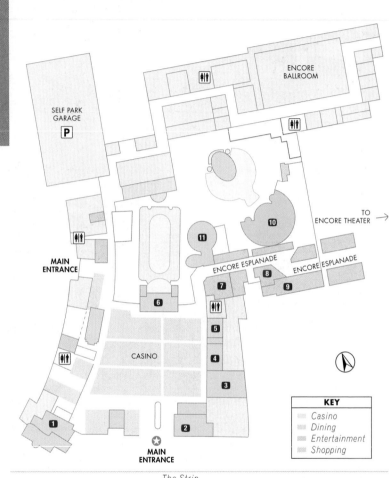

The Strip

NIGHTLIFE

Eastside Lounge, *Lounge* **6**

Southside Bar, *Bar* **4**

Surrender, *Dance Club* **2**

XS Nightclub, *Dance Club* **10**

SHOPPING

CHANEL, *Women's Clothing* **8**

Ensemble, *Women's Clothing* **9**

Hermés, *Women's Clothing* **7**

EXPENSIVE DINING

Botero, *Steakhouse* **11**

Sinatra, *Italian* **1**

MODERATE DINING

Society Cafe Encore,
American **3**

Wazuzu, *Asian* **5**

ENCORE

$ *Rooms from: $349* ⊠ *3131 Las Vegas Blvd. S, North Strip* ☎ *702/770–7000, 888/320–7123* ⊕ *www.encorelasvegas. com* ⤴ *2,034 suites* ⦿ *No meals.*

AMENITIES

■ The main hotel pools are surrounded by sculpted gardens, mosaic tiling, and feature Jacuzzi spas and 29 luxurious cabanas.

■ Todd-Avery Lenahan designed the Moroccan-theme Encore Spa, which features 37 treatment rooms, 14 naturally lighted garden rooms, a number of oversize couples' suites for massage, body treatments, and facials, as well as daily spin and yoga classes.

■ The beautiful Esplanade at Encore features Hermès, Chanel, and the first-ever Rock & Republic store.

■ In-room televisions include a channel that lists up-to-the-minute betting lines in the Wynn Las Vegas sports book.

★ **Fodor's Choice** Though smaller than its neighbor, Wynn Las Vegas, Encore combines the very best of all of Wynn's masterpieces. As far as luxury is concerned, Las Vegas simply doesn't get much better. Encore redefines the typical Vegas casino-resort experience with new levels of extravagance. All of the rooms are suites, and measure a minimum of 700 square feet (up to a maximum of 5,800 square feet). These accommodations come standard with spacious sitting areas, flat-panel televisions, floor-to-ceiling windows, and electronic curtain controls. Bathrooms feature Italian marble and Wynn's Desert Bambu signature bath products. Bedside control panels enable guests to operate nearly everything in the room. **Pros:** huge suites; glorious pools; fun (but intimate) casino. **Cons:** cab ride to other casinos; pricey.

HIGHLIGHTS

The details: Most Vegas casino resorts boast knock-offs of expensive antiques from all over the world; at Encore, however, designer Roger Thomas has invested in the real thing. A wall at Wazuzu Asian restaurant is decorated with a large dragon made from 90,000 Swarovski crystals.

The sunlight: Sunlit corridors with flower-filled atriums and sprawling pools are visible from throughout the property; there also are a number of signature mosaics.

The clubs: XS is a top club, combining an outdoor pool party with a sizzling club. Encore Beach Club and Surrender offer more of the same (though these two are heavier on the pool part).

Society Cafe: The hippest restaurant on property serves up dim sum on weekends and is famous for whimsical dishes such as pretzel bread and mac-and-cheese nuggets.

THE PALAZZO AT A GLANCE

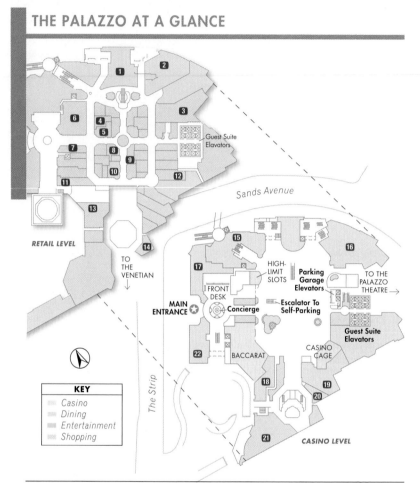

RETAIL LEVEL

TO THE VENETIAN

Guest Suite Elavators

HIGH-LIMIT SLOTS

Parking Garage Elevators

Escalator To Self-Parking

MAIN ENTRANCE ⭐ **Concierge**

FRONT DESK

TO THE PALAZZO THEATRE →

Guest Suite Elavators

CASINO CAGE

BACCARAT

Sands Avenue

The Strip

CASINO LEVEL

KEY
- Casino
- Dining
- Entertainment
- Shopping

THE PALAZZO RESORT HOTEL CASINO

$ *Rooms from: $239* ✉ *3325 Las Vegas Blvd. S, North Strip* ☎ *702/607–7777, 866/263–3001* ⊕ *www.palazzo.com* ⌁ *3,066 suites* ❧ *No meals.*

AMENITIES

■ Each suite comes standard with a sunken living room, marble bathroom, and linens from Anichini. Rooms also boast a printer/fax/scanner, DVD player, and iPod adapter.

■ A walkway connects the property to the Venetian.

■ The Canyon Ranch SpaClub includes a 40-foot-high climbing wall and Aquavana, the first complete suite of European-inspired thermal spa cabins, tubs, and aqua-thermal bathing in the United States.

■ On-site parking sits beneath the casino and is among the most accessible on the Strip.

"Palazzo" means "palace" in Italian, and the $1.8-billion, all-suites resort aims to bring new meaning to the word, ushering even more luxury to the north end of the Las Vegas Strip. Although it has struggled to keep restaurants, the hotel's an understated blend of style and sophistication. The floor plan for the Palazzo suites are almost exactly the same as the Venetian's. Each suite comes standard with a sunken living room, two plasma TVs, a dining area, sectional couch, and desk. Remote-controlled Roman shades and curtains add to the modern conveniences; let the sun in without getting out of bed! Bathrooms are appointed with marble and feature a separate shower and soaking tub. For $100 more per night, concierge-level rooms (known as "Prestige Suites") include breakfast, afternoon snacks, hors d'oeuvres, and business center services. **Pros:** state-of-the-art amenities; spacious suites; sumptuous linens. **Cons:** thin walls; deserted on weekdays.

HIGHLIGHTS

The Shoppes: With 50 international boutiques, including Barneys New York, Christian Louboutin, and Diane von Furstenberg, The Shoppes at The Palazzo are perhaps the No. 1 nongaming attraction at this palatial resort.

The pool: Palazzo has one of the Strip's largest pool decks, a humongous complex with private whirlpools, statues, and gardens galore.

The waterfall: A three-story waterfall graces the outskirts of the casino.

The green: With a top-quality energy conservation program and other green amenities, Palazzo has received LEED-Gold distinction from the U.S. Green Building Council.

THE VENETIAN AT A GLANCE

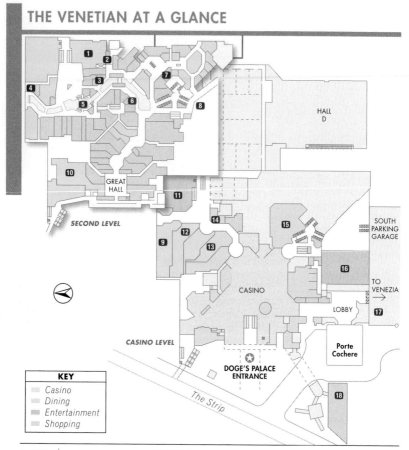

KEY
- Casino
- Dining
- Entertainment
- Shopping

SIGHTS
Gondola Rides **4**
Madame Tussaud's
Las Vegas **18**
Wedding Chapel **5**

SPAS
Canyon Ranch Spa Club **2**

SHOWS
Human Nature:
The Motown Show, *Theater* **16**
Rock of Ages, *Theater* **11**

NIGHTLIFE
Tao & Tao Beach, *Dance Club* ... **10**
V Bar, *Lounge* **14**

SHOPPING
Ca' d'Oro, *Jewelry* **3**
Grand Canal Shoppes, *Mall* **8**
Il Prato, *Gifts & Souvenirs* **7**
Simayof, *Jewelry* **6**

EXPENSIVE DINING
Aquaknox, *Seafood* **12**
Delmonico Steakhouse,
Steakhouse **9**
Postrio, *Contemporary* **1**

MODERATE DINING
Bouchon, *French* **17**
Canyon Ranch Cafe, *American* ... **2**
Pinot Brasserie,
Contemporary **13**
Tao, *Pan-Asian* **10**

INEXPENSIVE DINING
Grand Lux Cafe,
American-Casual **15**

THE VENETIAN RESORT HOTEL CASINO

$ Rooms from: $259 ⊠ 3355 Las Vegas Blvd. S, North Strip ☎ 702/414–1000, 866/659–9643 ⊕ www.venetian.com ⤴ 4,027 suites ⦿ No meals.

3

AMENITIES

■ The Canyon Ranch Spa Club offers the same lavish treatments as the spa resort's main campuses in Arizona and Massachusetts, and features a three-story climbing wall that guests can use for free. It's also open late on most weeknights, meaning you can spend more time at the tables before that workout.

■ The combination copier/scanner/fax/printer in every suite is perfect for business travelers who hope to get work done during their stay.

■ One of the best-kept secrets of Venetian's room-service: They'll bring you food from any restaurant on property, for a price.

★ **Fodor's Choice** This theme hotel re-creates Italy's most romantic city with meticulous reproductions of Venetian landmarks—including the Grand Canal. Some of the Strip's largest and plushest accommodations are found at this gilded resort that's a hit with foodies, shoppers, and high rollers alike. It's all about glitz and "wow" effect here, which makes it a popular property if you're celebrating a special occasion or looking for a quintessential over-the-top Vegas experience. Each 700-plus-square-feet suite offers a sunken living room with a coffee table and convertible sofa, walk-in closets, a separate shower and tub, three telephones (including one in the bathroom), two flat-screen TVs, and remote-controlled curtains. The even posher Venezia Tower has a garden, private entrance, fountains, and gargantuan suites. **Pros:** exquisite artwork; modern amenities; those remote-controlled curtains. **Cons:** the ostentatiousness isn't for everyone.

HIGHLIGHTS

The atmosphere: From the Strip you enter through the Doge's Palace, set on a walkway over a large lagoon. Inside, Renaissance characters roam the public areas, singing opera, performing mime, jesting, even kissing hands.

The scenery: Walking from the hotel lobby into the casino is one of the great experiences in Las Vegas: overhead, reproductions of famous frescoes—highlighted by 24-karat-gold frames—adorn the ceiling; underfoot, the geometric design of the flat marble floor provides an Escher-like optical illusion of climbing stairs.

The gondolas: On a lake in front of the casino visitors can take gondola rides and look out on the Strip. Inside, climb aboard with a gondolier who'll sing opera as he paddles you through canals that line the Grand Canal Shoppes.

WYNN AT A GLANCE

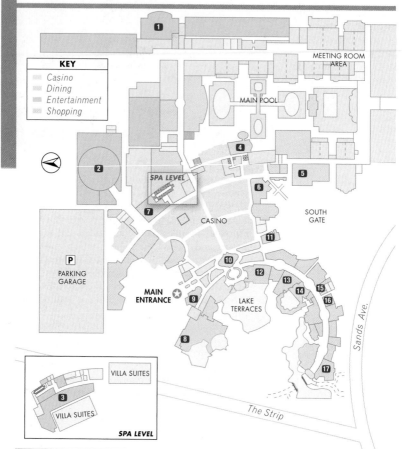

KEY
- Casino
- Dining
- Entertainment
- Shopping

MEETING ROOM AREA

MAIN POOL

SPA LEVEL

CASINO

SOUTH GATE

P PARKING GARAGE

MAIN ENTRANCE

LAKE TERRACES

Sands Ave.

VILLA SUITES

VILLA SUITES

SPA LEVEL

The Strip

SIGHTS

Wynn Las Vegas
Golf Course **1**

SPAS

The Spa Wynn Las Vegas **3**

SHOWS

Le Rêve, *Theater* **2**

NIGHTLIFE

Parasol Up and Parasol Down,
Lounge **10**

Tryst, *Dance Club* **8**

SHOPPING

Belts, Bags and Baubles,
Women's Clothing **9**

Brioni, *Men's Clothing* **17**

Cartier, *Jewelry* **11**

Chanel, *Women's Clothing* **12**

Louis Vuitton,
Luggage and Accessories **13**

Manolo Blahnik, *Shoes* **16**

Oscar de la Renta,
Women's Clothing **15**

EXPENSIVE DINING

Bartolotta, *Seafood* **14**

The Country Club, *Steakhouse* ...**1**

Tableau, *Contemporary* **4**

Wing Lei, *Chinese* **5**

MODERATE DINING

Red 8, *Chinese* **6**

The Drugstore Café, *Café* **7**

WYNN LAS VEGAS

$ *Rooms from: $319* ⊠ *3131 Las Vegas Blvd. S, North Strip* ☎ *702/770–7000, 888/320–7123* ⊕ *www.wynnlasvegas. com* ⇆ *2,359 rooms, 357 suites* ⊙ *No meals.*

AMENITIES

■ One of the most highly regarded spas in town, the Wynn Spa offers dozens of signature treatments, as well as relaxation and hydrotherapy rooms to while away a day. The spa specializes in facials, and therapists incorporate a number of Asian oils and herbs into each experience.

■ Men's barbershop services—including flat-razor shaves—are available in the salon. They incorporate products from Paris and New York's famous Hommage Atelier.

■ Relatively minor touches, such as richly appointed armchairs with ottomans and giant, fluffy Turkish towels, speak to the sheer sumptuousness of this place.

★ **Fodor's Choice** In a city that keeps raising the bar for sheer luxury, the Wynn—monolithic in both name and appearance—offers a discreet turn for the tasteful. The resort is a best-of-everything experience—a playground for jet-setters, high rollers, or anyone who wants to feel like one. Decked out with replicas of Steve Wynn's acclaimed art collection, the princely rooms, averaging a whopping 650 square feet, offer spectacular views through wall-to-wall, floor-to-ceiling windows. Rest your head on custom pillow-top beds with 320-thread-count linens, and call room service from the cordless phone. Bedside drapery and climate controls are another nice touch. The super-posh Tower Suites units have use of a separate pool and lanai, and some have opulent amenities such as granite wet bars, separate powder rooms, 42-inch flat-screen TVs, and walk-in closets. Downstairs, restaurants such as Wing Lei and Bartolotta Ristorante di Mare provide endless culinary delights. **Pros:** signature Desert Bambu bath products; access to gorgeous pool; on-site golf course. **Cons:** cramped casino walkways; slow elevators.

HIGHLIGHTS

The Esplanade: the Wynn Esplanade is as gorgeous as the Bellagio Conservatory, which Wynn helped design.

The golf course: The outstanding course incorporates 11 water hazards, including a 37-foot waterfall.

The chefs: Famous chefs don't just lend their name to Wynn's restaurants, they often take residence there, including Carlos Guia and Italian chef Paul Bartolotta.

The talent: *Le Reve* is a Cirque show created exclusively for Wynn that mixes ballet, acrobatics, and platform diving.

OTHER HIGHLY RECOMMENDED HOTELS

Hotel reviews have been shortened. For full information, visit Fodors. com.

SOUTH STRIP

$$$
RESORT
Fodor'sChoice
★

🏨 **The Delano.** If James Bond were staying on the Strip, something tells us he'd book a suite here. **Pros:** lavish suites; great views; separate and swanky entrance. **Cons:** long walk to main casino; dark elevator lobbies; hard-to-find entrance. Ⓢ *Rooms from: $299* ✉ *3950 Las Vegas Blvd. S, South Strip* ☎ *877/632–7800, 702/632–7777* ⊕ *www.mandalaybay. com/accommodations/thehotel* ➪ *1,117 suites* ⏺⏺ *No meals.*

$
RESORT
FAMILY

🏨 **Excalibur Hotel and Casino.** The giant Lego-like castle is popular with families—child-oriented attractions include the basement arcade (dubbed the "Fun Dungeon") and the medieval-theme Tournament of Kings dinner show—but recent makeovers in all of the property's rooms make much of the property look more grown-up. **Pros:** low table minimums make for more accessible gambling; easy access to Luxor and Mandalay Bay. **Cons:** low table minimums also attract huge crowds; most on-site dining options are not good. Ⓢ *Rooms from: $139* ✉ *3850 Las Vegas Blvd. S, South Strip* ☎ *702/597–7777, 800/879–1379* ⊕ *www.excalibur.com* ➪ *3,940 rooms, 41 suites* ⏺⏺ *No meals.*

$$$$
RESORT
Fodor'sChoice
★

🏨 **Four Seasons Hotel Las Vegas.** If peace and quiet are what you're after, this is your spot; after checking in at a separate ground-level lobby, guests are whisked up to the top floors of the main hotel tower at Mandalay Bay, cushioned from the general casino ruckus. **Pros:** kid-friendly; ultraposh; hotel-within-a-hotel vibe. **Cons:** pricey; far from rest of Vegas action; stuffy at times. Ⓢ *Rooms from: $429* ✉ *Mandalay Bay Resort, 3960 Las Vegas Blvd. S, South Strip* ☎ *702/632–5000* ⊕ *www. fourseasons.com/lasvegas* ➪ *343 rooms, 81 suites* ⏺⏺ *No meals.*

$$
RESORT
FAMILY

🏨 **Monte Carlo Resort and Casino.** The Strip could use more places like this—handsome but not ostentatious, elegant rooms outfitted with cherrywood furnishings. **Pros:** low-key way to have a fabulous Strip experience; exceptional rooms; easy to navigate casino. **Cons:** taxi entrance in the middle of nowhere. Ⓢ *Rooms from: $149* ✉ *3770 Las Vegas Blvd. S, South Strip* ☎ *702/730–7777, 888/529–4828* ⊕ *www.montecarlo. com* ➪ *2,768 rooms, 224 suites* ⏺⏺ *No meals.*

$$
RESORT

🏨 **Signature Suites at MGM Grand.** The three towers that comprise this spacious and well-appointed luxury resort adjacent to the MGM Grand are perhaps most notable for what they lack: a casino. **Pros:** relatively inexpensive room rates. **Cons:** inconvenient off-Strip entrance; a trek to nearest casino (at MGM Grand). Ⓢ *Rooms from: $199* ✉ *145 E. Harmon Ave., South Strip* ☎ *702/797–6000, 877/612–2121* ⊕ *www. signaturemgmgrand.com* ➪ *1,728 suites* ⏺⏺ *No meals.*

$$
RESORT

🏨 **Tropicana Las Vegas.** Today's "Trop" (as its been known for more than 50 years) features some of the most spacious rooms in town with a pleasant (and whitewashed) South Beach, Miami, style. **Pros:** views from the new Sky Villa Suites; Glow Spa; breezy style. **Cons:** small casino; interior layout can be confusing. Ⓢ *Rooms from: $169*

3801 Las Vegas Blvd. S, South Strip 702/739–2222, 800/462–8767 www.troplv.com 1,354 rooms, 109 suites No meals.

CENTER STRIP

$$ RESORT **Bally's Las Vegas.** Rooms at this old-school property were renovated in 2013, which makes the reasonably priced Bally's Resort, in the heart of the Strip, an underrated choice for a Vegas vacation. **Pros:** affordable rooms with a perfect Center-Strip location. **Cons:** construction in front of hotel through 2014. *Rooms from: $169 3645 Las Vegas Blvd. S, Center Strip 702/967–4111, 877/603–4390 www.ballyslasvegas.com 2,570 rooms, 244 suites No meals.*

$ RESORT **Flamingo Las Vegas.** This elaborately landscaped, pink, classic-era resort with a 15-acre pool complex is still one of the best choices in town, and "Go" rooms (which run about $50 to $100 more per night than standard rooms), with MP3 docking stations and 42-inch flat-screen TVs, are downright stylish. **Pros:** Margaritaville; heart-of-the Strip location; the pool lives up to its reputation. **Cons:** entrance is difficult to navigate by car or taxi; regular rooms are pretty old. *Rooms from: $119 3555 Las Vegas Blvd. S, Center Strip 702/733–3111, 888/902–9929 www.flamingolasvegas.com 3,190 rooms, 268 suites No meals.*

$ RESORT **Harrah's Las Vegas.** Old-school Vegas is alive and well at this affordable Center-Strip property. **Pros:** throwback vibe with some modern touches thrown in; affordable, reliable rooms; ideal location; Carnival Court is a great outdoor party. **Cons:** zero wow factor; small pool. *Rooms from: $119 3475 Las Vegas Blvd. S, Center Strip 800/214–9110 www.harrahslasvegas.com 2,293 rooms, 233 suites No meals.*

$$$ HOTEL Fodor's Choice ★ **Nobu Hotel.** The new hotel from celebrity chef Nobu Matsuhisa and partner Robert DeNiro is a sleek foodie haven tucked inside the Caesars Palace complex. **Pros:** foodie haven; insider access and VIP treatment; quiet haven in central Vegas. **Cons:** extra charges such as the $25 resort fee. *Rooms from: $269 3570 Las Vegas Blvd. S, Center Strip 702/785-6677 www.nobucaesarspalace.com 163 rooms, 18 suites No meals.*

$$ RESORT **Vdara.** This low-key property is actually a hotel-condo, with beautiful independently owned suites that have efficiency kitchens, pull-out sofas, and lots of extra space. **Pros:** quiet retreat right in the middle of the action; efficiency kitchens; spa. **Cons:** lacks the excitement of splashy resort properties; Market Cafe restaurant is ho-hum. *Rooms from: $209 2600 W. Harmon Ave., Center Strip 702/590–2111, 866/745–7111 www.vdara.com 1,495 suites No meals.*

NORTH STRIP

$ RESORT FAMILY **Circus Circus Las Vegas Hotel and Casino.** The hotel at the "Big Top" has renovated all of its rooms since 2009, giving some much-needed T.L.C. to some of the oldest rooms on the Strip (the resort opened in 1968). **Pros:** Adventure Dome Theme Park; pet-friendly. **Cons:** gaming atmosphere isn't nearly as elegant as most Strip properties. *Rooms* *from:* $89 ✉ 2880 Las Vegas Blvd. S, North Strip ☎ 702/734–0410, 800/634–3450 ⊕ www.circuscircus.com ⤳ 3,632 rooms, 135 suites ⦿ No meals.

$ 🏨 **Stratosphere.** The Stratosphere's 1,149-foot observation tower soars
RESORT over every other building in town, and it's an iconic part of the Las Vegas skyline. **Pros:** Top of the World restaurant and observation deck; Pin Up burlesque show; value for the rooms. **Cons:** surrounding neighborhood; nondescript casino. ⑤ *Rooms from:* $129 ✉ 2000 Las Vegas Blvd. S, North Strip ☎ 702/380–7777 ⊕ www.stratospherehotel.com ⤳ 2,294 rooms, 133 suites ⦿ No meals.

$$ 🏨 **Treasure Island** (*T.I.*). Whether you call it Treasure Island or T.I.,
RESORT what sets apart this resort is a dash of elegance mixed with a decid-
FAMILY edly unpretentious vibe. **Pros:** fairly modest price point; location; the long-running *Mystere* Cirque show. **Cons:** no real nightlife or standout amenities. ⑤ *Rooms from:* $169 ✉ 3300 Las Vegas Blvd. S, North Strip ☎ 702/894–7111, 800/944–7444 ⊕ www.treasureisland.com ⤳ 2,665 rooms, 220 suites ⦿ No meals.

$$ 🏨 **Trump International Hotel Las Vegas.** Units in Donald Trump's lavish,
RESORT nongaming 64-story condo-hotel are individually owned, but a major-
ity of them are rented out like hotel rooms and managed by Trump. **Pros:** apartment-style rooms make you feel right at home; Spa rivals best on the Strip. **Cons:** long walk through Fashion Island Mall to the nearest casino, especially at night. ⑤ *Rooms from:* $219 ✉ 2000 Fashion Show Dr., North Strip ☎ 702/982–0000, 866/939–8786 ⊕ www. trumplasvegashotel.com ⤳ 1,282 rooms ⦿ No meals.

DOWNTOWN

$ 🏨 **Four Queens Resort and Casino.** Named after former owner Ben Goff-
HOTEL stein's four daughters, the Four Queens is what Vegas regulars would consider an "oldie but goodie," one of the most iconic casinos on Fremont Street. **Pros:** gamblers welcome; kitsch factor; Hugo's; low table minimums. **Cons:** needs a better makeover; pool off-site. ⑤ *Rooms from:* $69 ✉ 202 Fremont St., Downtown ☎ 702/385–4011, 800/634–6045 ⊕ www.fourqueens.com ⤳ 650 rooms, 44 suites ⦿ No meals.

$ 🏨 **Golden Nugget Hotel & Casino.** The Golden Nugget has pretty much
RESORT reigned as Downtown's top property since the mid 1970s, evolving with the times, but maintaining classic appeal. **Pros:** legendary Vegas property; one-of-a-kind pool; great poker room. **Cons:** small sports book; although the best Downtown property it still doesn't quite measure up to the new mega-stars on the Strip. ⑤ *Rooms from:* $129 ✉ 129 E. Fremont St., Downtown ☎ 702/385–7111, 800/634–3454 ⊕ www. goldennugget.com ⤳ 2,148 rooms, 197 suites ⦿ No meals.

$ 🏨 **Main Street Station Casino Brewery & Hotel.** It's worth a visit to this pint-
HOTEL size property for the Victorian-era aesthetics alone, displaying stained glass and marble, and an antiques collection that includes Buffalo Bill Cody's private railcar, a fireplace from Scotland's Preswick Castle, and lamps that graced the streets of 18th-century Brussels. **Pros:** decor and quirky antiques; prices of rooms. **Cons:** no pool; no gym; no Internet in rooms (only Wi-Fi in lobby). ⑤ *Rooms from:* $69 ✉ 200 N. Main

Stroll beneath the soaring glass canyons of CityCenter and experience a serene streetscape insulated from the bustle of the surrounding Strip.

St., Downtown ☎ *702/387–1896* ⊕ *www.mainstreetcasino.com* ⏎ *392 rooms, 14 suites* ⏽⏽ *No meals.*

PARADISE ROAD, EAST SIDE, AND HENDERSON

$
RESORT
Fodor's Choice
★
Green Valley Ranch Resort & Spa. Locals have long known that Green Valley is a low-key, refined resort for the high-end crowd that prefers style over bustle (the Strip is a 25-minute drive away). **Pros:** gorgeous, airy casino; proximity to malls that offer great shopping. **Cons:** 25 minutes from the Strip and 10 minutes from downtown Henderson, there's not much in the immediate area. ⑤ *Rooms from: $129* ✉ *2300 Paseo Verde Pkwy., Henderson* ☎ *702/617-7777, 866/782-9487* ⊕ *https:// greenvalleyranch.sclv.com* ⏎ *417 rooms, 79 suites* ⏽⏽ *No meals.*

$$
RESORT
Hard Rock Hotel & Casino. This sprawling resort is a shrine to rock and roll—with rock tributes, exhibits, and authentic memorabilia everywhere. **Pros:** party central; great restaurants (Pink Taco and Ago) and pool; lively casino. **Cons:** rowdy crowd; minuscule sports book; close but not quite close enough to the Strip. ⑤ *Rooms from: $199* ✉ *4455 Paradise Rd., Paradise Road* ☎ *702/693–5000, 800/473–7625* ⊕ *www. hardrockhotel.com* ⏎ *1,412 rooms and 92 suites* ⏽⏽ *No meals.*

$$
RESORT
FAMILY
Hilton Lake Las Vegas Resort & Spa. After previous lives as the Ritz-Carlton Lake Las Vegas and Ravella, this property was rebranded yet again in late 2013, retaining its Mediterranean vibe and resplendent pool complex. **Pros:** relaxing; complimentary shuttle; golf nearby. **Cons:** still has a lack of identity; far from Strip. ⑤ *Rooms from: $219* ✉ *1610 Lake Las Vegas Pkwy., Henderson* ☎ *702/567–4700* ⊕ *www3.hilton. com* ⏎ *314 rooms, 35 suites* ⏽⏽ *No meals.*

$ ⊡ **Las Vegas Hotel & Casino.** Convention attendees have loved this hotel
RESORT   for decades; it's connected to the Las Vegas Convention Center. **Pros:**
great location for convention goers; classic sports book. **Cons:** no poker
room. ⑤ *Rooms from: $139* ⊠ *3000 Paradise Rd., Paradise Road*
☎ *702/732–5111, 888/732–7117* ⊕ *www.thelvh.com* ⟿ *2,700 rooms,*
300 suites ⟦◯⟧ *No meals.*

$ ⊡ **The M Resort.** Built by the Marnells, the same family that created
RESORT   the Rio, this resort is 6 miles south of McCarran Airport and is a
destination onto itself. **Pros:** huge rooms; convenient yet removed
from hubbub. **Cons:** cab ride to other casinos; planes roaring overhead. ⑤ *Rooms from: $119* ⊠ *12300 Las Vegas Blvd. S, Henderson*
☎ *702/797–1000, 877/673–7678* ⊕ *www.themresort.com* ⟿ *351*
rooms, 39 suites ⟦◯⟧ *No meals.*

$$ ⊡ **The Platinum Hotel and Spa.** This swank, nongaming, and LGBT-
RESORT   friendly condo-hotel has become a fashionable hideaway for Vegas
Fodor'sChoice   regulars who prefer top-notch amenities but don't need to stay on the
★   Strip. **Pros:** cocktail menu at STIR Lounge; lavish rooms with comfy
sofas and beds. **Cons:** no casino; location off the Strip makes it chal-
lenging to find a cab on busy nights. ⑤ *Rooms from: $179* ⊠ *211 E. Fla-*
mingo Rd., Paradise Road ☎ *702/365–5000, 877/211–9211* ⊕ *www.*
theplatinumhotel.com ⟿ *255 suites* ⟦◯⟧ *No meals.*

$$ ⊡ **Renaissance Las Vegas Hotel.** Everything is intimate at this nongaming
HOTEL   Rat Pack–inspired hotel off the Strip on Paradise Road. **Pros:** ENVY
steak house; fresh, stylish rooms. **Cons:** rooms a bit small; pool can get
overcrowded. ⑤ *Rooms from: $159* ⊠ *3400 Paradise Rd., Paradise*
Road ☎ *702/784–5700, 800/750–0980* ⊕ *www.renaissancelasvegas.*
com ⟿ *518 rooms, 30 suites* ⟦◯⟧ *No meals.*

$ ⊡ **Rumor.** Red ceilings, purple duvets, and many, many mirrors charac-
RESORT   terize the accommodations at this all-suites property across the street
from the Hard Rock Casino Resort. **Pros:** spacious and affordable
rooms; happening pool area. **Cons:** off the Strip; no casino. ⑤ *Rooms*
from: $139 ⊠ *455 E. Harmon Ave., Paradise Road* ☎ *877/997–8667,*
702/369–5400 ⊕ *www.rumorvegas.com* ⟿ *149 rooms* ⟦◯⟧ *No meals.*

$$ ⊡ **Westin Lake Las Vegas Resort & Spa.** This lavish resort on the shore of
RESORT   Lake Las Vegas has richly appointed rooms, with arched windows that
offer sweeping views of the glittering lake and desert. **Pros:** lake vistas;
Marssa restaurant; activity center on beach rents kayaks and paddle-
boats. **Cons:** casino is not for avid gamblers. ⑤ *Rooms from: $209*
⊠ *101 Montelago Blvd., Lake Las Vegas, Henderson* ☎ *702/567–6000*
⊕ *www.westinlakelasvegas.com* ⟿ *447 rooms, 46 suites* ⟦◯⟧ *No meals.*

WEST SIDE AND SUMMERLIN

$$ ⊡ **JW Marriott Las Vegas Resort & Spa.** If you have a penchant for pam-
RESORT   pering and personal service—or if your plans include golfing or hik-
ing—this stunner in Summerlin is for you. **Pros:** proximity to golf and
Red Rock National Conservation Area; terrific spa. **Cons:** a bit pricey
for a Marriott; casino sports book can fill up quickly during big events.
⑤ *Rooms from: $209* ⊠ *221 N. Rampart Blvd., Summerlin* ☎ *702/869–*
7777 ⊕ *www.jwmarriottlv.com* ⟿ *469 rooms, 79 suites* ⟦◯⟧ *No meals.*

$$ 🏨 **Palms Casino Resort.** Rooms at the Palms are large, opulent, and mod-
RESORT ern, with some unusual amenities for Las Vegas, such as beds with
ultrafirm mattresses, duvets, and ample minibars. **Pros:** renowned,
three-story spa; excellent coin games; low table-game minimums, any-
time check-in with advance notice. **Cons:** it's taxi-distance from the
Strip; doesn't quite have the of-the-moment hipness it had as recently
as five years ago. $ Rooms from: $159 ✉ 4321 W. Flamingo Rd., West
Side ☎ 702/942–7777, 866/942–7770 ⊕ www.palms.com ↪ 1,051
rooms, 259 suites.

$ 🏨 **Red Rock Casino Resort & Spa.** Way out on the western edge of the
RESORT Las Vegas suburbs, this swanky golden-age Vegas property looks out
on the ochre-red Spring Mountains, just a stone's throw from Red
Rock National Conservation Area. **Pros:** movies; bowling; VIP section
of sports book; proximity to Red Rock canyon. **Cons:** waitress ser-
vice in gaming areas can be slow; long distance from Strip. $ Rooms
from: $139 ✉ 11011 W. Charleston Blvd., West Side ☎ 702/797–7777,
866/767–7773 ⊕ https://redrock.sclv.com ↪ 732 rooms, 81 suites
⦿ No meals.

$ 🏨 **Rio All-Suite Hotel & Casino.** In Brazil, Rio is party central, and in
HOTEL Las Vegas so is this sprawling resort just west of the Strip. **Pros:**
mecca for poker fans; large rooms; festive atmosphere. **Cons:** just
off-Strip enough to be inconvenient; terrible house advantage for
gaming. $ Rooms from: $139 ✉ 3700 W. Flamingo Rd., West Side
☎ 702/777–7777, 866/746–7671 ⊕ www.riolasvegas.com ↪ 2,522
suites ⦿ No meals.

ELSEWHERE IN LAS VEGAS

AIRPORT AND SOUTH SIDE

$ 🏨 **Silverton Casino Hotel.** Don't overlook this Rocky Mountain lodge–
HOTEL themed hotel with popular attractions such as a huge Bass Pro Shop, a
117,000-gallon saltwater aquarium (complete with mermaid shows),
and the Shady Grove Lounge, complete with plasma-screen televisions
and a mini-bowling alley. **Pros:** Bass Pro Shop is a fisherman's heaven;
mermaid shows are one-of-a-kind; great value not too far from Strip.
Cons: casino underwhelms; mediocre dining options. $ Rooms from:
$89 ✉ 3333 Blue Diamond Rd., South Las Vegas ☎ 702/263–7777,
866/722–4608 ⊕ www.silvertoncasino.com ↪ 288 rooms, 12 suites
⦿ No meals.

$ 🏨 **South Point Hotel Casino & Spa.** Perk or quirk—the South Point is the
HOTEL only resort in the Las Vegas area to house an equestrian center, a venue
that frequently hosts rodeos and other horse-oriented shows. **Pros:**
pool area; equestrian center. **Cons:** proximity to airport; distance from
Strip hotels. $ Rooms from: $79 ✉ 9777 Las Vegas Blvd. S, South Las
Vegas ☎ 702/796–7111, 866/796–7111 ⊕ www.southpointcasino.com
↪ 2,079 rooms, 84 suites ⦿ No meals.

NORTH SIDE

$ ⊞ **Aliante Casino + Hotel.** Nestled in the beautiful Aliante planned com-
HOTEL   munity, this offering is as much a place for locals as for visitors looking
to escape from the hubbub of the Strip. **Pros:** intimate vibe; swanky
rooms; sexy pool. **Cons:** off the beaten path; casino a bit small. $ *Rooms
from: $69* ⊠ *7300 Aliante Pkwy., North Side* ☎ *702/692–7777* ⊕ *www.
aliantegaming.com* ⤳ *191 rooms, 9 suites* ⦿ *No meals.*

GAMBLING
AND CASINOS

Updated by
Dante Drago
and Matt
Villano

If the sum total of your gambling experience is a penny-ante neighborhood poker game, or your company's casino night holiday party, you may feel a little intimidated by the Vegas gambling scene. We're here to tell you that you don't need to be a gambling expert to sit and play.

All you need is a little knowledge of the games you plan on playing, the gumption to step up to the table, a bankroll, and the desire to have a great time. It would also be wise to remember that other than a very few extreme cases, the odds are always with the house. There are no foolproof methods, miracle betting systems, lucky charms, or incantations that will change this fact. So if you feel as though you can brave the risk, handle the action, and want to have some fun, roll up your sleeves and pull up a chair—it's gambling time.

GAMBLING PLANNER

CASINO RULES

Keep IDs handy. Dealers strictly enforce the minimum gambling age, which is 21 years everywhere in Nevada.

No kids. Children are only allowed in gaming areas if they're passing through on their way to another part of the resort.

No electronic distractions. As a general rule, casinos forbid electronic devices, or anything that distracts gamblers at the tables (e.g., phone, mp3 player). When you sit down at a table make sure to remove any listening devices from your ears, glasses-like computer devices from your head, and set phones on silent mode. If you must take a call, the dealer will hold your place while you step away from the table to take the call. Cell phones and any two-way communication devices are also strictly prohibited in the sports books, period.

Smoking. Smoke only in designated areas. Signs on the tables and around the casino will inform you whether it's okay to smoke in a specific area. If you're unsure, ask someone before lighting up.

CASINO STRATEGY

The right mind-set. There's nothing quite like the excitement you feel when you step into a Vegas casino for the first time. The larger-than-life sights and sounds draw you in and inspire fantasies of life-changing jackpots and breaking the bank on a game of chance. There's nothing wrong with dreaming about hitting it big. Plenty of folks win money every single day in Las Vegas, but most don't. Gambling should be entertainment, a pastime, a bonding activity with friends or family, and occasionally an intellectual challenge. It should never be an investment, job, or a way of making a quick buck. If you approach gambling in this way, you may leave Las Vegas without a shirt.

The best approach. Learn enough about the games so that you aren't simply giving away your money. A little education will prevent you from making terrible bets or playing out of control. The bad bets (i.e., high-risk, high payout) can be some of the most exciting to play at the tables, and great fun if you like the action. With luck, you may come out ahead, but understand that higher-risk games are much less likely to pay out over time.

Have fun! If you have reasonable expectations, set and keep to your financial goals, and play with proper strategy, you're bound to have a successful and enjoyable trip, and leave Las Vegas with your sanity, your dignity, and your shirt.

Notice how bets are advertised. A good rule of thumb for discerning good bets from bad bets at the tables is to look how/if the bet is advertised. Good bets generally aren't posted (e.g., odds in craps aren't even on the table). Bad bets will be in flashing lights, and their big payouts will be prominently shown on the table or on large printed cards. Or they'll be "sold" by the dealer (like insurance in blackjack, and proposition bets in craps).

HOW NOT TO GO BROKE

■ Create solid goals on what you're willing to lose, and what would be a satisfying amount to win.

■ Consider what you can afford to lose and stick to this number, *no matter what.*

■ Pace yourself when you play, so you don't spend all your money too early in your trip.

■ Break your play into sessions.

■ If you lose your allotted goal during a session, quit playing and accept the loss. Many gamblers get deep into debt trying to "chase" a loss, and end up betting more than they can afford.

■ Never gamble with money borrowed on your credit card! Check out this sobering math: Say you want a $500 cash advance. The casino will charge a fee (it varies but for our example, 5%), which makes the total $525. Then the (credit card) bank will charge you for the cash advance (usually 3%). You're now $45.75 in the hole before you even start playing. And if you're carrying a balance on previous purchases, the long-term costs of the *separate* finance charges on the cash advance can be staggering.

■ Make sure your winnings goal is realistic. If you wager $10 a hand at blackjack, it's not reasonable to think you'll win $5,000 in a session—$50–$100 would be a more obtainable goal. If you're fortunate enough to reach your realistic goal during one of your sessions, end that session immediately. You can put half of your winnings away, and gamble with the profit during another session.

■ Most important is to exercise discipline and not exceed your goals. Sticking to these basic rules, regardless of whether you're up or down, will contain your losses and preserve your winnings.

■ Go easy on the alcohol. We understand you want to let loose and have fun while you play, but overindulging at the tables can impair your judgment and cause you to make unwise decisions with your hard-earned money on the line. The only thing worse than a hangover is a hangover with an empty wallet.

THE GOOD, THE BAD, AND THE UGLY

Games you can actually beat under the right circumstances: Poker, Sports Betting, and Video Poker.

Games where you can lose money slowly: baccarat (bank), blackjack, craps (Pass/Don't Pass, Come/Don't Come), Pai Gow Poker/Tiles, Single-Zero Roulette, Three-Card Poker, and some slot machines.

The rest: There are many more games offered in Vegas casinos (e.g. Casino War, Asia Poker, Red Dog), and new ones seemingly pop up every day. We won't discuss many of these games in the following pages because they're not considered to be "core" games, and aren't carried in the majority of the casinos. These games were created to increase profits that the better odds games don't provide, so if you choose to play them, do so with caution.

Games with worst odds: Keno and the Big Six Wheel. Avoid these two like the plague.

THE HOUSE EDGE

Think of a coin-flip game paying you $1 on heads and taking $1 on tails. Over time, you'd win as much as you'd lose. But a *casino*-hosted game might only pay $0.98 on heads while still taking your $1 on tails. That difference is the "house edge." Two cents doesn't seem like much, but when enough people play, the casino earns millions over an extended period; it's a mathematical certainty. Another example: The "true odds" of rolling double sixes in craps is 1 in 36, but they only pay you 30 to 1, instead of $36 on a $1 bet. The extra $6 that should be paid to you is, in essence, kept by the house, making it a very bad bet. The house edge varies from game to game, so if you know the odds for each game you can minimize your losses.

COMPS, CLUBS, AND COUPONS

Nearly every establishment has a rewards program, or Players Club, used to identify and reward its loyal gamblers. Members of the casino's Players Club will get regular mailings advertising specials, discounts, contests, and other information. When you sign up you receive a card to present whenever you play. You may also get a PIN number so you can check your comp totals at one of the kiosks (a comp ATM) on the casino floor. The card is used to track your play at table games and slot machines. The amount of comps you're entitled to is based on factors such as the amount you buy in for, overall time played, average bet, and expected losses. Comps can be used for restaurants, gifts, rooms, or even cash in some places. In many cases one card is accepted at multiple casinos with the same owner. Sign up for a card at Harrah's, and use it at all of the Caesars-owned properties. Present your card every single time you play at a table or slot machine, and every time you move to a new one. Remember that comps are based on play, so don't expect to get a free meal if you only sit at a game for 15 minutes, and bet $10 a hand.

FUNBOOKS

Discount "funbooks" are another perk of joining a Players Club. Many casinos will offer you a book of coupons for discounts in their hotels, shops, and restaurants when you sign up. These books offer some excellent discounts of real value, and occasionally even freebies for drinks, food, or gift items, so it pays to take advantage of these while you are in town. Some hotels will give you the funbooks without signing up for the Players Card, but in others you will have to ask for them. Many of the best funbooks can be found at places that are off the Strip. The smaller casinos usually offer better deals in an attempt to lure you away from the big guys. You may also find some good coupon books in taxis, magazines in your room, hotel gift shops, and even from people handing them out on the Strip.

TIPS FOR COMPS

Get a Players Club card. You *might* get a comp without a club card, but it's not very likely.

Don't forget to ask. No one is going to come up and offer you a comp. Even if you're not sure you've played enough for a comp, you should ask the floor person, or pit boss. The worst they can do is politely say no.

Buy in often, buy in big. Your initial cash stake, and average bet at a table is often what gets you noticed by the casino supervisors. They'll usually log your average bet based upon your opening few bets at the table, so make your first bets larger when the supervisor is paying attention, then reduce them when he or she moves away from the table. When you're finished at one table, cash in your chips at the cashier, and use those bills to buy in at the next table.

Consider the value of the comp. Never increase what you intended to gamble just to earn comps. It'll cost you *much* less to pay for dinner than to risk losing enough money in order to get a comp for that same dinner.

BETTER BETTOR ETIQUETTE

Know a little before you play. Dealers are available for questions, but you should learn the basics. Watch for a while, or ask the casino host or supervisor about beginner's classes. Even better, find an empty table and ask the dealer if he or she or she would be willing to walk you through the game.

Understand betting minimums before you sit down. Each table has a plaque or digital display with table minimums, maximums, and specific gaming rules.

Sympathy for the dealer. Dealers can't take cash directly from your hand, so lay it down on the table when you buy in. Place your bet in the proper area, and stack your entire bet in one pile, with the largest denomination chips on the bottom, and the smallest on the top.

Ask for change as you need it. The dealers have a limited number of chips in their rack for payouts and making change, so they prefer to give you enough small chips for 10 to 20 minimum bets at a time. If you're at a $10 table and you buy in with $300; they'll give you 20 $5 chips and 8 $25 chips. If you run out of $5 chips, just ask them to change your $25 chips as needed.

BEST BEGINNER CLASSES

The whole gambling scene can seem intimidating for the first-timer. But casinos have worked hard to help newbies feel comfortable playing the games, in the hopes that once they get a taste of the excitement, they'll be back for more.

Free lessons in Vegas are widely available. One place to look is in your hotel room; many resorts play a running loop of gaming lessons on TV. If you prefer the in-person format, most resorts offer free group lessons where would-be gamblers gather around a real table game while a dealer or supervisor explains how it works. Classes usually take place at scheduled times during low-traffic hours (just ask the casino host or one of the supervisors). Venues we like include:

Excalibur offers poker lessons at 11 am, roulette at 11 am and 7 pm, blackjack at 11:30 am and 7:30 pm, and craps at noon and 8 pm.

Golden Nugget has lessons every weekday for the most popular games: Three-Card Poker at 10 am, Pai Gow at 10:30 am, craps at 10 am and noon, Texas Hold'em at 11 am, roulette at 11:30 am, and blackjack at noon.

HELPFUL WEBSITES

Perhaps the best time and place to learn how the games are played is before you leave for Las Vegas, on your home computer or tablet. There are tons of websites, and even phone and tablet applications that not only teach you how to play the games, but also provide simulations of the gaming experience. And unlike the brief lessons given at the casino, you can learn at your own pace and practice playing as much as you like, whenever you like.

Check your app store for free simulation game apps to download to your phone or tablet. If you choose to practice on the Internet without having to register or download any software, try **Linesmaker** (⊕ *casino. betlm.eu/free-casino*) for craps, baccarat, and Pai Gow poker.

For roulette: **Roulette Edu** (⊕ *www.rouletteedu.com*).

For blackjack, Pai Gow tiles, and video poker: **Wizard of Vegas** (⊕ *www. wizardofvegas.com/games*).

EASIEST GAMES TO PLAY

Roulette is considered the easiest table game, but it's also one with a high house edge. That's not a coincidence; players typically pay for easier games in the form of a larger advantage for the house. ■ TIP→ Play a single-zero wheel. It'll cut the house edge almost in half.

You can play **keno** while you eat in many casino coffee shops. Keno carries the worst odds in the whole casino, but it's extremely easy to play. You just mark numbers on a betting slip, give it to the keno runner with a buck or two, and watch the board on the wall to see if your numbers come up.

Bingo is also a fun, simple casino game. It's played in specialized parlors, mostly in the Downtown casinos, with a crowd of people sitting at tables in a large room listening for their lucky numbers to line up. The people you run into are often locals and casino workers, who like bingo's humble aesthetic after a long day filled with glitz and kitsch.

Newer **slot machines** are a little more complicated than traditional slots, but they still remain the easiest to play in the casino—put the money in (or bet your credits) and touch a button (or pull the handle if it's an older machine) and wait for the reels to stop spinning to see if you've won or lost.

BEST DEALERS

Dealers on the Strip keep the games moving fast and aren't prone to many mistakes, but they often don't go in for a lot of small talk. Many beginners feel more comfortable at tables that are social and lively. For that, try the folksy atmospheres of the locals' casinos off the Strip and away from Downtown, like Gold Coast or Sunset Station. Before you sit down, make sure the game's moving at a speed you're comfortable with. Do the dealer and players look happy? Do the players have big stacks of chips? Is there a friendly vibe? If you're feeling especially chatty, locate a dealer from a familiar or interesting city (their hometowns are often printed on their name tags) and strike up some friendly banter. Vegas dealers are trained, skilled professionals who run their games like clockwork, but they're also customer service experts. It's their job to make sure you have a good time whether you win or lose. Don't hesitate to ask questions, or seek advice if you're unsure of the rules, what to do on a particular hand, or even where is the best place to get a bite to eat. If you don't feel comfortable with a dealer for whatever reason, "color up" your chips and move on to another table.

Las Vegas Lingo

Bank. A row or group of similar gaming machines.

Bankroll. The amount of money you have to gamble with.

Buy-in. The amount of cash you exchange for chips during a gaming session.

Cage. The casino cashier, where you can exchange your chips for cash.

Cheques (or Checks). The chips with money-equivalent values, used to place wagers at the tables.

Color up. To exchange a stack of lower-denomination chips for a few high-denomination chips. Dealers will ask if they can "color you up" before you leave their table. Say yes.

Comp. Short for complimentary (i.e., a freebie). Can be a drink, room, dinner, or show tickets from the casino.

Cut. A ritual splitting of a deck of cards performed after shuffling.

Eye-in-the-Sky. The overhead video surveillance system and its human monitors in a casino.

Fill. When chips are brought to a table from the casino cage to refill a money rack that's low.

House. Another name for the casino's side of any bet, as in this sentence: "The house wins on any tie."

Layout. The printed felt covering of a particular table game, which states the game being offered, betting area, payout odds, and other pertinent information related to the playing of the game.

Marker. A player's IOU to the casino. Rather than buy in with cash, players who register for casino credit can sign a marker in exchange for chips.

Match Play. A one-time bet voucher for a table game, often given as a perk by casinos.

Pit. A subdivision of the casino floor, with several adjacent gaming tables.

Pit Boss. A senior casino employee who supervises the gaming tables in a casino pit, settles player disputes, and authorizes comps. The pit boss can usually be found at a computer console in the middle of the pit, or patrolling the entire pit he or she is assigned to.

Players Club Card. A card with a magnetic stripe on it used to track a gambler's activities in a casino.

Progressive. A special kind of jackpot, often available to multiple tables or game machines, that continues to grow until it's won.

Push. A Tie bet, where you neither win nor lose.

Rake. In poker, it's an amount the casino takes out of each pot as compensation for running the game. Usually it's 10% of the total pot, or a flat fee per hour, depending on the game or casino.

Shoe. A small box in a table game from which cards are dealt.

Sports Book. The casino area for sports betting.

Table Games. All games of chance such as blackjack and craps played against the casino with a dealer.

Toke. A tip (short for token of your esteem). Usually given to dealers during play, to reward outstanding service, or celebrate a player's good fortune.

Conversely, don't hesitate to throw the dealer a toke (tip), if he or she enhances your overall experience.

ELECTRONIC GAMING

So you feel like playing some blackjack, but it's a sunny day and you want to work on your tan? How about doing both! Now you can with the ino, or E-Deck. Pocket-Casinos are handheld, wireless portable devices that allow you to play certain games, such as blackjack, baccarat, and video poker, from places other than the casino floor. These devices are also revolutionizing sports book gambling, *as you'll see later in the Sports Betting section.* The devices are similar to computer games you play on your phone or tablet, with one major difference. Here, you're wagering real money, in the form of credits, that you deposit when you receive your device. The devices only work in certain areas of the casino, in order to prevent underage people from using them, so make sure you know where, and how to use it properly when you receive it. They're currently being offered at places such as **Venetian, Palazzo, Hard Rock, M Resort, Cosmopolitan,** and **Tropicana,** and can usually be found in the sports book.

LEARN BEFORE YOU GO

The Internet has resources galore: The Las Vegas Advisor (⊕ *lasvegasadvisor.com*) and Gaming Today (⊕ *gamingtoday.com*) are two publications that keep the rest of the world up to speed on the gaming industry, including where to find the best deals, promotions, and events. To find an in-depth discussion of game rules and odds, check out the Wizard of Odds (⊕ *wizardofodds.com*). Vegas visitors can stay informed on the latest news and tourism information from the two local newspapers' websites: The Las Vegas Review-Journal (⊕ *lvrj.com*) and Las Vegas Sun (⊕ *lasvegassun. com*).

BLACKJACK

Blackjack, aka "21," anchors virtually every casino in America. It's one of the most popular table games because it's easy to learn, fun to play, and has potentially excellent odds for the player.

The object of this classic card game is simple. You want to build a higher hand than the dealer without going over 21—a *bust*. Two-card hands, from one deck of cards up to eight decks of cards, are dealt to everyone at the table, including the dealer, who gets one card face down (the "hole" card) and one card face up for all to see. Play then proceeds from gambler to gambler. You play out your hand by taking additional cards ("hitting") or standing pat ("staying"). When all the players have finished playing out their hands, the dealer then plays the house hand following preset rules. Once that's complete, the dealer pays winning players and rakes the chips of the losers.

PLAYING THE GAME

The value of a blackjack hand is the sum of all the cards; aces count as 1 or 11 (whichever is more advantageous to your hand), and face cards (jacks, queens, and kings) have a value of 10. Suit plays no role in blackjack. If you bust, you lose your bet immediately, no matter what happens with the dealer's cards. The dealer can also bust by going over 21, in which case all players remaining in the hand get paid off. If you're dealt a combination of a 10-valued card (a 10 or any face card) and an ace on your first two cards, it's called a *natural* blackjack. If this is the case, you're paid a bonus on your bet, unless the house also has a blackjack. The payout is either 3 to 2 on your original bet, or 6 to 5, depending on the house rules where you're playing. The dealers use a little mirror or other device at the table to check their hidden card for blackjacks prior to dealing out extra cards.

For those who aren't lucky enough to be dealt blackjack, play starts with the person sitting to the dealer's left. Everyone plays out his or her hand by motioning to the dealer whether they want to hit or stand. Players *must* make specific motions to the dealer about their intentions:

■ If the cards have been dealt face up, which is the case at most casinos these days, you're not supposed to touch your cards, so you hit by tapping on the table with your finger(s) in front of your cards. To stand, you simply wave your hand side to side over your cards.

■ If the cards have been dealt face down, pick them up and hold them (with one hand only!). To hit, you "scratch" on the table toward yourself with the corner of your cards. To stand, you slide the cards face down under your chips. Don't fret if you knock over your chips in the process. The dealer will restack them for you if necessary. As long as your hand is less than 21, you can continue hitting and taking cards. If you bust, you must expose your cards immediately (if you are holding them), and the dealer will take your bet and remove your cards. At that point the dealer turns to the next player who repeats the same hit/stand process.

■ Once every player has a chance to act on his/her hand, the dealer reveals his or her hidden card and plays out the hand according to the following rules:

■ Dealer shows 16 or less: dealer must hit

■ Dealer shows 17 or more: dealer must stand (in most casinos)

Once the dealer's hand is complete, the bets are either paid (if the player's hand is higher than the dealer's) or raked (if the dealer's hand is higher than the player's). If the dealer has busted, all players remaining in the hand win their bets. In the event a player's hand value is equal to that of the dealer, it's a *push* (the dealer will knock on the table in front of the bet); the bet is neither paid nor raked.

DOUBLING DOWN

If your first two cards total 10 or 11, your chances of hitting and drawing a 10-value card to create a great hand are very good. To take full advantage of that, you can double down. It's a special bet you place after the hand has started, whose value can be any amount up to your initial bet. Doubling down for an amount not equal to your original bet is called "doubling for less," and the dealer will usually announce this when you do it. This confirms that you did not take the full amount of the double, so there are no discrepancies when you are paid. The upside of doubling is that you put more money in play for an advantageous situation. The downside is that you receive only a single card in lieu of the normal hit/stand sequence. Casino rules vary on which starting hands you can double down on, so ask the dealer before you slide a matching stack of chips beside your first bet. The most common rule variation says you can double down on any two cards.

SPLITTING

Splitting is another good way to raise your bet in a favorable situation. If your first two cards are of equal value (even two different face cards such as king and queen), you can split them apart and form two separate hands, then play each hand out separately as if it were a brand-new hand. When you want to split, push a stack of chips equal to your original bet into the betting circle, and tell the dealer your intentions. Never touch the cards yourself, unless you're playing a game that calls for it (like single deck), in which case you'll lay your cards down and place the extra bet. In some casinos you can re-split if you get another matching card for three or even four separate hands. You can draw as many cards as you want to make a hand when you split. In many casinos, you can't re-split aces and are only allowed to draw one card on each ace.

INSURANCE AND EVEN MONEY

When the dealer's up card is an ace, she'll ask if anyone wants to buy insurance. You can take insurance for up to half of your original wager. If the dealer makes black-

> ### BLACKJACK SWITCH
>
> Two is better than one right? That's the thinking behind Blackjack Switch, a Shuffle Master–owned game that started at Casino Royale but can now be found at just about every gambling hall in town. Instead of playing one hand, players are required to play two. Players can switch the second cards of their two hands to make two totally new hands. Standard splitting and doubling rules apply. Think the switcheroo favors the players? Think again. Blackjack Switch only pays even money, and when the dealer busts with 22, all bets push.

jack, the insurance bet pays off at 2 to 1 odds; if she doesn't, the insurance bet is lost and the hand is played normally. If you draw a blackjack when the dealer's up card is an ace, the dealer may ask if you want "even money" in some casinos. Taking even money is exactly the same as taking the insurance. It's offered this way in order to entice you to take the insurance (exactly what the house wants) instead of risking a push if the dealer has blackjack also. If you take even money the dealer will pay you 1 to 1 on your bet instead of the normal 3 to 2, and lock up your cards before he or she checks her hidden card for blackjack. Experts consider both insurance, and even money bad bets. Always pass on them.

STRATEGY

Although it's easy to learn, blackjack has varying layers of complexity that can be tackled, depending on your interest level. With practice and the perfection of basic strategy, you can reduce the house edge to about 0.5% (as opposed to about 2.5% for the average uninformed gambler), making blackjack one of the best bets of table games.

Basic strategy is simply the optimal way for a player to play his or her cards, based on the dealer's exposed card and a particular set of casino rules. We'll discuss these rules below (⇨ *The House Hedges*), because basic strategy changes as certain rules change.

At its *most* basic, basic strategy is the assumption that the dealer's hole card is a 10. If the dealer's up card is a 9, he or she likely has a 10 underneath to make 19. If the dealer shows a 4, he or she likely has a 14. You then act accordingly, standing pat or hitting depending on whether you can beat the dealer's hand. Learning and memorizing basic strategy is a must for professional gamblers, who can't afford to give up anything more to the house edge. For the casual or beginning gambler, the rules are printed on small charts (⇨ *example chart in this chapter*) that you can buy in any casino gift shop, or find and print online at one of the websites listed earlier. You're allowed to use these cards at the table for reference at any time, and you should every time you're not sure of whether to hit, stand, split, or double down on any given hand. You should, however, try to come with some basic knowledge of the game and strategy before you start playing, so you don't have to consult the card on *every* hand, which considerably slows down the game and enjoyment for other players at the table.

■ **TIP**➔ To practice basic strategy, try ⊕ www.hitorstand.net. If you make the wrong decision on a hand, the program will tell you.

4

If you don't have the patience to practice or memorize, or don't want to refer to a chart, you can always ask the dealer, who should have knowledge of basic strategy from his or her experience. Or, you can follow these basic rules-of-thumb based on the dealer's up card:

■ Ace, 10, 9, 8, 7—assume the dealer has a made hand (i.e., a hand totaling between 17 and 21 and will therefore not need to draw). If your hand is 17 or higher, stand. If your hand is 16 or lower, you should hit.

■ 2, 3, 4, 5, 6—assume that the dealer has an easily busted hand, so there's no need to take any risks. If your hand is 13 or higher, stand and hope the dealer busts. If your cards total 11 or lower, take a hit and then reevaluate using the same set of rules. If your hand totals 12 only hit against a dealer's 2 or 3.

■ If you have a "soft" hand (an ace with a value card; for example A,7) that totals less than 8 (or 18), you should always hit. If it totals 18 only hit against a dealer's 9, 10, or ace, and always stand on a soft total of 19 or 20.

■ If your hand total equals 11, you should consider doubling down against everything but a dealer ace. If your hand totals 10, you should consider doubling down against everything but a dealer 10 or ace.

■ Always split 8,8, and A,A, and never split 5,5, or 10,10.

THE HOUSE HEDGES

The casinos know that their edge in blackjack is very small, especially against those who employ basic strategy, so they have come up with ways to hedge their bets by adding certain rules, or restrictions to the once-standard rules. These things not only increase the house edge against you, but they can distort the odds for basic strategy decisions, and make your chart much less effective by changing some variables of the games. Because the variables change from game to game, and casino to casino, you must be sure your basic strategy card matches the game you're playing. Here are some general rules for choosing a good blackjack table and keeping the house edge low. Choose a table that:

■ Pays blackjack at 3 to 2, not 6 to 5 or anything else

■ Uses a smaller number of decks in the game. The fewer decks, the better for you

■ The dealer must stand on a soft 17 (A,6), instead of hitting

Blackjack Table

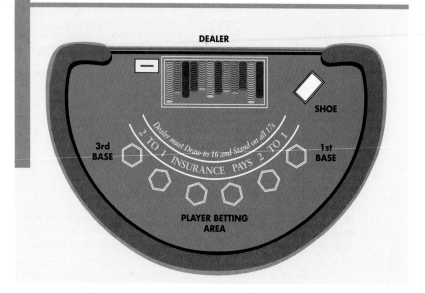

- Allows you to double down on any hand. Some casinos will only let you double on 10 or 11

- Allows you to re-split aces. The more times they let you split aces in one hand, the better

- Allows you to split aces, and receive more than one card if you choose

- Allows you to double down after splitting

- Has surrender. This allows you to surrender a bad hand before drawing extra cards. The casino will charge you half your wager for this privilege. Sometimes it's a good idea, and basic strategy will let you know when.

Now, chances are you won't find a game with all of these things in your favor. The trick is to find one that uses a combination of as many as possible.

THE SHUFFLE MATTERS

Some casinos now employ "continuous" shuffle machines at their blackjack tables. These machines recycle the used cards right back into the machine after every hand, where they're continuously shuffled and re-dealt nonstop directly from the machine, by the dealer. This should not be confused with an "automatic" shuffler, which uses a machine to shuffle the cards, but the cards are removed from the machine after the shuffle and placed in the shoe by the dealer. The difference? The continuous shuffler speeds up the game considerably, since there's no break for a shuffle, or a player cut. This increases the amount of hands you'll play in your allotted session, and gives the house edge more chances

SAMPLE BLACKJACK BASIC STRATEGY CHART

Your Hand	Dealer's Up Card									
	2	3	4	5	6	7	8	9	10	A
5–8	H	H	H	H	H	H	H	H	H	H
9	D	D	D	D	D	H	H	H	H	H
10	D	D	D	D	D	D	D	D	H	H
11	D	D	D	D	D	D	D	D	D	D
12	H	H	S	S	S	H	H	H	H	H
13	S	S	S	S	S	H	H	H	H	H
14	S	S	S	S	S	H	H	H	H	H
15	S	S	S	S	S	H	H	H	H	H
16	S	S	S	S	S	H	H	H	H	H
17	S	S	S	S	S	S	S	S	S	S
18	S	S	S	S	S	S	S	S	S	S
19	S	S	S	S	S	S	S	S	S	S
20	S	S	S	S	S	S	S	S	S	S
21	S	S	S	S	S	S	S	S	S	S
A,2	H	H	D	D	D	H	H	H	H	H
A,3	H	H	D	D	D	H	H	H	H	H
A,4	H	H	D	D	D	H	H	H	H	H
A,5	H	H	D	D	D	H	H	H	H	H
A,6	D	D	D	D	D	H	H	H	H	H
A,7	S	D	D	D	D	S	S	H	H	H
A,8	S	S	S	S	S	S	S	S	S	S
A,9	S	S	S	S	S	S	S	S	S	S
A,A	SP	SP	SP	SP	SP	SP	SP	SP	SP	SP
2,2	H	SP	SP	SP	SP	SP	H	H	H	H
3,3	H	H	SP	SP	SP	SP	H	H	H	H
4,4	H	H	H	D	D	H	H	H	H	H
5,5	D	D	D	D	D	D	D	D	D	H
6,6	SP	SP	SP	SP	SP	H	H	H	H	H
7,7	SP	SP	SP	SP	SP	SP	H	H	H	H
8,8	SP	SP	SP	SP	SP	SP	SP	SP	SP	SP
9,9	SP	SP	SP	SP	SP	S	SP	SP	S	S
10,10	S	S	S	S	S	S	S	S	S	S

H-Hit, S-Stand, D-Double Down, SP-Split

DID YOU KNOW?

With a bit of knowledge and the use of basic strategy (⇨ *see chart*), blackjack players can reduce the house's edge to less than 1%.

to work against you. Remember in blackjack, speed kills. If possible stick with the old-fashioned hand shuffle by the dealer, or even an automatic shuffler.

SIDE BETS AND VARIATIONS GAMES

Other strategies used by the casino to separate you from your money involve side bets and variation games. A side bet is a high-paying bet that's based on getting three 7s, a pair, a two-card 20, a three-card poker hand, and so on. This bet is usually placed before the cards are dealt, and isn't tied to the results of the main game. Like the bonus bets in poker table games (⇨ *below*), these bets carry a hefty house edge and should be avoided.

> ### SHOE BREAK
>
> If you see a sign on a table that reads, "No mid-shoe entry," you can't enter play in the middle of the shoe. You have to wait until the shoe ends to start play. Some players have the belief (unsupported by mathematics) that new people can bring bad luck or change the cards. Or they feel it just ruins the flow of the game. Casinos mostly put these signs at high-limit tables to keep their highest-betting customers happy.

Variation games like Double Attack Blackjack, Double Exposure Blackjack, or Spanish 21 use the rules of blackjack but change the dynamics of the game to stimulate more action and entice high-house-edge bets. For example, in Spanish 21 the deck has only 48 cards, because the 10s have been removed. Consequently, player 21s are paid immediately, and the rules allow players to do common blackjack things at strange times—you can surrender after your first two cards are dealt, or double down on any number of cards. Plus, hands like 6-7-8 and 7-7-7 pay automatic bonuses. There are so many different variation games and side bets these days that we won't describe them all here. The rules and bets are posted on the individual games. If you're interested in learning them, you can take a course or ask the dealer if he or she isn't busy. You should have a good understanding of how to play standard blackjack before attempting these games.

WHERE TO PLAY

In a bathing suit: Many hotels offer swim-up blackjack, but we like the game at Caesars, Flamingo, or the Hard Rock Hotel.

For the best odds: We can't list them all here, but, fortunately, someone else has. Check out the blackjack survey at ⊕ *wizardofvegas.com/guides/blackjack-survey* for the latest info. **El Cortez**, which is Downtown, has a single-deck game with very low house edge (0.19%), and it's only a $3 minimum to play. Also **MGM Grand, Monte Carlo,** and **Tropicana** have 3-to-2 (single-deck) games with a low house edge, but you often must be willing to play $15 or $25 per hand.

To learn the game: Downtown casinos are your best bet for low minimums, but **Circus Circus** also has a $3 game on the Strip.

POKER

Folks can't seem to get enough of poker. The top players are celebrities, and poker is on TV more than hockey. If you've played, you know why: it's an intellectual challenge to suit any size brain. And it has an egalitarian quality that beginners love; sometimes the cards fall just right for rookies and they win a tournament, or take home a huge pot.

BASIC RULES

In poker you win by being the last player standing at the end of the hand. That happens one of two ways: by betting more than anyone else is willing to bet and forcing other players to "fold" (drop out until the next hand), or by having the best hand of all players remaining in the game after the final round of betting. The two twists that make poker great are that the hands of each player evolve as more cards are dealt or revealed, and that some or all of the cards are hidden from view, so you can only speculate on the hand values of other players.

The variations played in casinos—Seven-Card Stud, Texas Hold'em, Omaha, and a smattering of others like Razz and Pineapple—all demand that the player create the best five-card hand from a deal that originates from a single standard deck of 52 cards. Five-card hands are valued in order of their statistical rarity:

■ Straight Flush: Five cards of the same suit in consecutive rank. A 10 to Ace straight flush is called a "royal flush," the rarest and highest of all hands.

■ Four of a Kind: Four cards of equal rank plus one nonmatching card.

■ Full House: Three cards of equal rank, and two of a different equal rank (e.g. 7-7-7-5-5). This hand is declared as "sevens full of fives." The value of the full house is dependent on the three equal cards, not the two. If two players both have full houses, the player whose three equal cards are higher value, will win (e.g. A-A-A-2-2 is better than K-K-K-7-7).

■ Flush: Five cards of the same suit, regardless of order.

■ Straight: Five cards in consecutive order, regardless of suit.

■ Three of a Kind: Three cards of equal rank, and two other nonmatching cards.

■ Two Pair: Two equal cards of one rank, two equal cards of a different second rank, with a fifth nonmatching card. Similar to the full house, the value of the highest-ranking pair wins (e.g., 10-10-4-4 beats 7-7-6-6).

■ Pair: Two cards of equal rank, and three other nonmatching cards.

■ High Card: Any five cards that don't fit into one of the *above* categories in which your highest card carries the value of your hand. If two hands have the exact same high card, the value of the next highest card is used, and so forth until the single largest value high card is revealed.

The high card will also determine a winner when hands have the same value, such as a straight, flush, two pair, or a pair. For example, if two players have a pair of 9s, the player with the highest value of the remaining three cards wins (which is referred to as a "kicker, as in "I have a pair of 9s with an Ace kicker"). Aces are the highest-ranked card with one exception: they can act as the low end of a straight (Ace, 2, 3, 4, 5). The 5 card is considered the highest ranked card for such a straight. In a final-round showdown that hand would lose to a 6-high straight (2, 3, 4, 5, 6). The suits are all equal in poker and totally identical hands split the pot.

The game starts when cards are dealt to all players at the table, who then take turns putting casino chips into a central "pot" during a predetermined number of betting rounds. When it's your turn to bet, you can decide to *fold,* which means you no longer participate in the hand. Any money you've already bet stays in the pot after you fold and will go to the winner of the hand. To stay in the game, each player must match, or *call,* the highest bet of that round to stay in the game. Players can also *raise,* which means that they are betting more than the round's current highest bet. After a raise, the betting round continues until everyone who wishes to stay in the game has contributed an equal amount to the pot.

Once all the betting rounds are over, if more than one player remains in the game there's a *showdown* where all cards are revealed. In most games the highest-value hand wins, although some poker games pay players for having the lowest hand, as you will soon see.

TEXAS HOLD'EM

Hold'em is *the* most popular form of poker. Each player (up to 10 can play one game) is dealt two cards face down, followed by a betting round. Then five community cards are dealt on the table in three groups, each followed by a betting round. First is a group of three cards (the *flop),* and then there are two more rounds of one card each (the *turn* and the *river).* You can use any combination of your cards and community cards to create your best five-card hand.

Position is very important in Hold'em. The deal rotates around the table after every hand, and with it, the *blinds* (minimum opening bets used to stimulate the betting action). Depending on house rules, either one or two players must automatically bet in the first betting round, regardless of their cards (that's why they're called blinds; you have to bet without even seeing your cards). To stay in and see the three cards of the flop, the other players must match (or raise) the blind bet. This ensures that no player sees the flop for free, and adds heft to the pot. The later your position, the better—players have an advantage if they can see what the players before them decided to do, and can better judge whether the size of the pot justifies the risk of betting and staying in the game.

> **AT A GLANCE**
>
> **Format:** Multiplayer card game, dealt by house dealer.
>
> **Goal:** Bet your opponents out of the game, or have the highest hand in the final showdown.
>
> **Pays:** Varies; each pot is determined by the amount of betting.
>
> **House Advantage:** None. The house "rakes" a small percentage of the total money played.
>
> **Best Bet:** Tournaments are a great way to stretch your poker dollar, even for novices.
>
> **Worst Bet:** Underestimating your competition.

■ TIP→ The dealer will hold your seat at a poker table for up to a half hour (for bathroom breaks, smoking, or just fresh air). Upon returning, you'll have to post the small and big blinds if you want to play immediately, or wait until the deal comes around to you naturally. If you don't return in the allotted time, you'll lose your seat at the table and your cheques will be collected and stored in the cashier cage until you claim them.

OMAHA

Omaha is dealt and played exactly like Hold'em except the player is given four cards instead of two, and *must* use two, and *only* two of the four cards, plus three of the community cards, to make his or her final hand. This adds another dimension to the game, as you must base your strategy on using only two of the four cards in your hand, and this strategy may change drastically from flop to river, because of the extra cards you're holding. You should have some experience playing Hold'em before taking on Omaha, in which reading hands is more complicated.

SEVEN-CARD STUD

In Seven-Card Stud there are no community cards; you're dealt your own set of seven cards over the course of five betting rounds: an initial batch of three cards (two down, one up); three more single up-cards; and a final down card. By the showdown, every player remaining in the game has three down cards and four up cards from which to make his or her best five-card hand.

POKER BETTING LIMITS

Casino poker rooms list ongoing games and soon-to-start tournaments on a large video monitor at their entrance. Before you get into a game, you should understand the betting limit nomenclature. Here are the basics:

Limit Games. Also known as a "Fixed Limit" game, the amount you can bet is listed with two numbers, like "$3–$6." This means you must bet and raise $3 in the first two rounds of play and $6 in the third and fourth rounds. The amount of the "big" blind bet is equal to the low limit ($3).

Spread Limit. This type of game gives the player a range for betting and raising. An example would be a "$1–$4–$8" game, where your bets must be at least $1 and at most $4 for the first two rounds, and between $1 and $8 in the later rounds.

Pot Limit. Players are allowed to wager any amount up to the total of what's currently in the pot.

No Limit. These games are exactly what they sound like; they usually have low betting minimums (they're listed as "$1–$2NL"). If you've got the chips on the table, you can bet them. This is the style of play you see on television, where players go "All In." Don't get involved in a No Limit game if you don't know what you're doing.

HI-LOW GAMES

Sometimes you'll see Omaha and Seven-Card Stud listed with Hi-Low. These games are played with the same rules as their relatives with one big exception. To win the entire pot, you must have the best high hand *and* the best low hand. A low hand is basically the lowest value you can make for your five cards. For example 5, 4, 3, 2, A (or "wheel" as it's referred to) is the lowest possible hand. In a regular game of Omaha, this would be a straight, and a fairly high-ranked hand. In Hi-Low the straight rank used for the high hand isn't also assumed when determining the low hand. If one player has the high hand, and another has the low hand, the pot is split between them. If more than one player has an identical winning low, or high hand, then half of the pot is split between them and so forth.

STRATEGY

If you're a beginner, focus on learning how to play the game at low-stakes tables or tournaments before you invest any serious bankroll. The old adage "if you can't spot the sucker at the table, it's you" is never truer than at a Las Vegas poker table. Playing free poker online is a valuable tool for players who are trying to learn the game prior to a Vegas trip, but the style of play is different. Playing online ignores a lot of the subtleties of playing live, including the all-important *tells*, outward quirks that reveal the contents of your hand to observant opponents. Also, remember that you're not betting real money when you play online, and may be inclined to play bad hands that you would be ill-advised to play in real money games.

POKER TOURNAMENTS

Poker tournaments are an excellent way for beginners to learn the game of poker in a real-life setting without the risk of losing large sums of money to more experienced players. Most casino poker rooms run tournaments in most of the popular games at different times throughout the day. Schedules can be found in the poker rooms, your room, or at the front desk. The listings will contain the game offered, the limits of the bets, if any, the amount it will cost you to enter plus the amount you pay the casino to run the game ($60+$15 for example), if you can rebuy any more chips when your first amount runs out, the time start, and any other pertinent information.

The entry fees of all the players that play in the tournament are put into a prize pool that pays out to a top number of finishers, which is determined by how many players enter (for example, the top 10 finishers out of 100 that entered will get prize money). The tournament is played just like the live game except the players use fake poker chips instead of real ones, and the blinds increase at fixed time intervals to speed the game along. When you've lost all your chips and re-buys, you're out of the tournament. The one left with all the chips is the winner of the tournament, and wins the top money prize out of the pool.

Although bluffing and big showdowns are part and parcel of the TV poker phenomenon, casino poker success in limit games and small tournaments comes with a steady, conservative approach. The most important thing to learn is how to calculate *pot odds*. You compare the amount of money likely to be in the pot—your potential win—with the relative odds that your hand will be improved as more cards are dealt or revealed. As with everything in life, if the payoff is big enough, the price you pay to stay in the game is worth the risk.

There are no shortcuts to learning poker strategy. Each variation of the game has its nuances. Part of learning the game is to understand how good your hand has to become in order to win a hand, given a certain pot size and number of opponents. You can get lucky, but it takes study and repetition to become consistently good at poker over the long haul.

POPULAR POKER VARIATIONS

All of the following games are played like traditional casino table games that use the elements of poker at their core. These games are found in the main casino area with the other table games instead of the poker room. Although there are other variations of poker games around Vegas, these five are the most common. Most of these games carry high house advantages, but move at a slower, more relaxed pace, so you won't lose as quickly as you might at blackjack or craps. Most of them also have a jackpot or bonus bet that can carry a very high payout for rarer hands, which makes the hefty house advantage seem worth it to many players. The bonus hands and payouts are always clearly listed at the table, and you can always ask the dealer how to play these bets if you're feeling frisky.

THREE- AND FOUR-CARD POKER

Three- and Four-Card Poker are two of the most popular poker table games, and at least one table of either can be found in virtually every casino in Vegas. Because you have fewer than the standard five cards to make your final poker hand in both of these games, the odds of making certain hands change. As a result, the ranking system of hands is adjusted. For example, in Three-Card Poker, a straight beats a flush. The hand rankings will be listed clearly right on the table layout in front of you for your convenience. As always, if you're not sure of something, ask the dealer.

Three-Card Poker. First, place a bet in the "Ante" spot. You and the dealer get three cards face down. After seeing your cards, you have the option to fold and surrender your Ante, or to play and make the "Play" wager (located directly beneath the Ante). The Play will always be equal to your Ante. The dealer will then reveal his or her cards. If the dealer doesn't have a total hand value of queen-high or better, he or she doesn't *qualify*. If this is the case, the dealer will return your Play bet to you and you'll get paid even money on your Ante. If you have a straight or better, you'll also get a bonus on your Ante for having a rare hand. If the dealer qualifies for the hand with a queen-high or better, and has a hand that's better than yours, he or she collects your Ante and Play bets. If he or she qualifies and your hand is better, you'll be paid even money on both your Play and Ante bets (and an Ante bonus if your hand qualifies).

Four-Card Poker. You start with an "Ante" wager and are dealt five cards, which you must use to make your best four-card hand. The dealer, however, will be dealt six cards to make his or her best four-card hand. Because of this extra card, there's no minimum hand needed for the dealer to qualify, as in Three-Card Poker, so you'll always have to beat the dealer to get paid. If you fold, you lose your Ante. If you decide to play, you can wager from 1 to 3 times your Ante wager in the spot marked "Play" (directly beneath Ante). If your hand beats the dealer's when it's revealed, you'll be paid even money on both Ante and Play bets. You'll be paid a bonus on your Ante if your hand is three of a kind or better. If your hand isn't better than the dealer's, you lose both bets. Because the house has a large advantage by receiving an extra card in this game, it'll pay you if you push, or tie, the dealer's hand.

BONUS BETS

Both of these games have a stand-alone bet that has nothing to do with whether you win the hand or not. These bets are the real reason that these games are so popular, and even though they're optional, they're placed by most people who play the game. They pay high odds for rare hands, adding the excitement of potentially hitting a small jackpot. In Three-Card Poker it's called Pair Plus (located above the Ante). If you choose this bet and get any hand that has a rank value of a pair or better, you get paid a bonus of up to 40 to 1 on your initial bet, depending on what the hand is. In Four-Card Poker the same bet is called Aces Up (also above the Ante). It pays if you get a hand that's at least a pair of Aces or better, and like the Pairs Plus bet in Three-Card, it's paid at increasing odds depending on how rare your hand is, up to 50 to 1. In both games the bonus hands, and what they pay, will be clearly marked on the table layout.

CARIBBEAN STUD

Caribbean Stud has waned in popularity as more exciting games like Three-Card Poker have emerged, so you might not find this game in every casino anymore. Each player places an initial Ante bet. You and the dealer are then dealt five cards face down. The dealer will expose one of her cards to entice you to play. You must then decide whether to remain in the game, in which case you place an additional wager in the "Bet" square equal to double your Ante, or fold, in which case you lose your Ante.

After you've placed your additional bet, or folded, the dealer reveals the rest of her hand. If the dealer's hand isn't better than a minimum value of ace-king high, he or she doesn't *qualify*, and you're paid even money on your Ante wager, and push on your Bet wager, even if the dealer's nonqualifying hand is better than yours. If the dealer has a hand that's better than a value of ace-king high, it qualifies. If it's better than your hand, you lose both bets. If your hand is better than the dealer's *qualifying* hand, you're paid even money on your Ante wager, and your additional wager will get paid at even money, or at increasing odds, depending on what the hand is (e.g., two pair pays 2 to 1, a straight pays 4 to 1). This game also offers a hard-to-resist $1 side bet for a progressive jackpot that pays bonuses for any hand better than a straight, and the jackpot (advertised in flashing lights) for a royal flush. This bet offers terrible odds, but adds to the excitement factor.

LET IT RIDE

You're dealt three cards; the dealer lays down two community cards. If your three cards, plus the community cards make a five-card hand that's a pair of 10s or better, you win. You start by placing three bets of equal size. On the first two bets you have the option to take them back or let them ride, as the community cards are revealed. When the second community card is revealed the dealer turns over your cards. If you don't have a pair of 10s or better, you lose your remaining bets. If you have the 10s or a better hand, you're paid even money, or at increasing odds based on what hand you have, on all the bets you let ride during the betting rounds. Like Caribbean Stud, there's a $1 bonus bet that will pay out if you get a hand that's three of a kind or better.

PAI GOW POKER

You're dealt seven cards from which you make one five-card and one two-card poker hand. The two-card hand can *never* have a better rank value than the five-card hand, so set your cards carefully. There's a joker, which can be used as an ace in either hand, or a wild card to complete a straight or flush in your five-card hand. You play against the dealer, who also makes two hands from seven cards, and will always set them according to a strict set of house rules. If both of your hands are beat by the dealer's hands, you lose. If you lose one and win one, you push. If you win both hands, you win even money on your bet, minus a 5% commission to the casino.

PAI GOW TILES

Many Vegas casinos offer Pai Gow Tiles, a distant cousin to poker. You'll recognize it right away because it's the only game in the house that uses a set of 32 dominoes (or "tiles") along with three dice. The goal of the game is to assemble a hand that beats the banker.

The dice are used to determine order of play, which begins with each player being given a stack of four tiles. The player then arranges them into two hands of two. Once everyone has set their pairs, the banker reveals the house hands and the players who beat both hands win even money, the players who win one and lose the other push, and the players who lose both hands lose their wager. There's also a 5% commission involved and a bank option for the players.

The twist, and what makes Pai Gow so addictive according to its adherents, is that there are different approaches to arranging your pairs. Because of this, and whether or not you bank the hand, the house edge can vary. What makes it a difficult game to learn is that the tile pairs have a specific—and nonintuitive—ranking system, which determines when hands win and lose.

WHERE TO PLAY

With the big boys: MGM Grand, which has a separate casino (dubbed "The Mansion") for whales (high rollers); and Bellagio, one of the jewels in the poker-room crown on the Strip.

Best all-around poker room: Aria, home of Phil Ivey's "Ivey Room."

SLOTS

Slot machines are the lifeblood of Vegas, earning the casinos mountains of cash. There's a reason why there are what seems like zillions of slot machines compared to table games—they guarantee a fixed rate of return for the casino with no risk. Some gamblers can't get enough of the one-armed bandits, and if you're one of them (a gambler, not a bandit), set yourself a budget and pray for those three 7s to line up.

BASIC SLOT PLAY

Playing slots is basically the same as it's always been: Insert money, see what happens. Over the years the look and feel of the games have changed dramatically. Machines that dispense a noisy waterfall of coins have all but given way to machines that pay with printed, coded tickets—gone are the one-arm-bandits of yore. Tickets are inserted like cash and redeemed at the cashier's cage or at ATM-like machines that dispense cash. If you're a historian, or sentimental, you may still find a few coin-dispensing relics in some of the Downtown or off-Strip casinos. Nearly all games are digital. The mechanical spinning reels that physically revolved have been replaced by video touch sensitive screens that are interactive. These screens offer fun bonus games for big bucks and excitement and make you feel like you played some role in the outcome. No matter which format you prefer, the underlying concept is still the same: you're looking for the reels—real or virtual—to match a winning pattern of shapes.

Each reel may have a few dozen shapes, creating an enormous number of possible patterns. The payout varies, depending on how rare the pattern is. The payout tables for each shape are usually posted above or below the "play" area of the machine. On some of the newer digital machines, there's a button marked "Payout Table." Prizes range from merely returning the bettor's initial stake, to multimillion-dollar *progressive* prizes.

STRATEGY

All slot machines, including every mechanical reel game, are run by onboard computers. The machine's computer brain generates a new random number thousands of times a second, which then determines where each reel will come to rest.

Although the casino can set the percentage an individual machine will retain for the house over the long term, each individual spin is an independent, random event. That means that if a jackpot reel pattern appears and pays a huge amount, the next jackpot is equally likely (or unlikely) to appear the very next spin. There's no such thing as an overdue machine, or a machine that's "tapped out."

Slot payout ranges can vary between 80% and 98%. A machine that pays out at 98% will, in the long run, pay back 98 cents out of every dollar you put in, as opposed to the paltry 80 cents you'll get back on the 80% machine. Picking the right machine can make the biggest difference in how fast you lose. Of course, information on which slot machines are the loosest (the ones that pay out the most) is hard to obtain, and can change often. Play the games you enjoy, but never lose sight of the fact that the payout percentage of that machine will usually determine how much you win or lose.

> **AT A GLANCE**
>
> **Format:** Bill- and ticket-operated electronic/mechanical machines.
>
> **Goal:** Line up winning symbols on machine's reels according to payout schedule.
>
> **Pays:** Varies by machine and casino.
>
> **House Advantage:** Varies widely, depending on how the machine is set.
>
> **Best Bet:** Playing "looser" higher-limit machines at the maximum coin bet.
>
> **Worst Bet:** Playing "tight" machines at noncasino locations.

■ TIP→ Make sure you always insert your player card into the appropriate slot before you insert cash or tickets. Slot players often enjoy lucrative promotions and comps that table-game players don't.

CHOOSING A MACHINE

■ Higher-denomination machines tend to have higher payback percentages.

■ Look for machines that advertise a higher payout, but beware of the fine print. The machines with the high progressive jackpots are usually the tightest. Resist the temptation, and avoid them.

■ If you want to take a shot at the jackpot, you need to play the *maximum* coins with *every play*. If that means stepping down to a lower-denomination machine (e.g., from dollars to quarters) so you can afford it, then do it. After all, we know that hitting the jackpot is the "reel" reason you're in Vegas.

VIDEO POKER

Video poker attracts a large following. Many gamblers enjoy the solo play of a slot machine, but prefer a slightly more complex set of rules, like to have a say in the outcome, and can't get enough of that feeling when that fifth card completes a full house. Make no mistake, video poker is not "live poker on training wheels." People love video poker because it's fun, convenient, and because the house advantage can be relatively low under the right circumstances.

BASIC RULES

Casino visitors will find video poker in long rows of machines just like slot machines. And many casino bars feature video-poker consoles for patrons to play as they sip. To play, just feed in bills or tickets to buy credits, then play the game until those credits run out or you decide to take the money and run.

Unlike regular poker, with its multiple betting rounds, bluffs, and competing players, video poker is all about you making the best possible five-card hand as the computer deals. Video poker comes in many different flavors like "Jacks or Better," "Double Bonus," and "Deuces Wild." Each game has a slightly different gimmick but follows the same basic sequence. After your bet (usually from one to five credits), you get dealt five cards, face up. You then have to choose which of the five cards to keep by either touching the card on the screen or by activating the appropriate button underneath each card. The cards you didn't keep are replaced with new cards. If it contains a winning combination, you get paid. It's that simple.

Or is it? Imagine you've bet one coin on a Jacks-or-Better game and you're dealt four hearts and one spade. Holding your four hearts and discarding your spade gives you a decent chance at making a flush (five cards of the same suit), which pays six coins. But before you throw it away, you realize the spade you hold is an ace, which matches your ace of hearts to make a pair. A pair only pays one coin but it's a guaranteed payout versus the possible payout of the flush. That dilemma—and others like it—is at the heart of video poker, and is what makes it so much fun for so many.

UNSPOKEN RULE

Veteran players can be territorial about their machines and often play several at one time. If you're unsure whether a machine is "occupied," politely ask before you sit down. Casino personnel can direct you to open machines.

STRATEGY

The first priority for any video-poker player is finding the best machines. That's because even though two machines may be identical in the game or games they offer, slight variations in the payoff table make one far more advantageous to play than the other.

PAYOUTS

Video-poker enthusiasts identify games by certain key amounts in their payout tables (displayed on the machine). For example, with Jacks-or-Better (JOB) games, the important values to look for are those for the payout on a full house and flush. Put simply, what you want are what's known affectionately as full-pay machines, and for JOB that means a 9/6 payout. If your game pays nine coins on a full house and six coins on a flush, you've found a 9/6 machine (that is "nine six" machine, not "nine-sixths" machine) and it's the most advantageous you'll find. So if the JOB game you just bellied up to pays less than 9/6 on a full house and flush, you should take your coins elsewhere.

Full pay for Double Bonus games are 10 coins to 1 on a full house and 6 coins on a flush. So if that's your game, look for 10/6 machines (if you're very lucky you might find a rare 10/7 machine). Full pay for a Deuces Wild game is 9/5, but these numbers actually refer to the single coin payout for a straight flush and a four-of-a-kind. If that seems low for such stellar poker hands, remember that the presence of wild cards makes the likelihood of an outstanding hand quite a bit higher. In fact, some experts go so far as to list the five-of-a-kind payout and define full-pay Deuces Wild as 15/9/5. Such machines are rare these days on the Strip, and when they're found, it's often for low-bet denominations. Why? Read on.

VIDEO POKER RULES

You'll find many video-poker variations in Vegas casinos; and a single machine can sometimes host several different game types, allowing the player to pick his or her poison from a menu. Here's a quick primer on the most popular:

Jacks-or-Better: The most common video-poker game, and the basis for many variations. The player must have at least a pair of jacks to be in the money.

Deuces Wild: Players must have three-of-a-kind to be in the money, but 2s are wild; that is, they become whatever card you need them to be to make your poker hand. Got two jacks, two queens, and a 2? The 2 can act as a jack or queen, so you've got a full house!

Double Bonus: Requires a pair of jacks or better to be in the money, but offers varied payouts on four-of-a-kind hands, with a bonus for getting four aces.

4

Certain video-poker games are considered positive advantage games, meaning the potential exists for players to actually win money over the long term (unlike just about every other game in the casino). ■ TIP→ To make the house edge negative though, the player must bet the maximum coins and make the statistically optimum choice during every single hand. In a 25¢ game, you can choose to play any multiple of 25¢ up to five times that amount (five quarters or $1.25) per hand. If you examine the payout schedule for most video-poker games, you'll see that the payout on the highest-value hands is inflated for maximum bet games. This is the casino urging you to bet more per hand.

For example, if you get a royal flush with four quarters in a common Jacks-or-Better game, the payout is 1,000 quarters. Bump your bet up to five quarters per hand and your royal flush is worth 4,000 quarters. The occasional windfall of a royal flush can boost the game's return up over 100%. The casino is betting on human behavior here—expecting many royal flush winners will have inserted less than the full bet. Nevertheless, the positive payout expectation is what makes video poker such an attractive game. However, the time and bankroll necessary to invest before hitting the full-pay royal flush can be prohibitive, so don't count on paying for your kid's college with video-poker proceeds.

WHERE TO PLAY

For the most full-pay machines: The Gold Coast (⊠ *4000 W. Flamingo Rd., West Side* ☎ *702/367–7111 or 800/331–5334* ⊕ *www.goldcoastcasino. com*) has a handful of full-pay machines, as do the **Red Rock Casino Resort Spa** and **The M Resort.**

For low-limit video poker: Fremont (⊠ *200 Fremont St., Downtown* ☎ *800/634–6460* ⊕ *www.fremontcasino.com*) has a great array of 25¢ machines.

ROULETTE

Roulette's an easy way to cut your teeth on the whole table-game experience. You select and bet on numbers, groups of numbers, or a color (red or black); watch the dealer drop a ball on a spinning wheel; and hope that the ball lands on your space. It doesn't get more straightforward than this.

BASIC RULES

The wheel's divided into red and black slots numbered 1 through 36 along with two green slots labeled 0 and 00 (zero and double-zero). The dealer (or croupier) drops a little white ball onto the spinning wheel, and as it loses momentum, it falls onto a series of randomizing obstacles until it settles into one of the numbered slots. You place your bet on a layout filled with numbers; the main betting area has 12 rows of three squares each, alternating red and black and covering numbers 1 through 36. There are also two green spaces for betting on 0 or 00. You can put chips on single numbers, or the lines that connect two, four, five (if 0/00 is involved), or six numbers together. You can also bet on entire categories of numbers, such as red/black, odd/even, and 1 through 18/19 through 36, or one of six different ways to bet on one-third of the numbers at one time.

INSIDE AND OUT

When you buy into roulette you're issued specialty chips so that each player at the table has his or her own color. When you want to stop, trade your roulette chips for regular casino chips. ■ TIP→ **Roulette chips are only good at the roulette table you bought them from. If you try to play at another table, or visit the cashier cage with them, you will be told to return them to the table you got them from.** As in any other game, you have to meet the table minimums when you're betting, but it gets a little confusing with roulette because the rules are different depending on what you want to bet on. Outside bets and inside bets are separate, and if you choose to bet on either or both, the table minimum

Roulette Table

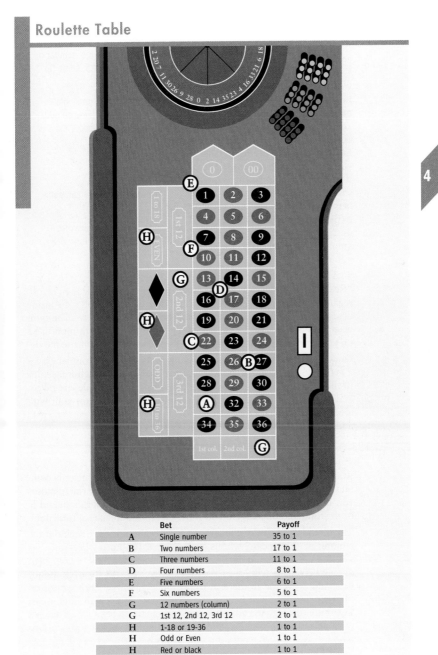

	Bet	Payoff
A	Single number	35 to 1
B	Two numbers	17 to 1
C	Three numbers	11 to 1
D	Four numbers	8 to 1
E	Five numbers	6 to 1
F	Six numbers	5 to 1
G	12 numbers (column)	2 to 1
G	1st 12, 2nd 12, 3rd 12	2 to 1
H	1-18 or 19-36	1 to 1
H	Odd or Even	1 to 1
H	Red or black	1 to 1

rules apply independently. An "outside" bet is made anywhere but on the actual area of the layout that contains the numbers 0, 00, and 1–36. Even, Odd, Black, and Red would be outside bets. An "inside" bet is any bet placed within the numbered area. Betting the 1, 22, and 36 would be considered inside bets. A $5 minimum roulette table means you must bet $5 per bet if you bet on the outside, and $5 total if you bet inside. You may bet in smaller denominations on inside bets, but all inside bets must add up to the minimum (even if you placed outside bets that make your total amount wagered over the table minimum).

AT A GLANCE

Goal: Place bet on the number or group of numbers that come up on the wheel.

Pays: From 35 to 1 on single numbers to even money on odd/even and red/black bets.

House Advantage: 5.26% for almost every bet on double-zero tables.

Best Bet: Playing at a European or single-zero table.

Worst Bet: The Five-way bet (0, 00, 1, 2, 3), which is close to an 8% house advantage.

So $5 on a single outside bet (like "Red") is legal, while five different $1 bets on the outside aren't. And regardless of whether you've placed an outside bet or not, a $1 inside bet is legal only if there are other inside bets that bring the total amount wagered inside to $5. So you could place $2 on your birth month, $2 on your birthday, then $1 on No. 21 in honor of your favorite movie.

Once betting is closed and the ball lands in its spot, the croupier places a marker on the winning number, on top of the stack of winning chips (if there are any). All the losing chip areas, inside and outside, are raked, and the croupier pays out each winning bet. Never reach for your winnings or start to make new bets until *all* the winning bets have been paid and the dealer has removed the marker from the table.

STRATEGY

Roulette is as simple a game as you'll find in the casino. The only complexity is in learning exactly where to place bets to cover the numbers you like. The odds, though, aren't good. The casino keeps over 5% of the total amount wagered on American (or double-zero) roulette.

The best plan, if you're going to get serious about it, is to seek out the handful of "European" wheels in Las Vegas. The Euro wheel only has a 0, and no 00. Also, if the 0 is hit, you will only lose half of your even money bets. This will lower the house edge to 1.3% for even money bets, and 2.7% for all the rest. Unfortunately the few Euro wheels on the Strip usually reside behind the velvet ropes of the high-limit areas, so be sure to weigh the advantages of playing this type of wheel against what you can afford to bet, and lose. Another option is the single-zero wheel. Like the Euro wheel, this wheel only has a 0, and no 00, but you lose 100% of your money on even money bets (unlike the Euro wheel). This wheel has a much better house edge (2.7%) than the double-zero wheel, and you can find these wheels in a few casinos on the main floor, with lower minimums.

RAPID ROULETTE

Rapid Roulette is an automated version of roulette. Instead of standing around a table, you sit at your own video terminal. Players give live dealers cash for credits, and make bets via the video screen. The ball is then spun on a live wheel, and the winning number is input into the machine. You're paid by credits for your winnings at your own terminal. When you cash out, the live dealer will give you chips for your winnings. You can find Rapid Roulette at many Strip casinos including Luxor, Caesars, and MGM Grand.

WHERE TO PLAY

For low-limit games: Try Sam's Town (✉ *5111 Boulder Hwy., Boulder Strip* ☎ *800/897–8696* ⊕ *www.samstownlv.com*).

For single-zero games: Most of the tables in town have disappeared, but the Venetian still offers single-zero games, both on the main casino floor and through its handheld electronic gaming device.

To go all night: Golden Nugget's croupiers will hold your spot while you run to the 24-hour Starbucks in the South Tower for a jolt of gambling gasoline.

4

CRAPS

Even if you've never played this game, you may have heard the roar of a delighted crowd of players from across the casino floor. Craps is a fun and fast-paced game in which fortunes can be made or lost very quickly, depending on how smart you play.

It can look intimidating or complicated to the beginner, because there are so many bets that can be placed on every roll, but this shouldn't deter you from stepping up to the table to play. Craps offers a couple of the best odds bets in the casino.

BASIC RULES

At its core, craps is a dice game. A dice thrower—a "shooter"—tosses two dice to the opposite end of a table and people bet on what they think the outcome or future outcome of the dice will be. It's the job of the "stickman" (the dealer with the stick) to keep the game moving, and to call out the dice totals so everyone knows them no matter what their vantage point at the table is. Two other dealers place bets for you, pay the winners, and collect from the losers. A "box man" sits or stands in the middle and supervises the action. The main layout is duplicated on the right and left sides of the table, although the middle section (the betting area in front of the stickman) is common to both wings of the craps table.

To play, step up to the table wherever you can find an open space. You can start betting casino chips immediately, but you have to wait your turn to be the shooter. If you don't want to "roll the bones" (throw the dice) when it's your turn, motion your refusal to the stickman and he or she will skip you. To roll the dice, you must place a bet first. Then choose only two of the five dice offered by the stickman.

DO'S AND DON'TS OF SHOOTING

Do: Use one hand to pick up the two dice you have chosen. Use the same hand to throw them.

Don't: Move the dice from one hand to the other before you shoot. It arouses suspicion of cheating.

Do: Throw both dice at the same time, and be sure to hit the far wall. A roll that doesn't hit the far wall will not count, and the box man will make you retry.

Don't: Slide the dice during your toss.

Do: Follow table etiquette when someone else is shooting.

Don't: Put your hands down into the table when someone else is shooting. If the dice hit your hand, it's considered bad luck. If a 7 "loser" is rolled after touching your hand, you may be blamed.

PASS LINE BETS

The game starts with the "come-out" roll. This is the first roll after someone rolls a 7, or if you happen to be the first one that comes to the table. The most common bet on the come-out roll is the Pass/Don't Pass Line, which can only be placed on the come-out roll, and which serves to illustrate the basic pattern the game follows.

RIGHT-WAY

Pass Line bettors bet *with* the shooter, or *right way*. If the come-out roll turns up a 7 or 11, it's an automatic win and they'll be paid even money on their Pass Line bet. If a total of 2, 3, or 12 (aka "craps") comes up on the come-out roll, they lose. The exact opposite applies for the Don't Pass bettor, who bets *against* shooter, or *wrong way*. For learning purposes, we'll focus more on right-way bets, which is the majority of bettors. Wrong-way bets are covered below.

If a shooter rolls a total of 4, 5, 6, 8, 9, or 10 on the come-out roll, it's known as hitting a "point." The point (5 for example) will be marked with a puck so everyone knows what it is. Once a point has been established, the players have the option to back up their Pass Line bets with "odds." The odds bet is probably the hardest bet for the beginner to understand. This is unfortunate because it's one of the best bets in the casino for the player and it's not marked on the layout for this reason. The odds bet is placed directly behind the Pass Line bet, and the maximum amount of odds you can take will be listed on the table and it varies by casino. "5x odds" means you can bet up to 5 times your Pass Line bet. *The odds bet is so great because it's the only bet that has a 0% house edge.* Because of this, you should always play maximum odds, if you can afford to. Many other bets can be made at this point as well, but we'll cover them separately. Once all odds bets and any other bets are placed, the shooter keeps rolling the dice until he or she rolls the point again, or a 7. Any other rolls in the meantime won't affect the

Line bets from winning or losing. If a point is hit before a roll of 7, it's called a *winner* and anyone who bet Pass will get paid even money on their Line bet, and the "true odds" on their odds bet. These are 2 to 1 for a roll of 4 or 10, 3 to 2 for a roll of 5 or 9, and 6 to 5 for a roll of 6 or 8. If the shooter rolls a 7 before he or she rolls the point, it's called a *loser,* and all Pass Line bets and the odds are lost. Once that happens, the dice are passed to the next player to "come out" and the sequence starts all over again.

OTHER BETS

In addition to Pass and Don't Pass bets, you can also make the following important wagers at craps:

COME BETS

Come bets can also be confusing for beginners, but if you understand how the Pass Line works, it's just as easy. The Come bet pays exactly the same as a Line bet and has the same great odds, so you should take the time to learn how to bet it. The main difference between a Line bet and a Come bet is that the Come bet is placed *after* the come-out roll, once a point has been established. Try to think of a Come bet as being just like its own little private Pass Line bet for you only, that you can place at any time during the roll (which you can't do with a Pass Line bet). Put your Come bet in the area marked "Come." The next roll is now the come-out roll for your Come bet only, which will win on 7 or 11, or lose on 2, 3, or 12. If the next roll is any other number, the dealer will put your Come bet on that number, and that number will now be the point for your Come bet only, not the Pass Line point (which has already been established). Now that the point has been established for your Come bet, you can take odds on it, just like the Line bet. This is done by placing your chips in the "Come" area and stating to the dealer that you want odds on your Come bet. The dealer will stack your Come odds on top of your Come point bet and a little offset, so he or she knows the amount of your original Come bet as opposed to your odds bet. Now that your Come bet has a point it's subject to the same rules as the Pass Line. If your Come point is rolled before a 7, you win and the dealer will pay you in the "Come" area. If a 7 is rolled before your Come point, you lose.

PLACE BETS

If you want to bet on a number without subjecting to the rules of the Pass Line or Come, you can "place" it. The casino pays reduced odds for this bet, as opposed to true odds on the Line or Come. A Place bet can be wagered at any time on any number in the squared boxes. If that number is rolled before the 7, you win. Otherwise you lose. If you place the 4 or 10, it'll pay 9 to 5; the numbers 5 or 9 pay 7 to 5, and the numbers 6 or 8 pay 7 to 6. If you win the Place bet the dealer will pay you your winnings only and leave your original bet on the number. Unlike a Come or Line bet, you can take down this bet at any time if you want. To make it easier for the dealers to figure the payouts, you must bet in multiples of $5 for the numbers 4, 5, 9, and 10, and multiples of $6 for the 6 or 8. The house edge is a very reasonable 1.52% for a Place bet on the 6 or 8 and a good option, but this isn't true for the other numbers. If you must place the 4 and 10, then "buy" them

Craps Table

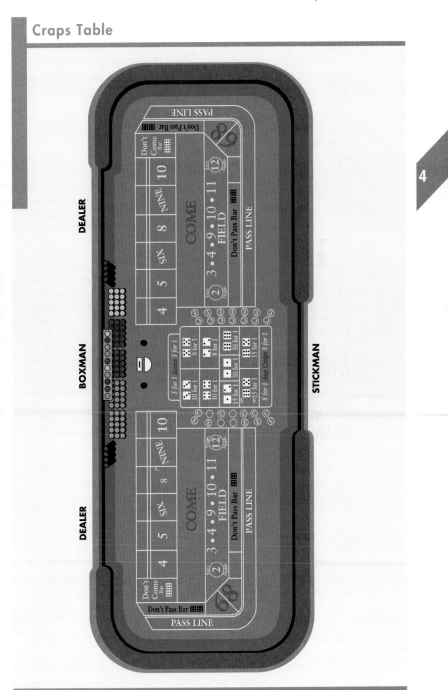

and you'll reduce the house edge on those bets. A "Buy" bet is a Place bet in which you pay a 5% commission to the house to get true odds on your money (in the case of 4 or 10, that's 2 to 1). Make this bet at least $20 or it won't be worth it. Never buy the 5, 9, 6, or 8.

■TIP→ Betting the Big 6 and 8 is exactly the same as placing the 6 and 8 with one important difference. Big 6 and 8 only pays you 1 to 1, as opposed to the 7 to 6 you'll get when you place them. This is the reason this bet is printed so huge and is closer to you on the table layout. The casino wants you to bet here, instead of making the better Place bet. Just say NO to the Big 6 and 8.

ONE-ROLL BETS OR PROPOSITION BETS

One-roll bets are exactly that, bets that win or lose on one roll of the dice (for example, Field, Eleven, or Double Sixes). Basically you bet what you think the next roll will be. If you happen to guess right you will be paid the odds listed on the table for that bet. These bets are located in front of you or the stickman, and you toss your wager in to him and tell him what you want. He or she will place your one-roll bet for you (except the Field, which you place yourself). One-roll and hard-way bets are also considered "proposition bets," so named because well-trained dealers will try to entice you to make these bets after every roll. The only proposition bet that's not a one-roll bet is a hard-way bet. A "hard" number is basically an exact pair on the dice (for example 2-2, 4-4). This bet will remain on the layout until a "soft" version of your number comes up (say 5-3 instead of 4-4), or a 7 is rolled. In this case you'll lose your hard-way bet. Hard-way bets can't lose on the come-out roll. Proposition bets carry an abysmal house edge (as much as 16.67% for some bets). Avoid these at all costs.

DON'T PASS BETTORS
WRONG WAY

Don't bettors, or wrong-way bettors as they're called, are betting against the shooter. They win when the shooter rolls a 7 (once the point is established), when everyone else at the table will lose. The wrong-way bets are the Don't Pass and Don't Come, and they work exactly opposite to the Pass and Come. You can "lay" odds on the Don't bets also, but since you have the advantage once the point has been established (because 7 is the most common roll), the casino will compensate for this by making you bet $6 to get $5 on the point of 6 or 8, $7 to get $5, on the 5 or 9, and $2 to get $1 on the 4 or 10. Many people avoid wrong-way betting because they don't like the idea of betting more to get paid less, or they don't like to "go against" everyone else at the table. This is understandable, but wrong-way betting carries slightly better odds than right-way betting, and should be considered once you feel comfortable playing the game.

STRATEGY

Getting an education first is a good strategy for all the games, but it's essential for craps. Before you step up to a craps table, learn and understand the rules and mathematics of the game, as well as table etiquette, betting procedures and placement, and which bets to stay away from.

CRAPS SAMPLE BETTING SEQUENCE

Here's a sample sequence of bets, starting with a new shooter coming out. You begin by placing a $10 chip directly in front of you on the Pass Line:

Roll 1. Come-out: shooter throws a 7, a winner for the Pass Line. The dealer pays you $10. Since no point was established by this roll, the dice are still in the come-out phase.

Roll 2. Come-out: shooter throws a 2—craps. Dealer takes your $10 Pass Line chip, which you must replace to keep playing. There's still no point, so the dice are still "coming-out."

Roll 3. Come-out: shooter throws a 4—a point. Pass Line bets now win only if another 4 is thrown before a 7. You take $10 odds behind your Pass Line bet, and decide to place a $10 chip in the "Come" betting area.

Roll 4. Shooter throws a 12—craps. Your Pass Line bet is unaffected, but your Come bet loses because it's still in the come-out phase. You replace it with another $10 Come bet.

Roll 5. Shooter throws a 9. Your Pass Line bet is unaffected. Dealer moves your Come bet chips onto the 9 square. You take $10 odds on your Come bet, and the dealer stacks it on top of your original $10 Come bet that's now in square 9, so you're now rooting for either a 4 (Pass Line bet) or a 9 (Come bet) to appear before any 7.

Roll 6. Shooter throws a 3—craps. Both of your bets are unaffected.

Roll 7. Shooter throws a 9. Your Come bet is a winner. The dealer will pay you $10 for your original bet, and $15 (3 to 2) for your odds bet, and place your winnings, original bet, and odds in the "Come" area for you to pick up. You now have no more Come bet.

Roll 8. Shooter throws a 7. Your remaining bet on the Pass Line loses.

Craps is by far the most complicated game to learn in the casino, and if you throw money blindly into it without understanding how it works, you'll lose fast. Our advice is to use the basics given here as a starting point, then build on that by getting a more advanced book, taking a lesson at a casino, or learning and playing online for free. Playing craps offers too much fun and excitement to be ignored, so take the next step and do your homework. You won't regret it.

For those who don't mind playing "without a net" (you know who you are), or don't have the time or patience to sit for a class, you can enjoy the game using the basics above. Keep in mind that only a few bets carry a low house edge. They are:

- Pass/Don't Pass Line with maximum table odds.
- Come/Don't Come bet with maximum table odds.
- Place bet on the 6 or 8.

Stick to these bets. It's best to bet the minimum on the Pass/Don't Pass line then make the odds bet for the maximum the table allows, or as much as you can afford to comfortably. If you feel you must bet proposition bets for some extra action, limit the amount you bet to single dollars. Even if you get lucky and hit some of these on occasion,

Las Vegas casinos never use dice with round corners. Check them out the next time you roll the bones in Sin City.

rest assured that over time these bad bets will eat a big chunk of your potential winnings.

WHERE TO PLAY

For the highest odds: Main Street Station Downtown offers up to 20-times odds and several $5 craps tables. On the Strip, **Casino Royale** (✉ *3411 Las Vegas Blvd. S, Center Strip* ☎ *702/737–3500* ⊕ *www. casinoroyalehotel.com*) has low minimums and generous 100-times odds on certain craps bets.

For the friendliest dealers: The crews at Treasure Island or Mirage will help you learn and keep your bets on track.

BACCARAT

4

Baccarat (pronounced bah-kah-rah) is a centuries-old card game played with an aristocratic feel at a patient rhythm. Baccarat is wildly popular around the world in all its varied forms and is gaining popularity in the United States. In fact in some Vegas casinos it's replaced blackjack as the most profitable table game for the house.

Although it's an easy game to play, baccarat has an air of mystery about it—perceived by many as a game played only by James Bond and powerful tycoons, behind closed doors with special access. Not so. The big version of the game may be the game of choice for many wealthy gamblers who like to play in roped-off areas or private rooms, and have very high betting limits, but the mini version of the game is becoming increasingly popular in Vegas, because it's extremely easy to play. Like the big game, it has reasonable betting limits and carries a very good house edge for the casual gambler.

PLAYING THE "BIG BAC"

Up to 14 players can squeeze into a baccarat table, but the game is played out with just two hands. Before play starts, you place your bet on one of three possible outcomes: the Player hand will win, the Bank hand will win, or that play will result in a Tie. The Tie bet can be placed along with a Bank or Player bet, or by itself. When it's your turn, you can either accept the responsibility of representing the Bank, or you can pass the shoe on to the next player in line.

The dealers, with an assist from the Bank player holding the shoe, start the game by dealing two two-card hands face down. The Player hand is dealt first and is traditionally placed in front of the gambler with the largest Player bet, who then turns them over and slides them back to the dealer. The player holding the shoe does the same with the Bank hand. These rituals are really only for ceremony, and to keep the game

Baccarat Table

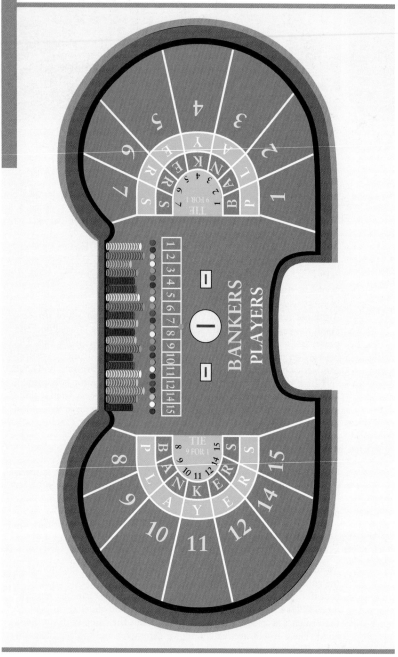

lively. Everyone at the table is tied to these two hands, regardless of how they're dealt and who gets to turn them over.

Depending on the value of the initial two-card hands, an extra card may be added to each hand according to a complicated set of drawing rules. Ask your dealer where you can get a copy of the rules when you sit down so you can follow the action. The winner of the hand is determined by which side has the higher total after all cards have been drawn. If you win on the Bank side, you must pay the house a 5% commission. The dealers keep track of this in the numbered boxes in front of them, which correspond to the numbered seats the players are sitting in. You can pay down this commission at any time during the shoe, but must pay any remaining balance after the last hand of the shoe has been played.

> ### AT A GLANCE
>
> **Format:** Multidealer card game usually played in roped-off areas.
>
> **Goal:** Player bets that one of two hands of cards will be closest to 9.
>
> **Pays:** Even money on Player and Bank bets. 8 to 1 on Tie bet. Bank bettors pay 5% fee.
>
> **House Advantage:** 1.06% on Bank bets, 1.24% for Player bets, 14+% for Tie bets.
>
> **Best Bet:** Bank bet.
>
> **Worst Bet:** Tie bet.

4

UNDERSTANDING THE HANDS

■ Face cards and 10s equal zero.

■ For any total more than 9, the first digit is ignored.

So if the cards are 7, 7, and Jack, the total would be 14: 7 + 7 + 0 = 14. The first digit [1] in 14 is ignored, so the final total is 4.

If you draw a total of 9 (a 10 + 9 for example) on the first two cards, it's called a "natural" and is an automatic winner, unless the other side draws a natural 9 for a tie. A total of 8 is also called a natural, and can only be beaten by a natural 9 or tied with another natural 8. If a tie does occur, the Bank and Player bets push and the Tie wagers are paid at 8 to 1.

STRATEGY

There's no play strategy in the North American version of baccarat; the game is carried out according to immutable rules. In essence it's like choosing heads or tails, and flipping a coin to see who wins. Baccarat players enjoy looking for patterns in previously dealt hands that might give them a clue what will win next, by keeping track of them on little scorecards. But in the end your guess is as good as theirs as to who'll win the next hand. ■ **TIP➜** The Bank bet, at a 1.06% house advantage, has good odds for such a simple game. Always avoid the Tie bet, because it has an excessive house advantage.

MINI-BACCARAT AND EZ-BACCARAT

The popularity of the big version of the game has waned over the years, and many casinos are removing the large tables altogether in favor of the smaller, more accessible version known as mini-baccarat. If you want to try baccarat, but can't handle the high minimum bets, the glacial pace, and the odd superstitious rituals of the big game, look for a mini-bac table. They're usu-

MISSING NUMBERS

You may notice that some of the baccarat layouts are missing numbers (usually 4, 13, and 14). This is because they're considered unlucky numbers in certain cultures.

ally in the main pit of any casino with the rest of the table games, or sometimes in a separate or Asian-theme room. Mini-bac follows the same rules as its blue-blooded cousin, but it's played at a much smaller blackjack-style table. The minimums are lower and a single dealer dispenses the hands, without the players ever touching the cards. The players merely place their bets for each new hand dealt. Midi-bac, or Macau-style mini-bac, is a hybrid of the big and mini-bac games. It's played at a slightly larger mini-bac table. In Midi, one dealer handles the shoe, but the players get to handle and reveal the cards as in the big game. These games sometimes employ an extra bet called "Dragon Bonus" or "Emperor Bonus." As with most side bets on table games, this one has a high house edge and should be ignored.

EZ-Baccarat is another version of mini-bac that plays the same, except there's no commission charged for winning Bank bets. In this game the casino makes its money on the "Dragon" bet. If the bank wins the hand with a three-card 7 total, it's called a "Dragon." When this occurs, the Player hand and Tie lose, and all Bank bets are pushes. If you bet on the "Dragon," you'll be paid 40 to 1 if it hits. Another side bet on this game is called the "Panda." If you bet the Panda, you'll be paid 25 to 1 if a three-card 8 on the Player side wins.

WHERE TO PLAY

Baccarat on a budget: Harrah's, the M Resort, and the Golden Nugget have tables with reasonable minimums.

With the whales: Try the new Aria at CityCenter; it's baccarat nirvana.

To be alone: Try wireless handheld electronic baccarat at the Venetian. Find a comfortable chair and play for stakes so low it makes the high rollers giggle.

SPORTS BETTING

4

Nevada is the only place in America where you can physically, legally bet on sporting events. The betting takes place in a sports book, a dedicated area of a casino that accepts wagers on upcoming games. Here you can try your luck on all the major team sports in America, plus a few individual sports. You can place a wide variety of wagers—from the outcome of a single game to a combination of events. You can even place "futures" wagers on a game that won't kick off for several months.

Sports books make money by taking a small percentage of the total amount bet on both sides of a game; this is called vigorish, or vig for short. Casinos adjust the odds they offer on a game to attract a similar amount to be bet on both teams. That ensures that they get their cut risk-free, regardless of who actually wins the game.

BASIC RULES

Placing a bet in a sports book is simple. Pick a game where you like the betting odds, either in the form of a "point spread" or a "money line," *both of which will be explained below*. The sports book will have a betting window or counter with a cashier who'll take your wager (you have to pay up front) and issue you a ticket that states the details of your bet. Don't lose that ticket! If your wager is a winner, return to the betting window after the game, turn in your ticket, and you'll get your initial bet plus your winnings.

The most common bet in a sports book are 11-to-10 bets and involve a point spread. That means for every $11 you risk (or lay), you win a profit of $10. Place an $11 sports bet, and you get back $21 if your team beats the spread.

Nevada is the only state where you can legally bet on sporting events. Bets must be placed in sports books, which you'll find in almost every casino on the Strip.

POINT SPREADS

An 11-to-10 bet indicates a nearly even-money bet. But if the two teams aren't evenly matched, the casino needs some way to prevent the public from betting heavily on the superior team. That's what a point spread is for; it provides a scoring "handicap" to make both teams equally attractive to a bettor.

When you read a point spread listing, one team is usually the favorite (denoted with a negative number), and one is the underdog (with a positive number). Consider this point spread listing:

Sooners

Longhorns -6.5

The spread on this game is 6½. They sometimes use half points to eliminate the possibility of ties. The sports books have determined that the public believes the Longhorns are more likely to win the game. To lure bettors to wager on the Sooners, the casino is effectively agreeing to take away 6½ points from the Longhorns' final score (or add 6½ points to the Sooners' score, depending on which way you look at it) when it evaluates bets placed on that game. Sports bettors will say that the spread on this game is "the Longhorns minus 6½" or "the Sooners plus 6½"—the two phrases mean the same thing. If you bet on the Longhorns, they'll have to have won by a margin greater than the point spread for you to win your bet. If you bet on the Sooners, your bet wins if the Longhorns win by less than the spread (e.g., Longhorns win 21–17, a margin of victory less than the point spread) or lose the game outright. If your point spread wager ends in a tie, the sports book will return your original bet, minus the vig, which it always takes.

OVER/UNDER

Here you're betting on whether the combined final score of the game will be either over or under a designated total. The total is determined by the sports book and usually appears in the point spread listing like this:

Giants 42.5

Eagles -7

The negative number is the point spread, and it has no effect on over/under bets. The other number, 42.5, is the total for this game. Bettors are welcome to bet on the point spread, the over/under, or both. Over/under bettors would try to predict whether the combined score of the Giants and Eagles will be higher or lower than the total (in this case, 42.5). If the Giants won 24–20, the combined score would be 44, so the over bets win and the under bets lose. An over/under bettor wouldn't care who won the game, as long as either lots of points were scored (over bettors) or few points were scored (under bettors).

4

■TIP→ **Betting odds vary from sports book to sports book, and they can change over time right up to the moment a sporting event starts. But once you place your bet, the point spread, money line, and/or payout odds are locked in place for that wager. Your bet is evaluated and paid according to the odds on your betting ticket.**

THE MONEY LINE

Money Line bets have no scoring handicap attached to them (such as a point spread). The bet wins if the team wins on the field. Sports books use money lines to entice you to bet on the underdog by increasing the payout in the event that team wins. And they discourage bettors from taking the better team by reducing the payout if they win. Let's take a look at an example:

Astros +150

Cubs -170

The two numbers represent money lines. The underdog has a positive number and the favorite has a negative number. For underdogs, the amount shown is the amount (in dollars) you'd win on a $100 bet. In this case, if the underdog Astros won and you bet $100, you'd win $150. On the other hand, the Cubs money line represents the amount you have to risk to win $100. Because the Cubs are seen to be more likely to win, the sports book asks a bettor to pay a premium to bet on them—to win $100, you'd have to bet $170.

NUMBER OF TEAMS	PARLAY BETTING ODDS	PAYOUT ODDS
2	13–5	3–1
3	6–1	7–1
4	10–1	15–1
5	20–1	31–1
6	40–1	63–1
7	75–1	127–1
8	140–1	225–1
9	200–1	511–1
10	400–1	1,023–1

Note: you don't have to bet $100 at a time. The money line just represents the proportions of amount risked to amount won (and vice versa). Most casinos require a $5 or $10 minimum bet.

PARLAYS

A parlay bet is a combination bet where two or more bets must win in order for your wager to pay off. A single parlay bet might include several different sports, as well as point spread, money line, and over/under bets. You can even parlay two games being played simultaneously. Standard parlay odds vary by casino, *but the table is a good example of what to expect:*

If you get all wins plus a tie on your parlay, the bet will still pay, just at the next lowest level of odds. For example, if you bet a four-team parlay and three of the bets beat the spread but the final game tied against the spread, you'd be paid 6 to 1 as if it were a three-teamer. If you get a win and a tie on a two-team parlay it pays as if it were a straight 11-to-10 bet.

⚠ Parlay cards are a quick way to bet on multiple games, but they sometimes have reduced payouts relative to normal parlay bets; sports books do not take vigs on parlay bets.

IN-RUNNING BETTING

In-Running Betting is a relatively new and exciting way of making sports bets, and it's changing the face of sports betting in Las Vegas as we know it. The term *In-Running Betting* describes a bet that you make on a game that's happening in real time. For example, you can make a bet on whether or not a player will make the next free throw in a basketball game that you're currently watching or which hockey team will score the next goal. Before this technology you had to make all of your final bets on a game before it started, and couldn't change or revise them once the game started. The In-Running Bet is made on a wireless, phone-size device known as an E-Deck or PocketCasino, that uses similar technology to those that update stock market prices. They're able to calculate and recalculate odds in real time. This enables the casino to change the odds tables, or lines, extremely quickly based on what's happening in the game being played at that time. How's this applied? Check out this scenario: You bet the "under" on a football game with an over/under of 40. At halftime the score is 27–10, which is already very close to the "over" of your original bet, and almost a certain loser. The computer has adjusted the over/under to 51 at halftime, enabling you to hedge (bet the other side in order to guard against a loss) your original bet, and now bet the "over." The benefit of this is that you have some information about how the game is being played because you're watching it as it's being played and can make better-educated guesses in the near future based on how the teams have already played in the past. The savvy bettor can also use information like momentum shifts, the resting of star players, and key injuries in real time to further enhance his or her chances. Of course, the downside is that you may still lose both bets and could get carried away placing too many bets in order to hedge your past losses as the game proceeds. Although this new type of betting may add some real excitement to watching and betting on sports, we recommend you have some knowledge and experience with sports betting, and know the sports you're betting on, before you try In-Running Betting.

4

TIPS

■ Betting against a team is just as valid—and profitable—as betting for a team.

■ Pick a few teams, become intimately acquainted with them, and be prepared to bet for and against them based on your expertise. Don't try to learn the habits of the entire league.

■ Be realistic. Sporting events include innumerable random events, so even the best sports bettors are thrilled to win 60% of their 11-to-10 bets over the long haul.

■ Avoid exotic bets. Casinos let you bet on almost anything; don't take them up on it. *Stick with the bets listed in this chapter.*

■ Beware of hype. It's often wrong. Do your own homework and draw your own conclusions and take joy in being a contrarian. The sports media have a way of making certain teams look utterly unbeatable. No team ever is. History is littered with examples.

■ Become an NCAA hoops fan. With so many teams in play leading up to March Madness, it's easy for odds-makers to get a point spread wrong, especially when smaller schools are playing each other.

■ Take a pass sometimes. Remember that a losing bet not placed is a win.

WHERE TO PLAY

For the best snacks: Every casino has plenty of eateries, but at Lagasse's Stadium, inside the **Palazzo**, the snacks are all gourmet and they're conceptualized by Emeril Lagasse. Reservations are required (usually with a $200 food-and-beverage minimum) for big events.

To watch the big game with your buddies: Hands-down it's **Caesars Palace**, followed by the **Mirage** and the **Wynn**. If you're in the hinterlands, head to **Red Rock**.

CASINOS

Vegas casino floors can vary dramatically in motif and interior design, but the basic play of the table games and slots, whether they're under decorative awnings, faux garden trellises, or mirrored ceilings, is the same. Odds, table limits, and machine "looseness" *(see Blackjack and Video Poker sections)*, however, can vary greatly from casino to casino, so it pays (literally) to do a little research on the casino in which you wish to play.

Rewards and loyalty programs also vary. Of course, none of that may be as important to you as the overall setting and crowd. Here's the lowdown on some of Sin City's most popular casinos, and a few gamblers' choices, too.

SOUTH STRIP

Luxor Las Vegas. Although the casino at Luxor has lost almost all of its Egyptian flare, the new modern gaming floor delivers a vibe that's genuinely hip and exciting. A swanky drinking establishment, Highbar, looks out over the casino's high-limit area, offering guests the opportunity to bet with the big boys or just watch. Then, of course, there's The Party Pit, where, on Friday and Saturday nights, girls in lingerie dance mere steps away from blackjack and a handful of other games. In the regular-limit area, table minimums are usually around $15 on weekends, but during the week you might find $10 tables. If poker's your game, heads up: the Luxor's room has received awards from local newspapers and offers special retroactive room rates for players who spend more than five hours at the tables. ⊠ *3900 Las Vegas Blvd. S, South Strip* ☎ *702/262–4444, 877/386–4658* ⊕ *www.luxor.com* ⤺ *3,958 rooms, 442 suites.*

Mandalay Bay Resort and Casino. Table limits start around $15; pits of table games are spread out across 135,000 square feet, and with rows and rows of slot machines, the casino floor is sprawling. The high-limit area is one of the fanciest big-stakes parlors on the Strip, but it offers little other than baccarat; in the Lotus Room, gamblers can play Pai Gow and other Asian games while sipping tea. Toward the entrance to Delano Las Vegas, the sports book has high ceilings but a noticeable dearth of seats. The poker room occupies a corner of the sports book with great views of the big screens (and free lessons Monday–Thursday at 2 pm). For those who wish to gamble in bathing suits, check out the Beachside Casino, which offers three stories of open-air gaming that overlooks the Beach. ⊠ *3950 Las Vegas Blvd. S, South Strip* ☏ *702/632–7777, 877/632–7800* ⊕ *www.mandalaybay.com.*

MGM Grand Hotel & Casino. The biggest of the Las Vegas casinos, the MGM has a staggering amount of gaming space, which includes more than 3,500 slot machines and 165 different table games. Table minimums on blackjack, craps, and roulette mostly start at $15; on weekends nearly all jump to $25. The Strip entrance is slot-heavy; one machine, the Lion's Share, notoriously hasn't hit a jackpot in more than 10 years. The main casino bar, Centrifuge, occupies the center of a giant rotunda room, with a remodeled sports book and stand-alone poker room nearby. The Mansion, the casino's high-roller area (with mostly baccarat), exists in separate wing with its own bar, kitchen, and entrance. You don't have to play to hang here; so long as you're respectful (and quiet), this casino-within-a-casino is home to some of the best whale-watching in Vegas. ⊠ *3799 Las Vegas Blvd. S, South Strip* ☏ *702/891–7777, 877/880–0880* ⊕ *www.mgmgrand.com.*

Monte Carlo. Perhaps the best thing about the Monte Carlo's casino is the layout; it's one of the few casinos with a clear pathway from the Strip-facing doors to the pits with table games. The entire gaming floor has been renovated since 2012, though the sports book (dubbed, "Score,") and poker room are almost disproportionately swanky in comparison to the rest of the casino. Also swanky: Hit Bar & Lounge, the new high-limit area, which offers single-zero roulette and blackjack games up to $5,000 per hand. A high-limit slots room offers maximum bets up to $100 per pull. ⊠ *3770 Las Vegas Blvd. S, South Strip* ☏ *702/730–7777, 888/529–4828* ⊕ *www.montecarlo.com.*

New York–New York Hotel & Casino. The casino at New York–New York is just like New York City itself: loud, boisterous, and incessant. The gaming floor has a decor that can be described as art deco meets neon-futuristic. Table limits are a little lower than the high-end Strip casinos, with most minimums starting at $10. Keep an eye out for the Party Pit, where (on Thursday, Friday, and Saturday nights) scantily clad women gyrate on platforms overlooking blackjack and roulette. Generally speaking, table games fan out from the Center Bar, while slot machines line the periphery of the casino. The oval-shaped high-limit table games and slots area feature ornate Murano crystal chandeliers and wood paneling. Sports bettors will be disappointed by New York–New York's race and sports book—the area sits in a corner by The Sporting House, and barely has enough seats for a professional basketball team. ⊠ *3790 Las Vegas Blvd. S, South Strip* ☎ *702/740–6969, 800/689–1797* ⊕ *www.newyorknewyork.com.*

CENTER STRIP

Aria Resort & Casino. CityCenter's lone casino is located at Aria. Oddly, however, while the rest of the hotel is bathed in sunlight, the main gaming floor (especially the middle pits) can at times feel too dark. Brighter gaming experiences can be had in the high-limit salons; there are separate rooms for American games (blackjack and roulette) and Asian games (mostly baccarat). Another popular spot to throw down cash is The Deuce Lounge, a part-nightclub, part high-roller room that also serves appetizers. Poker fans rave about Aria's spacious poker room, which has the private "Ivey Room" (named after Phil Ivey) for professionals. Perhaps the only disappointment is the sports book, which is oddly shaped and has sequestered horse betting in a closet-size satellite. ⊠ *3730 Las Vegas Blvd. S, Center Strip* ☎ *702/590–7757, 866/359–7757* ⊕ *www.aria.com.*

Bellagio Las Vegas. This roomy casino is luxurious and always packed. Under tassled, orange canopies you can sometimes spot high rollers betting stacks of black chips ($100 apiece) per hand. In Club Privé, the high-roller's area, wagers climb even higher. There are games for more typical budgets, too. Low-denomination slots are tucked in the back corners for low rollers and excellent blackjack games are offered for mid- to high-level players (table minimums usually start at $15). If you can find them, the $10-minimum craps tables also can get lively. The casino's epicenter remains its now-famous poker room, which rose to national notoriety as a key element of the TV poker fad. Players such as Daniel Negreanu and Phil Ivey are regulars here, though they frequently hit Bobby's Poker Room, a private room behind a closed door. Elsewhere in the casino, the race and sports book is small but cozy; each leather seat is equipped with its own TV monitor. ⊠ *3600 Las Vegas Blvd. S, Center Strip* ☎ *702/693–7111, 888/987–6667* ⊕ *www.bellagio.com.*

Caesars Palace. Considering how huge Caesars Palace really is, the actual gaming area feels remarkably small. The Palace Casino retains its 1966 intimacy, with low ceilings and high stakes. The Colosseum Casino offers a Pussycat Dolls–themed gaming pit and (creepy) ShuffleMaster automated table games. The Forum Casino boasts high ceilings, soaring marble columns, graceful rooftop arches, and embraces the middle market with 5¢ and 25¢ slots and lower limits (but more stringent rules) on table games. Across the board, video-poker pay schedules are liberal. The best place to gamble in Caesars Palace is in the race and sports book. With six 12-foot-by-15-foot oversize screens, a 20-by-50-foot LED board, and 12 50-inch plasma screens, the Caesars book is like an IMAX theater for sports. The spacious, adjacent poker room is pretty nice, too. ⊠ *3570 Las Vegas Blvd. S, Center Strip* ☎ *702/731–7110, 866/227–5938* ⊕ *www.caesarspalace.com.*

Casino Royale. The great odds are what make this no-frills casino (it's actually a Best Western!) across the street from The Mirage worth a

The Cosmopolitan's glitzy gaming floor

visit. The place is famous for offering 100x odds on craps, and is one of the few casinos in town to offer multiple Push-22 blackjack-derivative games, such as Blackjack Switch and Free Bet. Other options include $5 single-deck blackjack and a host of slot machines ranging in denominations from 1 penny to $5 a pull. With deals like these, Casino Royale isn't exactly known for top-shelf service; table-drink delivery can be painfully slow. Also, dining options are limited; if you're not into the Outback Steakhouse or Denny's, you're better off walking to The Venetian next door. ✉ *3411 Las Vegas Blvd. S, Center Strip* ☎ *800/854–7666* ⊕ *www.casinoroyalehotel.com.*

The Cosmopolitan of Las Vegas. Even with windows that look out to the Strip (rare for casino game floors), the casino at Cosmopolitan feels cozy; a sense of intimacy is created by its long, narrow layout. The vast majority of the table games here are blackjack, and the craps pit often gets lively after dark. Also, most slot banks have their own television monitors. Still, we miss the Blackjack Switch tables casino officials removed in late 2012. Other drawbacks: The light-up roulette tables and the cramped sports book, which is located on the second floor, near where clubbers line up for Marquee. For easier wagering, hit the satellite betting window on the main casino floor inside Book & Stage. ✉ *3708 Las Vegas Blvd. S, Center Strip* ☎ *702/698–7000* ⊕ *www.cosmopolitanlasvegas.com.*

The Mirage Hotel and Casino. The casino at the Mirage can be described as old-school fun. Blackjack and craps tables with $10 minimums are alongside tables with $500 minimums, bringing low rollers and high rollers together on the same gaming floor. A roulette pit overlooks the crowded poker room, which has some of the most active games in all of Vegas. Slots abound in just about every direction on the gaming floor. There's a high-limit lounge that offers blackjack, baccarat, and video poker. True gamblers come to the Mirage for its race and sports book. The book, to your left when you enter from the Caesars Palace side of the Strip, brags about 10,000 square feet of big-screen action and, well, it should—it resembles NASA's mission control. ⊠ *3400 Las Vegas Blvd. S, Center Strip* ☎ *702/791–7111, 800/374–9000* ⊕ *www. mirage.com.*

Paris Las Vegas. Dealers in this casino are trained to wish players *bonne chance,* which loosely translates into "good luck" in English. This catchphrase, coupled with the psychedelic sky-painted ceiling, conveys a dreamlike feeling that might distract you from the fact that some table rules are poor for the player (Hint: stay away from those single-deck blackjack tables; they only pay 6-to-5 for natural blackjacks). Livelier pits include the craps and baccarat sections; roulette is prevalent here, too—perhaps in keeping with the French theme. Slot machines are plentiful, though waitress service away from the tables can be spotty at best. The race and sports book is quaint but smoky. ⊠ *3655 Las Vegas Blvd. S, Center Strip* ☎ *877/796–2096* ⊕ *www.parislasvegas.com.*

Planet Hollywood Resort & Casino. Slots abound in the casino at Planet Hollywood; fittingly it's one of the few casinos on the Strip with Elvis-theme one-arm bandits. Table-game pits are clustered under Swarovski crystal chandeliers in the center of the main casino floor, and some feature scantily clad go-go dancers at night. On weekends the low-limit blackjack and Pai Gow tables stay busy for hours on end. The poker room, which comprises 11 tables on the main casino floor, is clean and spacious, and is outfitted with plenty of TVs to catch the big game when you're not staked in a pot. Nearby, the Playing Field, a modest race and sports book, is swanky and state-of-the-art. ⊠ *3667 Las Vegas Blvd. S, Center Strip* ☎ *702/785–5555, 866/919–7472* ⊕ *www. planethollywoodresort.com.*

NORTH STRIP

Encore. Instead of occupying one giant space, Encore's gaming floor is broken up into tiny salons, separated by columns and exquisite red curtains. Thanks to floor-to-ceiling windows, each of the parlor-style casino areas has a garden or pool view. The gaming is surprisingly diverse, with a variety of low-minimum tables and slots (yes, you can play $10 blackjack here). The main-floor high-limit room features mostly baccarat; upstairs, an even more exclusive area named the Sky Casino features tables with betting limits in the stratosphere. Noticeably absent from Encore's gaming operation are a sports book and poker room; to place these bets, head to Wynn Las Vegas. Guest room keys double as players' cards and track play over the duration of each stay. ⊠ *3131 Las Vegas Blvd. S, North Strip* ☎ *702/770–7000, 888/320–7123* ⊕ *www. wynnlasvegas.com.*

The Palazzo Hotel Resort Casino. While the Venetian's casino can be described as busy and buzzing, The Palazzo's has a more composed vibe.

Higher ceilings and wider walkways create a much slower pace on the casino floor; people are always gambling, but there's just more space to absorb their exuberance. Table games include roulette, Pai Gow poker, and Caribbean Stud; a separate high-limit room houses baccarat tables, assuming the biggest bettors will go here. There's blackjack, too, but a March 2014 policy to offer 3-to-2 blackjack payouts only to bettors wagering a minimum of $100 per hand (everyone else gets 6-to-5) has turned off all but the most amateur gamblers. The sports book, part of Lagasse's Stadium, provides mobile devices that enable bettors to wager from just about anywhere in the casino. Slots here are plentiful but otherwise nondescript. ✉ *3325 Las Vegas Blvd. S, North Strip* ☎ *702/607–7777, 877/283–6423* ⊕ *www.palazzo.com.*

Treasure Island Hotel & Casino. T.I. has a reputation for being one of the best places to learn table games. Dealers are patient and kind, and just about every table game has an hour of free lessons every day. The best tutorials are in craps, where some pit bosses will go so far as to explain odds on certain bets. There's also a decent offering of single-zero roulette. TI's slot machines aren't nearly as enticing; despite machines at just about every denomination, the mix is oddly generic. Poker fans like the modest poker room, though the facility only has a handful of tables. TI gives $2 per hour on food comps, and doles out weekly cash bonuses after only 10 hours of play. The sports book was renovated in June 2014. ✉ *3300 Las Vegas Blvd. S, North Strip* ☎ *702/894–7111, 800/288–7206* ⊕ *www.treasureisland.com.*

The Venetian Resort Casino. The Venetian's casino is a sprawling, bustling nexus of energy at just about every time of day. All told, the gaming floor boasts more than 120 games. Most table limits start at $25, though on weeknights you might find some with minimums of $15. The blackjack tables in particular have very good odds for high-level players—3-to-2 payouts if you're betting a minimum of $100 per hand—but a March 2014 policy change means blackjacks for players betting below that level pay out at the stingy 6-to-5. If you like slots, you're in luck—progressive machines abound. The Venetian has kept up with the poker craze and has a tremendous poker room. With more than 50 tables and daily deep-stack tournaments, it's currently the largest poker spot in town. Poker guests even get free valet parking. ✉ *3355 Las Vegas Blvd. S, North Strip* ☎ *702/414–1000, 866/659–9643* ⊕ *www.venetian.com.*

Wynn Las Vegas. Wynn's casino is a gorgeous, inviting place to play (and a great place to spot celebrities). Table limits can be dauntingly high, most starting at $25, and it's not uncommon to spot $500-minimum blackjack tables on the regular casino floor. Lest you dismiss Wynn Las Vegas as exclusively opulent, rest assured that a healthy number of 1¢ slots are out in a prominent area, rather than relegated to some remote corner. It may also surprise you that the coin games have some of the best pay schedules in town. Wynn also offers a variety of push-22 blackjack-derivative games such as Blackjack Switch. The poker room unfolds near the exotic car dealership, and there's a nice bar area next to the sports book, where plush chairs line individual viewing cubicles. ✉ *3131 Las Vegas Blvd. S, North Strip* ☎ *702/770–7000, 888/320–7123* ⊕ *www.wynnlasvegas.com.*

DOWNTOWN

The D Casino Hotel. Old meets new on the gaming floor at The D. The old: An entire floor of vintage slot-machine games, including Sigma Derby, a quarter-powered contest in which plastic horses race around a plastic track. The new: Points of sale around the casino that accept Bitcoin. The main gaming area is kitschy; female dealers tap out from behind table games and stand on tables to dance suggestively in lingerie. Thankfully, 3-to-2 payouts on blackjack and 10x odds at craps make the distractions worthwhile. ⊠ *301 Fremont St., Downtown* ☎ *702/388–2400* ⊕ *www.thed.com.*

Downtown Grand Hotel & Casino. In the olden days, the casino at The Lady Luck Hotel & Casino was considered one of the most happening spots in town. When the Downtown Grand opened on the same site at the end of 2013, they sought to create a similar buzz. Results are mixed. The preponderance of low-mininum table games and low-denomination slot machines is a home run. Design, however, with exposed brick and HVAC ducts, is curious. Save for the separate room for baccarat, perhaps the best gaming experience on property is upstairs under the tent at the Picnic rooftop pool deck. ⊠ *206 N. 3rd St., Downtown* ☎ *702/719–5100* ⊕ *www.downtowngrand.com.*

El Cortez Hotel & Casino. It's fitting that one of the oldest casinos in Las Vegas (circa 1941, to be exact) still offers blackjack the way it should be played: with natural blackjacks paying 3 to 2. Elsewhere on the gaming floor, you'll find single-zero roulette and stickmen offering up to 10x odds on craps. Slots here are plentiful. The sports book, however, is cramped and in desperate need of the same kind of overhaul the Cortez gave its rooms in 2012. ⊠ *600 E. Fremont St., Downtown* ☎ *702/385–5200, 800/634–6703* ⊕ *www.elcortezhotelcasino.com.*

Four Queens Resort & Casino. This isn't the fanciest casino in town, but locals and tourists alike love it for its approachable style and low table limits. At certain times of day, this means $3 blackjack (with single-deck games that pay 3 to 2 for blackjack), and 5x odds on craps. The casino also is home to a host of video poker options that pay out at 100%. The modest sports book is rarely crowded, making it a better option than some of the others in town. ⊠ *202 Fremont St., Downtown* ☎ *702/385–4011, 800/634–6045* ⊕ *www.fourqueens.com.*

Golden Nugget. This might be one of the oldest casinos in Downtown Vegas, but the place is as lively as ever. The biggest crowds tend to congregate in the older rooms, which are teeming with slot machines and lower-limit table games. This is also where companies such as ShuffleMaster like to pilot new games; a blackjack-derivative contest named Free Bet was a huge draw for most of 2013. The poker room, located in a corner of the main casino floor, holds regular daily tournaments, and offers free lessons daily at 10 am. It also hosts "Poker After Dark," a popular late-night poker show on NBC. Perhaps the only disappointment is the sports book, which is small and cramped. ⊠ *129 E. Fremont St., Downtown* ☎ *702/385–7111, 800/634–3454* ⊕ *www.goldennugget.com/lasvegas.*

Main Street Station Casino Brewery Hotel. Sure, Main Street grabs headlines for its brewery and antiques collection, but the gaming floor isn't too shabby either. The Victorian-theme 28,000 square-foot casino has the usual suspects of live-action tables, a bingo hall, and more than 800 of the latest video and reel machines. There's also an area of penny slots, as well as a daily slot tournament that usually draws a (surprisingly) huge number of entrants—this tournament is what prompted readers of *Strictly Slots* to vote Main Street's slot offerings best in Vegas in 2012. ✉ *200 N. Main St., Downtown* ☎ *702/387–1896, 800/713–8933* ⊕ *www.mainstreetcasino.com.*

PARADISE ROAD

Hard Rock Hotel & Casino. A favorite among the young and wealthy crowd, this hip casino revolves around table games, offering limits that are generally lower than elsewhere in town (which means you can stretch bankrolls longer). The result, however, is that slot machine offerings are pretty slim; if this is your game, it's best to gamble elsewhere. Hard Rock has spent gobs of money in recent years on a cavernous poker room and a new mobile system that enables bettors to wager on sports anywhere on property. If you've got the cash, the swanky high-limit rooms are worth exploring, too. ✉ *4455 Paradise Rd., Paradise Road* ☎ *702/693–5000, 800/473–7625* ⊕ *www.hardrockhotel.com.*

WEST SIDE

Palms Casino Resort. This casino is geared toward locals, with regular and generous promotions for those who sign up for the Club Palms gaming rewards program. Still, especially when visitors descend on the property for partying on weekend nights, the casino floor takes on a Strip-like vibe (and table limits rise accordingly). The best values on this floor are craps (with standard $10 minimums) and poker, where there's almost always a low-limit game of Hold'em being spread. On the east end of the gaming floor, Heraea combines the best of a sports book, a sports bar, and a swanky lounge for an environment that's geared toward a different clientele: women. ✉ *4321 W. Flamingo Rd., West Side* ☎ *866/942–7770* ⊕ *www.palms.com.*

Rio All-Suites Hotel and Casino. The casino floor at the Rio is one of Vegas's most lively places to play. The casino is perhaps best known for hosting the annual World Series of Poker, six weeks worth of poker tournaments that culminate with the "Main Event" in which one pro takes home millions of dollars in cash. Elsewhere, the gaming floor offers table games with some of the worst odds in town (it's one of the few Vegas casinos to spread Mississippi Stud). Perhaps the spontaneous performances by sexy "bevertainers" (cocktail waitresses who double as dancers) will provide a pleasant enough diversion for you to overlook the house edge. There's also more than 1,200 slot machines, including dozens of different statewide progressives. ✉ *3700 W. Flamingo Rd., West Side* ☎ *702/777–7777, 866/746–7671* ⊕ *www.riolasvegas.com.*

SUMMERLIN

Red Rock Casino Resort Spa. Without question, this locals casino in Summerlin is one of the best-kept secrets in the entire Las Vegas Valley. Swarovski Crystals sparkle over gamblers who wander around the circular gambling hall, creating a vibe of opulence and swank. There's even more bling inside the open-walled Lucky Bar, situated in the center of the casino. Despite all of these sparkles, betting minimums are low; it's not uncommon to stumble upon $5 craps and blackjack tables at peak hours. The real "gem" of the casino is the sports book, with its comfy chairs and giant big-screens. A cozy poker room, cavernous bingo hall, and ornate high-limit room (which promises blackjack as low as $25 per hand) also are worth a look. ✉ *11011 W. Charleston Blvd., Summerlin* ☎ *702/797–7777, 866/767–7773* ⊕ *https://redrock.sclv.com.*

WHERE TO EAT

BEST BUFFETS IN VEGAS

Despite Vegas's upscale culinary makeover, there's nothing we like more than the city's famous and fabulous buffets that continue to rake in the masses. Why? Because who doesn't love that uniquely American obsession—unlimited gorging for one set price?

Buffets originated in the late 1940s as an attention-grabbing loss leader that would attract hungry gamblers to the casinos (and keep them there). Now the buffet concept has grown into an important tradition at virtually every resort. Bargain-hunters will still find plenty of economical deals, but the top buffets typically charge upwards of $30, or even $45, per person at dinner. Hey, there are lobster tails, Kobe beef, and unlimited champagne at some of these spreads—you get what you pay for. With that in mind, here's a look at some of the best buffets in town.

TOP PICKS

✕ **Bacchanal Buffet.** Caesars Palace has completely revamped its buffet experience with the Bacchanal Buffet, a culinary extravaganza of more than 500 dishes daily, plus 15 chef's specials, with an emphasis on seasonality. Made-to-order sushi, baked-to-order soufflés, pizza made in a wood-burning oven, and individual portions of dishes that are served in steam tables elsewhere are consumed in three distinct dining areas with glass, wood, and steel decor themes. ⑤ *Average main: $40* ✉ *Caesar's Palace, 3580 Las Vegas Blvd., Center Strip* ☎ *702/731–7928* ⊕ *www. caesarspalace.com/restaurants.html* ⏰ *Breakfast $25.99; lunch $35.99;*

dinner $50.99 Mon.–Thurs., $53.99 Fri.–Sun. Champagne brunch weekends $45.99.

✕ **The Buffet at Bellagio.** Step into the regal dining room, tricked out with opulent chandeliers and elegant artwork, and any hesitation that a buffet could meet Bellagio's standards vanishes. Even the most discerning foodie should find something to like among urbane cuisine like venison chops, apple-smoked sturgeon, and (especially) elaborate pastries. Some say the Buffet is overrated and overcrowded, but don't be put off by the naysayers— if you skip items that you could easily get at any Vegas buffet (such as pizzas from the wood-fired oven), you'll do well here. The staff does a first-rate job tending to everybody's needs. If you want to try to avoid the dinner lines, show up right when dinner starts (3:30 pm daily). You might be eating earlier than normal, but the tradeoff is worth it. ■TIP→ For a special experience, try the Buffet Chef's Table. All the convenience and choice of the splendid Bellagio buffet plus a private audience with the executive chef, who oversees the delivery of a number of exclusive items, including caviar appetizers, table-side lamb and beef carving, and creamy chocolate fondue. Email buffetchef-stable@bellagioresort.com for reservations. ⑤ *Average main: $28* ✉ *Bellagio, 3600 Las Vegas Blvd. S, Center Strip*

☎ 702/693-7111 ⊕ *www.bellagio.com* ✉ *Breakfast $17.99; brunch $27.95; champagne brunch $35.99; lunch $20.99; dinner $31.99–$37.99.*

✕ **The Buffet at Wynn Las Vegas.** Steve Wynn prides himself on doing everything bigger and better than others in town, so the fact that buffet fans rave about his buffet is no surprise. The place boasts 16 live cooking stations, including those specializing in Asian, Indian, and Thai cuisine (to name a few). Across the board, the real star here is meat—veal short ribs, lamb T-bones, and char-grilled quail are just some of the options. Of course there usually are Alaskan King Crab legs, too. And the dessert table never disappoints. ⑤ *Average main: $32* ✉ *Wynn Las Vegas, 3131 Las Vegas Blvd. S, North Strip* ☎ 702/770–3463 ⊕ *www.wynnlasvegas.com* ✉ *Breakfast $19.99; brunch $31.99, champagne brunch $43.99; lunch $24.99; dinner $36.99 (weeknights), $39.99 (weekends).*

✕ **Le Village Buffet.** Let other buffets touch on international foods—Paris Las Vegas owns the world's foremost cuisine, and Francophiles unite jubilantly here to sample Vegas's take on French fare. The cooking stations are themed to the regions of France, such as Burgundy, Normandy, Alsace, and Brittany (head here for the delicious

dessert crepes). There's also an impressive spread of cheese (naturally). Drop by Le Flambé station for bananas Foster to top off your meal. The dining room, fashioned after a quaint French village, is a kick: stone walls and floors lend a charming feel, if not one that's especially conducive to quiet conversation, and the flattering, soft lighting is a rarity among Vegas buffet restaurants. ⑤ *Average main: $25* ⊠ *Paris Las Vegas, 3655 Las Vegas Blvd. S, Center Strip* ☎ *702/946–7000* ⊕ *www. parislasvegas.com* 🍽 *Breakfast $19.99 to $21.99; champagne brunch $30.99; lunch $21.99; dinner $33.99.*

✕ **Wicked Spoon.** Wicked Spoon quickly became a cult favorite for desserts such as gelato and homemade macaroons, and dishes such as Angry Mac N Cheese—traditional mac and cheese with a touch of spice. Unlike other buffets, which serve all of their items in large buffet pans, many of the items here are presented as individual portions, an improvement on a number of levels. The decor and music selection are modern and fun. Brunch costs $26–$34, and dinner $38–$41. ⑤ *Average main: $30* ⊠ *The Cosmopolitan Las Vegas, 3708 Las Vegas Blvd. S, Center Strip* ☎ *702/698–7000* ⊕ *www. cosmopolitanlasvegas.com* 🍽 *Reservations not accepted.*

Updated by
Heidi Rinella

LAS VEGAS IS ONE OF America's hottest restaurant markets. Nearly every big Strip property has at least one and often two or more celebrity-chef restaurants. Away from the Strip, the unprecedented population growth in the city's suburbs has brought with it a separate and continuous wave of new eateries, both familiar chains and increasing numbers of legitimate destination restaurants.

Casino-resort dining basically falls into one of three categories. In the top echelon are the properties that now have a half dozen or more bona fide star-status restaurants: Aria, Bellagio, Caesars, the Cosmopolitan, Mandalay Bay, MGM Grand, Venetian/Palazzo, and Wynn/Encore. At the next level are those resorts with one or two stellar restaurants and a smaller range of worthwhile but not quite top-of-the-line options. On the Strip, these include Mandarin Oriental, Mirage, Monte Carlo, New York–New York, Paris, Planet Hollywood, and Treasure Island. Off the Strip, you can add the Palms, the Hard Rock, M Resort, the Rio All-Suite Hotel, Green Valley Ranch, the JW Marriott, and Red Rock Resort. Then there's everybody else: casino-resorts with maybe a decent eatery or two but that simply aren't known for great food.

Downtown Las Vegas has seen a big revitalization in the past several years, and that extends to restaurants. Although Downtown still lacks a destination restaurant, notable spots are Le Thai and La Comida in Fremont East and Pizza Rock and the older Triple George Grill in the Downtown 3rd District.

Outside the tourism corridor, Las Vegas has a number of marquee restaurants with increasing cachet among foodies from out of town—places such as Todd's Unique Dining, Marché Bacchus, and Lotus of Siam. There's great food to be had off the beaten path in Las Vegas, and you'll pay a lot less in these areas, too.

If you haven't been to Vegas in three or four years, you'll notice some major changes. Names like Wolfgang Puck, Michael Mina, and Emeril Lagasse still have plenty of pull in this town, but the Vegas chefs commanding the most attention are French imports such as Pierre Gagnaire, Joël Robuchon, and Guy Savoy, along with vaunted U.S. chefs like Charlie Palmer and Mario Batali.

There's also a trend toward high-minded restaurants with exclusive-nightclub vibes. Note the success of see-and-be-seen Pan-Asian hot spots KOI Las Vegas and Tao Asian Bistro & Nightclub, the youthful late-night haunts LAVO and FIX, and bordello-chic establishments such as Strip House—to name just a few. Elsewhere in town, Las Vegas's growing international, and especially Asian, population has created a market for some of the best Chinese, Thai, Vietnamese, and Pan-Asian restaurants in the country.

5

LAS VEGAS DINING PLANNER

RESERVATIONS

As the Vegas dining landscape has become rife with showstopping, one-of-a-kind restaurants, reservations at dinner (and occasionally even at lunch) have become a necessity in many cases. Generally, if you have your heart set on dinner at any of the celeb-helmed joints at the bigger Strip casinos, you should book several days, or even a couple of weeks, ahead. On weekends and during other busy times, even at restaurants where reservations aren't absolutely essential, it's still prudent to phone ahead for a table.

WHAT TO WEAR

Although virtually no Vegas restaurants (with the exception of Joël Robuchon at the Mansion inside MGM Grand) require formal attire, men will likely feel a bit out of place at some of the top eateries on the Strip if not wearing a jacket—at the very least, avoid jeans in these spots. Dressing according to the mood of the restaurant (smart, stylish threads at the better ones) will generally help you out in terms of how you're treated and where you're seated. Casual attire is the norm at lunch, at less fancy venues, and virtually anywhere off the Strip or outside upmarket resorts.

HOURS

The majority of the top restaurants on the Strip are dinner only, although there are plenty of exceptions to this rule. Unless otherwise noted, the restaurants *listed in this guide* are open daily for lunch and dinner. Hours vary greatly from place to place, with 5 to 10 pm typical for dinner hours, but many of the more nightlife-driven venues serve until after midnight or even around the clock. Las Vegas is definitely a city where it's best to phone ahead and confirm hours.

TIPPING AND TAXES

In most restaurants, tip the waiter 16%–20%. (To figure the amount quickly, just double the tax noted on the check and add a bit more.) Bills for parties of eight or more sometimes include the tip already. Tip at least $1 per drink at the bar.

CHILDREN

Although it's unusual to see children in the dining rooms of Las Vegas's most elite restaurants, dining with youngsters doesn't have to mean culinary exile. *Some of the restaurants reviewed in this chapter are excellent choices for families, and are marked with "Family."*

PRICES

Las Vegas's status as a bargain-food town has evaporated steadily, even rapidly, as the restaurant scene has evolved and the city has been thrust into the gastronomic spotlight. Now at top restaurants in town it's unusual to experience a three-course meal (including a bottle of wine, tips, and tax) for less than $100 per person, and prices can be two to three times that at many establishments. You can save money by trying lunch at some of the top eateries, and by checking out the increasingly noteworthy crop of restaurants that have developed off the Strip. Credit cards are widely accepted, but some restaurants (particularly smaller ones off the Strip) accept only cash. If you plan to use a credit card, it's a good idea to double-check its acceptability when making reservations or before sitting down to eat.

WHAT IT COSTS			
$	$$	$$$	$$$$
under $12	$12-$20	$21-$30	over $30

Prices are the average cost of a main course at dinner or, if dinner isn't served, at lunch.

SOUTH STRIP

FOUR SEASONS RESORT LAS VEGAS

$$$$ ✕**Charlie Palmer Steak.** The whole concept of putting a Four Seasons
STEAKHOUSE hotel inside Mandalay Bay was to have a quiet enclave "hidden" within a busy hotel-casino complex. Charlie Palmer got the idea right away. Although his Aureole at Mandalay Bay can be something of a scene, this nearby steak house is easygoing and understated. The mahogany-paneled room off the Four Seasons lobby serves only beef that has been wet- or dry-aged for a minimum of 21 days. There's commendable seafood, too; options might include stuffed lobster, pan-roasted salmon, grilled swordfish, or oven-roasted mahimahi. Among the several first-rate desserts, try the house-made crème brûlée, the flavors of which change seasonally. A recent plus: The prix-fixe "cut of the week" menu with wine pairings at a comfortable price. ⑤ *Average main: $53 ⊠ Four Seasons Hotel, 3960 Las Vegas Blvd. S, South Strip* ☏ *702/632–5120* ⊕ *www.charliepalmer.com* ⊗ *Closed Sun. No lunch.*

THE LUXOR

$$$$ ✕**Tender Steak & Seafood.** Tender is the steak house that it seems every
STEAKHOUSE Las Vegas hotel-casino is required to have, but it offers much that's off the beaten path. Start with a cheese or charcuterie platter and consider moving on to the wild-game tasting of nilgai antelope osso buco, axis venison medallion, and wild boar loin with farro and fig chutney. The less adventurous can still indulge, in Lake Superior whitefish, free-range chicken or, of course, steaks. ■TIP➔ **The prix-fixe menu, available from 5 to 7 p.m. Sunday through Thursday, is a good value at three courses for $45.** ⑤ *Average main: $55 ⊠ Luxor, 3900 Las Vegas Blvd. S, South Strip* ☏ *702/262–4852* ⊕ *www.Luxor.com.*

MANDALAY BAY

$$$$ ✕**Aureole.** Celebrity-chef Charlie Palmer re-created his famed New York
AMERICAN restaurant for Mandalay Bay. He and designer Adam Tihany added a few playful, Vegas twists: a four-story wine tower, for example, holds more than 60,000 bottles that are reached by "flying wine angels," who are hoisted up and down via a system of electronically activated pulleys.

BEST BETS FOR LAS VEGAS RESTAURANTS

With hundreds of restaurants to choose from, how will you decide where to eat? Fodor's writers and editors have selected their favorites by price, cuisine, and experience in the following Best Bets list. The Fodor's Choice picks represent the "best of the best" across all categories.

Fodor's Choice ★

Alizé, p. 218
Burger Bar, p. 188
Capriotti's, p. 219
Comme Ca, p. 199
Hugo's Cellar, p. 210
Ichiza, p. 221
Jean Philippe Patisserie, p. 194
Joël Robuchon, p. 190
Lotus of Siam, p. 215
MIX, p. 189
Picasso, p. 195
Restaurant Guy Savoy, p. 198
Sage, p. 194
Sensi, p. 196
Wing Le, p. 209

Best by Price

$

Capriotti's, p. 219

$$

Burger Bar, p. 188
Dona Maria, p. 209
Ichiza, p. 221
La Comida, p. 210
Pizza Rock, p. 211

$$$

BLT Burger, p. 200
Border Grill, p. 188
Hash House A Go Go, p. 220
Lotus of Siam, p. 215
Raku, p. 221
Sushi Roku, p. 198
Tides Oyster Bar, p. 217

$$$$

Aureole, p. 183
B&B Ristorante, p. 205
Comme Ca, p. 199
ENVY Steakhouse, p. 213
Estiatorio Milos, p. 200
Joël Robuchon, p. 190
KOI Las Vegas, p. 202
Marché Bacchus, p. 221
Mastro's Ocean Club, p. 198
MIX, p. 189
Picasso, p. 195
Restaurant Guy Savoy, p. 198
Sage, p. 194
Sensi, p. 196

Spago Las Vegas, p. 198
Twist, p. 199
Wing Lei, p. 209

Best by Cuisine

AMERICAN

American Fish, p. 193
Aureole, p. 183
Mastro's Ocean Club, p. 198

ASIAN

Ichiza, p. 221
KOI Las Vegas, p. 202
Lotus of Siam, p. 215
Ping Pang Pong, p. 218
Raku, p. 221
Sushi Roku, p. 198
Wing Lei, p. 209

FRENCH

Alizé, p. 218
Comme Ca, p. 199
Joël Robuchon, p. 190
Le Cirque, p. 194
Restaurant Guy Savoy, p. 198
Twist, p. 199

ITALIAN

B&B Ristorante, p. 205
NOVE Italiano, p. 219
Sinatra, p. 203

MEXICAN

Border Grill, p. 188
Doña Maria, p. 209
Jaleo, p. 200
La Comida, p. 210
Pink Taco, p. 212

PIZZA

Grimaldi's, p. 217
Il Fornaio, p. 193
B&B Ristorante, p. 205
Pizza Rock, p. 211
Spago Cafe, p. 198

SEAFOOD

American Fish, p. 193
Bartolotta Ristorante di Mare, p. 207
Joe's Seafood, Prime Steak & Stone Crab, p. 196
Mastro's Ocean Club, p. 198

STEAK HOUSE

Carnevino Italian Steakhouse, p. 204
ENVY Steakhouse, p. 213
Jean Georges Steakhouse, p. 193
Prime Steakhouse, p. 195

5

Best by Experience

BREAKFAST

Bouchon, p. 206

Eat, p. 210

Hash House A Go Go, p. 220

Tableau, p. 208

CHILD-FRIENDLY

Grand Lux Cafe, p. 206

Grimaldi's, p. 217

Hofbräuhaus Las Vegas, p. 213

Honey Salt, p. 223

Village Eateries at New York–New York, p. 191

LATE-NIGHT DINING

FIX, p. 194

Ichiza, p. 221

MIX, p. 189

Mr. Lucky's, p. 212

Ping Pang Pong, p. 218

Raku, p. 221

STACK, p. 201

ROMANTIC

Alizé, p. 218

B&B Ristorante, p. 205

Bartolotta Ristorante di Mare, p. 207

Botero, p. 203

Mantra Masala, p. 221

Marché Bacchus, p. 221

MIX, p. 189

NOVE Italiano, p. 219

Shibuya, p. 190

Spiedini Ristorante, p. 222

Tableau, p. 208

Top of the World, p. 205

ARCHITECTURAL DESIGN/DECOR

Botero, p. 203

Joël Robuchon, p. 190

Mastro's Ocean Club, p. 198

MIX, p. 189

Shibuya, p. 190

Simon Restaurant & Lounge, p. 219

SUSHISAMBA, p. 205

Tableau, p. 208

T-bones Chophouse & Lounge, p. 222

Wing Lei, p. 209

COCKTAILS

Honey Salt, p. 223

LBS: A Burger Joint, p. 192

MIX, p. 189

NOVE Italiano, p. 219

SUSHISAMBA, p. 205

T-bones Chophouse & Lounge, p. 222

TASTING MENU

La Cave, p. 208

Julian Serrano, p. 193

Sage, p. 194

Shibuya, p. 190

VIEWS

Alizé, p. 218

Eiffel Tower Restaurant, p. 201

MIX, p. 189

Morels French Steakhouse & Bistro, p. 204

NOVE Italiano, p. 219

Top of the World, p. 205

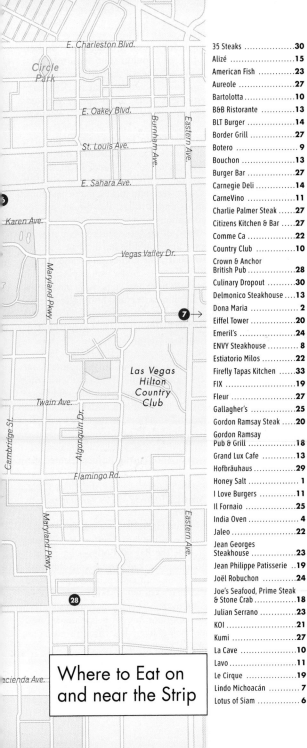

35 Steaks **30**
Alizé **15**
American Fish **23**
Aureole **27**
Bartolotta **10**
B&B Ristorante **13**
BLT Burger **14**
Border Grill **27**
Botero **9**
Bouchon **13**
Burger Bar **27**
Carnegie Deli **14**
CarneVino **11**
Charlie Palmer Steak **27**
Citizens Kitchen & Bar **27**
Comme Ca **22**
Country Club **10**
Crown & Anchor
British Pub **28**
Culinary Dropout **30**
Dona Maria **2**
Eiffel Tower **20**
Emeril's **24**
ENVY Steakhouse **8**
Estiatorio Milos **22**
Firefly Tapas Kitchen **33**
FIX **19**
Fleur **27**
Gallagher's **25**
Gordon Ramsay Steak **20**
Gordon Ramsay
Pub & Grill **18**
Grand Lux Cafe **13**
Hofbräuhaus **29**
Honey Salt **1**
I Love Burgers **11**
Il Fornaio **25**
India Oven **4**
Jaleo **22**
Jean Georges
Steakhouse **23**
Jean Philippe Patisserie ..**19**
Joël Robuchon **24**
Joe's Seafood, Prime Steak
& Stone Crab **18**
Julian Serrano **23**
KOI **21**
Kumi **27**
La Cave **10**
Lavo **11**
Le Cirque **19**
Lindo Michoacán **7**
Lotus of Siam **6**

Marrakech **32**
Mastro's Ocean Club **23**
Mesa Grill **18**
MIX **27**
Mon Ami Gabi **20**
Morels **11**
Mr. Lucky's **30**
N9NE STeakhouse **15**
Nobu **30**
NOVE Italiano **15**
Osteria del Circo **19**
Pamplemousse **5**
Payard Patisserie
& Bistro **18**
Pearl **24**
Picasso **19**
Ping Pang Pong **16**
Pink Taco **30**
Prime Steakhouse **19**
Raku **12**
Rao's **18**
Red Square **27**
Restaurant Guy Savoy **18**
RM Seafood **27**
Roy's **31**
Sage **23**
Scarpetta **22**
Sensi **19**
Shibuya **24**
Simon **15**
Sinatra **9**
Social House **23**
Society Cafe **9**
Spago **18**
STACK **14**
Strip House **21**
Sushi Roku **17**
SUSHISAMBA **11**
Tableau **10**
TAO Asian Bistro **13**
Tender Steak
& Seafood **26**
Todd English P.U.B. **23**
Top of the World **3**
Twist **23**
Wing Lei **10**

Where to Eat on
and near the Strip

The parallel-tasting menu ($85) includes a number of signature choices. À la carte, try the chef's signature French onion soup with foie gras, truffles, Gruyère, and puff pastry; or the chervil-crusted Alaskan halibut; or an 18-ounce dry-aged prime bone-in New York steak. $ *Average main: $55* ⊠ *Mandalay Bay Resort & Casino, 3950 Las Vegas Blvd. S, South Strip* ☎ *702/632–7401* ⊕ *www.charliepalmer.com* ⌕ *Reservations essential* ⊘ *No lunch.*

$$$ ✕ **Border Grill.** Mary Sue Milliken and Susan Feniger are the popular,
SOUTHWESTERN   green-minded chefs who created this cheery, sophisticated outpost of their Santa Monica restaurant. Starters include green-corn tamales, citrusy ceviche, and house-made guacamole, while grilled sustainable fish and hormone-free meats, such as skirt steak and turkey, make healthful, flavorful fillings for lunchtime tacos and tortillas. For dinner, opt for dishes such as sautéed shrimp and scallops with braised greens and rice, beef brisket taquitos with spicy slaw, or anchiote-spiced pork roasted in banana leaves. Service is snappy, and you'd be hard-pressed to find a tastier margarita in town—particularly the pomegranate and honeydew versions. The weekend brunch features creative small plates, such as Peruvian shrimp and grits, short-rib hash and eggs, and cinnamony, bite-size churros served with two dipping sauces (and bottomless mimosas!). At this writing, a Forum Shops branch is planned. $ *Average main: $30* ⊠ *Mandalay Bay Resort & Casino, 3950 Las Vegas Blvd. S, South Strip* ☎ *702/632–7403* ⊕ *www.bordergrill.com.*

$$ ✕ **Burger Bar.** There's a burger joint in every resort, but Hubert Keller's
BURGER   Burger Bar is truly a standout. You build your own burger at this jovial
Fodor's Choice   joint with marble tables and wood-paneled walls. First, start with your
★   meat; selections include merguez-style spiced lamb, buffalo, and Black Angus or Kobe beef (there is also a vegetarian alternative). Next, add cheese and pick a sauce (red wine-and-shallot reduction, for example, or peppercorn cream). Then pile on toppings like prosciutto, pan-seared foie gras, jalapeño bacon, fried egg, and grilled vegetables or shellfish; add fries, and open wide. Desserts continue the burger theme with choices such as the creamy cheesecake or chocolate burger. You can even get a spiked milk shake. $ *Average main: $15* ⊠ *Mandalay Place, 3930 Las Vegas Blvd. S, South Strip* ☎ *702/632–9364* ⊕ *www.burgerbar.com.*

$$$ ✕ **Citizens Kitchen & Bar.** At this 24-hour, circa-2013 pub, Brian Massie,
AMERICAN   a native New Yorker, serves up some of the best comfort food Vegas has to offer. Signature dishes include the Bag of Bones—dry-rubbed baby back ribs, crispy onions, and slow-cooked beans—and the Fatty Melt, a tomato grilled cheese sandwich with caramelized onions and Citizens' special sauce. "Citizens," as it's known, also offers a mélange of side dishes (the Smothered and Covered Tots are out of this world) and a list of signature cocktails including one with banana-infused rye and maple liqueur. The space itself is lively but casual; sometimes it can get loud during peak hours. $ *Average main: $25* ⊠ *Mandalay Bay, 3950 Las Vegas Blvd. S, South Strip* ☎ *702/632–7000* ⊕ *www.mandalaybay.com/dining.*

$$$$ ✕ **Fleur.** Chef Hubert Keller's Fleur has two dining spaces, one fairly
INTERNATIONAL   intimate and one open to Mandalay Bay's restaurant row, so you can

watch the world (or at least Las Vegas) go by. Small plates themed to the United States, China, Thailand, Spain, and France are served along with burgers and steaks. Menu items are seasonal, but signatures include "In the Shower" mac and cheese with lobster and shrimp, kushi oysters on green curry shaved ice, and a French onion tarte flambé. Then there's the Fleur Burger 5000, a Wagyu beef hamburger with foie gras, truffles, and a bottle of 1995 Chateau Petrus, costing—you guessed it—$5,000. Console yourself with pineapple carpaccio, or a brownie lollipop. [$] *Average main: $50 ⊠ Mandalay Bay Resort & Casino, 3950 Las Vegas Blvd. S, South Strip* ☎ *702/632–9400* ⊕ *www.mandalaybay.com.*

$$$$ ✕**Kumi.** Chef (and former professional snowboarder) Akira Back pres-
JAPANESE ents a Japanese menu with a slight Korean twist in a sleek space with
FUSION natural woods and hammered steel. Menu items include dishes such as Jidori chicken with kimchi green beans and hot-oil salmon carpaccio, as well as more conventional tataki, tempuras, and a wide variety of rolls and sushi. There's also Bar by Akira Back, showcasing the alchemy of the Light Group mixologists. [$] *Average main: $45 ⊠ Mandalay Bay, 3590 Las Vegas Blvd. S, South Strip* ☎ *702/632–7777* ⊕ *www. kumilasvegas.com.*

$$$$ ✕**MIX.** Dress to impress, arrive at 5, and tip into the lounge at MIX for
FRENCH a cocktail first; it's the best vantage point from which to see the stun-
Fodor's Choice ning view from Chef Alain Ducasse's 64th-floor perch atop the Delano
★ Las Vegas. ■TIP➔ **Skip the tiny, tightly spaced tables at dinner and reserve a seashell-shape booth instead.** Try a buttery roast cod or the seared scallops with sunchoke emulsion and roasted vermicelli and bacon. Portions are petite and prices are not, but you're also paying for the fine ambiance and great Strip views through the floor-to-ceiling windows. An attentive staff can help you navigate the more than 1,300 nightly wine options, but a glass of bubbly may be the perfect potion to sip underneath the 15,000 or so handblown spheres that cascade from the wondrous 24-foot-tall Murano-glass chandelier. [$] *Average main: $56 ⊠ The Delano Las Vegas, 3950 Las Vegas Blvd. S, South Strip* ☎ *702/632–9500* ⊕ *www.mandalaybay.com* ☾ *No lunch.*

$$$$ ✕**Red Square.** Renovated and refreshed during 2013, Red Square still
RUSSIAN marks its entrance with a headless statue of N. Lenin, while the interior has an imperial opulence with soaring ceilings and intricate chande-liers—as well as a bar made of ice. Start with a Siberian Night or Red Scare cocktail and choose among a half dozen sustainable caviars or their Siberian Nachos with smoked salmon and caviar. For entrées you can't go wrong with the chicken Kiev or beef Stroganoff. Somewhat ironically, they also serve a good all-American stuffed Maine lobster. Be sure to check out the walk-in vodka freezer, where you might even spot the statue's missing head. [$] *Average main: $45 ⊠ Mandalay Bay Resort & Casino, 3950 Las Vegas Blvd. S, South Strip* ☎ *702/632–7407* ⊕ *www.mandalaybay.com/dining* ☾ *No lunch.*

$$$ ✕**RM Seafood.** Rick Moonen is one of the culinary world's leading sus-
SEAFOOD tainability advocates, and in the downstairs portion Rx Boiler he oper-ates RM Seafood, a casual space complete with raw bar. You won't find overfished species on the menu, but you will find such dishes as Moonen's famous Catfish Sloppy Joe, RM Style Cioppino, whole

Dungeness crab, plus Wagyu steak frites, and even a few burgers. $ *Average main: $30* ✉ *Mandalay Bay Resort & Casino, 3950 Las Vegas Blvd. S, South Strip* ☎ *702/632–9300* ⊕ *www.rmseafood.com.*

MGM GRAND RESORT & CASINO

$$$$

SOUTHERN

✕ **Emeril's New Orleans Fish House.** Chef Emeril Lagasse's first restaurant in Las Vegas has been joined by three others, but it's still a popular choice and still puts the spotlight on the chef's creole-inspired cuisine, such as barbecued shrimp, Louisiana-style étouffée, or oysters on the half shell with cucumber champagne mignonette. Sides like jalapeño corn bread, bacon mac 'n' cheese, and jambalaya are hearty accompaniment for Black Angus rib eye with warm rémoulade sauce or crispy-skinned brick chicken. ■TIP➔ The central bar is great for a glass of white with hoisin-glazed duck wings or a beer with shrimp po'boy at lunch. Be sure to summon one of Emeril's bottled hot sauces for extra kick. Finish with a slice of banana cream pie. $ *Average main: $33* ✉ *MGM Grand Hotel & Casino, 3799 Las Vegas Blvd. S, South Strip* ☎ *702/891–7374* ⊕ *www.mgmgrand.com.*

$$$$

FRENCH

Fodor'sChoice

★

✕ **Joël Robuchon.** Chef Joël Robuchon employs his haute cuisine at two gorgeous, side-by-side restaurants. The less formal though still highly refined L'Atelier offers à la carte entrées plus a long list of small "tasting" portions that are whipped up in the central exhibition kitchen, with its gleaming, wraparound seating and startling organic flourishes. But it's the glamorous manse next door that has foodies buzzing. For the ultimate gastronomical rush, try the chef's 16-course, seasonal tasting menu—a waltz of rarefied creations, accented with sauces, froth, and froufrou, and costing $425 per person, sans wine. This is one impressive operation and a fitting venue for a celebratory meal, but a number of stellar restaurants in town deliver nearly as splendid service and food at a much lower price. $ *Average main: $204* ✉ *MGM Grand Hotel & Casino, 3799 Las Vegas Blvd. S, South Strip* ☎ *702/891–7925* ⊕ *www.mgmgrand.com* ⌦ *Reservations essential* 🎩 *Jacket required* ⊘ *No lunch.*

$$$$

CHINESE

✕ **Pearl.** Serving traditional Chinese cuisine (from Canton and Shanghai provinces) in crisp, contemporary surroundings, Pearl prepares its specialties using the four cooking methods: steam, braise, bake, and fry. Chef Kai Yau often adds seasonal offerings to the menu and presents classics such as Sichuan hot-and-sour soup with crispy noodles or his signature wok-charred Mongolian beef. Spider prawn dumplings and crispy garlic chicken are other signature dishes. $ *Average main: $45* ✉ *MGM Grand Hotel & Casino, 3799 Las Vegas Blvd. S, South Strip* ☎ *702/891–7380* ⊕ *www.mgmgrand.com* ⊘ *Closed Tues. and Wed. No lunch.*

$$$$

JAPANESE

✕ **Shibuya.** Dazzling Japanese fare, a vast selection of sake (more than 125, including three private labels), and splendid, urbane environs have contributed to the popularity of this spot modeled after Tokyo's Shibuya district. Skip the smoky teppanyaki station, reserve a regular table or choose a seat at the sushi bar, and opt for the sushi, sashimi, and salads. The Shibuya roll (soft-shell crab, spicy albacore, and ponzu) is brilliant, while great carnivorous dishes include Wagyu skirt steak with shiitake and black pepper teriyaki sauce; slow-cooked pork belly with

DINING WITH KIDS

Sin City dining has never been geared especially toward families, and the increasing numbers of high-end, ultrafancy restaurants at Strip casino resorts further the "adult-only" mentality. But you'll still find plenty of spots around town—both on and off the Strip—that happily welcome kids, from ubiquitous fast-food chains and something-for-everyone buffets to quite a few distinctive choices. Here's a look at several restaurants worth a trip if you have kids in tow.

Jean Philippe Patisserie, Aria and Bellagio, Center Strip.

The draw: a chocolate fountain, beautifully displayed cakes, cookies, gelati, and dessert crepes, and a fanciful Wonka-esque ambience.

Village Eateries, New York–New York, South Strip.

The draw: an outdoor food court that's designed to resemble the Big Apple's Greenwich Village—pizza, hot dogs, burgers, cheesesteaks, deli sandwiches, quesadillas, fried shrimp, and ice cream are among the many offerings.

LBS: A Burger Joint, Red Rock Casino, Summerlin.

The draw: classic burgers, grilled cheese, hot dogs, shakes, and fries,

set in a funky space with a ceiling made of pressed license plates. All kid meal items include a mini vanilla ice-cream sundae for dessert.

Hofbräuhaus Las Vegas, Paradise Road.

The draw: kitschy Bavarian decor, German bands playing oompah music, and decadent desserts, including a knockout Black Forest chocolate cake.

Honey Salt, Summerlin.

The draw: a menu created by kids for kids (age 10 and under), with both delicious (mac and cheese, organic chicken wings) and nutritious (grilled asparagus) offerings. There are rainbow snow cones for dessert and a Grow-Your-Own Sundae, where magic seeds (chocolate-covered sunflower seeds) grow a plant (scoop of vanilla ice cream) sprinkled with dirt (crushed cookies) and (Gummy) worms; served with a squeezable dispenser of warm chocolate fudge.

Grimaldi's, Palazzo, North Strip; Henderson.

The draw: exceptionally tasty pizza and a casual dining room with a cheery little patio that's good fun on a nice day.

jicama ceviche; and Wagyu short rib with foie gras. Try the tiramisu, with extra-creamy *kinako* ice cream and honey-like *kuromitsu* syrup, for dessert. ■ TIP➜ **Shibuya also offers sushi and sashimi dinners and omikase tasting menus.** ⑤ *Average main: $50* ⊠ *MGM Grand Hotel & Casino, 3799 Las Vegas Blvd. S, South Strip* ☎ *702/891–3001* ⊕ *www. mgmgrand.com* ⊗ *No lunch.*

Las Vegas Hamburger Roundup

A number of casino resorts have opened eateries dedicated to that most quintessentially American of cuisines—the compact and delicious hamburger. All of these restaurants are casual affairs; most don't even accept reservations.

BLT Burger. Burger choices in this Laurent Tourondel restaurant near the Mirage sports book include American Kobe, lamb, and turkey. Spiked milk shakes—including "Grandma's Treat" with Maker's Mark, caramel, and vanilla ice cream—make great accompaniments. ⊠ *Mirage Las Vegas, 3400 Las Vegas Blvd. S, Center Strip* ☎ *702/792–7888.*

Burger Bar. Chef Hubert Keller started the burger trend with this modest restaurant in 2004; the simple build-your-own-burger menu features a variety of different meats (beef, buffalo, lamb, turkey) and toppings. The Creamy Cheesecake and Chocolate burgers are sweet dessert treats. ⊠ *Mandalay Place, 3930 Las Vegas Blvd. S, South Strip* ☎ *702/632–9364.*

Holstein's. Chef Anthony Meidenbauer concocted the concept of this burger joint specifically for the Cosmopolitan with an emphasis on organic ingredients. Everything on the menu—from burgers to sausages, buns, and sides—is made in house. ⊠ *The Cosmopolitan, 3708 Las Vegas Blvd. S, Center Strip* ☎ *702/698–7000.*

I Love Burgers. This expansive burger joint inside the Shoppes at Palazzo features a variety of different gourmet burgers (including Wagyu beef, buffalo, salmon, and vegan varieties), as well as a large fry menu (try the fried pickles and mac and cheese). The shakes—virgin or spiked—are scrumptious (especially Blueberry Pan or Caramel Corn) and there's a great beer selection, too. ⊠ *The Shoppes at Palazzo, 3327 Las Vegas Blvd. S, North Strip* ☎ *702/242–2747.*

LBS. Happy Hour is indeed happy at this Anthony Meidenbauer burger joint inside Summerlin's Red Rock Resort; the eatery offers burgers for $7.77 and appetizers and cocktails for $5, Monday to Thursday from 2 to 6 pm. Gourmet burgers of beef, free-range turkey, and salmon are available all the time. ⊠ *Red Rock Casino Resort, 11011 W. Charleston Blvd., Summerlin* ☎ *702/835–9393.*

NEW YORK–NEW YORK RESORT & CASINO

$$$$
STEAKHOUSE

✕ **Gallagher's Steakhouse.** This credible remake of the famed 1927 Manhattan original offers an old-school carnivore experience inside the cleverly decorated New York–New York Casino. This convivial tavern's walls are lined with black-and-white photos of sports stars, actors, and politicos, and the hardwood floors and tray ceilings transport guests directly to Gotham. You can admire the aged steaks in a big cooler visible from the cobblestone promenade near the entrance. The menu's refreshingly simple: pick your main dish (Colorado lamb chop, center-cut filet mignon, and so on) and then one of the six sauces (béarnaise, brandied peppercorn, shallot and Beaujolais, Stilton blue cheese, wild mushroom, and caramelized onion) to accompany it. Gallagher's is open until midnight on Friday and Saturday, and serves lunch at the bar. [$] *Average main: $42* ✉ *New York–New York Hotel & Casino, 3790 Las Vegas Blvd. S, South Strip* ☎ *702/740–6450* 🌐 *www.newyorknewyork.com.*

$$$ ITALIAN ✕ **Il Fornaio.** Whether producing crusty loaves of freshly baked bread, house-made pasta, or dough for its excellent thin-crust, wood-oven pizzas, this soothingly neutral Italian restaurant will satisfy carb cravings as well as yearnings for dishes that Grandma used to make. Not only can you taste the love in your lasagna, but also feel the comfort that comes from watching it prepared in the exhibition kitchen, from whence seasoned fish, grilled meats, and juicy rotisserie, such as free-range rosemary chicken, are also created and plated with fresh ingredients. Tiramisu is a must and best enjoyed from the terrace, where you can watch passersby. Buy a loaf to go in the diminutive bakery, located just steps away; other foodie finds are also available. **■ TIP→ Il Fornaio is a great place for breakfast and brunch or for pastry take-out from the bakery.** [$] *Average main: $29* ✉ *New York–New York Resort & Casino, 3790 Las Vegas Blvd. S, South Strip* ☎ *702/650–6500* 🌐 *www.ilfornaio.com.*

5

CENTER STRIP

ARIA

$$$$ SEAFOOD ✕ **American Fish.** At Michael Mina's American Fish, which is designed to look like a lodge, fish orders are prepared one of four ways: salt-baked, wood-grilled, cast-iron griddled or, believe it or not, poached in ocean water. Entrées come from a list that might include branzino, rainbow trout, diver scallops, and big-eye tuna (there's a selection of meat as well, such as a Prime flat-iron steak or a Wagyu rib eye). Still, some of the menu's biggest treasures are in the appetizers section: dishes like New England lobster roll, seared scallops and foie gras, and crispy fish tostadas. Also pay attention to the side dishes, like crawfish hush puppies and truffle mac and cheese. [$] *Average main: $69* ✉ *Aria, 3730 Las Vegas Blvd. S, Center Strip* ☎ *877/230–2742* 🌐 *www.arialasvegas.com/dining* ⊙ *No lunch.*

$$$$ STEAKHOUSE ✕ **Jean Georges Steakhouse.** This steak house, named for famed chef Jean-Georges Vongerichten, serves up a modern spin on the traditional meat and potatoes. To wit: dishes such as the soy-glazed short rib with apple jalapeño puree and rosemary crumbs, and Dungeness crab cake with celeriac rémoulade. An early-evening menu and signature tasting menu are available in addition to the à la carte dinner menu. The restaurant also spotlights an extensive bar program that focuses on classic cocktails. During particularly busy weekends, look for pros on break from the nearby poker room; "J.G.," as it's known, has reportedly become one of the favorites of players such as Daniel Negreanu, Phil Ivey, and Phil Hellmuth. [$] *Average main: $69* ✉ *Aria, 3730 Las Vegas Blvd. S, Center Strip* ☎ *877/230–2742* 🌐 *www.arialasvegas.com/dining.*

$$$$ SPANISH ✕ **Julian Serrano.** Chef Julian Serrano—renowned for Picasso at Bellagio—chose to honor his homeland's tapas and paella traditions at his eponymous restaurant in Aria. Some of Serrano's signature dishes offered include tuna carpaccio with toasted pine nuts,

goat-cheese-and-mushroom-stuffed piquillo peppers, salmon with truffle béchamel, and Spanish tortilla with potatoes and eggs. The menu also features ceviche options and several large plates. For dessert, try the almond-infused Santiago's Cake. There's even a special three-course prix-fixe pretheater dinner menu for $39, as well as a signature $59 tasting menu. During lunchtime, seats on the edge of the "patio" that face hotel registration and the casino are great spots from which to people-watch. ⑤ *Average main: $39* ⊠ *Aria, 3730 Las Vegas Blvd., CityCenter, Center Strip* ☎ *877/230–2742* ⊕ *www.arialasvegas.com/dining.*

$$$$
MEDITERRANEAN
Fodor'sChoice
★

✕ **Sage.** Farm-to-table produce and artisanal meats flavored with innovative concepts from the Mediterranean are presented at Executive Chef Shawn McClain's swanky Aria restaurant. Exciting fare includes grilled Spanish octopus with charred pumpkin, and foie gras custard brûlée. Depending on when you visit, entrée options might include braised short rib with horseradish-smoked potato pave, bacon-wrapped Iberico pork loin, and Maryland black bass. A big attraction is the bar program; mixologists incorporate fresh-fruit purees, boutique liquors, and homemade bitters into cocktails, and the bar offers more absinthe than any other spot in Vegas. ⑤ *Average main: $49* ⊠ *Aria, 3730 Las Vegas Blvd., Center Strip* ☎ *877/230–2742* ⊕ *www.arialasvegas.com/dining* ⚅ *Reservations essential* ⊗ *Closed Sun.*

BELLAGIO

$$$$
AMERICAN

✕ **FIX.** The ceiling, constructed almost entirely of Costa Rican padouk wood, curves like a breaking wave at this upscale comfort-food restaurant, where childhood favorites get updated twists. Try the roasted tomato soup with grilled bacon-goat cheese, or the Kobe chile-cheese fries. Craving carbs? Indulge in the Adult Mac and Cheese with truffle oil and prosciutto or the smoked mashed potatoes. Entrées may include duck and waffles with fried egg and maple bourbon syrup, or crisp-skinned pork shank with sweet corn spoon bread and collards. Apple pie doughnuts or warm banana bread pudding are a perfect ending to your meal. The kitchen serves until 10:30 pm most evenings, and until 2 am on Friday and Saturday, and late-night and pre-"O" (Cirque du Soleil) menus are offered. ⑤ *Average main: $45* ⊠ *Bellagio Las Vegas, 3600 Las Vegas Blvd. S, Center Strip* ☎ *702/693–8865* ⊕ *www.bellagio. com/restaurants* ⊗ *No lunch.*

$
CAFÉ
FAMILY
Fodor'sChoice
★

✕ **Jean Philippe Patisserie.** Chocolate—dark, white, and milk—flows from a tall glass fountain at the entrance of this stunning pastry shop just off the Bellagio's iconic conservatory. This artful homage to chocolate has decadent desserts, including cakes, cookies, gelato, hand-dipped chocolate candies, and particularly memorable crepes (try the one filled with mango, coconut, passion-fruit, and pineapple sorbets). Seating is limited. It's open late, until midnight on Friday and Saturday and 11 pm the rest of the week. ⑤ *Average main: $8* ⊠ *Bellagio, 3600 Las Vegas Blvd. S, Center Strip* ☎ *702/693–7111* ⊕ *www.bellagio.com/ restaurants/jean-philippe.aspx.* ⑤ *Average main: $8* ⊠ *Aria, 3730 Las Vegas Blvd. S, Casino level, Center Strip*

$$$$
FRENCH

✕ **Le Cirque.** This sumptuous restaurant, a branch of the New York City landmark, remains one of the city's true temples of haute cuisine, despite increased heavy-hitting competition. The mahogany-lined room is all the more opulent for its size: in a city of mega-everything; Le Cirque seats only 80 under its draped silk-tent ceiling. Even with a view of the hotel's lake and its mesmerizing fountain show, you'll only have eyes for your plate when your server presents dishes such as the panko-crusted egg with osetra caviar, or sautéed foie gras with white chocolate and raisin brioche. Degustation, à la carte, and vegetarian menus are offered, and the wine cellar contains about 900 selections representing the major wine-producing regions of the world. One little-known secret: Le Cirque offers a reduced-price prix-fixe pretheater dinner menu. ⑤ *Average main: $89* ⊠ *Bellagio Las Vegas, 3600 Las Vegas Blvd. S, Center Strip* ☎ *702/693–8865* ⊕ *www.bellagio.com/restaurants* ⌂ *Reservations essential* ⊘ *Closed Mon. No lunch.*

$$$$ ✕ **Osteria del Circo.** With its expansive view of the lake, this is one of

ITALIAN Bellagio's prime dining spots. The colorful Circo sports velveteen harlequin-pattern seats and whimsically decorated chandeliers, and serves home-style Tuscan food. Appetizers might include citrus-cured smoked swordfish carpaccio with shaved fennel, or calamari with green beans and zucchini blossom fritti. The house-made pastas might include tortolloni filled with Maine lobster and butternut squash, while entrées include branzino, or veal chop Milanese. Caviar of various types is offered by the ounce for dinner, and the extensive wine cellar has selections from many of the major wine-producing regions of the world. It's the casual sister restaurant of next-door Le Cirque; food from Circo also can be purchased in Hyde Bellagio lounge. ⑤ *Average main: $52* ⊠ *Bellagio Las Vegas, 3600 Las Vegas Blvd. S, Center Strip* ☎ *702/693–8865* ⊕ *www.bellagio.com/restaurants* ⊘ *No lunch.*

$$$$ ✕ **Picasso.** Adorned with some original works by Picasso, this restau-

EUROPEAN rant raised the city's dining scene a notch when it opened in Bellagio

Fodor's Choice in 1998. Although some say Executive Chef Julian Serrano doesn't

★ change his menu often enough, the artful, innovative cuisine—based on French classics with strong Spanish influences—is consistently outstanding. Appetizers on the seasonal menu might include warm quail salad with sautéed artichokes and pine nuts, or poached oysters with osetra caviar and vermouth sauce. Roasted milk-fed veal or sautéed medallions of fallow deer with caramelized green apples are other potential entrée choices. Sometimes a seasonal specialty menu may feature Alba white truffles. Dinners are prix-fixe, with four- or five-course options; a vegetarian menu and a three-course pretheater menu also are available. ⑤ *Average main: $90* ⊠ *Bellagio Las Vegas, 3600 Las Vegas Blvd. S, Center Strip* ☎ *702/693–8865* ⊕ *www.bellagio.com/restaurants* ⌂ *Reservations essential* ⊘ *Closed Tues. No lunch.*

$$$$ ✕ **Prime Steakhouse.** Even among celebrity chefs, Jean-Georges Vongeri-

STEAKHOUSE chten has established a "can't touch this" reputation. Prime—with its gorgeous view of the fountains—is a place to see and be seen at Bellagio. In a velvet-draped gold, dark brown, and blue room, choice cuts of beef are presented with sauces from classic béarnaise to miso-mustard. You can also try seafood dishes such as Arctic char with roasted mushrooms, and appetizers such as sautéed foie gras with sweet and sour morels and Marcona almonds. ⑤ *Average main: $79* ⊠ *Bellagio Las Vegas, 3600*

5

Las Vegas Blvd. S, Center Strip ☎ *702/693–8865* ⊕ *www.bellagio.com/ restaurants* ⚱ *Reservations essential* ⊙ *No lunch.*

$$$$
ECLECTIC
Fodor's Choice
★

✕ **Sensi.** It's no easy feat coming up with a truly original restaurant in Las Vegas that offers more than just a gimmicky theme or celebrity-chef pedigree. Sensi, a casual but cosmopolitan spot that's secluded from Bellagio's noisy gaming areas and has sandstone and glass walls and soothing waterfalls, succeeds on all counts. Executive Chef Royden Ellamar presents a menu that's divided into four distinct culinary realms: Asian, Italian, American, and seafood, with an emphasis on sustainability and local sourcing. The seasonal menu might include poutine with goat barbacoa and St. Andre cheese, crispy shrimp with a rice-flake crust, or ricotta gnocchi with butternut squash and chestnuts. Quench your thirst with a glass of house-made ginger ale. If you have a few people in your party, try the Sensi Overload, "a towering assortment of everything sweet." Tasting, bar, and prix-fixe menus available. ⑤ *Average main: $49* ⊠ *Bellagio Las Vegas, 3600 Las Vegas Blvd. S, Center Strip* ☎ *702/693–8865* ⊕ *www.bellagio.com/restaurants* ⊙ *No lunch.*

CAESARS PALACE

$$$$
BRITISH

✕ **Gordon Ramsay Pub & Grill.** Three things stand out at this comfortable, casual restaurant, conceptualized by tyrannical celeb chef Gordon Ramsey: the libations, the cheery across-the-pond ambience, and the elevated British pub grub—in that order. The cocktails are strong and diverse, with names like "London Calling" and "God Save the Queen." Well, pip pip cheerio and all that rot. It's the beer here that's to die for. Slake your thirst with a Boddingtons imported draft or Strongbow cider. Choose from 99 brews and hum along with classic Brit pop and rock tunes and watch soccer on any of numerous flat-screen tellys. Seating is easy on the bum—the place settings are rich and lovely and rustic. Bread isn't complimentary and the service and food can be spotty, but when all goes well, it's smashing. Grilled burgers, sandwiches, soups, and salads follow notable starters such as shrimp cocktail; warm, salty pretzels with zesty cheese and mustard; and scotch or deviled eggs, with house-made horseradish and ketchup. The pot pie sampler (chicken, lamb, beef), grilled chops, seared scallops, crispy fish-and-chips, and lobster mac and cheese are standouts. Warm sticky toffee pudding has fans 'o' plenty. ⑤ *Average main: $31* ⊠ *Caesars Palace, 3570 Las Vegas Blvd. S, Center Strip* ☎ *702/731–7410* ⊕ *www.caesarspalace.com.*

$$$$
SEAFOOD

✕ **Joe's Seafood, Prime Steak & Stone Crab.** Drop by this bustling branch of the famed South Miami Beach restaurant for, at the very least, a pile of fresh stone crabs (they're available here year-round, unlike at the Florida location) and a beer. But Joe's is worth a try whether for a light lunch or snack (the bar menu features a nice range of raw-bar items, salads, and sandwiches) or a full meal to remember. Carnivores won't go hungry here, considering the leviathan bone-in New York strip steak or Colorado lamb chops. Waiters finish many dishes table-side. For dessert, save room for key lime pie or banana-cream pie with Foster sauce. ⑤ *Average main: $49* ⊠ *Forum Shops at Caesars, 3500 Las Vegas Blvd. S, Center Strip* ☎ *702/792–9222* ⊕ *www.joes.net/las-vegas.*

$$$$ ✕**Mesa Grill.** Playful splashes of bright green, blue, red, and yellow
SOUTHWESTERN offset the swanky curved banquettes and earth tones at Iron Chef and
grill-meister Bobby Flay's first restaurant outside New York City. The
menu's decidedly Southwestern, but with plenty of contemporary twists.
Options might include a starter of barbecued duck with habanero chile–
star anise sauce over blue-corn pancakes, and main dishes like mango-
and-spice-encrusted tuna steak with green peppercorn and green chile
sauce or ancho-chile honey-glazed salmon with spicy black-bean sauce
and roasted jalapeño crema. Some tables have views of the casino sports
book. There's also an impressive weekend brunch. ⑤ *Average main: $44*
✉ *Caesars Palace, 3570 Las Vegas Blvd. S, Center Strip* ☎ *702/731–
7731* ⊕ *www.caesarspalace.com/restaurants.*

$$$$ ✕**Nobu.** Celebrity chef Nobu Matsuhisa established a foothold in the
SUSHI Vegas market with a namesake restaurant (that still exists) at the Hard
Rock Casino Hotel, but in early 2013, he opened this modern location at the base of his new hotel tower at Caesars Palace. The result:
one of the hottest tables in town. The main restaurant serves up sushi,
sashimi, and other Japanese-inspired dishes à la carte (try the yellowtail sashimi with jalapeño). In the back, teppanyaki-style tables (think
Benihana) offer a prix-fixe experience that includes Waygu beef, fresh
seafood, and more. In the lounge, bartenders are happy to assist with a
dedicated sake menu, most of which has been hand-selected by Nobu
himself. ⑤ *Average main: $65* ✉ *3570 Las Vegas Blvd. S, Center Strip*
☎ *702/785–6628* ⊕ *www.caesarspalace.com* ⚊ *Reservations essential*
⊘ *No lunch.*

$$ ✕**Payard Patisserie & Bistro.** Dessert is king at this Las Vegas outpost of
CAFÉ the New York–based restaurant from celebrated chef François Payard.
Tourists and business travelers queue during lunch at the counter for
made-to-order crepes and treats that might include the Sweet Relief,
mango mousse with pineapple soufflé and roasted pineapple Swiss
meringue. The 46-seat dining room (dinner is served Wednesday
through Sunday) offers a lengthy wine list, savory items such as classic
croque monsieur (grilled ham-and-cheese sandwich), steak frites and
cheese soufflé, and a veritable bargain on the Strip: a $48 prix-fixe
menu of any appetizer, any entrée and any dessert. Breakfast offers an
array of croques, as well as quiches, brioche French toast, and omelets.
⑤ *Average main: $19* ✉ *Caesars Palace, 3570 Las Vegas Blvd. S, Center
Strip* ☎ *702/731–1292* ⊕ *www.caesarspalace.com.*

$$$$ ✕**Rao's.** While its 10-table New York counterpart is notorious for a jam-
ITALIAN packed reservation list, this 200-seat outpost at Caesars Palace offers
greater availability. Hearty portions of family-style, rustic, southern
Italian cuisine are featured on the menu, including traditional dishes of
baked clams, shrimp fra diavolo, and meatballs as well as the signature
dish, lemon chicken. The red walls are crammed with framed celebrity
photos—many of them digital replicas of originals back East. On warm
nights, diners can end their meal with friendly games of bocce on the
in-house (and first-come, first-served) court that overlooks the redone
Garden of the Gods pool oasis. ⑤ *Average main: $32* ✉ *Caesars Pal-
ace, 3570 Las Vegas Blvd. S, Center Strip* ☎ *702/731–7267* ⊕ *www.
caesarspalace.com* ⊘ *No lunch.*

$$$$ ✕ **Restaurant Guy Savoy.** In an ultraswank dining room on the second
FRENCH floor of the Augustus Tower, Michelin three-star chef Guy Savoy intro-
Fodor'sChoice duces gourmands to his masterful creations, such as turbot à la plancha
★ with cauliflower and green curry. The 14-course, $348 Innovation-
Inspiration Menu is the restaurant's crown jewel, featuring signature
dishes such as artichoke and black truffle soup, and pan-seared quails.
Prices are a little lower if you opt for the à la carte or nine-course Sig-
nature Menu or choose the three-course pretheater menu. The selections
from the Savoy's 15,000-bottle wine cellar only add to this restaurant's
epicurean mystique. $ *Average main: $150* ⊠ *Caesars Palace, 3570 Las
Vegas Blvd. S, Center Strip* ☎ *877/346–4642* ⊕ *www.caesarspalace.com*
☉ *Closed Mon. and Tues. No lunch.*

$$$$ ✕ **Spago Las Vegas.** Just as Steve Wynn ushered in the age of the Vegas
AMERICAN megaresort with the Mirage, Wolfgang Puck sparked the celebrity-chef
boom when he opened a branch of his famous Beverly Hills eatery at
Caesars Forum Shops in 1992. Spago Las Vegas has remained a fixture
in this ever-fickle city, and it remains consistently superb. It's fronted by
the less expensive café, which is great for people-watching at the Forum;
inside, the dinner-only dining room is more intimate. Both menus are
classic Puck: In the café, sample Puck's signature pizzas and dishes such
as Thai-style chicken salad. Options for the dining room might include
pan-seared duck breast with spinach and chanterelle mushrooms, and
grilled French sea bass with butternut squash puree. $ *Average main:
$49* ⊠ *Forum Shops at Caesars, 3500 Las Vegas Blvd. S, Center Strip*
☎ *702/369–6300* ⊕ *www.wolfgangpuck.com.*

$$$ ✕ **Sushi Roku.** On the top floor of the towering atrium at the Strip
JAPANESE entrance to the Forum Shops, Roku occupies an airy dining room lined
with bamboo stalks and tall windows facing the Strip. Sushi is the main
draw, and you can't go wrong with the sea bream or oyster nigiri, or the
baked lobster roll with creamy miso sauce. But greater rewards come
to those who venture deeper into the extensive menu. Seasonal items
worth considering: popcorn shrimp tempura in spicy creamy sauce,
filet mignon–wrapped asparagus, or Hakata ramen with pork Cha-shu.
$ *Average main: $30* ⊠ *Forum Shops at Caesars, 3500 Las Vegas Blvd.
S, Center Strip* ☎ *702/733–7373* ⊕ *www.sushiroku.com.*

CITYCENTER

CRYSTALS SHOPPING CENTER

$$$$ ✕ **Mastro's Ocean Club.** In addition to food that is upscale and delicious,
SEAFOOD Mastro's Ocean Club, inside Crystals complex at CityCenter, has two
major attractions: a piano lounge that serves stellar martinis and the
"Tree House," a two-story wooden sculpture that rises from the ground
level and houses the main dining room 30 feet above the ground. Menu
items range from vanilla-battered shrimp and ahi tuna tartare to New
York strip steak and rack of lamb. Side dishes tend to be predictable,
except for the Gorgonzola macaroni and cheese, and lobster mashed
potatoes. The signature Warm Butter Cake alone warrants repeat vis-
its. $ *Average main: $69* ⊠ *CityCenter, 3270 Las Vegas Blvd. S, Suite*

244, Center Strip ☎ *702/798–7115* ⊕ *www.mastrosrestaurants.com* ⊙ *No lunch.*

$$$$ ✕ **Social House.** Owned and operated by nightlife innovators Angel
SUSHI   Management Group, this eatery—tucked inside Crystals—is as much
a destination for good food as it is a spot to see and be seen. Cuisine
is pan-Asian with an emphasis on Japanese; Executive Chef John Lee
offers à la carte and small-bites menus for parties of just about every
size (there's also a special lunch menu). Standout items include Kobe
beef sashimi with wasabi crème fraîche, miso port short ribs, and seared
branzino with Kabocha "pasta" and chile-soy sauce. Happy Hour is
available from 5 to 8 pm daily; the best deal here is 12-ounce cans
of Sapporo or Kirin Light for $5. ⑤ *Average main: $45* ⊠ *3720 Las
Vegas Blvd., S, Center Strip* ☎ *702/736–1122* ⊕ *angelmg.com/venues/
social-house/.*

$$$ ✕ **Todd English P.U.B.** This sports bar represents four-time James Beard
BRITISH   Award winner Todd English's first pub concept—"pub," in this case,
stands for "public urban bar"—and it has become one of the Strip's
most popular casual spots. The menu takes playful approaches to tradi-
tional bar food; try the cocktail-sized corn dogs or the kettle chips with
bacon bits and fried chicken livers. The curved wooden bar features two
carving stations (don't miss the brisket, on your choice of bread with
your choice of sauces) and a raw bar, while bartenders serve more than
30 beers on draft. Throughout the room, plasma televisions are plentiful
but not obtrusive; there's also a spacious patio overlooking one of Aria's
"pocket parks" for outdoor dining. ⑤ *Average main: $24* ⊠ *Crystals,
3720 Las Vegas Blvd. S, CityCenter, Center Strip* ☎ *702/489–8080*
⊕ *www.toddenglishpub.com.*

MANDARIN ORIENTAL

$$$$ ✕ **Twist.** The 23rd floor of the Mandarin Oriental is the only place in the
FRENCH   United States to experience food from internationally renowned Chef
Pierre Gagnaire. The French chef pioneered the "fusion" movement in
cooking, and every dish blends flavor and texture in surprising ways. To
wit: appetizers such as sliced spiny lobster with olive oil mousseline and
mango salad, or the entrée of roasted veal chop with curry sweetbread
gratin. Desserts are just as appealing—consider the rum baba with red
currant syrup. Dinner can be ordered à la carte or as part of a four- or
six-course tasting menu ($135 or $175, respectively), or seven courses
with wine pairings for $777. The restaurant is sexy and sophisticated,
with an expansive wine loft (reached by a glass staircase) and nearly 300
illuminated globe-like spheres that float above the dining room like tiny
moons. ⑤ *Average main: $89* ⊠ *Mandarin Oriental, 3752 Las Vegas
Blvd. S, Center Strip* ☎ *888/881–9367* ⊕ *www.mandarinoriental.com/
lasvegas* ⩩ *Reservations essential* ⊙ *Closed Mon. No lunch.*

THE COSMOPOLITAN

$$$$ ✕ **Comme Ca.** The menu at this popular and comfy-casual David Myers
FRENCH   restaurant is approachable and innovative. There are daily chalkboard
Fodor'sChoice   specials, while the regular menu might include roasted beef marrow
★   and oxtail jam with parsley, lemon, and shallots; bouillabaisse teeming

with octopus, clams, shrimp, and mussels; and two styles of steak frites. With part of the dining room cantilevered over the sidewalk below, the restaurant has a commanding third-floor view of the Strip. $ *Average main: $39* ⊠ *The Cosmopolitan, 3708 Las Vegas Blvd. S, Center Strip* ☎ *702/698–7000* ⊕ *www.cosmopolitanlasvegas.com* ⌖ *Reservations essential.*

$$$$
MEDITERRANEAN

✕ **Estiatorio Milos.** The first Greek restaurant on the Las Vegas Strip certainly doesn't disappoint, although you'll pay well for the experience. Chef Costas Spiliadis flies in fresh fish from the Mediterranean; you pick out the piece of fish at market price and select how you'd like it prepared. Side dishes such as *chtipiti* (roasted red peppers and barrrel-aged feta cheese) are a nice complement to the main course. Also worth sampling: the Milos Special, lightly grilled zucchini with eggplant *tzatziki* and *kefalograviera* cheese. The dining experience itself is also a treat—the dining room is stark white, and the glass-enclosed terrace looks out on the Strip. $ *Average main: $55* ⊠ *The Cosmopolitan, 3708 Las Vegas Blvd. S, Center Strip* ☎ *702/698–7000* ⊕ *www. cosmopolitanlasvegas.com* ⌖ *Reservations essential.*

$$$$
SPANISH

✕ **Jaleo.** Chef Jose Andres was one of the first to capitalize on the tapas concept in the United States (at the Washington, D.C., version of Jaleo), and small plates are the highlights of the menu here, too. With choices such as *jamón ibérico* (Spanish ham) and *gambas al ajillo* (shrimp in oil), you haven't thoroughly explored the menu until there are stacks of plates on your table. Another highlight: paella, which changes daily. Bring a sense of humor to the main dining room, as some tables are fashioned out of foosball tables that still function perfectly (balls available upon request). For a more formal and intimate experience, try dining in the private room—an intimate, prix-fixe experience with seats that overlook a separate kitchen. $ *Average main: $49* ⊠ *The Cosmopolitan, 3708 Las Vegas Blvd. S, Center Strip* ☎ *702/698–7000* ⊕ *www. cosmopolitanlasvegas.com.*

$$$$
ITALIAN

✕ **Scarpetta.** In Italian, "scarpetta" refers to the process of using bread to soak up every last morsel of a dish, and Chef Scott Conant inspires diners to do just that when they eat at his casual and festive modern Italian eatery. Conant makes all of his own pasta, which takes front and center on the eclectic menu (the simple spaghetti with tomato and basil is, in a word, divine). Also worth trying: spiced duck breast with eggplant gratin and pine nuts, or farro risotto with roasted vegetables. Floor-to-ceiling windows that look out on the Bellagio and the Strip provide memorable views. For a more casual experience, try D.O.C.G., Conant's wine bar and light-bite eatery next door. $ *Average main: $35* ⊠ *The Cosmopolitan, 3708 Las Vegas Blvd. S, Center Strip* ☎ *702/698– 7000* ⊕ *www.cosmopolitanlasvegas.com.*

THE MIRAGE

$$$
BURGER

✕ **BLT Burger.** In the same space where Siegfried & Roy's white tigers once roamed, diners, not tigers, are on display at BLT Burger, which serves up the traditional burger, fries, and a shake—but with some tasty twists. For a sugar rush, start with a Twinkie Boy milk shake made with vanilla ice cream, caramel syrup, and real Twinkies. Or, spike that shake with bourbon (Maker's Mark, no less). Bite into a Wagyu truffle burger, or choose one made from lamb, turkey, or salmon. Sweet-potato fries are the perfect carbo sideshow for all this protein. BLT is open until 4 am on weekends. $ *Average main: $22* ⊠ *The Mirage, 3400 Las Vegas Blvd. S, Center Strip* ☎ *702/792–7888* ⊕ *www.mirage.com/restaurants.*

$$$ ╳ **Carnegie Deli.** The famed NYC source of matzoh-ball soup and mam-
DELI moth sandwiches has a bustling outpost inside the Mirage. Serious deli fans should try the smoked-sturgeon omelet or Harvey's Midnight Special (all-beef knockwurst with baked beans and sauerkraut) or a stacked-up-to-here Reuben. The prices are high, but not so much if you figure the meats by the pound. $ *Average main: $22* ⊠ *The Mirage, 3400 Las Vegas Blvd. S, Center Strip* ☎ *702/791–7310* ⊕ *www.mirage.com/restaurants.*

$$$$ ╳ **Onda Ristorante.** One of the few restaurants that have survived since
ITALIAN the opening of the Mirage in 1989, this venerable spot has been undated over the years and now is decorated in soothing pale neutrals that contrast the hardwood floor. The classics are here—the spaghetti and lasagna and gnocchi and veal osso buco—as well as updated dishes such as an indulgent burratta agnolotti with lobster and chanterelle mushrooms, or beef tenderloin with smoked barley risotto. $ *Average main: $45* ⊠ *The Mirage, 3400 Las Vegas Blvd. S, Center Strip* ☎ *866/339–4566* ⊕ *www.mirage.com/restaurants* ☺ *No lunch.*

$$$$ ╳ **STACK.** Curvy strips of exotic wood form the "stacked" walls of this
AMERICAN beautiful restaurant, owned by nightclub impresarios The Light Group. Inventively prepared comfort classics dominate the menu—start with the (totally modern) pigs in a blanket or the mini lamb gyros before tucking into the sea bass with lobster risotto or bone-in 24-ounce toma-hawk rib eye. Be sure to order a side of Adult Tater Tots with bacon and Brie. There's a live DJ in the lounge from 9 pm to midnight Tues-day, Friday, and Saturday, and dinner-and-show packages are available for Cirque du Soleil's *LOVE* as well as *Terry Fator, Boys II Men,* and *Aces of Comedy.* $ *Average main: $38* ⊠ *The Mirage, 3400 Las Vegas Blvd. S, Center Strip* ☎ *866/339–4566* ⊕ *www.mirage.com/restaurants* ☺ *No lunch.*

PARIS LAS VEGAS

$$$$ ╳ **Eiffel Tower Restaurant.** Paris Las Vegas Resort's best restaurant is a
FRENCH room with a view, all right—it's about a third of the way up the hotel's half-scale Eiffel Tower replica, with views from all four glassed-in sides (request a Strip view when booking for the biggest wow factor—it overlooks the fountains at Bellagio, across the street). But patrons are often pleasantly surprised that the food here measures up to the set-ting. The French-accented menu usually includes appetizers of cold foie gras torchon with duck prosciutto, or a Maine Peekytoe crab salad. On the entrée list, you might find individual Eiffel Tower Beef Wel-lingtons, charred spice-crusted venison, and vegetarian dishes such as baked herb crepes with artichoke and slow-roasted tomato coulis. The restaurant also offers a variety of caviar priced by the ounce, a tasting menu, and a gluten-free dinner menu. $ *Average main: $60* ⊠ *Paris Las*

Vegas, 3655 Las Vegas Blvd. S, Center Strip ☎ 702/948–6937 ⊕ *www. eiffeltowerrestaurant.com* ⌂ *Reservations essential.*

$$$$ ✕ **Gordon Ramsay Steak.** Gordon Ramsay's heavily British-theme Las
BRITISH Vegas flagship (which has been joined by Gordon Ramsay Pub & Grill at Caesars Palace and Gordon Ramsay BurGR at Planet Hollywood) bridges the geographic gap with a Chunnel-like entrance connecting it to Paris Las Vegas, and the culinary gap with a wide variety of cuts of beef, showcased before dinner on a rolling cart. Shellfish, caviar, and such luxe entrées as Roasted Beef Wellington are joined on this menu by fish-and-chips, short ribs, and other more earthy fare. Those with lighter appetites can try the bar menu; the Hell's Kitchen Limited Edition Tasting Menu is a more indulgent path. ⑤ *Average main: $100* ⊠ *Paris Las Vegas, 3655 Las Vegas Blvd. S, Center Strip* ☎ 877/346–4642 ⊕ *www. ParisLasVegas.com.*

$$$$ ✕ **Mon Ami Gabi.** This French bistro and steak house that first earned
FRENCH acclaim in Chicago has become much beloved here in Las Vegas, in large part because few restaurants have terraces overlooking the Strip. For those who prefer a quieter environment, a glassed-in conservatory conveys an outdoor feel, and still-quieter dining rooms are inside, adorned with chandeliers dramatically suspended three stories above. The specialty of the house is steak frites, offered a dozen ways, including classic, au poivre, bordelaise, and Roquefort. The skate wing with lemon-caper brown butter also is excellent, and the prices are, on the whole, reasonable for the Strip. ◼ TIP→ This place is a favorite for Sunday brunch; a kids' menu also is available. ⑤ *Average main: $35* ⊠ *Paris Las Vegas, 3655 Las Vegas Blvd. S, Center Strip* ☎ 702/944–4224 ⊕ *www.monamigabi.com.*

PLANET HOLLYWOOD RESORT & CASINO

$$$$ ✕ **KOI Las Vegas.** KOI has garnered a reputation as a see-and-be-seen
ASIAN restaurant in New York, Bangkok, Los Angeles, and Las Vegas. The cavernous 220-seat Las Vegas outlet offers sublime Asian-fusion fare that might include baked lobster roll with creamy sauce, Spicy Crunchy Yellowtail Tartare, and Kobe-style filet mignon. The main dining room can get noisy, so request a table along the back wall. After dinner, hit the swanky lounge to order a cosmo or martini, then head for the open-air patio to enjoy the Bellagio fountains across the street. ⑤ *Average main: $49* ⊠ *Planet Hollywood Resort & Casino, 3667 Las Vegas Blvd. S, Center Strip* ☎ 702/454–4555 ⊕ *www.planethollywoodresort.com.*

$$$$ ✕ **Strip House.** This lavish but cheeky steak joint with sisters in New York
STEAKHOUSE wears its bordello-chic atmosphere with a healthy touch of irony. The red-flocked wallpaper and dozens of vintage black-and-white boudoir photos may suggest you're inside an early-20th-century house of ill repute, but the menu of artfully presented chops and classic American foods reflects a highly skilled, contemporary kitchen. Appetizers such as warm garlic bread with Gorgonzola fondue and lobster bisque are indulgent starters. A broad variety of steaks including 20-ounce bone-in rib eyes and New York strips—veal rib chops, and Colorado lamb rack—don't disappoint. Feeling cuddly? Try the porterhouse for two. The 24-layer chocolate cake makes for a fittingly decadent end

to your meal. $ *Average main: $40* ⊠ *Planet Hollywood Resort & Casino, 3667 Las Vegas Blvd. S, Center Strip* ☎ *702/737–5200* ⊕ *www. planethollywoodresort.com* ⊗ *No lunch.*

NORTH STRIP

ENCORE

$$$$
STEAKHOUSE
✕ **Botero.** Panoramic windows, a huge Botero statue as a centerpiece, and a smattering of the master's paintings convey a sense of tasteful luxury inside this circular steak house overlooking the Encore pool area. Enjoyment of Chef Mark LoRusso's contemporary preparations of beef, poultry, and seafood is enhanced by the skilled, attentive service of the waitstaff. Enticing starters might include Dungeness crab agnolotti, a ham and cheese tasting, or baby-beet salad with warm chèvre. Of course, there are several steaks to choose from, with three styles of preparation: traditional or with pepper or chimichurri sauce. Consider sharing the chateaubriand, with a side of truffle mac and cheese. ■ TIP➔ Check out the vegan/allergen menus for their elevated options. $ *Average main: $54* ⊠ *Encore, 3131 Las Vegas Blvd. S, North Strip* ☎ *702/770–3463* ⊕ *www.wynnlasvegas.com/Restaurants* ⟡ *Reservations essential* ⊗ *No lunch.*

$$$$
ITALIAN
✕ **Sinatra.** Encore recalls the panache of vintage Vegas by dedicating one of its fine-dining venues to Frank Sinatra; a photo of the Chairman of the Board with the "other" chairman—Wynn/Encore owner Steve Wynn—even adorns one of the dining rooms. Chef Theo Schoenegger, formerly of L.A.'s celebrated Patina, turns out simple, elegantly presented Italian cuisine, such as Frank's Clams Posilipo and Ossobuco "My Way." Framed photos of Ol' Blue Eyes (as well as his Academy Award for *From Here to Eternity*) adorn the ivory-and-ruby-hued indoor dining room. The legendary crooner's music plays softly while well-dressed guests nibble their antipasto next to the fireplace on the outdoor patio. Some just pull up a seat at the swank bar to order a cocktail or postprandial limoncello or grappa. Go ahead and imbibe!— Frankie would approve. $ *Average main: $45* ⊠ *Encore, 3131 Las Vegas Blvd. S, North Strip* ☎ *702/770–3463* ⊕ *www.wynnlasvegas. com/Restaurants* ⟡ *Reservations essential* ⊗ *No lunch.*

$$$$
CAFÉ
✕ **Society Café.** This upscale café with lush banquettes and luxe draperies is perfectly suited for easy companionship, whether casual, intimate, or business. You can start your day off on a healthy note with the Green Machine or Gold Goddess freshly squeezed juice blends, or on a decadent note with the brioche monkey bread with caramel sauce and pecans. Those juice blends are offered at lunch as well, along with vegan choices and such dishes as a house pepper bacon BLT sandwich or Society Fish & Chips. There's an afternoon menu with lighter fare (and lighter prices) from 3 to 5 pm daily, and an extensive dinner menu, with food served until 11 pm Sunday through Thursday and 11:30 pm on Friday and Saturday. $ *Average main: $41* ⊠ *Encore, 3131 Las Vegas Blvd. S, North Strip* ☎ *702/770–5300* ⊕ *www.wynnlasvegas. com/Restaurants.*

THE PALAZZO

$$$$ ✕ **Carnevino Italian Steakhouse.** The giant bronze steer just inside the front
STEAKHOUSE   door of Chef Mario Batali's handsome restaurant attests to the primary
offering: melt-in-your-mouth beef. Steaks here are dry-aged, grilled until
the crust is slightly charred, then carved table-side by knowledgeable,
attentive servers. A favorite appetizer is the steak tartare, egg-free and
chopped to order. Fresh pastas, seafood, organic veal and pork, and
Colorado lamb are offered, as well as pretheater and tasting menus.
The fine wines are complimented by an equally impressive list of other
spirits, including beers, bourbons, and rums. When the bread arrives,
be sure to try the lardo, a savory spread made from pork fat, ginger,
allspice, and rosemary. The bar and more casual taverna serve lighter
fare daily, from noon until midnight. ⑤ *Average main: $46* ⊠ *The Pala-
zzo, 3325 Las Vegas Blvd. S, North Strip* ☎ *702/789–4141* ⊕ *www.
carnevino.com* ⊗ *No lunch in main dining room.*

$$ ✕ **I Love Burgers.** At lunchtime, many denizens of the surrounding mall
BURGER   like to relax and refuel in this large, lively restaurant that is short on
decor but long on flavor. Whet your appetite with the fried mac 'n'
cheese bites; crispy, dill tempura–battered fried pickle slices; or a trio
of sliders to share. There are several varieties of fries you can order
to accompany juicy beef or specialty burgers such as ground Wagyu
with truffle cheese. There are leaner choices, too, such as salmon, veg-
gie, turkey, and even buffalo burgers or soup and salad. Milk shakes,
slushies, and smoothies are addicting; especially the ones with booze.
A multitude of domestic, imported, and artisan beers are also available.
⑤ *Average main: $19* ⊠ *The Shoppes at Palazzo, 3327 Las Vegas Blvd.
S, North Strip* ☎ *702/242–2747* ⊕ *www.iloveburgers.com.*

$$$$ ✕ **Lavo.** The food at this Roman-styled see-and-be-seen restaurant/night-
ITALIAN   club often is overshadowed by the roaring club scene, but it's worth
a stop—especially if you go early to avoid the *thump thump* of the
music upstairs. The dishes, many of which are meant to be shared,
might include tuna tartare, Kobe beef carpaccio, and a lobster scampi-
style brick oven pizza. Entrées might feature grilled tuna with roasted
artichokes or a lobster stuffed with crabmeat. For dessert, try the Noce
cocktail with Nocello walnut liqueur, or the Oreo zeppole served with
a malted vanilla milk shake. There's also the Party Brunch from 2 pm
to 6 pm on Saturday, and the quieter Proper Brunch on Sunday. ⑤ *Av-
erage main: $38* ⊠ *The Palazzo, 3325 Las Vegas Blvd. S, North Strip*
☎ *702/791–1800* ⊕ *www.lavolv.com* ⊗ *No lunch.*

$$$$ ✕ **Morels French Steakhouse & Bistro.** Relaxed and dapper, Morels is Pala-
FRENCH   zzo's upscale yet unfussy all-day dining option. Its specialty is both tra-
ditional Parisian-inspired bistro fare and steak-house victuals. Except
for the pricey beef dishes, most of the food here is affordable by Strip
standards. And although the steak can be hit or miss, anything from
the seafood, cheese, and charcuterie bars is delicious, as well as dishes
such as crispy-skin Scottish salmon with bordelaise sauce, carrots, and
lentils. Cocktails are noteworthy as is the expansive (and expensive)
wine list, with more than 60 offerings—French, Italian, and Califor-
nian—available by the glass. Breakfast and weekend brunch are boffo.
■**TIP**→ VIP views of the Strip can be had from the patio (seasonal:

first-come, first-seated). $\boxed{S}$ *Average main: $42* ⊠ *The Palazzo, 3325 Las Vegas Blvd. S, North Strip* ☎ *702/607–6333* ⊕ *www.palazzo.com/Las-Vegas-Restaurants.*

$$$$ **✕SUSHISAMBA.** Come to this trendy, tricolor restaurant for its fresh
ASIAN sushi and sashimi, beautifully prepared and presented, with delightful dipping sauces and edible garnish. Dim lighting, hip music, voluptuous decor, and excellent cocktails complement the exotic fusion of flavors from Japan, Brazil, and Peru. A variety of small plates and brightly seasoned ceviches are served, as well as sizzling skewers of grilled meats, seafood, and vegetables. Try a side of purple-potato mash, coconut rice, or Peruvian corn with your tempura or temaki, and be sure to save room for yuzu tart cheesecake and house-made Peruvian donuts or ice cream. Try weekend brunch, or Samba Hour, from 4 to 7 pm every day but Saturday. $\boxed{S}$ *Average main: $43* ⊠ *The Palazzo, 3325 Las Vegas Blvd. S, North Strip* ☎ *702/607–0700* ⊕ *www.sushisamba.com.*

STRATOSPHERE

$$$$ **✕Top of the World.** Reserve a window-side table at twilight to see sunset
EUROPEAN melt into sparkling night while savoring Continental cuisine à la carte or from the four-course tasting menu (suggested wine pairings also listed). From 844 feet high, floor-to-ceiling windows display 360-degree views of the Vegas Valley as the entire 106th-floor dining room makes a complete revolution every 80 minutes. The jaw-dropping views are the big draw but the food is not overshadowed with a menu featuring such dishes as roasted Kurubuta pork belly with chimichurri and orange gastrique, a 10-ounce fillet with red wine sauce and wild mushrooms, or Colorado Rack of Lamb with Moroccan flavors. Generally quiet and romantic, the occasional bungee jumper hurtling past the windows from rooftop thrill rides provides some unexpected excitement. A stationary cocktail lounge for casual sipping is on the 107th floor. $\boxed{S}$ *Average main: $65* ⊠ *Stratosphere, 2000 Las Vegas Blvd. S, 106th fl., North Strip* ☎ *702/380–7711* ⊕ *www.topoftheworldlv.com* ⌨ *Reservations essential.*

THE VENETIAN

$$$$ **✕B&B Ristorante.** Ubiquitous food personality Mario Batali and his
ITALIAN trusty wine pro Joe Bastianich are the owners of this inviting (and underappreciated) tribute to the rustic foods of the Italian countryside. Along the Venetian's "restaurant row," B&B glows from within its dark-wood and leather confines (look for the bright orange Crocs on the host's podium). You can easily make a meal of several antipasti, with choices such as grilled octopus with limoncello vinaigrette, or warm lamb's tongue with chanterelles and a three-minute egg. Entrées might include crispy sweetbreads or olive oil–fried quail with mustard greens and mascarpone polenta. ■TIP➜ Batali and Bastianich also run the less expensive Otto Enoteca Pizzeria on St. Mark's Square in Venetian's Grand Canal Shoppes, where you can nosh on toothsome antipasti, pizza, cured meats, and artisanal cheeses while sipping on imported Italian wines. $\boxed{S}$ *Average main: $49* ⊠ *The Venetian, 3355 Las*

5

Vegas Blvd. S, North Strip ☏ *702/266–9977* ⊕ *www.bandbristorante. com* ⊘ *No lunch.*

$$$$ ✕ **Bouchon.** Ask many chefs to name their idol, and more than a few will
FRENCH cite French Laundry chef Thomas Keller, the star behind this stunning,
capacious French bistro and oyster bar in the Venezia Tower. Soaring
Palladian windows, antique lighting, a pewter-topped bar, and painted
tile lend a sophisticated take on French country design, a fitting setting
in which to dine on savory, rich cuisine. Menu options include classics
such as steak frites, mussels with white wine, and an extensive raw
bar. Finish with profiteroles, lemon tart, or crème caramel. A charming
garden outside is perfect for a post-meal stroll. Return for breakfast
or brunch, when you might try bread pudding–style French toast or
a smoked-salmon baguette. Bouchon has three free-standing bakeries
in the Venetian, offering breads, pastries, and confections. ⑤ *Average
main: $35* ⊠ *The Venetian, 3355 Las Vegas Blvd. S, Venezia Tower,
10th fl., North Strip* ☏ *702/414–6200* ⊕ *www.bouchonbistro.com.*

$$$$ ✕ **Delmonico Steakhouse.** Chef Emeril Lagasse gives a New Orleans touch
STEAKHOUSE to this big city–style steak house at the Venetian. Enter through 12-foot
oak doors. You'll find a sedately decorated, modern room in which to
relax and enjoy your slightly smoky, salty-sweet Bacon and Bourbon
Manhattan, along with appetizers such as butternut-squash ravioli;
Lagasse's signature barbeque shrimp, served with a fresh-baked rosemary biscuit; or the Caesar salad, prepared table-side for two. Among
the most popular entrées are the ample, tender cuts of beef, especially
the rib eye; and Emeril's Barbecue Salmon with potato and andouille
hash. When it's on the menu, don't miss the chocolate brioche bread
pudding for dessert. ⑤ *Average main: $48* ⊠ *The Venetian, 3355 Las
Vegas Blvd. S, North Strip* ☏ *702/414–3737* ⊕ *www.emerilsrestaurants.
com.*

$$$ ✕ **Grand Lux Cafe.** Warm earth tones, soft music and lighting, cloth
AMERICAN napkins, and marble-topped tables are an elegant milieu in which to
enjoy a glass of wine and mélange of appealing, freshly cooked flavors
and textures—Asian nachos, double-stuffed potato spring rolls, stacked
chicken quesadilla—24-hours a day. Located right off the main casino
floor, this convenient chain eatery offers eclectic menu items and famil-
iar crowd-pleasers: pizza, fried shrimp, BBQ chicken, burgers, BLTs,
and even wood-grilled filet mignon or rib eye. The "Lux" operates as a
subsidiary of The Cheesecake Factory, so not only is it a reliable option
for a budget-friendly meal, it also offers its signature cheesecake for
dessert. You can also get one to go in the adjoining bakery, as well as
coffee, pastries, and preordered food. ⑤ *Average main: $23* ⊠ *The Vene-
tian, 3355 Las Vegas Blvd. S, North Strip* ☏ *702/414–3888* ⊕ *www.
grandluxcafe.com* ⊂ *Also located in The Palazzo.*

$$$$ ✕ **TAO Asian Bistro & Nightclub.** The tunneled vestibule of this nightclub-
ASIAN cum-bistro is lined with stone tubs filled with water and rose petals,
leading patrons—including lots of celebrities, some of them hired to
host—into a dim space with black cobblestones, bamboo, and Buddhas
(one that's 20 feet tall is seated above a koi-filled pool). The quint-
essentially Asian decor compliments the expertly prepared sushi and
sashimi. Reserve a table early to enjoy dishes (spicy lobster roll with

black caviar, sake-braised shiitake mushrooms, roasted Thai chicken) in tranquillity before loud, young crowds and thumping music descend from the nightclub upstairs. ■TIP→ **Diners receive complimentary access to the nightclub, so ask your server for a stamp to stick around for cocktails, dancing, and celebrity-spotting.** [$] *Average main: $35* ⊠ *The Venetian, 3355 Las Vegas Blvd., North Strip* ☎ *702/388–8338* ⊕ *www.taorestaurantlv.com* ⊗ *No lunch.*

WYNN LAS VEGAS

$$$$ ✕ **Bartolotta Ristorante di Mare.** Fish
SEAFOOD flown in daily from the Mediterranean—complete with GPS tags, so location, temperature, and other conditions can be tracked along the way—are the hallmark of this elegant restaurant. It has a full bar and seating on the upper level, as well as a beautiful dining room downstairs and tables in cabanas along Wynn's Lake of Dreams. At the helm is two-time James Beard Award–winning Chef Paul Bartolotta, who serves his fish whole, to be filleted and plated at the table, or in dishes like Sicilian amberjack with radicchio and anchovy sauce or risotto with sea urchins and scallops. [$] *Average main: $85* ⊠ *Wynn Las Vegas, 3131 Las Vegas Blvd. S, North Strip* ☎ *702/248–3463, 702/770–3463* ⊕ *www.wynnlasvegas.com/ Restaurants* ⊗ *No lunch.*

> ### SWEET TREAT
>
> ✕ **Luv-it Frozen Custard.** Walking distance from the Stratosphere, this tiny take-out stand offers unbelievably delicious, velvety smooth frozen custard. The flavors change daily (check the website for the schedule), and sundaes are a popular offering—try the ever-popular Western, with hot fudge, caramel, and pecans or a Fruit Boat, with peach, pineapple, cherry, banana, marshmallow, and peanuts. It's been goin' strong since 1973. [$] *Average main: $5* ⊠ *505 E. Oakey Blvd., North Strip* ☎ *702/384-6452* ⊕ *www. luvitfrozencustard.com* ⊟ *No credit cards.*

$$$$ ✕ **The Country Club.** Removed from the din, this über-elegant, dark-wood
AMERICAN dining room is tucked down a corridor off the main casino floor. This clubby restaurant caters to golfers and is a locals' power-lunch spot, but it's a place every person can enjoy, especially when the weather is conducive to dining on the patio, where you can gaze at the huge waterfall cascading near the 18th hole at Wynn Golf Course. A mix of popular classics with dishes reflecting Chef Carlos Guia's New Orleans past are on the menu: shrimp and grits or kabocha squash ravioli, a King Creole burger, or County Club Sandwich. Seafood, poultry, chops, and charbroiled meats—veal porterhouse, for example, or a creole-spiced bison rib eye—are on the dinner menu. ■TIP→ **Book a table online and splurge for the Sunday brunch with live jazz, carving and shellfish stations, artisanal cheeses, and cured meats.** [$] *Average main: $55* ⊠ *Wynn Las Vegas, 3131 Las Vegas Blvd. S, North Strip* ☎ *702/248–3463* ⊕ *www.wynnlasvegas.com/Restaurants* ⊗ *Closed Sun. No dinner Mon. and Tue. No lunch Sat.*

CHEAP EATS

Don't forget about Sin City's terrific hole-in-the-wall dives, inexpensive regional chains, and cheap-and-cheerful take-out counters that serve tasty treats at rock-bottom prices.

✕ **Fatburger.** Billing itself immodestly "the Last Great Hamburger Stand," this fast-food joint across from Monte Carlo (with about a dozen locales elsewhere around town) cooks up toothsome charbroiled burgers, hefty chile dogs, and crispy "fat fries." The Strip location is open 24 hours. $ *Average main: $9* ⊠ *3763 Las Vegas Blvd. S, South Strip* ☎ *702/736–4733.*

✕ **In-N-Out.** The simple menu of fresh burgers, just-cut fries, and milk shakes makes this affordable West Coast fast-food joint a cult fave. If you're extra hungry (and we mean seriously so), go "off menu" and order a "4x4" (four beef patties with four slices of American cheese on a freshly baked bun), and maybe order it "animal style," with a mustard-grilled beef patty and extra spread with grilled onions. If you go through the drive-through you can watch them cutting the potatoes for fries, and choose your food packed for eating in the car (complete with lap mat) or taking out. $ *Average main: $7* ⊠ *4888 Dean Martin Dr., West Side* ☎ *800/786–1000* ⊕ *www.in-n-out.com.*

✕ **Jason's Deli.** Soups, sandwiches—including hero-style muffuletas and po'boys—and salads star on Jason's extensive menu, which focuses on healthful and often organic ingredients. Devotees swear by the "Ciabatta Bing": oven-roasted turkey, roasted tomatoes, purple onions, guacamole, Swiss cheese, and field greens on a ciabatta roll. $ *Average main: $9* ⊠ *3910 S. Maryland Pkwy., University District* ☎ *702/893–9799* ⊕ *www.jasonsdeli.com.*

$$$$
MEDITERRANEAN

✕ **La Cave Wine & Food Hideaway.** This intimate, casual restaurant focuses on wine and Mediterranean-inspired small plates such as sweet and salty bacon-wrapped dates with blue-cheese fondue and beef carpaccio with arugula and truffle aioli. The remarkable wine list reflects global selections, with an emphasis on Europe. The menu groups the offerings by provenance and preparation: From the Sea, Farm, Oven, Garden, Grill, Butcher, and so forth. A fiery artichoke, roasted pepper, and olives flatbread is ideal for sharing, while vegetable dishes, including warm salt-roasted beets with whipped goat cheese and pistachio, satisfy those with dietary restrictions. There also are charcuterie and cheese selections, and desserts such as beignets with raspberry jam and crème anglaise. ■ TIP➜ Select from their wine and beer flights for variety and value. $ *Average main: $36* ⊠ *Wynn Las Vegas, 3131 Las Vegas Blvd. S, North Strip* ☎ *702/770–7100, 877/321–9966* ⊕ *www.wynnlasvegas.com.*

$$$
AMERICAN

✕ **Tableau.** Isolated from the busier parts of the Wynn, this bright, airy restaurant overlooks a serene pool and well-manicured garden off the gleaming Tower Suites lobby. For breakfast you might try duck hash and eggs, banana sour cream pancakes drizzled with warm maple syrup, or eggs Benedict with smoked salmon and chive hollandaise. For lunch, try items such as the soft-shell crab sandwich or the steak salad with port wine onions and crispy potatoes. Or splurge for the fabulous Sunday brunch. $ *Average main: $26 ⊠ Wynn Las Vegas, 3131 Las Vegas Blvd. S, North Strip* ☎ *702/770–3463* ⊕ *www.wynnlasvegas.com/ Restaurants* ⊗ *No dinner.*

$$$$ ✕ **Wing Lei.** With all the panache of an Asian royal palace, this recently

CHINESE renovated fine-dining restaurant serves some of the choicest Chinese

Fodor'sChoice food on the Strip. Chefs present contemporary French-inspired cuisine

★ that blends the Cantonese, Shanghai, and Sichuan traditions. The decadent Imperial Peking Duck dinner, carved table-side, is a showstopper, but don't overlook options that could include prawns with caramelized walnuts and a honey-cream sauce, garlic beef tenderloin with black-pepper sauce, or the amazing Three Cup Sea Bass with ginger-soy reduction. Vegetarian, vegan, and allergen menus are available upon request. $ *Average main: $44 ⊠ Wynn Las Vegas, 3131 Las Vegas Blvd. S, North Strip* ☎ *702/248–3463* ⊕ *www.wynnlasvegas.com/Restaurants* ⊗ *No lunch.*

DOWNTOWN

Even during its heyday as the city's casino-gaming hot spot, Downtown was never much of a haven for gourmands. As the Strip and other parts of the city have become renowned for fantastic dining, Downtown's culinary reputation has become even more eclipsed. However, Downtown's big revitalization over the past few years includes a budding restaurant scene with a few places that are on par with the big Strip properties.

$$$$ ✕ **Andiamo Steakhouse.** This offshoot of Joe Vicari's nine restaurants in

ITALIAN the Detroit area is right at home in the loosely Detroit-theme D Las Vegas. There's atmosphere aplenty; customers enter through a long, arched brick passage to emerge into a candlelit room staffed by tux-clad waiters. And the food matches the elegant aura, with such starters as a rich lobster bisque with butter-poached lobster, or banana peppers with house-made sausage; entrées represent both Italian and stockyard cuisine with a half dozen steaks (and even a Pat LaFrieda Burger) along with Italian pastas and fish, chicken, and veal dishes. $ *Average main: $50 ⊠ The D Las Vegas, 301 Fremont St., Downtown* ☎ *702/388–2220* ⊕ *www.TheD.com.*

$$ ✕ **Doña Maria.** You'll forget you're in Las Vegas after a few minutes

MEXICAN in this relaxed and unpretentious downtown cantina with two locations in the area (the other is near Summerlin). Stop in on a Wednesday night and you might see a crowd gathered for the *fútbol* game on satellite-provided Mexican TV. All of the combinations and specials are good, but the best play here is to order tamales; in particular, the enchilada-style tamale (with red or green sauce), for which Doña Maria is justly renowned. You also won't go wrong with the *queso fundido con chorizo* (melted cheese with sausage). $ *Average main: $15 ⊠ 910 Las Vegas Blvd. S, Downtown* ☎ *702/382–6538* ⊕ *www. donamariatamales.com* $ *Average main: $15 ⊠ 3250 N. Tenaya Way, Summerlin* ☎ *702/656–1600.*

$$	✕ **Eat.** Eat may serve only breakfast and lunch but the food is so hearty
MODERN	(and so uniquely appealing), you may not feel the need for dinner.
AMERICAN	Among the specialties are cinnamon biscuits with warm strawberry
compote, shrimp and grits with bacon, and the DWBLTA, thick toasted
sourdough bracketing thick-sliced bacon, lettuce, tomato, and avocado.
■**TIP**➔ **The Killer Grilled Cheese with Kick Ass Tomato Soup lives up
to its name on both counts.** Ⓢ*Average main: $17* ✉*707 Carson St.,
Downtown* ☎*702/534–1515* ⊕*EatDTLV.com* ◷ *No dinner.*

$$$$	✕**Golden Steer.** In a town where restaurants come and go almost as
STEAKHOUSE	quickly as visitors' cash, the longevity of this steak house, opened
in 1958, is itself a recommendation. Both locals and visitors adore
this classic steak house with red-leather seating, polished dark wood,
and stained-glass windows for the huge slabs of well-prepared meat.
Steak, ribs, shrimp scampi, and Italian classics such as veal marsala
and chicken parmigiana are particularly popular. Some of the booths
are reputed to be the same ones where Elvis and members of the Rat
Pack—not to mention some infamous mob rats—used to sit. Ⓢ*Average
main: $45* ✉*308 W. Sahara Ave., Downtown* ☎*702/384–4470* ⊕*www.
goldensteersteakhouselasvegas.com* ◷ *No lunch.*

$$$$	✕**Hugo's Cellar.** Four Queens is home to Hugo's, a venerable restaurant
AMERICAN	that dates to the Rat Pack era. The "cellar" aspect (it's about a half-
Fodor'sChoice	flight below ground) gives it a cozy feel, as do old Vegas touches like
★	table-side salad preparation with every dinner (you choose what you
want from the cart), a red rose for each woman, and formal, impeccable
service. The menu presents a '60s vibe, with dishes like Duck Anise
Flambe, chateaubriand, and lobster for two, and table-side Cherries
Jubilee and bananas Foster. But entrées are prepared with modern sen-
sibilities and are joined by new-era choices like a grilled stuffed porta-
bella mushroom and ahi tuna. Ⓢ*Average main: $50* ✉*Four Queens,
202 Fremont St., Downtown* ☎*702/385–4011* ⊕*www.HugosCellar.
com* ⌫ *Reservations essential.*

$$	✕**La Comida.** This Baja-rustic restaurant and lounge from Michael and
MEXICAN	Jenna Morton, late of the N9NE Group, serves updated Mexican food
on what looks like Abuelita's old china with mismatched furniture and
plenty of depictions of the Virgin of Guadalupe. The cut-from-the-cob
Mexican street corn or tostada with tuna, red onions, and microgreens
are a great way to start; consider moving on to Gulf shrimp with butternut squash, chorizo, cherry tomatoes, and roasted corn, or mesquite-
smoked pork shoulder with plantain chips. And don't forget to try a
tamarind or prickly-pear margarita. Ⓢ*Average main: $20* ✉*100 6th
St., Downtown* ☎*702/463–9900* ⊕*LaComidaLV.com.*

$$$	✕**Le Thai.** Noodles are the house specialty at this intimate restaurant in
THAI	the Fremont East district of Downtown. While most of the dishes are
Thai (try the Awesome Noodles; the name isn't hyperbole), others lean
more toward Chinese and Japanese influences. Also worth trying: the
decadent Short Rib Fried Rice. Whatever you order, request "spicy"
dishes at your own risk; chefs here spice things up the way they'd like
to eat them, not the way you'd like to eat them. The restaurant itself
is truly tiny, with only a handful of tables and seating at the bar, but a
large patio with pergola covering is complete with misters for summer

and heaters for winter. $Average main: $25 ✉ 523 Fremont St. E, Downtown ☏ 702/778–0888 ⊕ www.lethaivegas.com ⊘ Closed Sun.

$$ ✕ **Lillie's Asian Cuisine.** This longtime Golden Nugget favorite specializes
ASIAN   in Cantonese and Szechwan dishes but its menu is really Pan-Asian, with such dishes as chicken satay, vegetable tempura, and sushi in addition to old favorites like beef chow-fun, General Tso's chicken, and sweet-and-sour pork. There's a touch of the authentic in specialties such as fish maw and crabmeat soup, and like many Chinese restaurants in Las Vegas it's open late, until midnight. $Average main: $20 ✉ Golden Nugget Hotel & Casino, 129 E. Fremont St., Downtown ☏ 702/386–8131 ⊕ www.goldennugget.com ⊘ No lunch.

$$ ✕ **Pizza Rock.** Eleven-time world pizza champion Tony Gemignani
PIZZA   installed four ovens in this heavily renovated industrial-chic space in the Downtown Third district so he could produce all styles of pizza: Neapolitan, Romano, American, New York, classic Italian, Californian, New York/New Haven, Sicilian, and Chicago. Don't neglect the starters, though; the fried green beans with garlic and olive oil and Moretti-battered fried artichokes are worth the trip alone. It's open until 2 am on Friday and Saturday. $Average main: $20 ✉ 201 N. 3rd St., Downtown ☏ 702/385–0838 ⊕ www.PizzaRockLasVegas.com.

$$ ✕ **Second Street Grill.** The art deco–style dining room in this venerable
SEAFOOD   Downtown casino restaurant is dark and intimate, with oversize chairs and elegant wood paneling, and the menu is much more new Vegas than old, with a Pacific Rim emphasis. There's decent variety in the menu, though, with dishes such as scallop and shrimp dim sum and Peking duck and shrimp tacos joined by a Buffalo mozzarella salad and a selection of steaks and chops. $Average main: $19 ✉ Fremont Hotel and Casino, 200 E. Fremont St., Downtown ☏ 702/385–6277 ⊕ www.fremontcasino.com ⊘ Closed Tues. and Wed.

$$$ ✕ **Triple George Grill.** You won't find too much in the way of nouvelle
AMERICAN   flourishes or ultramod decor at this San Francisco–style restaurant, and that's just how both visitors and locals prefer it—the elegant dining room is a favorite haunt for power-lunching and hobnobbing. Triple George is known for its commendably prepared traditional American fare such as oysters on the half shell, classic "wedge" salad, oh-so-tender pot roast, and truly stellar sourdough. Seafood and chops dominate the fancier parts of the menu, from shellfish cioppino and traditional fish-and-chips to Filet Oscar and a hefty pan-seared porcini-crusted rib eye. ■TIP➔ **The vegan menu is one of the best in town.** $Average main: $30 ✉ 201 N. 3rd St., Downtown ☏ 702/384–2761 ⊕ www.triplegeorgegrill.com.

PARADISE ROAD

HARD ROCK HOTEL & CASINO

$$$$ ✕ **35 Steaks + Martinis.** The key number at this always-buzzing hot spot
STEAKHOUSE   is 35. All steaks are aged for at least 35 days, and the signature dish, the Tomahawk, is a 35-day-aged, 35-ounce prime steak "carved for two or just for you." The menu includes a bevy of openers such as

charcuterie, crab cake, and a whole artichoke with boursin and spinach and tomato dip. Further along in the meal you might opt for a salmon, chicken, or lamb. Steaks, of course, reign supreme, and you can add lobster, king crab legs, or prawns to any order. Drinks here are exquisite, and include flavor-infused martinis and a stellar wine list (dubbed "Wines that Rock"). ■ TIP→ **Get a complimentary wine pour, from 5 to 6 pm daily.** ⑤ *Average main: $69* ⊠ *Hard Rock Hotel & Casino, 4455 Paradise Rd., Paradise Road* ☎ *702/693–5000* ⊕ *www.hardrockhotel. com* ⊘ *No lunch.*

$$$$
AMERICAN

╳ **Culinary Dropout.** Five-time James Beard Award finalist for Outstanding Restaurateur Sam Fox has put a unique stamp on this irreverent hangout inside the Hard Rock. Menu items range from such whimsical choices as Yesterday's Soup, house potato chips with onion dip, and the Cheap House Salad, to culinary wonders including *jamon Iberico*, burrata with persimmon, and Korean-style rib eye. During brunch on weekends, consider the Cap'n Crunch Crusted French Toast, a chicken-fried pork chop, or smoked salmon hash brown with salmon crème fraîche. ⑤ *Average main: $35* ⊠ *Hard Rock Hotel & Casino, 4455 Paradise Rd., Paradise Road* ☎ *702/522–8100* ⊕ *www.hardrockhotel.com.*

$$
ECLECTIC

╳ **Mr. Lucky's.** The hippest casino coffee shop in Las Vegas is still inside the Hard Rock Hotel, overlooking the main gaming area. Light-wood floors and vintage rock-and-roll posters highlight this bubbly, circular café. You can have a Rehab Omelet, flatbread burger, or pasta. More substantial items include the Hot Rotisserie Turkey Plate, rice bowls, and prime rib. Or you could go for The King—14 banana pancakes, 14 strips of bacon, a peanut butter glaze, and maple syrup. Lucky Shots and Spiked Milk Shakes add to the fun. This place is open 24/7. ⑤ *Average main: $19* ⊠ *Hard Rock Hotel & Casino, 4455 Paradise Rd., Paradise Road* ☎ *702/693–5000* ⊕ *www.hardrockhotel.com.*

$$$$
JAPANESE

╳ **Nobu.** Executive Chef Nobu Matsuhisa has replicated the decor and menu of his Manhattan Nobu in this slick restaurant with bamboo pillars, a seaweed wall, and birch trees. Dishes might include spicy Kumamoto oyster with Nobu sauce, monkfish pâté with caviar, rock shrimp tempura, and Maine lobster with wasabi-pepper sauce. The menu comprises small or moderate-size plates, making Nobu perfect for sharing, but an easy place to drop a wad of cash (as all those artful food presentations add up). If you're feeling brave (and flush), opt for the Omakase multicourse tasting menu and let the chef make the decisions for you. ⑤ *Average main: $49* ⊠ *Hard Rock Hotel & Casino, 4455 Paradise Rd., Paradise Road* ☎ *702/693–5000* ⊕ *www.hardrockhotel. com/las-vegas-restaurants* ⊘ *No lunch.*

$$$
MEXICAN

╳ **Pink Taco.** Nothing inside the Hard Rock Hotel is boring, and that goes for this over-the-top take on a Mexican cantina, which evokes a playful, even rollicking, vibe. The Tex-Mex food takes a decided backseat to the party scene, which includes a huge four-sided bar, patio doors that open onto the hotel's elaborate pool area, and waitresses in low-cut tops. Still, the grub is good. Fill up on lobster tacos with mango pico de gallo, chile relleno, slow-roasted pork carnitas, and enchiladas with chicken, steak, or shrimp. There are low-cal, vegetarian, vegan, and gluten-free choices as well. Come during happy hour (weekdays from

4 to 7 at the bar) for $5 beers and $5 to $9 food specials. ⑤ *Average main: $22 ✉ Hard Rock Hotel & Casino, 4455 Paradise Rd., Paradise Road ☎ 702/693–5000 ⊕ www.hardrockhotel.com.*

RENAISSANCE LAS VEGAS HOTEL

$$$$
STEAKHOUSE

✕ **ENVY Steakhouse.** A hip restaurant at the elegant Renaissance Las Vegas, ENVY offers an update of the steak-house concept. The glamorous contemporary dining room is bathed in jewel tones, and the young and knowledgeable staff is quick to explain the creative cuisine or suggest wines from the 1,500-bottle repertoire. Among the sides, consider the positively addictive truffle-Parmesan fries; pair them with a 40-ounce Tomahawk chop, or any of a number of more average-size steaks. Other choices include pan-seared Chilean sea bass with a truffle-butter crust, braised oxtail spaghetti, and vegetarian lasagna. ENVY's Seafood Crepes are a decadent choice at Sunday brunch. ⑤ *Average main: $39 ✉ Renaissance Las Vegas, 3400 Paradise Rd., Paradise Road ☎ 702/784–5716 ⊕ www.envysteakhouse.com ☽ No lunch.*

NON-CASINO RESTAURANTS

$$$
MEDITERRANEAN

✕ **Firefly Tapas Kitchen.** As the name suggests, this hip bistro focuses on small plates reflecting most of the world's cuisines, few of which cost more than $10. Order a few and you've got a meal, made even better with one of Firefly's signature sangrias or mojitos, available by the glass or pitcher. On any given day, options might include ham-and-cheese croquettes, meatballs in a sherry-tomato sauce, marinated and grilled octopus, and shrimp in lemon-garlic-butter sauce. There are usually a few heartier entrées, such as a rib-eye steak or paella, offered as well. For dessert, order the rich chocolate-and-cherry bread pudding with a port wine reduction. Dine in the colorful dining room or outside on the cheerful patio. They have locations in Henderson and the West Side, too. ⑤ *Average main: $29 ✉ 3824 Paradise Rd., Paradise Road ☎ 702/369–3971 ⊕ www.fireflylv.com.*

$$
GERMAN

✕ **Hofbräuhaus Las Vegas.** Enjoy a heavy dose of kitsch at this gargantuan offshoot of Munich's most famous brewery. The interior beer garden is the perfect spot to down a brew in those notorious liter mugs, especially on too-hot Vegas evenings. Pair your beer with hearty Bavarian classics, including Bavarian potato soup with sausage, Wiener schnitzel, goulash, and *Schweinebraten,* or updated dishes such as Caesar salad with pretzel croutons. For dessert, try apple strudel or Black Forest chocolate cake. They've covered the oompah here, too: bands brought in from Germany keep things as lively as they are back in Munich. ⑤ *Average main: $19 ✉ 4510 Paradise Rd., Paradise Road ☎ 702/853–2337 ⊕ www.hofbrauhauslasvegas.com.*

$$
INDIAN

✕ **India Oven.** You have to brave a neighborhood of illicit-looking 24-hour "massage" parlors to find this remarkably natty restaurant that serves surprisingly good food. It's in a shopping center north of the former Sahara casino, site of the soon-to-be opened SLS Resort, and the space is filled with imported antiquities. Tandoori meats and naan bread are prepared in the tandoor (oven), and other specialties include lamb korma with cashews, almonds, and raisins, as well as Goa-style fish curry with an aromatic coconut sauce. For dessert, try the homemade kulfi, also known as pistachio ice cream. $ *Average main: $19* ⊠ *2218 Paradise Rd., Paradise Road* ☎ *702/366–0222* ⊕ *www. indiaovenlasvegas.com.*

$$$$ ✕ **Marrakech.** Sprawl out on soft floor cushions and feel like a pam-
MOROCCAN pered pasha as belly dancers shake it up in a cozy Middle Eastern–style "tent" with a fabric-covered ceiling and eye-catching mosaics. The $45 prix-fixe feast is a six-course affair that you eat with your hands; it usually includes Moroccan-spiced shrimp scampi, vegetable salad, len-til soup, Cornish game hen, lamb shish kebab, and the tasty dessert *B'stilla,* which is baked phyllo dough layered with apples, peaches, and pecans. Algerian wines flow freely in this upbeat spot where servers wear Moroccan robes and patrons are invited to join the belly dancers if they feel the urge. $ *Average main: $40* ⊠ *3900 Paradise Rd., Para-dise Road* ☎ *702/737–5611* ⊕ *www.marrakechvegas.com* ☾ *No lunch.*

$$$$ ✕ **Roy's.** A popular import from Hawaii, Roy's is plush without feeling
HAWAIIAN pretentious or overdone—a good bet for a relaxed, elegant meal. You enter the restaurant along a torch-lighted lane, and a highly profes-sional, friendly staff works the bustling dining room. Executive Chef Roy Yamaguchi has become synonymous with creative Hawaiian fusion fare, such as the ahi poke, lilikoi pear salad, or sesame-crusted ono. There's a full sushi bar, as well. The food bar overlooking the action in the kitchen is perfect for those dining alone. On Monday nights in winter, try the three-course price-fixe meal for $36.95. $ *Average main: $36* ⊠ *620 E. Flamingo Rd., Paradise Road* ☎ *702/691–2053* ⊕ *www. roysrestaurant.com* ☾ *No lunch.*

$$$$ ✕ **Table 34.** Run by Laurie Kendrick and Stan Carroll, two highly
ECLECTIC respected Vegas chefs who trained under Wolfgang Puck, this intimate, modern restaurant with clean lines, blond-wood floors, and high ceil-ings looks like something you'd find in California wine country. Espe-cially good among the reasonably priced, outstanding bistro creations are the fresh pastas and thin-crust pizzas (try the one topped with pro-sciutto, figs, and blue cheese). Entrées such as herb-roasted chicken with apple-sage dressing and all-beef meatloaf with mashed potatoes and onion gravy each score high marks. An impressive wine list has nearly 100 selections. Note: the restaurant sits just south of where Paradise Road intersects with Interstate 215 (south of the airport), and the con-stant planes overhead contribute a bit of unpleasant noise. $ *Average main: $39* ⊠ *600 E. Warm Springs Rd., Paradise Road* ☎ *702/263–0034* ☾ *Closed Sun. No lunch Sat.*

EAST SIDE AND UNIVERSITY DISTRICT

UNIVERSITY DISTRICT

$$ ✕ **Blueberry Hill.** This local mini-chain feels a bit like Denny's but serves
DINER far superior food, including hearty Mexican specialties, fruit-topped pancakes and waffles, and a number of "diet delight"–type platters. Blueberry Hill has four locales within a short drive of the Strip, two of

them open 24 hours. 💲 *Average main: $15* ✉ *1505 E. Flamingo Rd., University District* ☎ *702/696–9666* ⊕ *www.blueberryhillrestaurants. com.*

$$
BRITISH

✕**Crown & Anchor British Pub.** With 24-hour service and graveyard specials, Crown & Anchor is uniquely Las Vegas (and a favorite haunt of students from nearby UNLV). Most of the food is British, including the steak-and-kidney pie, bangers and mash, and authentic fish-and-chips. Sandwiches with American and British flavors are plenty, and nightly specials make this spot even more of a bargain proposition. There are beers from all over the world and a "shoppe" selling Anglophile favorites like Branston pickle. The decor and faux-cottage exterior are decidedly British, and special events add to the fun: on New Year's Eve the celebration starts when it's midnight in the United Kingdom, which is 4 pm in Las Vegas. The Little Crown & Anchor on Spring Mountain Road is, as the name implies, a smaller version. 💲 *Average main: $12* ✉ *1350 E. Tropicana Ave., University District* ☎ *702/739–8676* ⊕ *www.crownandanchorlv.com.*

EAST SIDE

$$
MEXICAN

✕**Lindo Michoacán.** Javier Barajas, the congenial owner and host of this colorful cantina chain, named it for his home in Mexico. He presents outstanding specialties that he learned to cook while growing up in the culinary capital of Michoacán. Many menu items are named for his relatives, including *flautas Mama Chelo* (corn tortillas filled with chicken). Michoacán is known for its carnitas, so don't miss them. Or try the *cabrito birria de chivo* (roasted goat with red mole sauce). Guacamole is made table-side. Finish with the flan, a silken wonder. Barajas has two other locations around the city, and has had a hand in two other similar restaurants—Bonito Michoacán and Viva Michoacán—on Decatur Boulevard and Sunset Road, respectively. 💲 *Average main: $19* ✉ *2655 E. Desert Inn Rd., East Side* ☎ *702/735–6828* ⊕ *www.lindomichoacan.com* 💲 *Average main: $19* ✉ *10082 W. Flamingo Rd., West Side* ☎ *702/838–9990* 💲 *Average main: $19* ✉ *7870 W. Tropical Pkwy., North Side* ☎ *702/385–4636* 💲 *Average main: $19* ✉ *645 Carnegie St., Henderson* ☎ *702/837–6828* 💲 *Average main: $19* ✉ *3715 S. Decatur Blvd., West Side* ☎ *702/257–6810.* 💲 *Average main: $19* ✉ *2061 W. Sunset Rd., Henderson* ☎ *702/492–9888*

$$$
THAI
Fodor'sChoice
★

✕**Lotus of Siam.** This simple Thai restaurant has attained near-fanatical cult status leaving some to wonder what's all the fuss? Consider the starter of marinated prawns, which are wrapped with bacon and rice-paper crepes, then deep-fried and served with a tangy sweet-and-sour sauce. For a main course, try dishes such as charbroiled beef liver mixed with green onion and chile, or the chicken and vegetables with Issan-style red curry. Be warned—this is some of the spiciest food you'll ever try. But another of Lotus's surprises is the phenomenal wine list, on which you might find a vintage to cool your palate. 💲 *Average main: $25* ✉ *953 E. Sahara Ave., East Side* ☎ *702/735–3033* ⊕ *www. saipinchutima.com* ⊘ *No lunch weekends.*

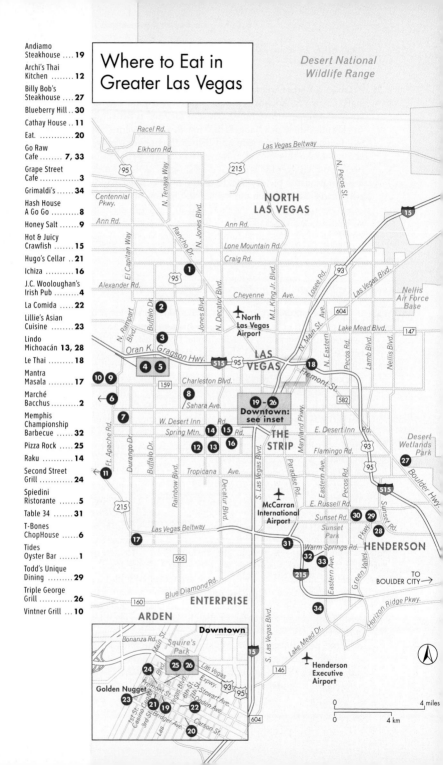

Where to Eat in Greater Las Vegas

Desert National Wildlife Range

Racel Rd.

Elkhorn Rd.

Las Vegas Beltway

Centennial Pkwy.

NORTH LAS VEGAS

Ann Rd.

Ann Rd.

Lone Mountain Rd.

Craig Rd.

Alexander Rd.

Cheyenne Ave.

North Las Vegas Airport

Lake Mead Blvd.

Nellis Air Force Base

Oran K. Gragson Hwy.

LAS VEGAS

Charleston Blvd.

Downtown: see inset

Sahara Ave.

W. Desert Inn Rd.

Spring Mtn. Rd.

THE STRIP

E. Desert Inn Rd.

Desert Wetlands Park

Flamingo Rd.

Tropicana Ave.

McCarran International Airport

E. Russell Rd.

Sunset Rd.

Sunset Park

HENDERSON

Las Vegas Beltway

Warm Springs Rd.

BOULDER CITY

ENTERPRISE

Blue Diamond Rd.

ARDEN

Horizon Ridge Pkwy.

TO BOULDER CITY →

Downtown

Bonanza Rd.

Squire's Park

Golden Nugget

Henderson Executive Airport

0   4 miles

0   4 km

$$ ✕**Memphis Championship Barbecue.** Barbecue the old-fashioned way:
BARBECUE that's what fans are looking for, and that's what Memphis Champi-
onship Barbecue delivers. The owner–founder, a winner of numerous
barbecue competitions, hails from Murphysboro, Illinois, which is
between St. Louis and Memphis. If you've got a big appetite—or a
big family—try Mama Faye's Down Home Supper, a family-style din-
ner for four; you won't go away hungry. Other choices include burnt
ends, barbecued pork shoulder, rib-eye steak, and fried or blackened
catfish. Oh, and on the side, treat yourself to some fried dill pickles.
There's another location out near Nellis Air Force Base. $ *Average
main: $16* ✉ *2250 E. Warm Springs Rd., East Side* ☎ *702/260–6909*
⊕ *www.memphis-bbq.com* $ *Average main: $16* ✉ *4379 Las Vegas
Blvd. N, North Side* ☎ *702/644–0000* $ *Average main: $16* ✉ *1401
S. Rainbow Blvd., Summerlin* ☎ *702/254–0520.*

$$$$ ✕**Pamplemousse.** The name, which is French for "grapefruit," was
FRENCH chosen on a whim by the late singer—and restaurant regular—Bobby
Darin. The dominant color at this old-school restaurant notable for its
kitschy pink-glowing sign is burgundy, orchestral music is played over
the stereo system, and the food is classic French. An elaborate crudité
basket sets the tone for the good things to come. Specialties include
roast duckling with cranberry and Chambord sauce and grilled wild
salmon with champagne sauce; a five-course prix-fixe menu is avail-
able for $56. $ *Average main: $39* ✉ *400 E. Sahara Ave., East Side*
☎ *702/733–2066* ⊕ *www.pamplemousserestaurant.com* ⌣ *Reserva-
tions essential* ⊗ *Closed Mon. No lunch.*

BOULDER HIGHWAY

$$$$ ✕**Billy Bob's Steak House.** Big food is the name of the game at this giddy,
STEAKHOUSE locally beloved steak joint at Sam's Town, known as much for its campy
Old West decor as it is for its genuinely juicy chops. The massive slabs
of bone-in rib eye, porterhouse, and prime rib could feed a rodeo and
the loaded baked potato is mammoth (although there are more mod-
est choices for more modest appetites). And then there's dessert: the
chocolate éclairs are a foot long, and the chocolate cake could fill up a
good chunk of the Grand Canyon. Sharing is recommended. A porch
area adjacent to the bar provides a great view of the Sunset Stampede,
the animatronic and laser show in the resort's indoor Mystic Falls Park.
$ *Average main: $32* ✉ *Sam's Town Hotel and Gambling Hall, 5111
Boulder Hwy., Boulder Strip* ☎ *702/456–7777* ⊕ *www.samstownlv.com*
⊗ *No lunch.*

HENDERSON

GREEN VALLEY RANCH RESORT & SPA

$$$ ✕**Tides Oyster Bar.** For affordable seafood, this sleek update of a classic
SEAFOOD coffee shop does the trick. The space is groovy and inviting, with a long
stone counter facing the kitchen and big-screen TVs showing sporting
events. Here you can sit on a blond-wood bar stool and slurp clams and

oysters on the half shell or a dinner-size bowl of gumbo. A particular specialty is the traditional pan roast of crab, shrimp, or lobster (or all three), prepared in an old-timey steam kettle with tomato, herbs, butter, and brandy. Also consider the all-you-can-eat crab leg dinner for $29.95. $ *Average main: $21* ⊠ *Green Valley Ranch, 2300 Paseo Verde Pkwy., Henderson* ☎ *702/617–7075* ⊕ *greenvalleyranch.sclv.com.*

HENDERSON NON-CASINO RESTAURANTS

$$ ╳ **Grimaldi's.** A branch of the legendary coal-fired pizza-baker nestled
PIZZA beneath the Brooklyn Bridge, this casual little joint in Henderson (with
FAMILY four other outposts in the valley) doesn't quite conjure up the atmosphere of the original, despite exposed-brick walls and red-checked tablecloths—it's in a suburban strip shopping center, after all—but it does have a wine list and a martini menu. What counts, of course, is the pizza, and in this regard, Grimaldi's deserves high praise. The oven-hot pies come in three sizes and with such staple toppings as spicy sausage, meatballs, and ricotta cheese and more updated ones like baby spinach and jalapeños. Finish off your meal with a cannoli or some flavor-of-the-month cheesecake. $ *Average main: $15* ⊠ *9595 S. Eastern Ave., Henderson* ☎ *702/657–9400* ⊕ *www.grimaldispizzeria.com* $ *Average main: $15* ⊠ *750 S. Rampart Blvd., Summerlin* ☎ *702/479–1351* ⊕ *www.grimaldispizza.com.*

$$$$ ╳ **Todd's Unique Dining.** What's really unique (for Vegas) about this inti-
ECLECTIC mate spot a short drive southeast of the airport is that artful, creative contemporary cuisine is served in an easygoing space with an unpretentious vibe. The dining room has been updated but still is decorated simply, perhaps to show off colorful fare such as goat-cheese wontons with raspberry-basil sauce, and duck breast with pomegranate red wine sauce and mashed sweet potatoes. This place, from a former Strip executive chef, used to be something of a sleeper, but it's becoming better known, so book a couple of days ahead if you want to dine Thursday through Saturday. $ *Average main: $39* ⊠ *4350 E. Sunset Rd., Henderson* ☎ *702/259–8633* ⊕ *www.toddsunique.com* ⊗ *Closed Sun. No lunch.*

WEST SIDE AND SUMMERLIN

WEST SIDE CASINO RESTAURANTS

GOLD COAST HOTEL AND CASINO

$$ ╳ **Ping Pang Pong.** Delicious regional (mostly Cantonese) fare, includ-
CHINESE ing marvelous dim sum made fresh daily, compels discerning diners—many who hail from Vegas's large Asian community—to brave the smoky, low-roller's gaming area of the Gold Coast. Named for three characters in Puccini's opera *Turandot* (Pong is head chef of the imperial kitchen), this well-regarded restaurant comprises a pair of circular dining rooms decked with red lanterns. ▪TIP→ **Request a table in the back of the left-hand dining room to avoid casino noise, open-kitchen clatter, and take-out traffic.** Order authentically prepared dishes such

as minced squab–lettuce cups, Empire seafood stew, preserved-egg porridge, or fresh, braised abalone, along with a glass of chrysanthemum iced tea and sweet pineapple buns for dessert, soft and warm from the oven. The lobster Macau (in caper-butter sauce) also has plenty of fans. Chefs will cater to customers' requests for small, unique offerings not on the menu, as long as the ingredients are on hand. The restaurant is open nightly until 3 am. $ *Average main: $19* ⊠ *Gold Coast Hotel and Casino, 4000 W. Flamingo Rd., West Side* ☎ *702/247–8136* ⊕ *www.goldcoastcasino.com/dine.*

PALMS CASINO RESORT

$$$$ ✕ **Alizé.** This fine French restaurant with soaring glass walls set high
FRENCH atop the Palms Resort offers one of the best views of the city, includ-
Fodor'sChoice ing the Strip. At the helm is André Rochat, a French expatriate who's
★ been in Las Vegas long enough to have earned the title of home-grown celebrity chef. The seasonal menu might begin with Rochat's seared foie gras with caramelized pear and vanilla custard or his rich Maine lobster bisque. Entrées include his signature Dover sole Veronique, veal loin with goat cheese ravioli, or prime rib eye with smoked potatoes. Pretheater, à la carte, and tasting menus are available. $ *Average main: $59* ⊠ *The Palms, 4321 W. Flamingo Rd., West Side* ☎ *702/951–7000* ⊕ *www.palms.com* ⌕ *Reservations essential.*

$$$$ ✕ **N9NE Steakhouse.** A trendy, attractive clientele often populates this
STEAKHOUSE sleek and upscale-but-unstuffy restaurant, newly renovated in late 2013; keep your eyes wide open for the occasional celebrity sweeping in for face time, champagne, and caviar. (Note: Background music and conversation can be loud at times.) A dozen high-quality cuts of beef are listed on the menu as well as several à la carte sides—potato gnocchi, sweet creamed corn, button mushrooms, and so forth—but there are other superb entrées, too, such as juicy grilled lamb chops with a Parmesan-and-pine-nut crust, or moist organic Fire Chicken with lemon-rosemary sauce, garnished with red and green slow-roasted jalapeños. The pricey Lobster Thermidor is 3 pounds of sautéed lobster, with Gruyere cheese sauce and toasted garlic bread crumbs. ■ TIP➜ Order the prix-fixe meal before 7 pm, a delicious value with wine pairings and dessert ($59 per guest). $ *Average main: $54* ⊠ *The Palms, 4321 W. Flamingo Rd., West Side* ☎ *702/933–9900* ⊕ *www.n9nesteak.com* ⊗ *No lunch.*

$$$$ ✕ **NOVE Italiano.** Head to the Palms's decadent Fantasy Tower to try
ITALIAN out this see-and-be-seen Italian restaurant with an excellent view of the Strip, vaulted ceilings, classical statuary, and ornately upholstered armchairs—there's an intentionally gaudy look about the place, and that's part of its allure among high rollers and poseurs. The modern Italian food, however, is seriously good and surprisingly restrained: several heirloom tomato caprese salads, crudo (sliced raw fish) of the day, daily risotto and gnocchi, or Veal Nove, which is scaloppine with prosciutto, arugula, and lemon. The 24-ounce bone-in rib-eye steak with a Gorgonzola crust is a particularly memorable treat. $ *Average main: $45* ⊠ *The Palms Fantasy Tower, 4321 W. Flamingo Rd., 51st floor, West Side* ☎ *702/942–6800* ⊕ *www.palms.com* ⊗ *Closed Sun. and Mon. No lunch.*

$$$$ ✕**Simon Restaurant & Lounge.** You'll find fresh, seasonal ingredients
AMERICAN including organic eggs and chicken at Chef Kerry Simon's stylish, modern restaurant. Servers wearing sneakers bring a menu that's chock-full
of traditional fare with creative twists and a long list of sushi specialties. Seekers of comfort food might also find Mama Simon's Meat Loaf
with succotash, or chicken with farro and barley risotto among the
entrées. The dessert offerings include a giant bowl of freshly spun cotton candy—a Simon signature. Frosted flake–crusted French toast and
lobster eggs Benedict are favorites at Sunday brunch. The bright and
airy restaurant features floor-to-ceiling windows that look out onto the
adjacent swimming pool. ⑤ *Average main: $49* ⊠ *Palms Place, 4381 W.
Flamingo Rd., take elevator up, cross skyline walkway, take elevator
up, West Side* ☎ *702/944–3292* ⊕ *www.palms.com.*

WEST SIDE NON-CASINO RESTAURANTS

$$ ✕**Archi's Thai Kitchen.** Fans of Thai food flock here for spot-on excep-
THAI tional chow with few surprises—just expertly prepared curries, tom
yum soups, fish cakes, and pad thais. In particular, the shrimp "ginger
ginger ginger" (or you can choose it with meat or tofu) has drawn
raves; yes, it really is that gingery. ⑤ *Average main: $13* ⊠ *6360 W.
Flamingo Rd., West Side* ☎ *702/880–5550* ⊕ *www.archithai.com*
♥ *Closed Mon.* ⑤ *Average main: $13* ⊠ *6345 S. Rainbow Blvd., West
Side* ☎ *702/870–5558*

$ ✕**Capriotti's Sandwich Shop.** This East Coast transplant satisfies Sin City's
DINER cravings for giant sub sandwiches, including a Philly-style cheese steak,
Fodor'sChoice a hot pastrami sandwich, and a divine creation called the Bobbie—basi-
★ cally Thanksgiving dinner on a bun. Numerous locations around town
include outposts in a couple of outlying casinos, such as Red Rock,
Aliante, Santa Fe, and Green Valley. ⑤ *Average main: $10* ⊠ *322 W.
Sahara Ave., West Side* ☎ *702/474–0229.*

$$ ✕**Cathay House.** Set in a strip mall of popular Asian eateries and busi-
CHINESE nesses among Las Vegas' Chinatown, Cathay House stays open late and
combines the feel of a mom-and-pop operation with a sleek atmosphere
and an à-la-carte menu of varied traditional Chinese favorites that
emphasize the fiery flavors of Sichuan and Hunan. It's open daily for
dim sum (10:30 am until 5 am), which attracts diners not only because
of selections such as crispy chicken wings and shrimp or pork dumplings, but also for its fair prices and liberal portions. Among other local
favorites are items such as squid with black bean sauce, thousand-year-
old egg porridge, and salt-baked shrimp, served with heads and shells
still on and garnished with fried chiles and garlic. ⑤ *Average main: $19*
⊠ *5300 Spring Mountain Rd. W, Suite 107, West Side* ☎ *702/876–3838.*

$$ ✕**Go Raw Cafe.** The name of this all-vegan, all-organic café refers to the
VEGETARIAN fact that nothing is cooked at temperatures higher than the 100°F-plus
it takes to make flat breads and pizza dough. Devotees of living food—
as well as vegans and vegetarians—find much to like here. Enjoy a
healthy lunch with dishes such as organic kale salad; savory mush-
room, nut, and herb loaf; or lasagna made with zucchini, spinach,
carrots, marinara sauce, and nut "cheese." A satisfying selection of
refreshing fruit and veggie beverages are juiced to order. ⑤ *Average*

main: $14 ✉ *2910 Lake East Dr., West Side* ☎ *702/254–5382* ⊕ *www. gorawcafe.com* Ⓢ *Average main: $14* ✉ *2381 E. Windmill La., East Side* ☎ *702/450–9007.*

$$$ ✕**Grape Street Cafe, Wine Bar & Grill.** This smart neighborhood restau-
MEDITERRANEAN rant serves food intended to coordinate nicely with the restaurant's interesting, affordable, and plentiful (as in, 80 selections by the glass) wine list. The menu features salads, sandwiches, pizzas, pasta, and seafood, as well as traditional dishes such as rack of lamb and chicken Parmesan or marsala. Desserts range from austere Stilton and port to positively decadent dark-chocolate fondue. The dining room at Grape Street is brick-lined, candlelit, and cozy, and there's a patio for pleasant evenings (if you don't mind the parking-lot view). Ⓢ *Average main: $26* ✉ *7501 W. Lake Mead Blvd., West Side* ☎ *702/228–9463* ⊕ *www. grapestreetcafe.com.*

$$$ ✕**Hash House A Go Go.** Hearty appetites and a dash of patience will be
AMERICAN richly rewarded at this quirky purveyor of so-called twisted farm food. Heaps of savory comfort food are cooked to order in this spacious restaurant done up in industrial, urban-farmhouse decor. Breakfast skillets runneth over with tender, house-cured hashes, fresh eggs, house-made biscuits and jam, and sage-fried chicken Benedict with smoked bacon, griddled mozzarella, spinach, tomato, and chipotle cream. Loaded dinner platters include chicken and waffles; stuffed meatloaf, burgers, or roasted butternut squash; seafood; potpie and pastas; and pork tenderloin and barbecued ribs. No room for dessert? Get the fresh-fruit cobbler or bread pudding to go. Additional locations are in the Quad Resort & Casino, the Plaza Hotel & Casino, and at the Rio, which only serves breakfast and lunch. Ⓢ *Average main: $25* ✉ *6800 W. Sahara Ave., West Side* ☎ *702/804–4646* ⊕ *www.hashhouseagogo.com.*

$$ ✕**Hot & Juicy Crawfish.** This busy, bare-bones eatery has developed a loyal
SEAFOOD following for its delicious, fresh seafood, where crawfish from Louisiana is delivered regularly and available with five seasoning choices at four heat levels. The shellfish (Dungeness, blue, King, or snow crab; lobster, clams, shrimp, and, of course, crawfish), priced at the going market rate, is ordered by the pound. When your shellfish boil appears in its plastic bag, put on the plastic bib and dig in! Baskets of fried poultry and seafood are neater alternatives and come with Cajun fries. Sides include corn-on-the-cob, potatoes and sweet potato fries, plus a credible étouffée. There are two other locations, one just a little closer to the Strip on Spring Mountain Road (at 3863) and one on Eastern Avenue in Henderson. Ⓢ *Average main: $14* ✉ *4810 Spring Mountain Rd., Suite C, West Side* ☎ *702/891–8889* ⊕ *www.hotnjuicycrawfish.com.*

$$ ✕**Ichiza.** Modest, little Ichiza has developed a cult following for serving
JAPANESE sublimely delicious, authentic Japanese food and drink in a casual social
Fodor's Choice environ that borders on controlled chaos. Located on the second floor
★ of a shopping center in the city's China Town section, this boisterous pub is crammed with tourists, students, and local hipsters who love a good value and the chance to chow down on a variety of tasty small-plate offerings (aka "Japa tapas") until 3 am, 4 am Thursday through Sunday. Forget the menu and study the walls instead, where dozens of haphazardly taped signs list the daily specials, or ask your server for

suggestions, which might include black cod with grated white radish; stir-fried calamari with ginger butter; a seaweed or salmon-skin salad; and deep-fried, breaded quail eggs. From dinner to desert, it's best to order with a sense of adventure. $ *Average main: $19* ✉ *4355 Spring Mountain Rd., Suite #205, West Side* ☎ *702/367–3151* ⊘ *No lunch.*

$$ ✕ **Mantra Masala.** Indian-food purists insist it's no big deal to drive 15
INDIAN minutes from the Strip to the back of a bland strip mall for exceptionally authentic cuisine. The sparely lighted space comprises a pair of rooms sprinkled with exotic paintings, dark wood, and richly upholstered booths. Sitar music twangs softly overhead. Enter the dining room and smell the aroma of lamb chunks simmering in a rich cardamom sauce—a signature dish. The usual tandoori and biryani favorites are here, plus offerings such as Goa prawn curry (cooked in a tamarind-coconut sauce). The house makes its own yogurt and cheese and eschews preservatives and processed foods, emphasizing a healthy approach. A dozen vegetarian dishes are offered, too. $ *Average main: $19* ✉ *Durango Springs Plaza, 8530 W. Warm Springs Rd., West Side* ☎ *702/598–3663* ⊕ *www.mantramasala.com* ⊘ *Closed Mon.*

$$$$ ✕ **Marché Bacchus.** The list of wines at this French bistro-cum-wineshop
FRENCH in a quiet northwest neighborhood is nearly 1,000 deep, and free tastings are held on Saturday afternoon from 11:30 until 1:30. You can buy a bottle at retail prices in the store and then drink it while dining ($10 corkage fee) in the cozy dining room or on the expansive lakeside terraces. When you're ready to eat, dine on the fare of Michelin two-star chef Alex Stratta, who consults with the restaurant, starting with a cheese or charcuterie tray and moving on to seared foie gras with vanilla bread pudding or an heirloom beet salad with goat cheese mousse. Entrées might include a classic steak frites or a lobster and rock shrimp risotto. Hear live music most Wednesday, Friday, Saturday, and Sunday nights. $ *Average main: $31* ✉ *2620 Regatta Dr., Suite 106, West Side* ☎ *702/804–8008* ⊕ *www.marchebacchus.com.*

$$$ ✕ **Raku.** Seating is at a premium in this softly lighted strip-mall *robata*.
JAPANESE At 6 pm sharp every day but Sunday, doors open for small-plate offerings of creamy house-made tofu, fresh sashimi (no sushi), and savory grilled meats, fish, and veggies (cooked over charcoal imported from Japan) that reflect the culinary mastery of its Tokyo-born owner-chef. An efficient waitstaff will visit your table to describe the spendy chalkboard specials and also to suggest which seasonings—which include five soy sauces, three salts, and four sugars—will best accent a particular dish. An ample list of sake (including a monthly sampler of three) and à-la-carte menu items, such as the sashimi salad, Kobe beef liver sashimi, and steamed foie gras egg custard, is also provided. Raku also offers omakase, which showcases the chef's choice of the best dishes each day. $ *Average main: $28* ✉ *5030 W. Spring Mountain Rd., Suite 2, West Side* ☎ *702/367–3511* ⊕ *www.raku-grill.com* ⊘ *Closed Sun. No lunch.*

$$ ✕ **Viva Mercado's.** Locals-favorite Viva Mercado's, by longtime local
MEXICAN restaurateur Bobby Mercado, features 12 house-made salsas and a well-executed seafood-heavy menu. Dishes include shrimp and nopales salad; tostadas with shrimp, langostino, tilapia and avocado; and

Ensenada-style fried fish tacos, plus offerings including steak picado and veggie fajitas. $ *Average main: $19* ✉ *9440 W. Sahara Ave., West Side* ☎ *702/454–8482.*

SUMMERLIN CASINO RESTAURANTS

JW MARRIOTT LAS VEGAS RESORT & SPA

$$ ✕ **J.C. Wooloughan's Irish Pub.** What do you get when you build a pub in
IRISH Ireland, dismantle it, and ship it across the ocean, to be reconstructed in the desert? An Irish pub in one of the city's most elegant off-Strip resorts that looks like a wee bit o' the Emerald Isle. J.C. Wooloughan's offers Irish beers and beer blends, several fine Irish whiskeys, and a happy hour from 3 to 6 pm daily with $2.50 draft beers and $5 food specials. Authentic Irish fare, such as bangers and mash, corned beef and cabbage, savory pies (shepherd's or beef-and-Guinness), and beer-battered fish 'n' chips, ensure all eyes will be smiling. $ *Average main: $15* ✉ *JW Marriott Las Vegas Resort & Spa, 221 N. Rampart Blvd., Summerlin* ☎ *702/869–7725* ⊕ *www.jwlasvegasresort.com.*

$$$ ✕ **Spiedini Ristorante.** Longtime local chef Gustav Mauler serves tradi-
ITALIAN tional favorites including his signature osso buco, shrimp fra diavolo and chicken saltimbocca—along with house-made pastas, risotti, and gnocchi. Starters likeTuscan Hummus and beef carpaccio make way for chicken involtini and wild Alaskan halibut. Don't miss the gelato and sorbet for dessert, or Emilio's Famous Cheesecake. There's a full bar in front and patio out back for dining by a burbling waterfall. Wine dinners ($69) are often hosted on the fourth Tuesday of the month; four selections of wine paired with four small plates. $ *Average main: $30* ✉ *JW Marriott Las Vegas Resort & Spa, 221 N. Rampart Blvd., Summerlin* ☎ *702/869–7790* ⊕ *www.spiedini.com* ☾ *No lunch.*

RED ROCK CASINO RESORT SPA

$$$$ ✕ **T-bones Chophouse & Lounge.** Well-dressed local professionals are
STEAKHOUSE drawn in by the striking slabs of dragon onyx guarding the entrance to this upscale steak house. During the "T-Time" happy hour from 4 to 7 daily signature cocktails and bar snacks such as sea-salted roasted beets or the Vegas shrimp cocktail are served on the cheap. Much pricier, however, is the à-la-carte dinner served in the seductive dining room—the perfect spot for a romantic or celebratory meal, especially Wednesday through Saturday when live music enhances the ambience. The menu features oversize wet-aged prime steaks, seafood, and poultry, and, for an old-Vegas touch, table-side preparations of dishes including chateaubriand, Dover sole, and a T-bone for two. $ *Average main: $55* ✉ *Red Rock Casino Resort Spa, 11011 W. Charleston Blvd., Summerlin* ☎ *702/797–7576* ⊕ *RedRock.SCLV.com* ☾ *No lunch.*

SUMMERLIN NON-CASINO RESTAURANTS

$$$ ✕ **Honey Salt.** Frequented by local professionals and ladies-who-lunch,
ECLECTIC this spacious suburban spot serves farm-to-table–inspired dishes that combine ingredients such as free-range poultry, whole grains, and seasonal produce. Chic, rustic decor—soft hues, reclaimed wood, and

antiqued mirrors—lends a casual airiness to the dining room and conveys sophistication, despite its gingham-clad waitstaff. Appetizers, sides, and salads are stars here: My Wife's Favorite Salad combines arugula and frisée with duck confit, pine nuts, and pomegranate, crowned with a sunny-side egg. In addition to caramelized sea scallops, grass-fed filet mignon, and Nana's Tiffin Chicken Curry, there are several offerings for the lighter appetite (and budget). Indulge in the Brown Bag Baked Apple Pie for dessert. A light afternoon menu bridges the gap between lunch and dinner. ⑤ *Average main: $23* ✉ *Rampart Commons, 1031 S. Rampart Blvd., West Side* ☎ *702/445–6100* ⊕ *www.honeysalt.com.*

$$$$
MEDITERRANEAN

✕ **Vintner Grill.** Once you get past the bland office-park setting, you'll find that this sumptuously decorated spot near Red Rock Resort has plenty to recommend in the way of contemporary Mediterranean fare. Start with one of the wood-fired flat breads, or an item such as pan-seared crab cakes with tarragon cream and roasted peppers. From here the menu branches out to pastas and risottos on one side, and a range of meat and seafood grills on the other. A highlight is the venison saddle with caramelized sweet potato hash. As the restaurant's name suggests, there's an impressive wine list here—and many wonderful cheeses. At midday, look for the power-lunchers who escape the beaten path. On nice evenings, ask for a table on the outdoor patio, where the view is better than you might expect. ⑤ *Average main: $32* ✉ *Summerlin Centre, 10100 W. Charleston Blvd., Suite 100, Summerlin* ☎ *702/214–5590* ⊕ *www.vglasvegas.com.*

SHOPS AND SPAS

Updated
by Susan
Stapleton

VEGAS IS AN INTERNATIONAL SHOPPING destination. The square footage in the Forum Shops at Caesars alone is the most valuable retail real estate in the country; bankrolls are dropped there as readily as on the gaming tables. It's the variety that has pushed Las Vegas near the ranks of New York City, London, and Rome: you could send home a vintage slot machine or tote back a classic Hermès handbag.

Most Strip hotels offer designer dresses, swimsuits, jewelry, and menswear; almost all have shops offering logo merchandise for the hotel or its latest show. Inside the casinos the gifts are often elegant and exquisite. Outside, all the Elvis clocks and gambling-chip toilet seats you never wanted to see are available in the tacky gift shops. Beyond the Strip, shopping in Vegas can encompass such extremes as finding a couture ball gown in a vintage store and, in a Western store, a fine pair of Tony Lamas boots leftover from the town's cowboy days. Shoppers looking for more practical items can head for neighborhood malls, supermarkets, shopping centers, and specialty stores. Bargain-hunters seeking to avoid the stratospheric prices on the Strip, and not averse to traveling a bit, can usually find the same high-ticket items at discounted prices in the local or nearby factory outlet malls.

SHOPPING PLANNER

GETTING AROUND

Shopping in Las Vegas—so demanding, yet so rewarding. With malls encompassing millions of square feet of retail space, you won't have any trouble finding ways to part with your cash. But to make the most of your time and money, you should map out your shopping safaris. Distances are deceiving because of the scale of the resort casinos. What looks like a quick walk might take a half hour, or more. Due to crowd-control measures, you'll find yourself squeezing around barriers and leaping over bridges instead of just crossing a street. Grab a cab or ride the monorail ($5 a trip) and save the time for shopping. Buses, which are $8 for 24 hours along the Strip, are a cheaper option, but crowded at all hours.

Got a car? All resorts offer free parking and free valet service (don't worry—they'll still get your money).

SEND THEM PACKING

Who wants to lug packages from store to store? Most stores are happy to send your purchases back to your hotel, or even ship them back home for you.

HOURS OF OPERATION

Although Las Vegas may be up all night, the people who work in the retail establishments need a little rest. Many places are open from 10 am to 11 pm during the week, and stay open an hour later on weekends. And the shopping, like the gambling, goes on every day.

FIND OUT WHAT'S GOING ON

The city's daily newspaper, the *Las Vegas Review-Journal* (⊕ *www. reviewjournal.com*) and weekly publications, *Las Vegas Weekly* (⊕ *www. lasvegasweekly.com*) and Vegas Seven (⊕ *www.vegasseven.com*), offer guides to local malls and discount coupons. Many malls supply their own coupon booklets at on-site customer service or information desks as well. Some will discount even further on presenting a student ID or AAA member card. Social networking sites, such as Twitter, Foursquare, and Facebook, are also excellent resources for on-the-spot discounts and freebies, detailed product information, and exclusive product previews and offerings. Online, head to Racked Vegas (⊕ *vegas.racked.com*) for the most up-to-date information on new stores opening, shops closing, and maps stores that carry handbags, watches, beauty supplies and more.

MALLS ON THE STRIP

Appian Way Shops. A majestic replica of Michelangelo's *David* in Carrara marble marks the entrance to the Appian Way Shops, where a dozen stores sell wares such as luggage, home goods, gifts, eye wear, skin care, cigars, condiments, and apparel. P*q sells all sorts of novelty goods such as home accessories, games, and children's products while King Baby brings a wealth of rock and roll handcrafted sterling silver pieces with elements of precious stones. Take home some olive oils and vinegars from around the world at Olive & Beauty. Carina can spiff up your wardrobe with brands such as Joseph Ribkoff, True Religion, Betsey Johnson, Jessica Simpson, and Vince Camuto. HOME showcases decorative accents and antiques dating back to ancient Chinese dynasties. ⊠ *Caesars Palace, 3570 Las Vegas Blvd. S, casino floor near Forum Tower elevators, Center Strip* ☏ *866/227–5938* ⊕ *www. caesarspalace.com.*

6

Fodor'sChoice
★

The Shops at Crystals. Two levels of opulent boutiques, restaurants, and artistic flourishes are housed within the dramatic steel-and-glass structure that envelops The Shops at Crystals shopping venue at CityCenter. True to its gleaming façade, scads of swanky designer apparel and accessories from fashion's crème de la crème line the clean, minimalist confines within. Touch-screen directories guide you to brands such as Pucci, Prada, Bulgari, Lanvin, Miu Miu, Balenciaga, Bottega Veneta, Stella McCartney, Nanette Lepore, and Tom Ford. Come dressed to impress if you intend to do anything more than ogle the latest and greatest offerings; some of the salespeople here can be more haughty than the couture.

Roberto Cavalli has a two-story boutique that sells everything Cavalli—even the pet line—and features a built-in catwalk. One of Louis Vuitton's largest locations in North America is here, with two levels that extend beyond leather goods to include men and women's ready-to-wear, shoes, jewelry, textiles, ties, and more.

Among the places to dine are Pinkberry; Bobby Flay's Bobby's Burger Palace; boutique steak house and nightclub SHe by Morton's; Mastro's Ocean Club sitting inside a tree house; and Wolfgang Puck Pizzeria & Cucina. Afterward, stroll outdoors to cross the CityCenter Sky Bridge to Gallery Row (near the Mandarin Oriental and giant, 4-ton sculpture of a blue-and-red typewriter eraser by Claes Oldenburg and Coosje

van Bruggen), where three galleries feature the work of Seattle glass master Dale Chihuly, bronze sculptures by Richard MacDonald, and wilderness photography by Rodney Lough Jr.

■**TIP**➔ **For a fun way to access The Shops at Crystals, ride the sleek and silent Aria Express, City-Center's free electric tram with a fantastic elevated view of the complex.** ⊠ *CityCenter, 3720 Las Vegas Blvd. S, adjacent to Aria, Center Strip* ✛ *By Car: Cross Las Vegas Blvd. via E. Harmon Ave. to enter Aria's South Parking garage. Park on its southwestern side for the closest elevator access to Monte Carlo's casino level. Once inside, turn right on Monte Carlo's shopping walkway, Street of Dreams, for the short walk to the tram's boarding platform. Board and travel one stop to Crystals Station; the downward escalator will deposit you onto Level 2 of Crystals* ☎ *866/754–2489* ⊕ *www.crystalscitycenter.com.*

NONSTOP SHOPPING

Can't wait to hit another mall? A pedestrian bridge from the Fashion Show mall to the Wynn Esplanade gives you access to millions of square feet of retail bliss. Start at the Fashion Show, which houses such heavy hitters as Neiman Marcus and Nevada's only Nordstrom as well as hip boutiques such as Louis Vuitton, Topshop, and Henri Bendel. Head across to the Esplanade, where you can pick up high-end goodies at Oscar de la Renta, Manolo Blahnik, or Outfit.

Fashion Show. The frontage of this fashion-devoted mall is dominated by *The Cloud*—a giant, oblong disc that looms high above the entrance. Ads and footage of the mall's own fashion events are continuously projected across the expanse of this ovoid screen. Inside, the mall is sleek, spacious, and airy; a nice change from some of the claustrophobic casino malls. The mall delivers on its name—fashion shows are staged in the Great Hall on an 80-foot-long catwalk that rises from the floor, Friday–Sunday., every hour from noon to 6 pm.

Although you can find many of the same stores in the casino malls, there's a smattering of different fare, such as bareMinerals, which carries many different types and shades of natural, mineral-based cosmetics, and the yoga-inspired Lululemon Athletica. Topshop and neighboring TopMan bring British fashions to the dessert. Neiman Marcus, Saks Fifth Avenue, Macy's, an expanded Macy's Men's Store, Nordstrom, Forever 21, and Dillard's serve as the mall's anchors. ⊠ *3200 Las Vegas Blvd. S, next to Trump Hotel, North Strip* ☎ *702/369–8382* ⊕ *www. thefashionshow.com* ☞ *Free valet and self-parking.*

Fodor's Choice ★ **Forum Shops.** Amazing ambience, architecture, and design means visitors won't have to drop a single dime to enjoy touring this highly accessible mid-Strip mall. Leave the high heels at home to better roam three levels of restaurants and retail—some paths cobblestoned—that resemble an ancient Roman streetscape, with scattered statuary, immense columns and arches, two central piazzas with ornate fountains, and a cloud-filled ceiling-sky that changes from sunrise to sunset over the course of three hours (to subconsciously spur shoppers to step up their pace of acquisition, perhaps?). ■TIP→ The Mitsubishi-designed freestanding Spiral Escalator is a must-ride for the view.

Of course, shopaholics will rejoice at the selection of designer shops and traditional standbys, from high-end heavy hitters such as Tahari, Brooks Brothers, Gucci, Fendi, Michael Kors, Christian Louboutin, Jimmy Choo, Ferragamo, Pucci, Louis Vuitton, Marc Jacobs, and Balenciaga, to more casual labels like Lucky, Juicy Couture, Bebe, Diesel, Nike, Guess, and Gap/Gap Kids. Armani fans will find an Emporio *and* Exchange for menswear, along with John Varvatos, Valentino Red, Hugo Boss, and Thomas Pink. Gaze at stunning jewelry, watches, and crystal works at Baccarat, Cartier, Hearts on Fire, Tourneau, DeBeers, Pandora, Swarovski, and David Yurman. Apple offers a whole host of electronics, too. Cosmetics queens will keep themselves busy at Dior Beauty, Kiehl's, and MAC Pro Store. And don't miss the flagship Victoria's Secret for lingerie and swimwear, or Agent Provocateur and LaPerla, for that matter.

When all this walking/shopping brings on the inevitable hunger, head to The Palm or Wolfgang Puck's Spago. The Cheesecake Factory is popular, as well as bistro Max Brenner Chocolate: divine smells, luscious crepes, waffle sandwiches, and chocolate martinis and fondue—what's not to love? ⊠ *Caesars Palace, 3500 Las Vegas Blvd. S, Center Strip* ☎ *702/893–4800* ⊕ *www.simon.com.*

Grand Bazaar Shops. In front of Bally's Las Vegas, a "21st-century bazaar" inspired by the world's great outdoor markets showcases 150 shops over 2 acres. A giant crystal star burst by Swarovski re-creates Times Square, New York's New Year's Eve nightly while the booths feature glowing, mosaic, undulating rooftops over a broad selection of retail covering apparel, footwear, accessories, electronics, jewelry, and beauty. Already signed on in addition to Swarovski: Swatch, Superdry, Havaianas, and Campo Marzio. ⊠ *Bally's Las Vegas, 3645 Las Vegas Blvd. S* ☎ *702/967–4111* ⊕ *www.grandbazaarshops.com.*

Fodor's Choice ★ **Grand Canal Shoppes.** This is one of the most unforgettable shopping experiences on the Strip. Duck into shops like Dooney & Bourke, Lior, Sephora, the Art of Shaving, or Peter Lik's rustic gallery of fine-art photography. Amble under blue-sky ceilings alongside the Grand Canal. All roads, balustraded bridges, and waterways lead to St. Mark's Square, an enormous open space filled with Italian opera singers and costumed performers. Watch for the living statues, who will intrigue and amuse. If you need to take a load off, hail a gondola! ($19 per person) The mall is open late (until 11 pm Sunday–Thursday, until midnight Friday and Saturday).

On the Palazzo side, find powerhouse names such as Diane von Furstenberg, Michael Kors, Chloé, Bottega Veneta, and Tory Burch. Shoe lovers will swoon over the Christian Louboutin and Jimmy Choo boutiques, and jewelry aficionados will delight in Piaget and Cartier. The main attraction for many, though, is the mall's anchor, Barneys New York. The reputable department store brings in up-and-coming, cutting-edge designers as well as established, exclusive ones such as Balenciaga and

Lanvin. ☒ *Venetian Resort Casino, 3377 Las Vegas Blvd. S, North Strip* ☎ *702/414–4500* ⊕ *www.thegrandcanalshoppes.com.*

The LINQ. Caesars Entertainment debuted a 300,000-square-foot entertainment district replete with the High Roller, the world's tallest observation wheel at 550 feet. The world's largest Kitson, with men's and women's clothing for the pool or the nightclub, anchors this shopping center modeled after the Meatpacking District in New York City. Rapper Nas presents Midnight Run, his ode to sneakers, while Koto sells oddities. Polaroid Fotobar revives an old way of making photographs for the 21st century. Chilli Beans brings sunglasses and Brazil's largest eyewear brand. ☒ *3475 Las Vegas Blvd. S, Center Strip* ⊕ *www. thelinq.com.*

Miracle Mile Shops. The shops here line an indoor sidewalk built around the circular The Axis, the theater where Britney Spears has her residency. Along the way, you'll find such notable and diverse fashion names as Herve Leger, Bebe, American Apparel, Urban Outfitters, H&M, and Bettie Page. Beauty lovers will enjoy Bath & Body Works and Sephora, the authority in beauty retail stores, which is well worth the walk on the cobblestone flooring. Miracle Mile does an admirable job of balancing fashion designer boutiques with modestly priced shops. Many of the stores are at your local mall, but you still may discover a treasure here. ☒ *Planet Hollywood Resort & Casino, 3663 Las Vegas Blvd. S, Center Strip* ☎ *702/866–0703, 888/800–8284* ⊕ *www. miraclemileshopslv.com.*

The Shoppes at Mandalay Place. Request the savings booklet at the north end of this sky-bridge mall, which spans the gap between Mandalay Bay and the Luxor, to receive immediate discounts at 40 shops and eateries. Get a free shot of hooch at Minus5 Ice Bar, for example, or a free facial at Lush, an all-natural cosmetics boutique with its own "cosmetic deli." Or get 15% off any purchase at Elton's Men's Store or Ron Jon Surf Shop. You can practice your golf swing with Nike irons and drivers at the first-ever Nike Golf store, or pick up sterling-silver razors at the Art of Shaving, a high-roller "barber spa" and grooming emporium. Music fans will love the Art of Music, where vintage concert T-shirts, autographed instruments, and oil paintings of lauded musicians are on display. Rock stars, athletes, and other celebs drop in for occasional meet-and-greets, too. Fashionistas will be drawn to hip boutique Nora Blue, where beautiful dresses and hot designs from Sue Wong and Frank Lyman can be found. Iconic Frederick's of Hollywood carries all manner of lingerie. For relief from eye-popping price tags, head to budget fashion stores Maude or Fashion 101. ☒ *Mandalay Bay, 3930 Las Vegas Blvd. S, South Strip* ☎ *702/632–9333* ⊕ *www.mandalaybay.com.*

FAMILY   **Showcase Mall.** "Mall" is a bit of a misnomer here, where stores are more like highly evolved interactive marketing concepts. First off, there's M&M's World, the four-story homage to the popular candy, where huge dispensers with every color and type line one wall. More sugar awaits you at Everything Coca-Cola, where $8 buys either the Around the World sampler of 16 colorful, international soda flavors or 8 flavors of floats. Branded apparel, accessories, and interesting collectibles are also for sale. Post-sugar buzz, you can head to the Hard Rock Cafe to browse the interactive video Rock Wall or buy T-shirts, Las Vegas–branded clothing, and souvenirs. An inexpensive place to buy souvenirs, snacks, water, and booze is in the Grand Canyon Experience, with its faux rocks and wooden rope bridge. The Showcase Mall's parking structure ($3) is right next to MGM Grand; the best access is from the fifth floor, where a pedestrian bridge crosses into the mall. A less hectic option is to park at any of the surrounding hotels for free (MGM, NY–NY, Monte Carlo) and walk here. ✉ *3785 Las Vegas Blvd. S, near the corner of Tropicana Ave., South Strip* ☎ *702/597–3122.*

Via Bellagio. Steve Wynn spared no expense to create the Bellagio, so be prepared to spare no expense shopping at its exclusive boutiques. Elegant luxury stores, such as Prada, Chanel, Giorgio Armani, Gucci, Harry Winston, and Tiffany & Co., line a long passage. When you're ready to cool your heels, dine on the balcony at Olives, right in the promenade, to snag the best patio seat (first come, first served) for watching the Fountains of Bellagio (aka dancing waters). Children, with few exceptions (such as those of hotel guests), aren't allowed anywhere in the Bellagio casino areas. ✉ *Bellagio Las Vegas, 3600 Las Vegas Blvd. S, Center Strip* ☎ *702/693–7111, 888/987–6667* ⊕ *www.bellagio.com.*

SPECIALTY SHOPS ON THE STRIP

BOOKS

Bookstores aren't exactly as ubiquitous in Las Vegas as video-poker machines, but if you venture out into the greater metro area, you inevitably find them. They're stashed among the many strip malls and neighborhood shopping centers. The more rarified, albeit pricier, offerings are found on the Strip.

Bauman Rare Books. Housing an exquisite collection of first-edition titles in pristine condition, this antiquarian book store carries such classics as Dr. Seuss's *The Cat in the Hat,* Truman Capote's *Breakfast at Tiffany's,* and *A Farewell to Arms,* inscribed by Hemingway himself. A large-folio 1679 edition of the King James Bible contains meticulous engraved-plate illustrations, as does Ellen Willmott's rare first-edition printing of *The Genus Rosa,* with its full-page color pages of roses. Historical documents showcase the original signatures of Jung, Edison, and presidents Lincoln and FDR, among other notables. Special binding services are also offered. You may have seen this bookshop on the History Channel's *Pawn Stars.* ✉ *Grand Canal Shoppes, 3377 Las Vegas Blvd. S, North Strip* ☎ *702/948–1617, 888/982–2862* ⊕ *www. baumanrarebooks.com.*

FOOD AND DRINK

FAMILY **M&M's World.** Every day, till midnight, all manner of M&M merchandise is sold here—a slot machine that dispenses M&M jackpots is a best seller—and the popular candy may be purchased by the pound.

Shopping on and off the Strip

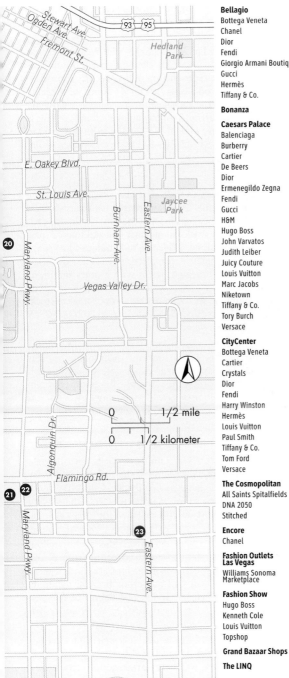

6

Four levels of air-conditioned, colorful, milk-chocolate goodies attract crowds of families with children (and strollers). Those who use the personalized printing machine can create and print custom messages on M&Ms, or select from unique Las Vegas images (the Welcome to Las Vegas sign or a deck of cards). NASCAR champion Kyle Busch hails from Las Vegas, and a full-size reproduction of his M&M's-sponsored #18 racing Toyota Camry is on display (floor 4) along with racing merchandise. About every half hour, the short 3-D movie, *I Lost My M in Vegas* (G-rated, free), starring spokescandies Red and Yellow, is screened on floor 3. ⊠ *Showcase Mall, 3785 Las Vegas Blvd. S, next to the MGM Resort, South Strip* ☎ *702/736–7611* ⊕ *www.mymms.com.*

GIFTS AND SOUVENIRS

Bonanza "World's Largest Gift Shop". Okay, so it may not, in fact, be the world's largest, but at more than 40,000 square feet, it's Vegas's largest souvenir store. And although it carries most of the usual junk, this peddler of pop-culture kitsch also stocks some most unusual junk. A pair of fuzzy pink dice? Check. Blinking "Welcome to Fabulous Las Vegas" sign? Check. Elvis aviator sunglasses complete with black sideburns? Check. How about a battery-operated parrot with a potty mouth or 3-inch plastic slot machine that squirts water? They're all here, seven days a week, open till midnight. As the store likes to say, "If it's in stock, we have it." ⊠ *2440 Las Vegas Blvd. S, North Strip* ☎ *702/385–7359* ⊕ *www.worldslargestgiftshop.com.*

House of Blues. Blues music is an original American art form. Buy music, books, hot sauce, and T-shirts at the souvenir shop in the popular bar–restaurant at Mandalay Bay, where an expansive, remarkable collection of colorful folk art decorates the walls. ■ TIP➜ Show your restaurant receipt to save an additional 10%. ⊠ *Mandalay Bay, 3950 Las Vegas Blvd. S, South Strip* ☎ *702/632–7600* ⊕ *www.houseofblues.com/lasvegas.*

JEWELRY

Most malls and shopping centers on and off the Strip have jewelry stores, including such national chains as Ben Bridge, Gordon's, Lundstrom, Whitehall Co., and Zales. More exclusive jewelers can be found in several of the Strip hotels, most notably Bellagio, the Shops at Crystals, and the Venetian.

Ca'd'Oro. Fittingly named after a Venetian palace, this exclusive boutique specializes in European jewelry and carries collections from Aaron Basha, Gucci, Marco Bicego, Hearts on Fire, Ippolita, and Wellendorff. Lovers of fine watches will find numerous brands, including Ebel, Movado, Longines, TAG Heuer, Tissot, and Baume & Mercier. ⊠ *Grand Canal Shoppes, 3377 Las Vegas Blvd. S, Venetian Resort, North Strip* ☎ *702/696–0080* ⊕ *www.cadorojewelers.com.*

Cartier. There are three outposts of this venerable jeweler in Las Vegas: at the Forum Shops, Wynn Las Vegas, and The Shops at Crystals. You'll find a fine collection of jewelry, watches, leather goods, accessories,

CLOSE UP

Where to Refuel

If you're on a shopping mission, keep your strength up at one of these delicious pit stops.

MALLS ON THE STRIP
Bellagio: Olives

Caesars Palace: Mesa Grill

Fashion Show: Stripburger

The Forum Shops at Caesars: Il Mulino New York, Sushi Roku, the Palm, or Spago

Paris Las Vegas: Mon Ami Gabi

Planet Hollywood Resort & Casino: Pink's Hot Dogs or Gordon Ramsay BURGR

The Shoppes at Mandalay Place: Burger Bar

Showcase Mall: La Salsa Cantina

The Venetian: Postrio Bar and Grill or Sushisamba

OUTLET MALLS
Fashion Outlets of Las Vegas: Hot Dog on a Stick

Las Vegas Premium Outlets—North: Great Steak & Potato Company

Town Square: California Pizza Kitchen or Capriotti's Sandwich Shop

6

and fragrances. ✉ *The Forum Shops, 3500 Las Vegas Blvd. S, Caesars Palace, Center Strip* ☎ *702/418–3904* ⊕ *www.cartier.us.*

De Beers. The store may be small but its wow-factor is huge. This jeweler appeals to the diamond connoisseur. Engagement rings, pendants, and high-fashion jewelry are abundant here. ✉ *The Forum Shops, 3500 Las Vegas Blvd. S, Level 1, near Spiral Escalator, Center Strip* ☎ *702/650– 9559* ⊕ *www.debeers.com.*

Harry Winston. Celebrities continually turn to this exclusive jeweler for red-carpet-worthy diamonds and rare gemstones. ✉ *The Shops at Crystals, 3720 Las Vegas Blvd. S, Level 2, CityCenter* ☎ *702/262–0001* ⊕ *www.harrywinston.com.*

Tiffany & Co. Browse through a full selection of Tiffany's timeless merchandise as well as the exclusive jewelry designs of Elsa Peretti, Paloma Picasso, and Jean Schlumberger. Cleaning and repair services are also offered. Additional store locations include the Forum Shops, Crystals, and Fashion Show Mall. ✉ *Via Bellagio, 3600 Las Vegas Blvd. S, Center Strip* ☎ *702/697–5400* ⊕ *www.tiffany.com.*

FAMILY **Vilebrequin.** If there's a daddy's boy in the family, this is the place to shop for him. Vilebrequin specializes in matching father-son swim trunks with a stylish aesthetic and speedy drying technology. ✉ *Forum Shops, 3500 Las Vegas Blvd. S, Center Strip* ☎ *702/894–9460* ⊕ *us. vilebrequin.com/.*

MEN'S CLOTHING

You can't walk into the shopping areas of Strip hotels without encountering high-end men's clothing stores. If the price tags on the Strip are too out of reach, the outlet malls have brand names for less, such as Tommy Hilfiger, Perry Ellis, Hugo Boss, Van Heusen, Polo Ralph Lauren, and DKNY.

Elton's. Exclusive men's designers, both high profile (Hugo Boss, Diesel, D. J. Pliner) and obscure (Cult of Individuality, George Roth L.A., Great China Wall) come together in this premium men's boutique. Additional location at the Shoppes at Mandalay Place. ⊠ *Grand Canal Shoppes, 3377 Las Vegas Blvd. S, North Strip* ☎ *702/853–0571.*

Ermenegildo Zegna Boutique. You'll find the finest in Italian men's suits on this store's racks. Quality craftsmanship, superior fit, and impeccable style dominate here. Made-to-measure service, small leather goods and accessories, and a selection of apparel from fashion lines Z Zegna and Zegna Sport are also available. Additional location at Crystals. ⊠ *The Forum Shops, 3500 Las Vegas Blvd. S, Center Strip* ☎ *702/369–5458* ⊕ *www.zegna.com.*

Giorgio Armani Boutique. Italian designer Armani cuts a cloth like nobody's business. Clean lines, quality fabrics, expert stitching—all evident in the luxury formalwear displayed throughout this elegant store. The maestro's signature spiffy sportswear, shoes, handbags, and accessories are sold here, too, as well as fragrances and cosmetics. ⊠ *Via Bellagio, 3600 Las Vegas Blvd. S, Center Strip* ☎ *702/893–8327* ⊕ *www. armani.com/giorgioarmani.*

Hugo Boss. Men's fashions straight from European and New York runways, with two additional local branches (The Venetian and Fashion Show Mall), plus three factory store outlets. ⊠ *The Forum Shops, 3500 Las Vegas Blvd. S, Center Strip* ☎ *702/696–9444* ⊕ *www.hugoboss. com.*

John Varvatos. Casual-chic men's clothes and a slew of shoes, belts, and messenger bags make up the offerings here. The Forum Shops location also carries formalwear. The version at the Hard Rock Hotel is a boutique store modeled after their New York City Bowery location (former site of the iconic rock club CBGB). ⊠ *The Forum Shops, 3500 Las Vegas Blvd. S, Center Strip* ☎ *702/939–0922* ⊕ *www.johnvarvatos.com.*

Kenneth Cole. The store provides a sleek, realistic approach to men's runway trends. A healthy supply of footwear and accessories is also sold. Additional location at the Grande Canal Shoppes. ⊠ *Fashion Show, 3200 Las Vegas Blvd. S, Zone B, Upper Level, North Strip* ☎ *702/794–2653* ⊕ *www.kennethcole.com.*

Paul Smith. The designer hails from England and his British-inspired menswear makes that quite clear. Emphasizing understated patterns and colors, Paul Smith's designs have a cool, relaxed quirkiness to them. Some call it geek chic. In addition to accessories and shoes, this Daniel Libeskind–designed store also carries women's wear. Books, art, vintage furniture, and other curios are also for sale. ⊠ *The Shops at Crystals,*

3720 Las Vegas Blvd. S, Level 1, Center Strip ☎ *702/796–2640* ⊕ *www. paulsmith.co.uk/us-en/shop.*

Stitched. Men who want the best of the latest and greatest fashions will be right at home here. Jacks & Jokers, Zachary Prell shirts, and the XXXX Stitched collection of suits and sports coats are carried here. An on-site tailor can personalize garments. Made-to-measure suits are a specialty. ✉ *The Cosmopolitan, 3708 Las Vegas Blvd. S, Center Strip* ☎ *702/698–7630* ⊕ *www.stitchedlifestyle.com.*

Tom Ford. The designer put his stamp on the fashion world when he brought Gucci back from the dead. Since then the outstanding craftsmanship of his modern menswear line has suited Brad Pitt, George Clooney, and Jay-Z on the red carpet. Men's eyewear, accessories, and fragrances are offered, as well as women's ready-to-wear. Neiman Marcus in Fashion Show has an impressive counter of Tom Ford Beauty products for both men and women. ✉ *The Shops at Crystals, 3720 Las Vegas Blvd. S, Level 1, Center Strip* ☎ *702/740–2940* ⊕ *www. tomford.com.*

SPORTING GOODS AND CLOTHING

Adidas Performance Center. The coolest Adidas technology is displayed with minimalist design at this two-story store, one of only a handful of Performance Centers in the country. Scads of merchandise are divided and organized by sport throughout and touted on interactive screens and text tickers. Women shouldn't miss British designer Stella McCartney's signature line of fashion-inspired sportswear. You won't know whether to hit the gym or the runway (same difference?) in her designs. For old-school style with new-age engineering, scope out the Adidas Originals collection. ✉ *Showcase Mall, 3785 Las Vegas Blvd. S, South Strip* ☎ *702/262–1373* ⊕ *www.adidas.com.*

Niketown. This multilevel Nike theme park features attractive displays, inspirational slogans, and giant swoosh symbols amid the latest cool technology in athletic shoes. Flashy and crowded, it's full of "Nike athletes" yelling into two-way radios. ✉ *The Forum Shops, 3500 Las Vegas Blvd. S, Center Strip* ☎ *702/650–8888* ⊕ *www.nike.com.*

WOMEN'S CLOTHING

Vegas shopping will impress the most jaded of shoppers. Prepare to find an abundant selection of women's wear at area hotel-casino malls and outlet centers. Go ahead, name a designer. The odds are high that you'll find a signature shop in this town.

Alexander McQueen. The British designer's store on the Wynn Esplanade features men's and women's attire as well as shoes and handbags, including the coveted brass knuckle clutches. ✉ *Wynn Esplanade, 3131 Las Vegas Blvd. S, North Strip* ☎ *702/369–0510* ⊕ *www. alexandermcqueen.com.*

AllSaints Spitalfields. The British brand uses vintage themes as its inspiration for graphic tees and embellished dresses that cater to a youthful demographic. Celebrities like Vanessa Hudgens, Jessica Alba, and

Dakota Fanning have been known to wear the edgy styles here. ⊠ *The Cosmopolitan, 3708 Las Vegas Blvd. S, Center Strip* ☎ *702/722–5252* ⊕ *www.us.allsaints.com.*

Balenciaga. The highly stylish Italian fashion house brings an architectural approach to men's and women's ready-to wear fashions, handbags, and accessories. Additional location at Crystals. ⊠ *The Forum Shops, 3500 Las Vegas Blvd. S, Center Strip* ☎ *702/732–1660* ⊕ *www. balenciaga.com.*

Bottega Veneta. Renowned for its modern, sophisticated take on the classics, this Italian fashion house melds elegant style with leather fabrics. The line appeals to the woman with a taste for timelessness. Additional locations at Via Bellagio and the Grand Canal Shoppes. ⊠ *The Shops at Crystals, 3720 Las Vegas Blvd. S, North Strip* ☎ *702/369–0747* ⊕ *www. bottegaveneta.com.*

Burberry. The luxury British brand features its famous trench coats and rain gear as well as hot fashion accessories. Additional location at the Forum Shops. ⊠ *Grand Canal Shoppes, 3377 Las Vegas Blvd. S, North Strip* ☎ *702/382–1911* ⊕ *us.burberry.com.*

Chanel. The boutiques for this fine French couturier at Bellagio and Wynn stock the latest women's ready-to-wear fashions, accessories, sunglasses, leather goods, shoes, jewelry, cosmetics, and fragrances. The boutique at Encore carries a smaller, ultralux selection and is home to Chanel's Fine Jewelry Collection. Additional locations at Encore Esplanade and Via Bellagio. ⊠ *Wynn Esplanade, 3131 Las Vegas Blvd. S, North Strip* ☎ *702/765–5055* ⊕ *www.chanel.com.*

CH Carolina Herrera. Chic sophistication is the name of the game at this fashion boutique where you can find the acclaimed designer's bridge collection. ⊠ *The Forum Shops, 3500 Las Vegas Blvd. S, Level 2, Center Strip* ☎ *702/894–5242.*

Chloé. This high-end French fashion house sports a large selection of women's ready-to-wear collections, as well as gorgeous handbags, shoes, and accessories for the Bohemian in every woman. Additional location at Wynn Esplanade. ⊠ *Grand Canal Shoppes, 3377 Las Vegas Blvd. S, North Strip* ☎ *702/266–8122* ⊕ *www.chloe.com.*

Diane von Furstenberg. Head here for something figure-flattering, comfortable, and high on the style scale. Diane von Furstenberg, or DVF as she's known to longtime followers, first made her fashion presence known in 1972 with her iconic wrap dress, which is still a staple in her collections to this day. Additional location at the Forum Shops. ⊠ *Grand Canal Shoppes, 3377 Las Vegas Blvd. S, North Strip* ☎ *702/818–2294* ⊕ *www.dvf.com.*

Dior. Clothes from this storied fashion house appeal to the sophisticated woman who still wants to stand out in a crowd. The Wynn boutique and the one at The Shops at Crystals also carry the collection of Dior Homme menswear. Additional locations at Via Bellagio and the Forum Shops. ⊠ *Wynn Esplanade, 3131 Las Vegas Blvd. S, North Strip* ☎ *702/735–1345* ⊕ *www.dior.com.*

DNA 2050. Shopping for jeans has never been so easy. This 2,305-square-foot branch specializes in denim, carrying all the old faithfuls such as True Religion, Hudson, and J Brand as well as the latest trendsetters such as Nudie, G-Star, Current Elliott, and Fidelity. Don't overlook the handbag collection here. ⊠ *The Cosmopolitan, 3708 Las Vegas Blvd. S, Center Strip* ☎ *702/698–7610* ⊕ *www.emporiumdna.com.*

Fendi. The Italian designer offers elegant garments, furs, shoes, and handbags that transcend trends. The boutique at The Shops at Crystals features a replica of Rome's Trevi Fountain inside, while the Forum Shops' boutique features a jewel box of a glass-enclosed store with its handbags and shoes as well as a traditional shop across the aisle. Additional locations at the Grand Canal Shoppes and Via Bellagio. ⊠ *The Forum Shops, 3500 Las Vegas Blvd. S, Center Strip* ☎ *702/732–9040* ⊕ *www.fendi.com.*

Gucci. The Italian luxury designer features the men's and women's clothing and shoes collections as well as leather goods, luggage, jewelry, timepieces, silks, and eyewear. Additional locations at Via Bellagio and Crystals. ⊠ *The Forum Shops, 3500 Las Vegas Blvd. S, Center Strip* ☎ *702/369–7333* ⊕ *www.gucci.com.*

H&M. The crème de la crème of fast fashion, this Swedish retailer features affordable apparel and accessories that rival what you'll see on high-profile runways. Diffused lines from acclaimed designers are also prevalent here, and generally only make an appearance at this location. The store contains three floors, three checkout stations, an elevator, and a cut-open façade. ■TIP→ The location at the Forum Shops is the second biggest H&M in the country. Additional location at the Miracle Mile Shops. ⊠ *The Forum Shops, 3500 Las Vegas Blvd. S, Center Strip* ☎ *702/207–0167* ⊕ *www.hm.com.*

Hermès. The Parisian brand's iconic Birkin bags are so exclusive you could be on a waiting list for several years—yes, years—before securing one. The fine silk scarves and well-crafted clothes carry the same prestige without the waiting game. Additional locations at Via Bellagio and Crystals. ⊠ *Encore Esplanade, 3121 Las Vegas Blvd. S, North Strip* ☎ *702/650–3116* ⊕ *usa.hermes.com.*

Herve Leger. Expect to find the famous, sexy, strappy bandage dresses that put this brand on the map. The clothes aren't modest and neither are the price tags. Additional location at the Grand Canal Shoppes. ⊠ *Miracle Mile Shops, 3663 Las Vegas Blvd. S, Center Strip* ☎ *702/732–4529* ⊕ *www.herveleger.com.*

Juicy Couture. To think, it all started with a velour tracksuit. This L.A. line has since evolved into a full-fledged lifestyle brand of flirty, irreverent fashion. ⊠ *The Forum Shops, 3500 Las Vegas Blvd. S, Center Strip* ☎ *702/892–9600* ⊕ *www.juicycouture.com.*

Kitson. The largest Kitson, at 12,000 square feet, anchors the LINQ with a two-story store serving up fashions for the pool on up to the nightclub. Look for men's, women's and kids' clothing, accessories, gifts, apothecary, books and novelties as well as exclusives from Homies, Boy London, Sol Angeles, Yosi Samra, Lauren Moshi, and others. ⊠ *The LINQ, 3545 Las Vegas Blvd. S, Center Strip* ⊕ *www.shopkitson.com.*

Lanvin. The creative window decor here alone is reason enough to check out this boutique that carries men's and women's fashions and accessories. Inside you'll be dazzled by the bold, sophisticated fashions. ⊠ *The Shops at Crystals, 3720 Las Vegas Blvd. S, Center Strip* ☎ *702/982–0425* ⊕ *www.lanvin.com.*

Louis Vuitton. Stash your winnings in a designer bag from one of five Vegas branches of this famous French accessories maker. Hot-stamping services are offered at all branches. The store at The Shops at Crystals is the largest in North America and has an exclusive invitation-only James Turrell Akhob exhibit, a walk-in light installation, the artist's largest Ganzfeld exhibit to date. Additional locations at Wynn Esplanade, The Forum Shops, Via Bellagio, and Fashion Show. ⊠ *The Shops at Crystals, 3720 Las Vegas Blvd. S, Center Strip* ☎ *702/262–6262* ⊕ *www.louisvuitton.com.*

Marc Jacobs. The Forums Shops offers two branches: Marc by Marc Jacobs features the American designer's cutting-edge female fashions, coveted handbags, beauty products, and accessories. The Marc Jacobs Collections is split down the middle with men's and women's ready-to-wear fashions and accessories, as well as a small selection of handbags and shoes near the main Strip entrance. ⊠ *The Forum Shops, 3500 Las Vegas Blvd. S, Center Strip* ☎ *702/734–0220, 702/369–2007* ⊕ *www.marcjacobs.com.*

Oscar de la Renta. Stop here for couture wear as well as informal wear from this sophisticated red carpet designer. ⊠ *Wynn Esplanade, 3131 Las Vegas Blvd. S, North Strip* ☎ *702/770–3487* ⊕ *www.oscardelarenta.com.*

Outfit. If it's graced the pages of *Vogue*, it's hanging on the racks of Outfit. Names such as Lanvin, Ungaro, Zac Posen, Narciso Rodriguez, and Nina Ricci all call this place home. ⊠ *Wynn Esplanade, 3131 Las Vegas Blvd. S, North Strip* ☎ *702/770–3465.*

Topshop. Eclectic British style meets high fashion at this London clothier's U.S. outposts. Men's fashions also find a home inside neighboring TopMan. The stores carry limited edition items for Vegas only such as hot pants and shimmering dresses. ⊠ *Fashion Show, 3200 Las Vegas Blvd. S, North Strip* ☎ *702/866–0646* ⊕ *us.topshop.com.*

Tory Burch. Rich textures, zippy colors, perky prints, and Bohemian spirit infuse the stylish, wearable clothing and accessories at Tory Burch. The handbags, pumps, and ballet flats are staples here. Additional location at the Grand Canal Shoppes. ■**TIP**→ **The Forum Shops branch is the largest and carries a wider selection.** ⊠ *The Forum Shops, 3500 Las Vegas Blvd. S, Center Strip* ☎ *702/369–3459* ⊕ *www.toryburch.com.*

Versace. This boutique features a body-conscious, seductive line of ready-to-wear clothes that speak to a confident woman. Additional location at Crystals. ⊠ *The Forum Shops, 3500 Las Vegas Blvd. S, Center Strip* ☎ *702/932–5757* ⊕ *www.versace.com.*

SPAS ON THE STRIP

The Bathhouse. Dark slate and suede-covered walls wrap this modern and sexy boutique spa at the Delano. A 16,000-square-foot spa here features a nightclub-like scene sans the thump, thump, thumping music. Instead, replace that with the serene melody of water trickling. Baths are a specialty here with treatments such as the Moor mud bath that beautifies and soothes arthritis, respiratory issues and more, while the signature fizz bath bubbles with fragrances that turn into essential oils. ☒ *Mandalay Bay, 3950 Las Vegas Blvd. S, South Strip* ☎ *877/632–9636* ⊕ *www.mandalaybay.com* ☞ *Body treatments $90–$250; facials $85–$265; manicure/pedicure $45–$110; waxing $30–$35; tanning $90–$150. Services: Swedish, aromatherapy, deep-tissue, reflexology, prenatal, jade guasha, accupoint, parafin, dry brush, hot stone. Beauty treatments: anti-aging, facials, waxing. Exfoliation: body polish, salt glow, sugar polish, waxing. Facilities: sauna; steam room; heated whirlpools; cold plunge. Gym with: Precor equipment; free weights.*

Fodor's Choice ★ **Canyon Ranch SpaClub at the Venetian and the Palazzo.** Vegas's largest spa—one of the best day spas in the country—is this outpost of Tucson's famed Canyon Ranch connected to the Venetian and the Palazzo. The extensive treatment menu here covers any desire, including Vibrational Therapy and an ayurvedic herbal rejuvenating treatment. The real treat here is the Aquavana, a European-inspired space that offers a host of water-related experiences. The Wave Room simulates ocean waves under a domed canopy; the Finnish sauna infuses colored light into a dry heat sauna; and the Igloo cools guests off with three arctic mist experiences and sparkling fiber optics. Weekend warriors love the health club, the Strip's largest, with its 40-foot climbing wall and frequent fitness and yoga classes. The nutrition, wellness, and exercise physiology departments also offer free lectures, Lifetime Nutrition Consultation, and acupuncture. An adjoining café serves healthy cuisine and smoothies. ☒ *The Venetian, 3355 Las Vegas Blvd. S, North Strip* ☎ *877/220–2688* ⊕ *www.canyonranch.com* ☞ *Body treatments $165–$345; facials $190–$305; manicure/pedicure $50–$155; waxing $30–$110. Services: Swedish, aromatherapy, stone, couples massage, ashiatsu, deep-tissue, prenatal, ayurvedic rejuvenation, reflexology. Beauty treatments: anti-aging, facials, manicure, pedicure, haircutting, waxing, hair extensions, makeup. Exfoliation: body polish, salt glow, sugar polish, waxing. Facilities: Vichy shower; Pilates and Kinesis studio; cycling studio; yoga and dance studio; rock climbing wall; thermal cabins; soaking tubs. Gym with: boot camp; Zumba classes; barre workouts.*

ESPA at Vdara. ESPA at Vdara is the first of the brand's ventures to the West Coast and only its third in the United States. With it comes a line of products with natural ingredients that ties in with Vdara's commitment to organic and natural spa treatments and skin-care products. Try the Desert Rose, a 110-minute body treatment that includes a welcoming foot bath, body scrub, shower, and massage with body butter. On the Rocks uses a body brush followed by a massage using hot stones. ESPA takes care of the men with treatments such as a purifying facial and a fitness massage. ☒ *Vdara, 2600 Harmon Ave., Center Strip*

6

☎ 702/590–2474 ⊕ *www.vdara.com/spa/espa.aspx* ☞ *Body treatments $170–$325; facials $160–$260; waxing $15–$95. Services: Swedish, aromatherapy, deep-tissue. Beauty treatments: anti-aging, facials, hair-cutting, waxing, makeup. Exfoliation: body polish, salt glow, sugar polish, waxing. Facilities: sauna; steam room; hot plunge; co-ed meditation lounge. Gym with: cardio equipment; personal trainers.*

MGM Grand Spa. Though this well-managed spa lacks the stunning architecture of other Strip spas, it makes up for it with accommodating attendants and a serene, feng shui–designed atmosphere. The Ritual Experiences menu offers creative treatments from around the world, including the Dreaming Ritual inspired by Aborigines in Australia, or the Nirvana that combines Abhyanga massage with ayurvedic oils and hot stones. Too adventurous? Detox your hangover with the Morning Latte, an exfoliating scrub with coffee, or the Citrus Splash with salt grains. ■ TIP➜ Spa services are available to nonguests Monday through Thursday only. ⊠ *MGM Grand, 3799 Las Vegas Blvd. S, South Strip* ☎ 702/891–3077 ⊕ *www.mgmgrand.com/amenities* ☞ *Body treatments $75–$325; facials $75–$340; manicure/pedicure $60–$250; waxing $70–$140. Services: Swedish, aromatherapy, deep tissue, pregnancy massage, shiatsu, stone, reflexology, ayurvedic treatments. Beauty treatments: anti-aging, haircutting, facials, manicure, pedicure, waxing. Exfoliation: sugar and coffee scrubs. Facilities: steam rooms; saunas; whirlpools; relaxation lounge. Gym with: cardio and weight equipment.*

Nurture Spa. Perhaps one of the most accessible spas on the Strip, Nurture Spa features a bright and airy setting giving it an inviting, earthy feel. Try one of the signature treatments such as the peppermint leg therapy to recuperate from a long day of walking the Strip or the bubalina sugar scrub, a 20- or 50-minute treatment that nourishes skin all over your body. ⊠ *Luxor, 3900 Las Vegas Blvd. S, North Strip* ☎ 800/258–9308 ⊕ *www.luxor.com/amenities* ☞ *Body treatments $70–$200; facials $75–$155; manicure/pedicure $40–$100; waxing $20–$75. Services: Swedish, aromatherapy, deep-tissue, Moroccan oil, reflexology, prenatal, Hawaiian shamanic, ashiatsu, tandem, hot stone. Beauty treatments: anti-aging, facials, haircutting, hair color, waxing, makeup. Exfoliation: body polish, salt glow, sugar polish, waxing. Facilities: sauna; steam room; whirlpools. Gym with: cardio equipment; circuit training equipment; free weights.*

Fodor's Choice ★ **Qua Baths & Spa.** This behemoth of a spa at Caesars Palace bases its philosophy on the calming properties of water. Many of the treatments and special features here draw heavily on this element, beginning with the Roman Baths. Qua's social spa-ing concept of encouraging guests to verbally interact comes naturally when indulging in these three soothing baths. For guests suffering from heat exhaustion, the Arctic Room offers the perfect solution: snow falling from a glass sky. If traditional treatments bore you, consider visiting the Crystal Body Art Room. You won't completely experience Qua's water benefits until you've had a Vichy shower treatment that uses seven different showerheads called the Dancing Waters. Qua also has Men's Zone, a salon for men, and the Tea Lounge where an in-house tea sommelier blends you a cup. Color, a phenomenal hair salon from colorist to the stars Michael Boychuck, is right next door. ■TIP➔ The Nobu Hotel flexes its influence with a whole series of treatments including the Nagomi Ritual with a welcoming foot bath, aroma nectars, and massage. ✉ *Caesars Palace, 3570 Las Vegas Blvd. S, Center Strip* ☎ *866/782–0655* ⊕ *www.caesarspalace.com* ☞ *Body treatments $100–$520; facials $180–$350; waxing from $25. Services: Swedish, stone, deep-tissue, Thai, reflexology, shiatsu, Biofreeze, Hawaiian healing, raindrop therapy, chakra rebalancing, couples, prenatal. Beauty treatments: facials, waxing. Exfoliation: herbal, microderm, champagne grape seed. Facilities: Vichy shower; hydrotherapy tubs; arctic ice room; ultraheated room. Gym with: Technogym equipment; fitness concierge.*

Sahra Spa and Hammam at the Cosmopolitan. Omnipresent slot machines and neon lights can make you forget that you're in the desert, but Sahra Spa is designed to return you to the peace and solitude of the Southwest. It starts with the Space Between, the serenity lounge that makes you feel transported to the peak of a canyon, and stretches all the way to the metallic ceilings that twinkle like only a nighttime desert sky can. Highlights here include the extensive skin-care treatments, special baths, and hammam, only one of three on the Strip. Two of the "transformations," the Sahra Journey and the Sahra Select, incorporate the heat-infused hammam to address the body's needs and all its senses. At the center of the hammam is a heated slab of stone that feels like it's been sitting in the warm sun for hours. Follow this up with the Red Flower Bathing Ritual, which exfoliates and moisturizes your desert-dried skin. ✉ *The Cosmopoliton, 3708 Las Vegas Blvd. S, Center Strip* ☎ *855/724–7258* ⊕ *www.cosmopolitanlasvegas.com* ☞ *Body treatments: Sahra Signature Massage, 50–80 mins $150–$255; bath treatments start at $160; skin treatments $95–$435. Services: baths, hammam, body wraps, facials, aromatherapy, massage, scrubs. Fitness center with: cardiovascular machines, free weights, weight-training equipment. Classes and programs: yoga, Zumba, Pilates.*

The Spa and Salon at Aria. Aria provides a contemporary way to spa, starting with the design, which is all clean lines and modern furniture. Some of the furniture is even functional to your pampering, like the Japanese *gabanyoku* beds. Comprised of warm stones, the beds are designed to balance metabolism, circulation, and muscle movement. The services are just as innovative, like the ashiatsu massage that has therapists using ceiling bars to balance as they walk on your back. The Shio Salt Room uses lamps and a brick wall to emit salt to improve breathing as guests lounge. A customized men's menu includes the Man Tan and extensive barber services. A Vichy rain bar enhances certain body treatments and facial add-ons include a firming system for décolletage, an eye mask, and hand and feet massages. ✉ *Aria, 3730 Las Vegas Blvd. S, Center Strip* ☎ *877/312–2742* ⊕ *www.arialasvegas.com* ☞ *Body treatments from $175; 50-min signature Thai Poultice massage $190–$290; facials $95–$360. Services: aromatherapy, flexology, massage, Vichy rain bar, therapy pool, tanning, waxing. Facilities: hair salon; hot tub; sauna; steam room. Gym with: cardiovascular machines; free weights; weight-training equipment. Classes and programs: personal training, indoor hikes, yoga.*

The Spa at Encore. The opulent Spa at Encore feels like a splendid outdoor retreat destination, with natural sunlight, limestone, and water features. Try the Nalu Body Ritual with its relaxing Polynesian fusion massage, full-body exfoliation, and scalp treatment with coconut oil or the Encore Escape, a massage that incorporates a multitude of techniques. Perhaps the only drawback is the exorbitant prices that go along with a luxury place like Encore. ⊠ *Encore Las Vegas, 3121 Las Vegas Blvd. S, North Strip* ☎ *702/770–4772* ⊕ *www.wynnlasvegas.com* ☞ *Body treatments $185–$425; facials $170–$350; waxing $85–$170. Services: Swedish, Bodhi and visualization, nalu, stone, aromatherapy, deep-tissue, prenatal. Beauty treatments: anti-aging, facials, waxing. Exfoliation: body polish, salt glow, sugar polish, Moroccan mud wrap, waxing. Facilities: sauna; steam room; heated whirlpools; cold plunge. Gym with: personal training; fitness classes including yoga, Pilates, core fusion, and sculpting.*

The Spa at Mandarin Oriental. It's luxury all the way at this spa, where every imaginable form of pampering is offered. Upon entering the two-story space, guests take in the art deco–style of 1930s Shanghai and prepare to be catered to hand and foot, emphasis on foot. One of the optional add-ons for treatments here is the foot spa, where guests can have those long walks on the Strip forgiven through a cleansing ritual and foot and leg massage. Other features include a hammam with showers for cooling off, a vitality pool, and a women's rhassoul that combines mud, heat, and steam for exfoliation and toxin-purging. Treatments here, many of which start with a consultation, are tailored to individual needs. Journeys combine treatments for a full body experience, and the Time Rituals vary from two to six hours. Topping off the experience here is the beautiful view of the Strip from the relaxation room. ⊠ *Mandarin Oriental, 3752 Las Vegas Blvd. S, Center Strip* ☎ *702/590–8888* ⊕ *www.mandarinoriental.com/lasvegas* ☞ *Body treatments:Journeys start at $240; Time Rituals start at $300; facials $180–$400. Services: hammam, rhassoul, aromatherapy, foot spa. Facilities: hair salon; hot tub; sauna; steam room. Gym with: cardiovascular machines; free weights; weight-training equipment. Classes and programs: yoga, Pilates, body sculpt, kinesis circuit training, boot camp.*

Spa at Trump. Customization is the name of the game at Trump's spa. Services are based upon your wishes—Do you want to be calm, balanced, healed, purified, or revitalized?—which then determines everything from your massage oils and candles, to the tea you drink and the music you'll hear during your visit. Services exclusive to this location include the Vegas Recovery Massage and the Royal Facial. The spa's skin-care treatments use Kate Somerville products. There's also couple- and men-specific services. Last but not least, an attaché service takes care of your every need from shoe shining to clothes steaming. ⊠ *Trump International Hotel, 2000 Fashion Show Dr., North Strip* ☎ *702/982–0000* ⊕ *www.trumphotelcollection.com* ☞ *Body treatments $150–$250; wraps/baths $40–$250; facials $150–$300; manicure/pedicure $45–$70; waxing from $20. Services: Swedish, aroma-infused, prenatal, ayurvedic, reflexology, Thai herbal, hot-stone, gemstone massages. Beauty treatments: haircut and color, manicure,* *pedicure, facials, eyelash and brow tinting, waxing, makeup lessons. Exfoliation: Javanese Lulur, salt scrub, herbal body scrub, yogurt, mud. Facilities: eucalyptus-infused sauna. Gym with: Technogym machines; personal trainers.*

Fodor's Choice ★ **The Spa at Wynn Las Vegas.** Designed according to feng shui principles, and set away from the bells and jangles of the Strip, this spa exudes an elegant Zen calm while remaining very cozy. There's a fireplace and flat-screen TV in the lounge areas, and the hot and cool plunge area is naturally lighted and lush with thriving palms and orchids. Treatments, such as the Choco Latte Body Buff, are Asian-inspired. The Good Luck Ritual is based on the five elements of feng shui, and includes a fusion massage, an ultramoisturizing hand therapy, and a wild lime botanical scalp treatment. For the ultimate in combating the drying desert clime, try the Hydrating Collagen Booster Therapy facial, which infuses phytonutrients, ceramides, and plant-based minerals. ⊠ *Wynn Las Vegas, 3131 Las Vegas Blvd. S, North Strip* ☎ *702/770–3900* ⊕ *www.wynn. com* ☞ *Body treatments $100–$375; facials $170–$300; manicure/ pedicure $45–$105; waxing $30–$75. Services: aromatherapy, deep tissue, couples massage, prenatal, reflexology, waxing. Beauty treatments: anti-aging, haircutting, facials, manicure, pedicure, waxing, hot-lather shaves for men. Exfoliation: body polish, salt glow, sugar polish. Facilities: plunge pools; atrium. Gym with: cardio machines; weights; personal training; yoga.*

Spa Bellagio. Besides the calming reflecting pools and the Reflexology Pebble Walk, this swank Zen sanctuary has treatments such as Thai yoga massage and Gem Therapy. The 6,000-square-foot fitness center has a gorgeous view of the Mediterranean gardens and the pool. There's even a candlelit meditation room with fountain walls. If over-indulging and the dry climate have gotten to you, try the Thermal Seaweed Body Wrap for a seaweed- and water-based detoxifying and hydrating treatment. Spa Bellagio offers Watsu, an aquatic massage using shiatsu techniques that takes place in a warm pool while floating. ■**TIP→** Spa services are exclusive to Bellagio guests Friday–Sunday. ⊠ *Bellagio, 3600 Las Vegas Blvd. S, Center Strip* ☎ *702/693–7472* ⊕ *www.bellagio.com/spasalon* ☞ *Body treatments $85–$400; facials $85–$350; manicure/pedicure $40–$135; waxing $25–$100. Services: Swedish, aromatherapy, stone, couples massage, Watsu, ashiatsu, Thai yoga, deep-tissue, prenatal, Jamu, Indian head massage, reflexology. Beauty treatments: anti-aging, facials, manicure, pedicure, hair cutting, waxing, hot-lather shaves for men. Exfoliation: body polish, salt glow, sugar polish, coconut scrub Vichy shower, Moor Mud, seaweed, gold, coffee. Facilities: private suites; aquatic therapy room; Vichy showers. Gym with: strength training equipment; yoga classes; spinning; barre classes.*

Spa Mandalay. Modeled after Turkish-style baths, the hot, warm, and cold plunges at this spa are surrounded by marble, fountains, and plenty of places to lounge. Try the Aromatherapy Massage that uses essentials oils and Swedish massage techniques. The spa offers what may be the only hot-stone pedicure in town. ⊠ *Mandalay Bay, 3950 Las Vegas Blvd. S, South Strip* ☎ *877/632–7300* ⊕ *www.mandalaybay.*

6

com ☞ Body treatments $85–$265; facials $85–$250; manicure/pedi-
cure $45–$150; waxing $30–$185. Services: aromatherapy, Swedish,
deep-tissue, prenatal, shiatsu, stone, reflexology. Beauty treatments:
anti-aging, haircutting, facials, manicure, pedicure. Exfoliation: herbal,
mud, sugar, and salt scrubs. Wraps/Baths: herbal wrap, aromatherapy
wrap. Facilities: hydrotherapy baths; sauna; eucalyptus steam room.
Gym with: Precor exercise equipment; redwood sauna; relaxation
lounge.

MALLS OFF THE STRIP

Fashion Outlets of Las Vegas. Make the 35-mile drive south of McCarran
International Airport to Primm, Nevada, for more than 100 manu-
facturer-owned-and-operated outlet stores under one roof. The shops
along this bright, spacious, and easy-to-navigate looping layout offer
savings of up to 70% off department store prices. Aeropostale, BCBG
Max Azaria, Bath & Body Works, DKNY, Kate Spade New York, Kenneth Cole, Lucky Brand Jeans, Lacoste, Gap, and Williams-Sonoma
Marketplace are among the popular brands. Neiman Marcus Last Call
stocks designer labels as well as its private labels. A shopping tour bus
runs daily from on-Strip locations. The $15 round-trip fare includes a
discount card with $800 in total savings at participating stores. (Reserve
seats online to save $3.) ■ TIP➜ Discount cards are free for AAA mem-
bers and also available for $5 at the customer service center in the
food court. And lest you think you've strayed too far from the action,
there's escalator access into the Primm Valley hotel-casino at the north
end of mall, offering no-frills gambling. There's also a free shuttle (every
45 minutes, 24/7) that crosses over Interstate 15 to hotel-casinos Buffalo Bill's and Whiskey Pete's. The bullet-riddled car driven by infamous crime duo Bonnie Parker and Clyde Barrow is often displayed at
Whiskey Pete's. ⊠ *32100 Las Vegas Blvd. S, Primm* ☎ *702/874–1400*
⊕ *www.fashionoutletlasvegas.com ☞ Free parking.*

Fodor'sChoice **Las Vegas Premium Outlet—North.** The upscale mix at this racetrack-
★   shaped Downtown outlet mall includes names you can find at your
own mall, such as Nine West, Charlotte Russe, and Quiksilver, but
with better discounts; and rarely seen outlets of fashion heavyweights
such as Dolce & Gabbana, St. John Company Store, Brooks Brothers
Factory Store, Kate Spade, Ted Baker London, Tory Burch, and Salvatore Ferrgamo. Fashion jeweler David Yurman and coveted handbag
designer Coach are also here. This is one of the few outdoor malls in
town, and there's plenty of shade as well as misting towers to help keep
you cool in the Vegas heat. Take a taxi or ride a regional bus: Purchase
tickets aboard for $2 (single ride), $5 (2-hour Access Pass), or $7 (24-
hour Access Pass), with pick-up/drop-off at several Strip locations. Call
RTC for more information. Two parking garages afford easy access
to the mall but tend to fill up quickly; valet parking available in main
garage. ⊠ *875 Grand Central Pkwy. S, Downtown* ☎ *702/474–7500,*
702/228–7433 RTC ⊕ *www.premiumoutlets.com.*

FAMILY **Las Vegas Premium Outlet—South.** Like its northern sister outlet, this
branch has a vast selection of popular brands such as Bose, Fossil,

Easy Spirit, Lucky, Ann Taylor, Brooks Brothers, Calvin Klein, DKNY, Jones New York, Nautica, Nike, Sketchers, Wet Seal, Wilson Leather, and Zales. (Saks Fifth Avenue Off 5th occupies the Annex, a small separate building on the south side.) But these shops, located 2½ miles south of the Strip, are indoors and air-conditioned, with plenty of free on-site parking. ■ TIP→ **Stop at the Information Center for a layout and listings brochure, which includes coupons and daily specials. Moreover, AAA card members receive a free discount card for additional savings.** Some stores offer student discounts as well. The Disney store, Carter's, and Gymboree stocks stuff for kids, and there's a carousel ride, too. Regional buses will pick up or drop off shoppers at Silverton and South Point hotel-casinos, as well as from several on-Strip locations. (Call RTC at ☎ 702/228–7433 for information.) ⊠ 7400 *Las Vegas Blvd. S, Airport* ☎ 702/896–5599 ⊕ *www.premiumoutlets.com.*

FAMILY **Town Square.** Constructed to resemble Main Street America with open-air shopping and dining, this 100-acre complex contains more than 150 shops, including La Nora, MAC and Sephora cosmetics, Juicy Couture, H&M, Apple, and Patty's Closet fashion boutique. When you tire of shopping (or the kids do anyway), there's also a children's play area, multiplex cinema, and rides on the Town Square train. Gastropub English's serves British fare and high tea every afternoon. There's also a Capriotti's, Tommy Bahama's, Nestle Toll House Café, and several other on-site eateries, including a Whole Foods Market. Stoney's Rockin' Country dance and live-music venue opens every evening at 7 pm, with free two-step lessons offered on Tuesday. ■ TIP→ **Need to make a quick stop? Town Square offers curbside parking so you don't have to schlep all the way from one of three parking garages to your shopping destination.** ⊠ 6605 *Las Vegas Blvd. S, at junction of I–15 and 215 Beltway, Airport* ☎ 702/269–5000 ⊕ *www.townsquarelasvegas.com.*

6

SPECIALTY SHOPS OFF THE STRIP

BOOKS

Psychic Eye Book Shop. Behind the innocuous strip-mall façade are all sorts of esoteric books, lucky talismans, tarot cards, and candles. Get a psychic reading or an astrological chart on where to place your bets. Additional locations in North Las Vegas, the Airport area, and Henderson. ⊠ 6848 *W. Charleston Blvd., West Side* ☎ 702/255–4477 ⊕ *www.pebooks.com.*

FOOD AND DRINK

FAMILY **Ethel M Chocolates Factory and Cactus Garden.** The M stands for Mars, the name of the family (headed by Ethel in the early days) that brings you Snickers, Milky Way, Three Musketeers, and M&M's. Come here for two special reasons: one, to watch the candy making, and two (more important), to taste free samples in the adjoining shop. As for the other half of this place's name, yes, there is, indeed, a cactus garden—Nevada's largest—with more than 350 species of succulents and desert plants. It's at its peak during spring flowering. ■TIP→ The factory tour and gardens are free, but if you forget to go, McCarran International Airport features branches at all gates after airport security. ⊠ *2 Cactus Garden Dr., Henderson* ☎ *702/435–2655, 702/435–2608* ⊕ *www.ethelm.com.*

HOME FURNISHINGS

Williams-Sonoma Marketplace. Need a cool bottle-opener for that duty-free liquor back at the room? How about a gift for your favorite gourmand or foodie? Many cleverly designed and stylish cooking tools, gourmet goodies, and home-decor items are suitcase-friendly. Perhaps you simply want to pass a pleasant hour before going to lunch. Call the branch for a rundown on its monthly cooking demos, hands-on workshops, or other technique classes. Additional location in Summerlin. ⊠ *The District at Green Valley Ranch, 2255 Village Walk Dr., Suite 129, Henderson* ☎ *702/897–2346.*

MEN'S AND WOMEN'S CLOTHING

The Bungalow. It's equal parts cozy and contemporary at this women's lifestyle boutique that comes from the former owner of Vegas's famed but now-defunct Talulah G boutiques. The small space features cocktail dresses and gowns from the likes of Anna Sui and Malene Birger. Tables throughout the boutique feature the kind of sportswear and casual looks that take a boho turn. Mighty Fine vintage tees meet Viscose tie-dyed scarves. Intimates and jewelry are also sold here, as well as decorative pillows and towels from Missoni Home that boast the famous zigzag knits. ⊠ *7024 W. Charleston Blvd., West Side* ☎ *702/303–3353* ⊕ *www.thebungalowlv.com.*

Fruition. Kanye West heads to this off-the-Strip locale when he's in Vegas. Why? The owners have a great eye for the next big thing. That's why they've styled videos for Li'l Kim and M.I.A. The look here is accomplished by fusing the old with the new. Men's and women's vintage Yves Saint Laurent, Christian Dior, Alexander McQueen, and more can be found here. You'll also uncover up-and-comers just making their mark at this urban-meets-tribal-meets-geek-meets-hipster store. Have a look around while Diggable Planets blasts overhead and a furry little dog runs around the racks. ⊠ *4139 S. Maryland Pkwy., East Side* ☎ *702/796–4139* ⊕ *shop.fruitionlv.com.*

Undefeated. This store is the authority on premium sneakers and street wear. Look for classic brands sitting next to limited edition pieces as well as UNDFTD, their own label that collaborates with the big boys to create lustful objects such as the Air Jordan IV Retro and Nike Dunk Hi NL. ⊠ *Paradise Esplanade, 4480 Paradise Rd., Suite 400, Paradise Road* ☎ *702/732–0019* ⊕ *undefeated.com.*

MUSIC

Zia Records. This store is for the music lover who enjoys shopping for tunes the old-fashioned way—thumbing through title after title, hoping to get that lucky break. The vinyl selection at Zia is diverse and vast, but the real gems here are in the pop and rock genres. That goes for CDs, too, which can be found at rates as low as four for $10. Whether it's Wilson Phillips, Fleetwood Mac, Elvis, or a little Richard Marx, you'll find what you didn't know you were looking for in this store that feels like the basement where the ol' band once practiced. In fact, you might get lucky on your visit and enjoy local talent performing live. Take advantage of the knowledgeable staff who can test your music trivia or offer recommendations based on your current collection. Additional location in Northwest Las Vegas. ⊠ *4225 S. Eastern Ave., East Side* ☎ *702/735–4942* ⊕ *www.ziarecords.com.*

VINTAGE CLOTHING

Buffalo Exchange. This is a thrift store must-stop for the terminally hip. The extensive collection of great vintage and used clothing at reasonable prices makes for satisfying shopping. You also can find great recycled discards and, since we all could use the help, lots of suggestions from the staff. ⊠ *4110 S. Maryland Pkwy., East Side* ✛ *At Flamingo Rd.* ☎ *702/791–3960* ⊕ *www.buffaloexchange.com.*

Electric Lemonade. In the heart of the Arts District, this two-level store feels like a fashion work of art. The vintage pieces have been carefully edited to bring the same looks the runways feature, only from the original decade that inspired them. High-waist shorts from the '80s, check swing coats from the '60s, and maxi dresses from the '70s meet here for a blast from the past. ■ TIP→ After shopping this eclectic boutique, make time to stroll the surrounding art galleries. ⊠ *Arts District, 220 E. Charleston Blvd., Downtown* ☎ *702/776–7766* ⊕ *www. electriclemonadeshop.com.*

WESTERN WEAR

Shepler's. Since 1946, thousands of cowboys (and cowgirls) have bought their Wranglers and Stetsons here. Additional location at Sam's Town on Boulder Highway. ⊠ *4700 W. Sahara Ave., West Side* ☎ *702/258–2000.*

SPAS OFF THE STRIP

The Spa at Red Rock. For some, a spa experience simply translates into relaxation, and that can take many forms. Here, in this sleek 25,000-square-foot haven flanked by mountains, it may mean the robe, slippers, and massages. For those who prefer to stick with decisions more along the lines of Swedish versus deep tissue, there are 13 massages to choose from. The Zone lets you get in and get out, concentrating on the neck, back, or legs and lasting a brief but efficient 25 minutes. There's also Customized To You, which blends massage techniques to provide an experience designed exclusively for, well, you. Both acne and aging are addressed through 17 different facials, offering vitamin C treatments, microdermabrasion, and the Volcanic Deep Purifying facial that concentrates on extractions. ■TIP→ The Spa at Red Rock offers the Adventure Spa, a separate experience that includes horseback riding, Black Canyon river rafting and kayaking adventures, guided hikes, and rock climbing, all off-site. ⊠ *Red Rock Casino, Resort & Spa, 11011 W. Charleston Blvd., Summerlin* ☎ *702/797–7878* ⊕ *www.redrock. sclv.com* ☞ *Body treatments $85–$285; 25-min massage $90; facials $90–$245. Services: aromatherapy, reflexology, microdermabrasion. Facilities: hair salon; hot tub; sauna; steam room. Gym with: cardiovascular machines; free weights; weight-training equipment. Classes and programs: adventure spa-ing.*

ONLY IN LAS VEGAS

Fodor's Choice ★ **Gambler's General Store.** This gambling superstore can design and manufacture custom poker chips, then ship them out for that big game or family gathering back home. Gambling books galore compete with casino-quality merchandise—bingo supplies, roulette wheels, cloth layouts, playing cards, chips, and dice—and novelty items, such as an acrylic dealing shoe designed to hold business cards. The special player in your life will love the professional chip cases/trays and high-quality gaming sets and furniture here, such as a poker table with a green-suede overlay and built-in stainless-steel drink holders. This 8,000-square-foot store is less than a mile south of the Plaza Hotel on Main Street. ⊠ *800 S. Main St., Downtown* ☎ *702/382–9903, 800/322–2447* ⊕ *www. gamblersgeneralstore.com.*

FAMILY **Houdini's Magic Shop.** Magicians are hot tickets in Vegas, so it's no surprise that Houdini's corporate headquarters are in town. Get the popular UFO illusion, or Ultra Floating Object, which enables you to "float" cards and other small objects. The $24 set includes instructional booklet and DVD. There are smaller branches in the Grand Canal Shoppes at the Venetian, Miracle Mile Shops at Planet Hollywood Resort, New York–New York, and MGM Grand resorts. ⊠ *Houdini's Factory Store, 6455 Dean Martin Dr., Peterson Center, Suite L, Airport* ☎ *702/798–4789* ⊕ *www.houdini.com* ⊗ *Closed weekends* ☞ *Free parking.*

Serge's Wigs. If you always wished for the sleek tresses of the stunning Vegas showgirls (or female impersonators), or if you want to try a daring new look for the clubs, head to this bright and spacious Vegas institution. You'll find an expansive selection of natural hair and synthetic wigs and hairpieces available in many styles, lengths, and colors, as well as accoutrements such as Styrofoam heads, hair adhesives, shampoos, scarves/turbans, and eyelashes. ■TIP→ A hair covering must be worn (scarf, bandana, nylon stocking) or purchased ($2) before trying on wigs. Allow additional time for cutting, styling, and proper fitting of your hairpiece if planning to wear it on the same day of purchase. ⊠ *4515 W. Sahara Ave., West Side* ☎ *702/207–7494* ⊕ *www.sergeswigs. com* ⊗ *Closed Sun.*

7

SHOWS

Updated
by Mike
Weatherford

THE VERY NAME "LAS VEGAS" has been synonymous with a certain style of showbiz ever since Jimmy Durante first headlined at Bugsy Siegel's Flamingo Hotel in 1946. Through the years this entertainment mecca has redefined itself a number of times, but one thing has remained consistent—doing things big.

The star power that made the old "supper club" days glitter with names like Frank Sinatra and Dean Martin is making a latter-day comeback in showcases by veteran concert acts Rod Stewart and Elton John. Nationally known performers such as Penn & Teller and Boyz II Men have come to roost on the Strip after years of living out of a suitcase. While *Jubilee!* hangs in there as a shimmering example of the "feather shows" that made an icon of the showgirl, Cirque du Soleil dominates the Strip with its technologically advanced shows presenting little or no language barrier to the city's large numbers of international tourists. Contemporary entries such as the break-dancing Jabbawockeez try to lure younger audiences the nightclubs have skimmed from the ticketed shows.

In the not-so-olden days, shows were loss leaders intended to draw patrons who would eventually wind up in the casino. Nowadays the accounting's separate and it can cost you more than $100 to see name performers such as Donny and Marie Osmond and $250 for Celine Dion. Meanwhile, the lesser names and production shows that run year-round have become a confusing, "never pay face value" circus of discount outlets and offers.

The new generation of resident headliners ranges from ventriloquist Terry Fator to "mindfreak" Criss Angel to pop star Britney Spears. There's still no other place in the world to find such a concentration of female impersonators, "dirty" dancers, magicians, and comedians—all continuing the razzle-dazzle tradition Las Vegas has popularized for the world.

SHOWS PLANNER

RESERVED-SEAT TICKETING

Most hotels offer reserved-seat show tickets, and nearly all the Las Vegas shows are available through corporate ticketing networks such as Ticketmaster or Vegas.com. If you don't buy in advance, an old-fashioned visit to the show's box office is still your best bet for minimizing add-on charges. It's advisable to purchase tickets to concerts or the hotter shows, such as the Colosseum at Caesar's Palace headliners, ahead of a visit. For smaller shows or spontaneous decisions, visit the various discount kiosks along the Strip; most producers "mark 'em up to mark 'em down" at these outlets anyway. Only pay full face value for a headliner name or a show you really want to see. Remember, too, that for the popular titles, casinos control their inventory and make sure their big players are always taken care of. If advance tickets are no longer available, check for last-minute cancellations. Your chances of getting a seat are usually better when you're staying—and gambling—at the hotel.

If you plan on spending a fair amount of time at the tables or slots, call VIP Services or a slot host to find out what their requirements are for getting a comp, paid tickets that have been withheld for last-minute release, or perks such as premium seating or a line pass (it allows you to go straight to the VIP entrance without having to wait in line with the hoi polloi).

CONTACTS AND RESOURCES

Ticketmaster. As most of the venues in town are part of Ticketmaster, you can buy tickets at any Ticketmaster outlet or on the website. All Caesars Entertainment properties now use Ticketmaster exclusively. ☎ *800/745–3000* ⊕ *www.ticketmaster.com.*

Tickets & Tours. Tickets & Tours, operated by Entertainment Benefits Group, sells tickets online and in more than 30 booths or kiosks around town, including the airport, the Venetian, Planet Hollywood, and the Golden Nugget. See their website for all locations. They also sells tickets for tours, including backstage peeks at some of the shows. ☎ *702/617– 5595* ⊕ *www.ticketsandtours.com.*

Tix4tonight. With 10 locations and counting, Tix4tonight is the place to visit for most ongoing shows (but not the hot concert acts or headliners). There's a service charge for each ticket and the majority of business is for same-day walk-up sales. Strip locations include Bally's, Circus-Circus, Slots-A-Fun, the Fashion Show Mall, the Hawaiian Marketplace shopping center, the Showcase Mall (look for the giant Coke bottle), Planet Hollywood, and the Casino Royale. The Downtown location's inside the Four Queens casino. Another outlet is on Las Vegas Boulevard, way south of the pedestrian part of the Strip, in the popular Town Square shopping center. Originally, prices were half price across the board and only for that day's performance. But the company's now such a dominant source that some producers try to get away with lesser discounts and some make their titles available a day in advance or via phone reservations. ☎ *877/849–4868* ⊕ *www.tix4tonight.com.*

Vegas.com. Vegas.com is a major sales outlet for full-priced tickets and discount offers. "Convenience" and "processing" fees are spelled out clearly before you hit the final button to place your order. ⊕ *www. vegas.com.*

FIND OUT WHAT'S GOING ON

Information on shows, including their reservation and seating policies, prices and suitability for children (or age restrictions), is available by calling or visiting box offices. It's also listed in several local publications or websites.

The **Las Vegas Advisor** (✉ *3665 S. Procyon Ave., West Side* ☎ *800/244– 2224* ⊕ *www.lasvegasadvisor.com*) is available as a monthly printed newsletter at its office for $5 per issue or $50 per year. An online membership is $37 and the website has become a font of free news and coupons. It's a bargain-focused consumer's guide to Las Vegas dining, entertainment, gambling promotions, comps, and news.

The stories tend to be of the fawning press-release variety, but two free visitor publications are filled with show listings and discount coupons:

Today in Las Vegas (⊕ *www.todayinlv.com*) and *What's On, the Las Vegas Guide* (⊕ *www.whats-on.com*) are available at hotels and gift shops.

The *Las Vegas Review-Journal,* the city's morning daily newspaper, publishes a pullout section each Friday called *Neon*, with free distribution separately. It provides entertainment features and reviews, and showroom and lounge listings with complete time and price information. In the tourist corridor, the daily *Review-Journal* is wrapped inside a Daily Visitor's Guide that includes show listings. The newspaper also maintains a website (⊕ *www.lvrj.com*), and entertainment reporters blog about the latest developments. The *Las Vegas Sun,* a competing daily that once had separate distribution, is now a section inside the *Review-Journal* but maintains its own editorial staff and website, ⊕ *www.lasvegassun.com.*

Two weekly newspapers are distributed at retail stores and coffee shops around town and maintain comprehensive websites. They tend to be the best source for coverage of the nightclub scene and music beyond the realm of the casinos: Vegas Seven (⊕ *www.vegasseven.com*), and *Las Vegas Weekly* (⊕ *www.lasvegasweekly.com*).

WHAT'S NEW?

Cirque du Soleil's Michael Jackson tribute Michael Jackson ONE landed at Mandalay Bay in 2013 as Cirque's eighth resident Vegas title. That magic number finally seemed to level off the company's local ambitions. The Cosmopolitan attempted to fuse traditional shows and nightclubs with a themed "social club" called Rose.Rabbit.Lie., which offers both roving entertainers for diners and a ticketed show, "Vegas Nocturne."

Celine Dion, Rod Stewart, Elton John, and Shania Twain continued to rotate dates in the 4,300-seat Colosseum at Caesars Palace, which pointed the way to a tier of venues seating 3,000 to 5,000 people. Planet Hollywood remodeled its theater to host **Britney Spears,** who kept her dance-oriented *Piece of Me* off the road to play exclusively at Planet Hollywood for two years. Limited runs by the likes of **Def Leppard** at the Hard Rock Hotel continued to promote that venue as a place to see customized, only-in-Vegas showcases as well as major tours. And the Cosmopolitan also opened a 4,000-capacity venue called the Chelsea at the end of 2013 to host concert acts including eight shows by **Bruno Mars.** In mid-2014 these new venues were joined by a Las Vegas branch of the **Brooklyn Bowl** at the new retail complex the **LINQ.**

The LINQ aims to unify in one location the nightclubs, restaurants, and shops that relegated the Las Vegas show to near obscurity. But depending on how you count comedy clubs and short-haul headliners such as Spears or Olivia Newton-John, who also decided to test the waters in 2014, the number of shows can still top 100. It seems the city isn't ready to surrender its self-appointed status of "The Entertainment Capital of the World" just yet.

AFTERNOON SHOWS

Las Vegas has become a wider-reaching and more family-friendly destination. But at the same time, evening show prices can be in the triple digits. These factors are sometimes at odds with one another and help explain a few afternoon shows that hold their ticket prices down or discount heavily with promotional coupons. The following are the most proven and popular.

Legends in Concert. The durable *Legends* is one of the longest-running shows in Las Vegas and it inspired many imitators. But its production values seemed more modest as the big shows got bigger. In 2013 it moved to the Flamingo and became the rare show to split its schedule between afternoons and evenings, with the matinees avoiding competition from the big-budget spectacles. It's still the same basic formula of "mini-concerts" by a rotating lineup of celebrity impersonators, and can still attract the best in the profession. The Elvis Presley finale used to be the only constant, but occasionally a rousing Michael Jackson tribute is the dramatic closer. There's no lip-syncing and always a band. ⊠ *Flamingo Las Vegas, 3555 Las Vegas Blvd. S, Center Strip* ☎ *702/777–7776* ⊕ *legendsinconcert.com* ✉ *$58–$93* ⊘ *Sat.–Thurs. 4 pm; Tues.–Thurs. and Sat. 10 pm (late show schedule can vary).*

FAMILY
Fodor's Choice
★

Mac King. The reigning king of Las Vegas afternoons—playing at Harrah's Las Vegas since 2000—seems more like a Ragtime-era court jester with his plaid suit and folksy "Howdy!" King stands apart from the other magic shows on the Strip with a one-man hour of low-key, self-deprecating humor and the kind of close-up magic that's baffling, but doesn't take the focus away from the running banter. But watch out for that bear! ⊠ *Harrah's Las Vegas, 3475 Las Vegas Blvd. S, Center Strip* ☎ *702/369–5111* ⊕ *mackingshow.com* ✉ *$38–$49* ⊘ *Tues.–Sat. 1 and 3.*

FAMILY
Nathan Burton Comedy Magic. The likable magician whom many came to know on *America's Got Talent* puts a fun spin on familiar illusions—behold! The "Microwave of Death"—and is family-friendly for those with older children. ⊠ *Saxe Theater, 3667 Las Vegas Blvd. S, Miracle Mile Shops, Planet Hollywood, Center Strip* ☎ *702/260–7200* ⊕ *www. nathanburton.com* ✉ *$55–$75* ⊘ *Tues.–Sun. 4.*

COMEDY CLUBS

Even when Las Vegas wasn't the hippest place to catch a musical act, it was always up-to-the-minute in the comedy department. From Shecky Greene to Daniel Tosh, virtually every famous comedian has worked a Las Vegas showroom or lounge. The Strip still has dependable comedy rooms that copy the club format of multiple-act formats featuring top names on the circuit. Cover charges are in the $40 range, but two-for-one coupons are easy to come by in freebie magazines and various coupon packages.

Brad Garrett's Comedy Club. Brad Garrett has returned to his stand-up roots in a classic comedy-club setting—a bar with plenty of photos of Brad Garrett on the walls. He hand-picks the comedians and headlines

DID YOU KNOW?

Le Rêve, at the Wynn, is an aquatic theater-in-the-round with 85 cast members.

RAVES AND FAVES

Splashiest opening: It's a curtain war. The beginning of *O* gets things off to an astonishing start when a regal curtain is whooshed away into the backstage recesses as though sucked into a giant vacuum cleaner. Not to be outdone, Celine Dion's intro drops and then whisks away a 2,000-pound white scrim to reveal the orchestra.

Best finale: The climactic scene of *LOVE* just had to be "A Day in the Life." Cirque du Soleil rises to the challenge of the famous orchestral buildup with a symbolic, moving scene featuring an angelic, floating mother figure. (Remember that both John Lennon and Paul McCartney's mothers died young.)

Best band in town: The blue baldies in the *Blue Man Group* never talk, so it's even more important that their silent antics be backed by a rocking sound track. The seven-piece band keeps the sound percussive and otherworldly.

Most words per minute: Penn & Teller discuss everything from "ocular hygiene" to "petroleum by-products" (meaning Solo cups), conveniently overlooking the fact that most Vegas shows push spectacle over words. What's even more amazing? Only one of them (Penn) talks.

Most deliberately provocative: There was much speculation about whether a man-to-man kiss would stay in Cirque du Soleil's *Zumanity*. It did, although now it's later in the show and placed in a more comedic context.

Best guilty pleasure: The title says it all: *Evil Dead the Musical*. Campy attitude and deliberately bad acting rule the day. It's the only lo-fi musical (yes, the gory cult movie really has been set to show tunes) in Vegas show that douses its audience in stage blood. Well, those who pay extra anyway.

several times per year himself: "It was either this or 'Jews on Ice' at the Stratosphere," he likes to tell audiences. ☒ *MGM Grand, 3799 Las Vegas Blvd. S, South Strip* ☎ *702/891–7777* ⊕ *www.bradgarrettcomedy. com* ☼ *Daily pm.*

The Improv. Comedy impresario Budd Friedman oversees the bookings for this 300-seat showroom on the second floor of Harrah's. It has the occasional bigger name comedians and is frequently packaged with room or player's club discounts. ☒ *Harrah's Las Vegas, 3475 Las Vegas Blvd. S, Center Strip* ☎ *702/369–5223* ⊕ *www.improv.com* ☼ *Tues.– Sun. 8:30 and 10 pm.*

Sin City Comedy. Veteran comedian-turned-producer John Padon gave the usual stand-up formula a new twist by mixing (covered) burlesque numbers in between comedians. It's a fun variation that might sway gents who are unfamiliar with the stand-up names on any particular lineup, in a modest but appealing space. ☒ *Planet Hollywood, 3663 Las Vegas Blvd. S, Center Strip* ☎ *702/777–2782* ⊕ *www.sincitycomedy. com* ☼ *Daily 7 and 9 pm.*

Blue Man Group is a show for the whole family.

EVENING REVUES

Absinthe. Sometimes it's not the elements, but how they are combined. Perhaps the setting, too. *Absinthe* takes circus acrobatics, raunchy comedy, and a couple of saucy burlesque numbers, and puts them all under a tent in front of Caesars Palace. (At least it's a tentlike structure; once it was decided the show would stick around, fire inspectors insisted on a sturdy, semi-permanent pavilion.) The audience surrounds the performances on a small, 9-foot stage. The show is hosted by a shifty insult comic known as the Gazillionaire. This is cheap raunch for a discerning audience. And, like Penn & Teller's show, it's on some level a knowing salute to show business itself. ⊠ *Caesars Palace, 3570 Las Vegas Blvd. S, Center Strip* ☎ *800/745–3000* ⊕ *www.absinthevegas.com* ✉ *$109–$136* ⊗ *Wed.–Sun. 8 and 10 pm. Showtimes vary seasonally.*

FAMILY
Fodor's Choice
★

Blue Man Group. The three bald, blue, and silent characters in utilitarian uniforms have become part of the Las Vegas landscape. At the end of 2012, *Blue Man Group* moved from the Venetian to the Monte Carlo, updating the show by about half. New sequences include a female "showbot" and two scene-stealing assembly-line robots. The updated satire of technology and information-overload merges with classic bits from the group's humble off-Broadway origins: paint splattering, mouth-catching marshmallows, and rollicking percussion jam-sessions that includes banging on PVC pipe contraptions to their unique brand of interstellar rock and roll. ⊠ *Monte Carlo, 3770 Las Vegas Blvd. S, Center Strip* ☎ *702/730–7010* ⊕ *www.blueman.com* ✉ *$88–$236* ⊗ *7 and 9:30 pm daily (schedule varies seasonally).*

Chippendales: The Show. Score one for the ladies: The Rio builds a theater dedicated to the men of Chippendales, surrounds it with a lounge and gift shop, and gives the historically male-oriented entertainment in this town a jolt. The show has fancier staging than any G-string revue traveling on the nightclub circuit, and the bow-tied hunks keep it respectable enough to let Mom tag along with the bachelorette party. The Chips have taken to the occasional guest host, such as Jeff Timmons of the boy band 98 Degrees, and two of its company members (Jaymes Vaughan and James Davis) came in second on "Amazing Race" in 2012. ✉ *Rio All-Suite Hotel & Casino, 3700 W. Flamingo Rd., West Side* ☎ *702/777–7776* ⊕ *www.riolasvegas.com* 🎫 *$55–$80* ⊗ *Daily 9 pm, Fri. and Sat. 9 and 11 pm.*

Criss Angel—Believe. When no one seemed to appreciate the odd-couple pairing of Cirque du Soleil and the star of television's *Mindfreak*, Cirque backed off and left Angel on his own to rework the show in 2010. He stripped down the production, eliminated most of the artsy theatrics, and transformed it into a more predictable magic showcase—one that's rockin' loud and full of pyrotechnics as Angel bustles through one illusion after another like a young(er) David Copperfield. Consider the changes a good thing if you're a fan of his, maybe less so if it was Cirque's name and contribution that intrigued you. ✉ *Luxor Las Vegas, 3900 Las Vegas Blvd. S, South Strip* ☎ *702/262–4400* ⊕ *www.official. crissangel.com* 🎫 *$75–$208* ⊗ *Tues., Fri., and Sat. 7 and 9:30 pm; Wed. and Thurs. 7 pm.*

Defending the Caveman. Comedian/author Rob Becker's anthropological take on the battle of the sexes is a popular touring show that brought something new to Las Vegas: theatrical long-form comedy, delivered by a lone actor (lately Chris Allen) mixing jokes with real scientific insight. It's an extended monologue by one likable schlub (enhanced with lighting and sound cues) that preaches greater understanding on a set that looks like it's right out of *The Flintstones.* ■ TIP➔ Two of the weekly performances are in the afternoon and slightly discounted (4 pm Sunday and Monday). ✉ *Harrah's Las Vegas, 3475 Las Vegas Blvd. S, Center Strip* ☎ *702/777–2782* ⊕ *www.defendingthecaveman. com* 🎫 *$49–$74* ⊗ *Daily pm, Sun. and Mon. 4 pm.*

Fantasy. *Fantasy* is a topless show (un)dressed up as a variety show, with power-pop singing by its female host and, most nights, impressions and clowning from Sean Cooper. It's not uncommon to see couples in the audience here. ✉ *Luxor Las Vegas, 3900 Las Vegas Blvd. S, South Strip* ☎ *702/262–4400* ⊕ *www.fantasyluxor.com* 🎫 *$46–$68* ⊗ *Nightly 10:30 pm.*

Human Nature: The Motown Show. *Human Nature* features a vocal quartet that enjoyed '90s fame as an Australian "boy band" and has reinvented itself as keepers of the Motown sound, complete with an official sanction from Smokey Robinson (who pops up for a video introduction and duet). These friends from childhood sing together almost instinctively in a flashy showcase, which touches on both their own curious history and that of the Detroit label. The four aren't famous outside Australia, but they've filled a niche for an old-school musical group with a year-round presence on a Strip crowded with circus shows and stand-up comedy. ⊠ *The Venetian, 3355 Las Vegas Blvd. S, Center Strip* ☎ *702/414–9000* ⊕ *www.humannaturelive.com* ✉ *$74–$117.*

Jabbawockeez PRiSM. The only Las Vegas performers who don't show their faces star in this rare show, one that greatly appeals to the younger nightclub demographic. The masked hip-hop dance collective has steadily improved its showmanship and expanded its appeal since it settled on the Strip in 2010. There's plenty of break dancing, but the Jabbawockeez also make like lounge crooners and Motown stars and wrap their show in positive themes of brotherhood and inclusiveness. A cozy 830-seat theater opened with the new show in 2013, putting at least a third of the audience right on top of the action. Imaginative video and multimedia effects give it all a fun-house vibe. ⊠ *Luxor, 3900 Las Vegas Blvd. S, South Strip* ☎ *702/262–4400* ⊕ *www.jbwkz.com* ✉ *$70–$99.99* ⊙ *Thurs.–Mon. 7 and 9:30 pm.*

Jersey Boys. Las Vegas proved to be a fine location for a permanent company of the runaway hit biography of Frankie Valli and the Four Seasons. The show has become a phenomenon, thanks to familiar music combined with the little-known story of the group's rough-and-tumble beginnings, a surprising saga that contrasts dynamically with the familiar songs. It's all told at a cinematic clip with an edge of grit. One of the actors says the creators always reminded the cast, "You're in a Scorsese film. You're not in 'Guys & Dolls.'" The Vegas version is slightly trimmed but still runs in two acts. ⊠ *Paris Las Vegas, 3325 Las Vegas Blvd. S, Center Strip* ☎ *702/777–2782* ⊕ *www.jerseyboysinfo. com* ✉ *$59–$200* ⊙ *Wed.–Fri. and Sun. 7 pm; Tues. 6:30 pm; Sat. 5 and 8:15 pm.*

Jubilee!. This may be the last bastion of showgirls on the Strip, at least in the classic context of a giant "feather show" with dancing on lighted staircases, dazzling costumes and headdresses, and gargantuan sets and props, such as the sinking of the *Titanic*. An overhaul in early 2014 supervised by Beyonce's career-long choreographer, Frank Gatson Jr., brings a modern over-the-top vision to the classic over-the-top Vegas revue. ∎TIP→ The early show on Saturday is "covered" (i.e. a bit more chaste) if you want to take the whole family. ⊠ *Bally's Las Vegas, 3645 Las Vegas Blvd. S, Center Strip* ☎ *702/777–2782* ⊕ *www.ballyslasvegas. com* ✉ *$65–$132* ⊙ *Sat.–Thurs. 7:30 and 10:30 pm.*

KÀ. KÀ is Cirque du Soleil's bold interpretation of live martial-arts period fantasies like *Crouching Tiger, Hidden Dragon* in the adventures of two separated twins. The spectacle includes huge puppets and a battle on a vertical wall. A fixed stage is replaced by an 80,000-pound deck that's maneuvered by a giant gantry arm into all sorts of positions, including vertical. Though no Cirque that followed rivals it for sheer spectacle, the operatic tone remains divisive; those not sitting close enough to see faces can be confused by the story, which is told without dialogue. If nothing else, it's an amazing monument to the sky's-the-limit mentality that fueled Vegas in the go-go 2000s. ⊠ *MGM Grand Hotel & Casino, 3805 Las Vegas Blvd. S, South Strip* ☎ *702/891–7777* ✉ *$85–$174* ⊙ *Tues.–Sat. 7 and 9:30 pm.*

Le Rêve. Perhaps befitting the surreal dream implied in the title, it has been a long, strange voyage for this aquatic spectacle created by original *O* and *Mystere* director Franco Dragone. *Le Rêve* was heavily revised after it was deemed too reminiscent of *O*, and the theater-in-the-round now has a deluxe seating area with champagne service. The circular seating configuration pulls everyone in close for the tale of a female dreamer adrift in a surreal journey to find love. Max Chmerkovskiy from *Dancing with the Stars* added a ballroom element to the water-based stunts and aerial acrobatics. You're likely to remember the sensual image of the dreamer in her dripping-wet dress as much as the 80-foot dives from an upper bell tower. ⊠ *Wynn Las Vegas, 3131 Las Vegas Blvd. S, North Strip* ☎ *702/770–9966* 🖃 *$115–$214* ☾ *Fri.–Tues. 7 and 9:30 pm.*

Fodor's Choice ★

LOVE. Meet the Beatles again—well sort of, in a certified home run for Cirque du Soleil. Before he died, George Harrison convinced the surviving Beatles (and Yoko Ono) to license the group's music to Cirque. The remixed music by Beatle producer George Martin and his son Giles is revelatory on the state-of-the-art sound system, often like hearing the songs for the first time. Coming up with visuals to match was more of a challenge. Cirque created a theatrical and fanciful version of Liverpool, loosely telling the story of Beatlemania and the postwar generation without literally depicting the Fab Four. It's a lot to absorb, and one's attention can be split between the aerial stunt work and the action on the ground. But that just gives Beatles fans a reason to see it twice. ⊠ *Mirage Las Vegas, 3400 Las Vegas Blvd. S, Center Strip* ☎ *702/792–7777* ⊕ *www.cirquedusoleil.com* 🖃 *$85–$174* ☾ *Thurs.–Mon. 7 and 9:30 pm.*

FAMILY

Michael Jackson ONE. After traveling the world as "The Immortal," Cirque du Soleil's salute to Michael Jackson took on its second iteration in a remodeled Mandalay Bay theater. The touring version was designed as more a pop concert for sports arenas, but Cirque officials wanted the permanent installation to be more theatrical. Instead of a live band, the show opts to remix Jackson's actual recordings in earth-shaking sound delivered by more than 7,000 speakers. The story follows the journey of four misfits who discover Jackson's "agility, courage, playfulness, and love." It appeals to casual fans by ignoring the creepier aspects of the legacy and capturing Jackson in his '80s heyday, when he appears on video now and then as the quartet's spirit guide. ⊠ *Mandalay Bay, 3950 Las Vegas Blvd. S, South Strip* ☎ *877/632–7400* ⊕ *www.cirquedusoleil. com* 🖃 *$87–$209* ☾ *Sat.–Wed. 7 and 9:30 pm.*

Million Dollar Quartet. A retro-rock energy crackles through this Broadway hit inspired by a real moment in history—when Elvis Presley, Johnny Cash, Carl Perkins, and Jerry Lee Lewis convened for a jam session at Sun Records studio in Memphis. The Las Vegas version is shorter and tighter than the already intermission-free Broadway version, and the cozy vintage showroom at Harrah's Las Vegas is a perfect fit for a different kind of "legends in concert." ⊠ *Harrah's Las Vegas, 3475 Las Vegas Blvd. S, Center Strip* ☎ *702/777–2782* ⊕ *www. harrahslasvegas.com* 🖃 *$63–$87* ☾ *Tues., Wed., and Fri. 7 pm; Mon. and Thurs. 5:30 and 8 pm.*

Continued on page 266

THE LAS VEGAS SHOWGIRL

By Matt Villano

Move over, Old Blue Eyes. Sit down, Wayne Newton. You may be legends, but no one embodies the spirit of Sin City better than showgirls and their sequins, fishnets, and feathers.

For generations, these sexy, confident ladies have been the subject of boyhood (and manhood) fantasies. Whether entirely topless or merely scantily clad, showgirls have a timeless pinup-girl allure. What could be more Vegas?

Perhaps the best place to find the quintessential showgirl is Donn Arden's *Jubilee!*, a show that has played nonstop at Bally's Las Vegas for almost 25 years. It employs nearly 100 showgirls and still incorporates some of the costumes that Bob Mackey (creator of Cher's current Vegas show costumes) designed for the show's 1984 debut. For a rundown of showgirl accessories and attire, see opposite page.

DID YOU KNOW?

Over the course of a 90-minute *Jubilee!* show, the girls make between 7 and 11 costume changes. To reach the right parts of the three-level stage, they also run an average of 400 steps per night.

Top & Above, Don Arden's *Jubilee!*, Bally's Las Vegas

HEADDRESSES

Made of goose and rhea feathers, Swarovski crystal, and a whole lot of fabric, some of these headdresses can soar 5 feet and weigh up to 35 pounds.

WINGS

During the *Jubilee!* show, girls appear on stage with angel-like wings that are attached to tiny backpacks—the combination weighs 30 to 40 pounds.

FEATHER BOAS

Made from dyed ostrich feathers, these boas stretch up to 4 feet in length and can weigh as much as 5 or 6 pounds.

SEQUIN DRESSES

According to *Jubilee!*, the average costume contains 100,000 sequins in silver, gold, and a kaleidoscope of other colors. Each dress weighs 7–8 pounds.

G-STRINGS

This is a showgirl must. *Jubilee!* G-strings are made with a nude-colored fabric so they appear invisible to audience members.

FISHNETS

Jubilee! employs sewing technicians exclusively to keep fishnets looking good. In an average week, showgirls go through as many as six pairs.

HEELS

What's a showgirl without towering heels? Most dancers stomp around in three- or four-inchers; shorter gals opt for heels that are even higher.

JEWELRY

These pieces might contain rhinestones rather than diamonds but they're still substantial. Some of the jewelry can weigh up to 20 pounds.

Discount Tickets Vegas Style

It seemed like a welcome idea at the time. Visitors had long wondered when Las Vegas would get those kiosks for discount show tickets that people are used to looking for in New York's Broadway theater district.

When the first such outlet finally arrived on the Strip, producers were assured that they would remain in control of their own ticket inventory. Sell all the full-priced seats you can, the argument went, but why not fill any remaining seats at half price once it appeared full-price sales had peaked for the day?

And so it went. For a time. What the producers learned they couldn't control was the number of discount outlets. But, isn't that a win-win for the consumer, finding 10 or more of these booths all along the Strip now? Sort of. What happens now is that producers mark 'em up to mark 'em down. A middle-tier show such as *Fantasy* charges $46 to $68 in order to get half that. Now, any budget-minded person is almost forced to seek out the discount outlets for all but a handful of shows that still sell out at full face-value: Cirque du Soleil's *O*, usually, or headliners such as Celine Dion with a limited number of performance dates, or touring concert acts.

And discount vendors changed what once used to be simple, across-the-board pricing—all seats half price, plus a service charge—to offer discounts of less than 50% and some shows available a day in advance or by telephone. "Half-price outlets are like crack," noted one veteran of the ticket wars. "You start with a few and get that easy sale, so you start doing more and more."

The same-day outlets still make it deliberately inconvenient with no Internet sales, prodding those who have their hearts set on a title to buy ahead. But other discounts are out there as well, from coupon ads to room-and-show promotions bundled by the hotels. All of these, one producer explained, factor in to get prices from one number—the face value of a full-price ticket—to the real number a producer uses after averaging all the various discounts.

One magician says another who was new to town told him, "I figure if I can get just 100 full-priced sales a day, I'll be fine."

"Do you know how rare that is?" The veteran told him. "You will be lucky to get 30 on a good day."

—Mike Weatherford

FAMILY **Mystère.** Since 1993 Cirque du Soleil's new-age circus has been the town's most consistent family show. *Mystère* most purely preserves the original Cirque concept, and has held up to the increased spectacle of its sister shows by being the funniest of the bunch, and by keeping the spectators close to the action and the human acrobatics in the spotlight. Perhaps more than the other Cirque productions, you're intimately involved with this surreal wonderland and the comic characters who interact with the audience. In early 2012, the show swapped out the climactic trapeze number for an aerialist display from a closed show in Japan, providing new incentive to re-explore *Mystère*. ☒ *Treasure*

Island, 3300 Las Vegas Blvd. S, North Strip ☎ *800/392–1999* ⊕ *www.cirquedusoleil.com* ✉ *$86–$141* ☉ *Sat.–Wed. 7 and 9:30 pm.*

FAMILY

Fodor's Choice

★

O. More than $70 million was spent on Cirque du Soleil's theater at Bellagio back in 1998, and its liquid stage is the centerpiece of a one-of-a-kind show. It was money well spent: O remains one of the best-attended shows on the Strip. The title is taken from the French word for water (*eau*), and water is everywhere—1.5 million gallons of it, 12 million pounds of it, contained by a "stage" that, thanks to hydraulic lifts, can change shape and turn into dry land in no time. The intense and nonstop action by the show's acrobats, aerial gymnasts, trapeze artists, synchronized swimmers, divers, and contortionists takes place above, within, and even on the surface of the water, making for a stylish spectacle that manages to have a vague theme about the wellspring of theater and imagination. To catch all that's going on, many people become repeat visitors. ✉ *Bellagio Las Vegas, 3600 Las Vegas Blvd. S, Center Strip* ☎ *702/693–8866* ⊕ *www.cirquedusoleil.com* ✉ *$119–$181* ☉ *Wed.–Sun. 7:30 and 10 pm.*

Rock of Ages. The unlikely Broadway hit, a salute to '80s-era hard metal and power ballads, actually played on the Strip very briefly in 2006 before it went on to the Great White(snake) Way. Now it's back where its producers always wanted it to be, in spite of the lackluster response to the movie version starring Tom Cruise as an over-the-top rocker. The spoofy stage version alternates high-school humor with fist-pumping '80s hits such as "Sister Christian" and "Don't Stop Believin'," telling a story as old as rock and roll itself: The kids try to save their beloved club from greedy developers. ✉ *The Venetian, 3355 Las Vegas Blvd., North Strip* ☎ *702/414–9000* ⊕ *www.rockofagesmusical.com* ✉ *$69–$167* ☉ *Tues.–Fri. and Sun. 8 pm, Sat. 7 and 10 pm.*

FAMILY

Tournament of Kings. One of the last vestiges of Las Vegas's "family" phase is 20-plus years of this Arthurian stunt show in a dirt-floor arena, with the audience eating a basic dinner (warning: no utensils) and cheering on fast horses, jousting, and swordplay. Those familiar with Medieval Times around the country will recognize it in all but name. But it's still a great family gathering—especially for preadolescents, who get to make a lot of noise—and the realistic stunts speak to the commitment of the cast. Those who haven't seen it in a few years may notice some long-delayed upgrades in the costumes and props. ✉ *Excalibur, 3850 Las Vegas Blvd. S, South Strip* ☎ *702/597–7600* ⊕ *www.excalibur.com* ✉ *$71 with dinner; $53 show only* ☉ *Wed.–Mon. 6 pm; Wed., Thurs., and weekends 8:30 pm.*

Vegas Nocturne. The return of the social club! In the old days, you went to a nightclub to see a show. The Cosmopolitan is reuniting the night-club and show experience with the retro-theme "supper club" called Rose.Rabbit.Lie. House performers entertain diners before the feature show, *Vegas Nocturne.* As a stand-alone product, "Nocturne" is a bit upstaged by its environment; those who don't pony up for a ticket in the main room get much of the same entertainment in adjacent areas. But "Nocturne" is still a fun parade of variety and burlesque performers, with humor that swings from winking wit to shock-value raunch.

SAVE OR SPLURGE

SAVE

Mac King. The comedy magic of Mac King is worth every penny of the full $38 ticket price, and full-price tickets send you to the front of the line. But if you look for coupon-dispensing showgirls within Harrah's or check in at a promotions booth, you can often get in for much less.

Fremont Street Experience. Dazzling video shows on Fremont Street's overhead canopy aren't the only thing happening in Glitter Gulch. The street itself has become a midway, from sidewalk artists to an overhead zip line. Every weekend live performers—heavy on costumed tribute bands with names such as Fan Halen or Led Zepagain—play free gigs on two stages; select weekends even bring in acts with name recognition (breakout country stars Lady Antebellum and Eric Church have played the weekend of the Academy of Country Music Awards). Stages are on 1st and 3rd streets. ☎ 702/678–5777.

Frankie Moreno. A piano-pounding showman with old-Vegas charisma who has the looks and the chops, but he doesn't have the name recognition to compete with the big-ticket stars. So full-price tickets are $44, and half price for Stratosphere hotel guests.

SPLURGE

Le Rêve. Wynn Las Vegas experimented with an "upsell" ticket for its water show in-the-round, adding a "VIP Indulgence" section of seating that's been so successful, the producers say they wish there was room for more seats. The top $214 ticket includes champagne, chocolate-covered strawberries, and video monitors offering backstage and underwater views of the action.

LOVE. A $150 sound-and-vision extravaganza that delights old Beatles fans—and with a sound track that pumps from 6,500 speakers, creates new ones.

O. Cirque's big water show has been around since 1998, but you won't ever see it go on tour. Pony up the $180 and save on your water bill when you get home.

$\boxtimes$ *The Cosmopolitan of Las Vegas, 3708 Las Vegas Blvd. S, South Strip* ☎ *877/667–0585* ⊕ *www.roserabbitlie.com* ✉ *$134–$156.*

V — The Ultimate Variety Show. This mid-priced variety show has held its own against the splashier Cirque productions for more than 10 years. It has magic, juggling, and acrobatics such as hand balancing. But its success is due to its "front of curtain" atmosphere with likable performers making direct contact with the audience. $\boxtimes$ *Miracle Mile Shops at Planet Hollywood, 3667 Las Vegas Blvd. S, Center Strip* ☎ *702/260–7200* ⊕ *www.vtheaterboxoffice.com* ✉ *$71–$104.*

X Burlesque. This is no old-timey burlesque. Instead, an edgy modern-rock attitude permeates this dance-intensive topless revue. A comedian doing a 10-minute set is the only spoken contact with the audience. It's much closer to a strip-club vibe than the more theatrical *Fantasy* at Luxor, which should serve as a recommendation to some and a warning to others. But even the more intense gyrations are leavened with a winking humor. ⊠ *Flamingo Las Vegas, 3555 Las Vegas Blvd. S, Center Strip* ☎ *702/777–2782* ⊕ *www.xburlesque.com* ✉ *$49–$62* ☉ *Daily 10 pm.*

Zarkana. When *Viva Elvis* left the building as Cirque du Soleil's first certified Las Vegas flop, the company replaced it with a proven ticket seller: *Zarkana*, which was created for New York City's Radio City Music Hall and spent two summers there. Because it wasn't initially intended to sit among seven other Cirques on the Strip, it's more like a "greatest hits" show in the company's original style. That general approach makes it a bit repetitive, particularly of O and *KÀ*, and lacking the grand distinctions of the Beatles and Michael Jackson–themed titles. But for Cirque newbies, the concept of an abandoned theater coming back to life with the ghosts of circuses past will nonetheless deliver the company's trademark sense of wonder. ⊠ *Aria, 3730 Las Vegas Blvd. S, Center Strip* ☎ *855/927–5262* ⊕ *www.cirquedusoleil. com* ✉ *$76–$198* ☉ *Fri.–Tues. 7 and 9:30 pm.*

Zumanity. For its third Las Vegas production, Cirque du Soleil deliberately turned away from the family market to indulge in an erotic, near-naked exploration of sexuality. The end product also followed the lead of Baz Luhrmann's movie *Moulin Rouge* by fusing Cirque acrobatics with European cabaret and English music-hall tradition. *Zumanity* has evened out over the years with a stronger balance of comedy, omnisexual titillation, and the familiar Cirque acrobatics to literalize metaphors for love and sex: taking flight, soaring, etc. Softer curves replaced the original edge and *Zumanity* doesn't try so hard to shock anymore, but it's still (somewhat proudly) not meant for everyone. ⊠ *New York–New York, 3790 Las Vegas Blvd. S, South Strip* ☎ *702/740–6815* ⊕ *www. cirquedusoleil.com* ✉ *$87–$148* ☉ *Fri.–Tues. 7 and 9:30 pm.*

RESIDENT HEADLINERS

The turn of the 21st century took Las Vegas back to one of the traditions from its past. The explosion of new room volume on the Strip combined with the hassles of modern air travel opened the doors to a wave of resident headliners, those who live in Las Vegas and perform on a year-round schedule comparable to the revues. Donny and Marie Osmond, George Wallace, and Carrot Top all bet that audiences were ready to embrace the down-front performing tradition (not letting anything get between the performer and the audience) that put Las Vegas on the map.

Now Las Vegas is returning to its '60s and '70s-era concept of stars who don't live here, but come in several times a year for extended stretches. Rod Stewart and Elton John assembled custom showcases, and Celine Dion returned with her second Las Vegas residency in 2011. Plenty of other stars seem willing to get in line, with Britney Spears, Boyz II Men, Meat Loaf, and Olivia Newton-John the latest to test the waters. With nonstar production shows having hit a creative wall outside of Cirque, count on this star-plus-spectacle formula to continue for some time.

Celine Dion takes center stage at Caesars Palace for a limited number of must-see special engagements.

Britney Spears: Piece of Me. Pop princess Britney Spears has opted to present a *Piece of Me* exclusively in Las Vegas for two years. Fans of her live shows will recognize this hit parade as a continuation of past arena tours rather than an attempt to conform to a traditional Vegas residency. That means a host of athletic dancers and eye-popping video, but little live singing or banter from the star. Casual fans might feel a little like disconnected party crashers, wondering what all the fuss is about. But those who grew up with Britney will cheer her on as she descends to the stage in an orb to conquer an alien planet or swings Tarzan-like from a giant tree. ⊠ *Planet Hollywood, 3667 Las Vegas Blvd. S, South Strip* ☎ *800/745–3000* ⊕ *www.planethollywoodresort. com* ⊠ *$59–$179.*

Carrot Top. After years on the college circuit, the prop comic moved his trunks full of tricks into the Luxor, where a lot of people realize he's funnier than they thought he would be. The Florida native known off-stage as Scott Thompson still is most unique when wielding his visual gags, but he sells them with a manic energy, a tourist's street-level view of Vegas, and a whole running commentary on the act itself, perhaps a sly nod to his eternal lack of respect. ⊠ *Luxor Las Vegas, 3900 Las Vegas Blvd. S, South Strip* ☎ *702/262–4400* ⊠ *$60–$71* ⊙ *Wed.–Sat. and Mon. 8:30 pm.*

Fodor's Choice
★

Celine Dion. Celine Dion became a divisive pop star in the '90s, and so may be singing to the converted at this point. Too bad, because those willing to approach with an open mind will be treated to a universally entertaining showcase. Dion goes beyond her expected hits and steers her powerhouse voice into challenging new directions. The new show puts the focus squarely on the music, trading the large ensemble of dancers from the five-year run of *A New Day* for an onstage orchestra and a few visual enhancements. The song list provides fun surprises, from a medley of James Bond movie themes to Ella Fitgerald and Michael Jackson tributes. ■TIP➜ Those planning a trip around Celine should know the 150 or so annual performances of "A New Day" have been cut back to a modest 70-plus shows a year. Check the schedule on her website (www.celinedion.com) or thecolosseum.com. ✉ *Caesars Palace, 3570 Las Vegas Blvd. S, Center Strip* ☎ *877/423–5463* ⊕ *www.celinedion. com* ✉ *$55–$250* ⊘ *7:30 pm selected dates (no shows Mon.).*

David Copperfield. The master magician has made Las Vegas a part of his career since the 1980s, but only in recent years has he settled into playing the MGM Grand for more than 40 weeks per year. At this point, Copperfield is sort of the Rolling Stones of magic; you sense his authority and submit to it from the minute the show opens, and trust him to wow you. He varies the pace with illusions that can be touching or funny, but most of all they still genuinely fool you. ✉ *MGM Grand Hotel & Casino, 3799 Las Vegas Blvd. S, South Strip* ☎ *702/891–7777* ⊕ *www.davidcopperfield.com* ✉ *$83–$116* ⊘ *7 and 9:30 pm (4 pm shows at seasonal times of year).*

Donny and Marie Osmond. The Mormon siblings who grew up in front of America still look and sound great, and their variety training on the Strip back in the 1970s allows them to work this old-school showroom setting with ease. The two are quick to split into lengthy solo sets that let Marie sing opera and rock out to Aerosmith, while Donny gives the old Osmonds pop ditty "Yo-Yo" a Justin Beiber treatment. The time apart just makes their time together more valuable. The production numbers with a campy squad of badly costumed dancers will rekindle memories of their toothier, bad-hair days on variety TV. ✉ *Flamingo Las Vegas, 3555 Las Vegas Blvd. S, Center Strip* ☎ *702/733–3333* ⊕ *www. donnyandmarie.com* ✉ *$104–$135* ⊘ *Tues.–Sat. 7:30 pm.*

Elton John. The pop and rock legend's return to Caesars Palace is called *The Million Dollar Piano*, based on imbedded video panels that display everything from Versace design patterns to old videos. But the show as a whole is longer and more subdued than his previous "Red Piano" run at Caesars. The band is larger—including a couple of string players, soul singer Rose Stone, and longtime percussion sidekick Ray Cooper—and the focus more upon his early '70s classics, with even a few rarities to please serious fans. ■TIP➜ Check the schedule at the Colosseum at Caesars Palace as John rotates dates with Celine Dion, Rod Stewart, and others. ✉ *Caesars Palace, 3570 Las Vegas Blvd. S, Center Strip* ☎ *888/929–7849* ⊕ *www.eltonjohn.com or www.caesarspalace.com* ✉ *$55–$250* ⊘ *7:30 pm select Sun., Tues., Wed., Sat.*

Gordie Brown. The Canadian impressionist has been a Las Vegas presence for years, with a needed jolt of exposure as the opening act for Celine Dion's U.S. arena tour in 2009. Women will warm up to a guy good-looking enough to be a retro crooner, while men will recognize the kid from their middle school who memorized *MAD* magazine. Brown's terrain is the song parody, delivered with a manic silliness that sometimes goes by so fast you're not sure if it even makes sense. But you won't take the effort for granted. ⊠ *Golden Nugget, 129 E. Fremont St., Downtown* 🕾 *866/946–5336* ⊕ *www.gordiebrown.com* 🖾 *$37–$75* ⊙ *Tues.–Sat. 7:30 pm.*

Fodor's Choice
★

Penn & Teller. Eccentric comic magicians Penn & Teller once seemed an unlikely fit for Las Vegas, but they're more popular now than when they came to town more than a decade ago. The two have spread into mainstream culture beyond the Strip, thanks to Penn (the big loud one to Teller's short mime) becoming a cable news pundit and *Celebrity Apprentice* contestant. Their off-kilter humor now seems less jarring as they age gracefully at the Rio. Their magic in a gorgeous 1,500-seat theater is topical and genuinely baffling, the only show in town to push the form into new creative directions. And their comedy is satiric, provocative, and thoughtful. ⊠ *The Rio, 3700 W. Flamingo Rd., West Side* 🕾 *702/777–7776* ⊕ *www.pennandteller.com* 🖾 *$92–$116* ⊙ *Sat.–Wed. 9 pm.*

Rod Stewart. Wearing the second half of his 60s as comfortably as a mop of sandy hair, Rod Stewart breezes through a gentle-rocking showcase of his hits. You can almost see him winking from the back row as he still agitates the ladies with a bit of the soft shoe on "Tonight's the Night." And yet, in some of his shows, Stewart also buckled down in a few places to remind audiences of the more credible moments of his past, offering more serious tunes such as "The Killing of Georgie." ■TIP➔ Fans will want to plan in advance a Las Vegas visit around Stewart's blocks of shows at the Colosseum; he's only there a couple of stretches per year. ⊠ *Caesars Palace, 3570 Las Vegas Blvd. S, Center Strip* 🕾 *888/929–7849* ⊕ *www.caesarspalace.com* 🖾 *$55–$250* ⊙ *Select dates 7:30 pm.*

Shania Twain: Still the One. Live horses? Flying motorcycles? It's everything you would expect in a custom-Vegas showcase for the superstar who fused country music with MTV video glam back in the '90s. Shania Twain's comeback, staged exclusively for the Colosseum at Caesars Palace, is a fun update of the Ann-Margret variety shows of the '70s, down to the sequined bodysuits and male buckaroos. The visuals can overwhelm the singing, yet it's all grounded in a sincerity that will please fans who held on through the years. ⊠ *Caesar's Palace, 3570 Las Vegas Blvd., Colosseum, Center Strip* 🕾 *888/929–7849* ⊕ *www. shaniainvegas.com* 🖾 *$55–$250.*

Terry Fator. Las Vegas has long been a haven for impressionists, only this one lets his puppets do the talking. Fator is the likable second-season winner of *America's Got Talent* who does singing impressions as well as ventriloquism. During his run at the Mirage he's added new puppets to the act, including Vicki the Cougar (on the prowl for younger men) and a beetle who sings the Beatles. In just a few years, Fator has become one of the more accomplished and consistent headliners on the Strip. ■TIP➔ Fator's Christmas show, during the holiday stretch when many titles go on vacation, is even more charming. It tones down some of the humor that makes the year-round version less suitable for children than you'd think a puppet show would be. ⊠ *Mirage, 3400 Las Vegas Blvd.*

O, at the Bellagio, is one of Las Vegas's eight Cirque du Soleil shows.

S, Center Strip ☎ 702/792–7777 ⊕ *www.terryfator.com* ✉ *$75–$174* ⊙ *Mon.–Thurs. 7:30 pm.*

Vinnie Favorito. Don Rickles has an heir apparent in this insult comic who devotes all but the first five minutes of his set to working the crowd, singling out victims for all sorts of racial profiling and raunchy interrogation. The politically correct should stay far away or try to hide in the back of the room, but it usually doesn't help. He will find you. And most people end up not minding so much, or forgetting they should know better. ⊠ *Flamingo Las Vegas, 3555 Las Vegas Blvd. S, Center Strip* ☎ 702/777–2782 ⊕ *www.flamingolasvegas.com* ✉ *$69–$125* ⊙ *Nightly 8 pm.*

FINE ARTS

Although it's known more for theatrical spectacles than serious theater, Las Vegas does have a lively cultural scene. The arrival of the Smith Center for the Performing Arts center Downtown in 2012 was a game-changer, giving new prominence to the city's ballet and philharmonic, which offer full seasons of productions each year. And while some musicals such as "Jersey Boys" dig in for long runs on the Strip, The Smith Center also filled the previously missing niche of touring Broadway musicals that drop in for a week or so.

BALLET

Nevada Ballet Theatre. The city's longest-running fine-arts organization (this being Las Vegas, it only dates from 1973) stages three or four productions each year, anchored by an annual December presentation of

The Nutcracker. ✉ *1651 Inner Circle Dr., Summerlin* ☎ *702/243–2623, 702/982–7805 for tickets* ⊕ *www.nevadaballet.com.*

CLASSICAL MUSIC

Las Vegas Philharmonic. Formed in 1998, the Philharmonic performs both a "Masterworks" and "Pops" series, the latter often using guest vocalists from shows on the Strip. ✉ *361 Symphony Park A, Downtown* ☎ *702/258–5438 for schedule information, 702/749–2000 for tickets* ⊕ *www.lvphil.org.*

THEATER

Away from the Strip, a booming community theater scene caters to the area's many new residents, from retirees to hipsters, who are looking for a low-cost alternative to the pricey shows. With the exception of Las Vegas Little Theatre, most don't have their own performance spaces and instead rent municipal auditoriums or the offbeat Onyx Theatre for their productions.

Las Vegas Little Theatre. Las Vegas's oldest community theater has branched out beyond the Neil Simon basic. Its main-stage season is augmented by a "Black Box" season of smaller, more adventurous works and it hosts the Vegas Fringe Festival of new works in June. The productions are staged in a cozy, comfortable theater in a strip mall. ✉ *3920 Schiff Dr., West Side* ☎ *702/362–7996* ⊕ *www.lvlt.org.*

Onyx Theatre. Some wild and challenging theater has emerged in the back of a fetish store in a rundown shopping center. The small venue has presented everything from Shakespeare to *Naked Boys Singing* and *Twisted Cherry Burlesque.* The theater also hosts concerts by singers and cabaret acts. ✉ *953 E. Sahara #16b, East Side* ☎ *702/732–7225* ⊕ *www.onyxtheatre.com.*

University of Nevada–Las Vegas Theater Department. UNLV's Nevada Conservatory Theatre brings in outside professionals and holds community-wide auditions for a full season of five productions each academic year, one of them a musical. Most performances are held in the Judy Bayley Theatre on campus. ✉ *4505 S. Maryland Pkwy., University District* ☎ *702/985–2787 for tickets* ⊕ *www.theatre.unlv.edu.*

NIGHTLIFE

Updated by Susan Stapleton

FUELED BY THE "WHAT HAPPENS in Vegas, stays in Vegas" ethos (read: "All your sins here get expunged completely as soon as you pay your bookie, loan shark, and/or credit card bill"), nightlife impresarios keep dipping into their vast pockets in order to create over-the-top experiences where party-mad Visigoths—plus, well, you and me—can live out some wild fantasies. The number of high-profile nightclubs, trendy lounges, and sizzling strip bars continues to grow, each attempting to trump the other in order to attract not just high rollers, but A-list celebrities and the publicity that surrounds them. Many of the newest clubs even have gambling. Though, we ask: Why bother when you can lounge beside the pool by day and bellow at the moon by night while dancing half clad at a club until noon the following day (when it's back into the pool you go)?

In the late 1990s, once the Vegas mandarins decided that the "family experience" just wasn't happening, Sin City nightlife got truly sinful again, drawing raves from clubbers worldwide. A wave of large dance clubs, such as the Luxor's (now-defunct) Ra, opened their doors, followed by a trendy batch of cozier ultralounges—lounges with dance floors and high-tech amenities.

The game of one-upmanship has continued—recent additions that have kept the city hopping include Light Nightclub at Mandalay Bay and the mammoth Hakkasan at the MGM Grand. What's more, bawdy '50s-era burlesque lounges are continuing their comeback with a gaggle of clubs now dedicated to the art of striptease.

Few cities on Earth match Vegas in its dedication to upping the nightlife ante. So with all these choices, no one—not even the Visigoths—has an excuse for not having fun, however you define the "f" word.

NIGHTLIFE PLANNER

FIND OUT WHAT'S GOING ON

With the number of nightlife options in Las Vegas, it's not hard to be overwhelmed. *These local publications can steer you in the right direction and help you plan your ultimate Vegas night out.* Remember that party schedules—as well as the popularity of any one spot—can change overnight, *so the best way of keeping current is to consult these publications.*

Eater Vegas (⊕ *www.vegas.eater.com*) provides invaluable information on dining and nightlife, many times long before the newspapers.

Anthony Curtis' *Las Vegas Advisor* (☎ 702/252–0655 ⊕ *www.lasvegasadvisor.com*) is a monthly newsletter that's invaluable for its information on Las Vegas dining, entertainment, gambling promotions, comps, and news. If you're here for a short visit, pick up free copies of *Vegas, Today in Las Vegas,* and *What's On in Las Vegas* at hotels and gift shops.

The *Las Vegas Review-Journal,* the city's daily newspaper, publishes a tabloid pullout section each Friday. It provides entertainment features and reviews, and showroom and lounge listings with complete time and price information. The *Review-Journal* maintains a website

LAS VEGAS NIGHTLIFE BEST BETS

BEST OUTDOOR PATIO
With cabanas, private tables, a deejay, and a dance floor, **Encore Beach Club**, part of the indoor/outdoor **Surrender** day- and nightclub is the perfect way to spend a night under the stars.

BEST VIEWS
Rooftop and high-rise lounges with amazing views include the **Voodoo Rooftop Nightclub, Mandarin Bar, Ghostbar, Level 107 Lounge**, and the **Foundation Room.**

BEST LOCAL LOUNGE
Peppermill's Fireside Lounge, with its lethal Scorpion cocktail.

BEST ALL-AROUND "HANG"
The **Chandelier** at the Cosmopolitan, where mixologists serve up dozens of handcrafted cocktails in a three-story bar—all inside the world's largest chandelier.

BEST ANTIDOTE TO THE STRIP
For an alternative scene, the no-frills **Double Down Saloon** rules, although charming lounges like **Commonwealth, Downtown Cocktail Room**, and the **Lady Silvia** are giving it a run for its money.

(⊕ *www.lvrj.com*) where show listings are updated each week. The *Las Vegas Sun*, once a competing daily, is now a section inside the *Review-Journal* but maintains its own editorial staff and website: ⊕ *www. lasvegassun.com.*

Two excellent alternative weekly newspapers are distributed at retail stores and coffee shops around town and maintain comprehensive websites. *Las Vegas Weekly* (⊕ *www.lasvegasweekly.com*) and *Vegas Seven* (⊕ *www.vegasseven.com*) offer some timely and incisive reflections on the nightclub scene and music outside the realm of the casinos.

HOW TO GET IN

Nobody comes to Las Vegas to wait in line. So how exactly do you get past those velvet ropes? Short of personally knowing the no-nonsense bouncers and serious-looking women holding clipboards that guard the doors, here are a few pointers.

First, know that even though this is a 24-hour town, lines start forming around 10 pm (or earlier). If you're not on a list, get there after dinner and dress the part—which is to say, don't expect to go straight from the pool to the club. Vegas bars and clubs have pretty strict dress codes, so leave those T-shirts, baseball caps, and ripped jeans in your hotel room (unless you're headed to the Griffin Lounge or some other hipster haven). Arguing that your sneakers were made by Alexander McQueen probably won't help, either. At most of the trendier spots, at least for women, skin is in—this *is* Sin City, after all. And needless to say, the universal rule of big-city nightlife also applies in Vegas: groups of guys almost always have a harder time getting in without a few women in the mix. If your group is gender impaired, consider politely asking some unaccompanied women to temporarily join you, perhaps in exchange for some drinks once you're all inside. Too shy, you say? If there was ever a place to check your shyness at the airport, it's this town.

Most spots have two lines: a VIP line (for those on the guest list or who have a table with bottle service reserved) and a regular line. You can either ask your hotel concierge for help contacting a club to get on a guest list, or contact the club directly. Some websites such as ⊕ *www. vegas.com* sell passes they guarantee will get you past the crush, but save your money for the door—better to slip the bouncer $20 per person than hope they'll acknowledge the Internet ticket you've bought for the same amount. If you have a few people in your group, it might be worth it to splurge on a table reservation: without one, a group of five could easily spend $20 each getting in good with the bouncers, plus $20 each for the cover charge, and then there's always the expensive drinks.

A further note on going deluxe: If you're getting a table with bottle service, note that your VIP host will expect something from you, as will the busboy who actually lugs over your booze. On holiday weekends and New Year's Eve, expect to multiply what you plan to give them by at least two.

ON THE STRIP

BARS AND LOUNGES

"ULTRALOUNGES" AND THEN SOME

The lounges of the Las Vegas casino-hotels were once places where such headliners as Frank, Dean, and the gang would go after their shows, taking a seat in the audience to laugh at the comedy antics of Shecky Greene or Don Rickles. For a while lounges were mostly reduced to small bars within the casino where bands played Top 40 hits in front of people pie-eyed from the slots. The turn of the 21st century, however, brought an explosion of hybrid nightspots—the so-called ultralounges—that aimed for the middle ground between dance club and conventional lounge. Some of the best of them—the Beatles Revolution Lounge in the Mirage, Bellagio's Hyde Lounge, and the Mandarin Oriental's Mandarin Bar—are worth a separate trip, given how much of a pleasure-jolt they offer.

Fodor's Choice ★   **The Beatles Revolution Lounge.** Designed for synergy with Cirque du Soleil's Beatles-theme *LOVE*, the "Rev" wows tourists and locals alike with its private alcoves, hippie-outfitted servers, beanbag chairs, and eye-popping, ever-shifting psychedelic fractal wall projections (which patrons can control at their tables). The high volume deemphasizes the "lounge" aspect here, and the classic rock and Fab Four tunes begin to give way to pumping dance music as the night wears on. The lounge has different DJs every night it's open. On weekends, it's also one of the most crowded spots in the Mirage. ⊠ *The Mirage, 3400 Las Vegas Blvd. S, Center Strip* ☎ *702/693–8300* ⊕ *www.mirage.com/nightlife* ⊗ *Closed Mon.–Wed.*

Fodor's Choice ★   **The Chandelier.** True to its name, this swanky lounge sits in a chandelier with 2 million crystal beads, making it the largest chandelier in town

Out at 4 am

Vegas is a 24-hour town, and when the party starts to wind down in some places, the doors to others are just opening. The following are our picks for after-hours hot spots. Remember, even after 4 am, expect lines—sometimes very long ones—to get in. And bring your sunglasses to protect those bleary eyes from the morning rays when you finally stumble out.

Since the closing of Drai's, the **Artisan Lounge** has become the after-hours king, with killer deejays and cocktail specials after 2 am.

Another late-night option is even smaller and more intimate: **Savile Row** inside the Luxor's **LAX** nightclub.

There's no set menu here; instead, mixologists come by and ask you what sorts of drinks you like, then they concoct cocktails based on your preferences.

For those seeking a different kind of decadence, go to Sin City's best strip joint, the gloomy yet glorious **Spearmint Rhino**.

Finally, if you're looking for a chill atmosphere rather than a club or strip joint, check out The Cosmopolitan's **Chandelier** for three levels of cocktail splendor, or hang and gamble at Aria's lounge/high-limit room, the **Deuce Lounge.**

(and, perhaps, the world). The bar is separated into three separate levels, and each has different themes. The ground floor—dubbed "Bottom of the Chandelier," for those of you scoring at home—is dedicated to intricate specialty drinks, the kinds of cocktails you'll only find here. The second floor pays homage to molecular gastronomy in cocktail form; spiked sorbets and dehydrated fruits are common in drinks here. Finally, at the top of the Chandelier, everything's coming up floral, with rose and lavender syrups and violet sugar. If you're particularly adventuresome (and you can get a seat on the first floor), try the off-menu Verbena cocktail with a "Szechuan button." This desiccated flower from Africa numbs your mouth to make flavors more potent; it also prompts you to down your cocktail in mere seconds. ⊠ *The Cosmopolitan, 3708 Las Vegas Blvd. S, South Strip* ☎ *702/698–7000* ⊕ *www. cosmopolitanlasvegas.com.*

The Deuce Lounge. Part bar, part high-roller pit, The Deuce Lounge is a great spot for revelers who like to mix business (that is, high-stakes gambling) and pleasure (that is, boozing) all night long. Bartenders serve up custom cocktails, with pretty much whatever liquors you prefer. There's also appetizer service until 10 pm every night. Before 8 pm, The Deuce is a great spot to take in a ball game, especially since Aria's sports book is so small (yet close enough to run in those last-minute wagers). ⊠ *Aria, 3730 Las Vegas Blvd. S, Center Strip* ☎ *702/693–8300* ⊕ *www.aria.com/nightlife.*

eyecandy. High technology hits the Strip at this vast "interactive" ultralounge in the center of Mandalay Bay's casino floor. For "future shock" freaks, there are tented "touch tables" onto which you can draw messages, words, and images projected onto video screens above

"Turn off your mind, relax . . . " Beanbag chairs and modern psychedelic touches such as fractal wall imagery are what make the Beatles Revolution Lounge the future of retro.

the dance floor, and "sound stations" that let you send music of your choice to the deejay. More important than the technology here, though, is the cocktail menu; crafted by master mixologist Tony Abou-Ganim, drinks are so scrumptious they could call the place "mouthcandy," too. ✉ *Mandalay Bay, 3950 Las Vegas Blvd. S, South Strip* ☎ *702/632–4760* ⊕ *www.mandalaybay.com/entertainment.*

Fizz Las Vegas. Drink like Sir Elton John and his husband, David Furnish, at this chichi and very private champagne bar decked out with more than 50 provocative photos from the famous couple's private collection. Champagne obviously is the name of the game at this bubblicious lounge replete with lighting under the sofas to highlight the ladies' high, high heels. Furnish, the creative director for the lounge, and Sir Elton lent their own private chef to create a small -ites menu of caviar (natch), gourmet paninis, and more. The cocktail menu even includes a $2,500 libation for those inclined to drop some Benjamins. ⚠ **Everyone's a celebrity here, including you, so no photos are allowed inside.** ✉ *Caesars Palace, 3570 Las Vegas Blvd. S, Center* ☎ *702/776–3200* ⊕ *fizzlv.com.*

Fodor's Choice ★ **Foundation Room.** Ancient statues, tapestry-covered walls, pirated Mississippi road signs—the Foundation Room gets high marks for aesthetic appeal. Though it used to be open to members only, this secluded subsidiary of the House of Blues is now open to everyone seven nights a week—provided you're willing to wait on line. The venue itself is a series of different rooms, each with its own set of design themes and type of music that could range from Top 40 hits to house, depending on the night. A main attraction is the view of the Strip; because the club is on the 43rd floor, it provides panoramic vistas of the entire town, one of the best in the city. ✉ *Mandalay Bay, 3590 Las Vegas Blvd. S, South Strip* ☎ *702/632–7631* ⊕ *www.houseofblues.com.*

HIT Lounge. Located next to the high-limit area on Monte Carlo's main casino floor, the swanky and intimate HIT Lounge doubles as the classroom where members of MGM's M Life Rewards Club can experience a hands-on mixology class. The two-hour tutorial, available for the member and up to nine friends, essentially is a private session with the director of beverages, who'll teach the secrets behind mastering the perfect cocktail. Students don't only learn how to make cocktails; they also drink them. The price for the class: $75 per person. ✉ *Monte Carlo Resort & Casino, 3770 Las Vegas Blvd. S, Center Strip* ☎ *702/730–7777* ⊕ *www.montecarlo.com.*

INDUSTRY NIGHTS

Although most bars, clubs, and strip bars rely primarily on out-of-towners for their income, locals—especially those who work in the nightlife biz—bring much welcome spirit, sex appeal, and insider-hipness to the mix, so many hot spots feature special (always nonweekend) nights in which these folks get free admission, free drinks, and so on. Don't be put off by "Industry" or "Locals" parties—they tend to be even cooler than "regular" evenings.

Hyde Bellagio. SBE founder and CEO Sam Nazarian made a splash in the local nightlife scene with this posh ultralounge, famous for its front-and-center view overlooking the Bellagio Fountains. Inside, the theme is library chic—there are actual books on the walls. Outside, a small patio harbors what some deem the most romantic table in Vegas—a two-top that looks out on the water show. The real star at this swanky lounge, however, is the cocktail program, complete with roving Bellini carts. ✉ *Bellagio, 3600 Las Vegas Blvd. S, Center Strip* ☎ *702/693–8700* ⊕ *hydebellagio.com.*

Koi Lounge. Circles are a big theme at this lounge that fronts Koi restaurant. More than 20 Tibetan hand-carved prayer wheels are positioned around the room, interspersed with circular banquettes that are great for big groups and lousy for small ones. Be sure to visit during happy hour, when mixologists oblige by offering half price on signature drinks and select appetizers. Unlike other lounges around town, this joint's happy hour runs seven days a week (with limited late-night hours on weekends). ✉ *Planet Hollywood, 3667 Las Vegas Blvd. S, Center Strip* ☎ *702/454–4555* ⊕ *koirestaurant.com.*

Level 107 Lounge. The Stratosphere might be downscale compared to other Vegas hotels, but there ain't nothing "down" about the high-in-the-sky experience to be had here. From this sleek, attractive room, the view of Sin City is truly amazing (if slightly remote). For an even bigger thrill, head upstairs and outside (to level 108, of course) to AirBar. The signature drink: something called Jet Fuel served in a souvenir cup. Consider yourself warned. ✉ *Stratosphere, 2000 Las Vegas Blvd., North Strip* ☎ *702/380–7777* ⊕ *www.stratospherehotel.com.*

Light Nightclub. Combining the acrobatics of co-creators Cirque du Soleil with a nightclub environment gives this hot spot an element of theatrics. State-of-the-art lighting, sound, and special effects give this deejay-driven nightclub the upper hand, while resident deejays such as Axwell and Sebastian Ingrosso drive the EDM-frenzied crowds. The aerialists floating over the masses tip it over the edge. Even if you're not ordering bottle service, the video screens behind the deejay booth will wow. ⊠ *Mandalay Bay, 3950 Las Vegas Blvd. S, South Strip* ☎ *702/693–8300* ⊕ *thelightvegas.com.*

Lily Bar & Lounge. This colorful (hence the name) ultralounge is quite literally at the center of the action in Bellagio; it's smack-dab in the middle of the casino floor, which you can view through windows on two sides. Community-style ottomans lend themselves to conversation. At the bar, expert mixologists pour cocktails made with seasonally fresh ingredients. DJs spin most nights until the venue closes around 4. ⊠ *Bellagio, 3600 Las Vegas Blvd. S, Center Strip* ☎ *702/693–8300* ⊕ *lilylasvegas.com.*

Mandarin Bar. Few views of the Strip are as breathtaking as the one you'll get from this über-chic lounge on the 23rd floor of the Mandarin Oriental at CityCenter. The room is wrapped with floor-to-ceiling windows, meaning just about every one of the plush banquettes is a winning seat. Mixologists concoct cocktails based on individual preferences, though Dom Perignon is always on hand. There's a small menu of bite-sized appetizers and hip live music on weekends. Business-casual dress is recommended. ⊠ *Mandarin Oriental, 3752 Las Vegas Blvd. S, Center Strip* ☎ *888/881–9367* ⊕ *www.mandarinoriental.com/lasvegas.*

Minus5 Ice Bar. Did you ever think you'd be wearing a winter parka in the Las Vegas desert? If not, then you've underestimated just how gimmicky these 21st-century bars can be. So don that parka, pay attention to your orientation speech, buy those drink tickets, and step into Minus5's bar area, where the temperature is always minus five below zero. This frosty clime ensures that you'll have a "cool" time here, but it also keeps the walls, bar, cocktail glasses, chairs, couches, and decorative sculpture in their frozen-solid state. Expensive fun for the sheer weirdness of it? Definitely! The drinks are tasty, too. Additional location at the Monte Carlo. ⊠ *The Shoppes at Mandalay Place, 3930 Las Vegas Blvd. S, South Strip* ☎ *702/632–7714* ⊕ *www.minus5experience.com.*

Mix Lounge. Floor-to-ceiling windows, an appealing curved bar, an equally appealing staff—what could top all that? An outdoor, 64th-floor deck that offers stunning views of the Strip, that's what. At this spot atop the Delano, even the glass-walled restrooms give you a window onto the city. Dark brown faux leather accented by red lighting creates a hipper-than-thou vibe. ⊠ *Mandalay Bay, 3590 Las Vegas Blvd. S, South Strip* ☎ *702/632–4760* ⊕ *www.mandalaybay.com.*

Fodor'sChoice **Parasol Up.** Not to be confused with sister lounge "Parasol Down," this
★ exquisite-looking—and exquisitely tranquil—setting near the entrance of Wynn Las Vegas ensures you can indulge in that most endangered of all pleasures: a good conversation. Tufted leather chairs and an extensive menu of house martinis certainly contribute to the vibe. Best of

all, the menu features a handful of snacks, and the place stays open all night. ⊠ *Wynn Las Vegas, 3131 Las Vegas Blvd. S, North Strip* ☎ *702/770–7000* ⊕ *www.wynnlasvegas.com.*

Fodor's Choice
★

Peppermill's Fireside Lounge. Pining for a genuine taste of retro Las Vegas? This kitschy and shagadelic lounge remains one of the town's truly essential nightspots. Just north of Encore, this evergreen romantic getaway serves food, but what you're really here for is the prismatic fire pit and signature cocktails such as the Key Lime Pie Martini and the lethal, 64-ounce Scorpion. ⊠ *2985 Las Vegas Blvd. S, North Strip* ☎ *702/735–4177* ⊕ *www.peppermilllasvegas.com.*

Petrossian Bar. Leave your designer handbags on the bar; this is a place to see and be seen. Sophisticated clientele frequent this piano lounge with experts tinkling the ivories of a one-of-a-kind, art deco–styled Steinway grand while patrons sup on three refined versions of the gin and tonic. Whether you're catching your breath or going for full elegance at this 24-hour lounge overlooking the grandiose entrance to the Bellagio, you can sip on sublime cocktails such as the Beluga vodka martini with a cube of namesake Petrossian caviar at the bottom of the glass or pair up your vodkas with caviar in a tasting of three of each. ⊠ *Bellagio, 3600 Las Vegas Blvd. S, Center Strip* ⊕ *www.bellagio.com.*

Press. The very swanky but very inviting Press features fire pits with seating overlooking the private pool at the Four Seasons, cooled off by misters in the hotter months. Like everything at the upscale resort, the libations and accompanying bites are near perfection. Must-orders include the Jalisco Smash, an intoxicating mix of Patron Reposado Tequila, pear liquor, smoked honey, mint, and lemon or the clever Maple Crown Frost with Crown Royal Maple, fresh mint, rock candy, and crushed ice. Free high-speed Internet, 12 charging docks, and access to 2,000 digital newspapers and magazines from 100 countries in 56 languages highlight the complimentary services here. ⊠ *Four Seasons, 3960 Las Vegas Blvd. S, South Strip* ☎ *702/632–5000* ⊕ *www.fourseasons.com/lasvegas.*

Talon Club. This swanky little pocket bar is open to everyone, but its spot in the high-limit gaming area on the second floor of the casino (no, you don't have to play) makes it a well-kept secret for drinkers who want some privacy. Mixologists don't usually offer a cocktail menu; instead they simply ask you what you like and craft drinks from there. Perhaps the only downside is the prices, befitting the decadent setting. ⊠ *The Cosmopolitan, 3708 Las Vegas Blvd. S, Center Strip* ☎ *702/698–7000.*

Vesper. The Chandelier Bar at Cosmopolitan may be the bar of the moment, but you shouldn't overlook the sleek Vesper Bar, the true mixologist space here. Name an ingredient, any ingredient, and the talented staff behind the bar can come up with a drink for you. Long-forgotten cocktail recipes are a specialty at this very modern square bar sitting alongside hotel registration. ⊠ *Cosmopolitan, 3708 Las Vegas Blvd. S, Center* ☎ *702/698–7000* ⊕ *www.cosmopolitanlasvegas.com.*

8

SPECIALTY BARS AND LOUNGES

CIGAR BAR

Casa Fuente. Casa Fuente, a full-service cigar shop, reproduces the decor and atmosphere of El Floridita, Ernest Hemingway's favorite Havana watering hole. Its sophisticated lounge is a great place to enjoy your smoke. ⊠ *Forum Shops, 3500 Las Vegas Blvd. S, Center Strip* ☎ *702/731–5051* ⊕ *www.casafuente.com.*

IRISH BARS

Nine Fine Irishmen. Don't be surprised to see patrons break into impromptu bouts of step-dancing at this authentic Irish pub inside New York–New York. It's so authentic that the place was built in Ireland, shipped over, and reassembled in Vegas. Today, barkeeps pour all sorts of Irish whiskeys, and cooks crank out Irish food and traditional Irish breakfast all day long. Live Irish music rounds out the toe-tapping sing-along entertainment here. ⊠ *New York–New York, 3790 Las Vegas Blvd. S, South Strip* ☎ *702/740–6463* ⊕ *www.ninefineirishmen.com.*

Rí Rá Irish Pub. Like the Statue of Liberty, this pub was constructed in Europe, then shipped over piecemeal and reassembled in Mandalay Place (yes, Lady Liberty is in New York; you know what we mean). Highlights include the music—which regularly comprises Irish sessions—and the menu, which boasts enough sausage rolls and fish-and-chips to make you feel like you've flown to Dublin. ⊠ *The Shoppes at Mandalay Place, 3930 Las Vegas Blvd. S, South Strip* ☎ *702/632–7200* ⊕ *www.rira.com.*

PIANO BAR

Napoleon's Dueling Piano Bar. This baroque Paris piano bar can get loud, but it's all good fun. Free performances nightly at 9 pm. It's also home to live entertainment from *American Idol* winner Taylor Hicks, so check before heading over. ⊠ *Paris Las Vegas, 3655 Las Vegas Blvd. S, Center Strip* ☎ *702/946–7000* ⊕ *www.parislasvegas.com.*

SPORTS BAR

Lagasse's Stadium. Jumbo video screens on the walls, more than 100 high-def TVs, and delicious down-home cooking (from celebrity chef Emeril Lagasse!) are all found at Lagasse's Stadium. Add in mobile sports betting devices from the Palazzo's sports book (located next door) and there's no better place to enjoy a game. ⊠ *Palazzo, 3325 Las Vegas Blvd. S, North Strip* ☎ *702/607–2665* ⊕ *www.emerilsrestaurants.com.*

TEQUILA BAR

Tequila Bar & Grille. Latin music, Mexican meals, and more than 60 types of tequila—all these are found at Tequila Bar & Grille, one of the few legitimately rollicking spots inside Bally's Las Vegas. The $2 menu (tacos, margaritas, shots, and draft beers) offers great value. ⊠ *Bally's Las Vegas, 3645 Las Vegas Blvd. S, Center Strip* ☎ *702/967–4111* ⊕ *www.ballyslasvegas.com.*

DANCE CLUBS AND NIGHTCLUBS

Vegas dance clubs come in three basic flavors—up-to-the-moment trendy (e.g., Marquee, 1 OAK, Chateau, and XS), established classic (Tao, LAX, Tryst, and Bank), and fun for the great unwashed masses (PURE and Moon). The usual Catch-22 of nightlife applies: the more "in" the place, the harder it is to get in and the more oppressively crowded and noisy it'll be once you do. Cover charges have crept into the $20 to $30 or $40 range—and don't be surprised to find that, even in these enlightened times, men pay higher cover charges than women. Although the level of capital investment gives these clubs a longevity their New York counterparts don't enjoy, dance clubs are still by nature a fickle, fleeting enterprise, so check with more frequently updated sources (such as the Fodor's website as well as local periodicals) to ensure they're still hot.

1 OAK. The "OAK" in this nightclub's name is an acronym for "Of A Kind," and, indeed, it's darker and louder than just about any other dance club in Vegas. And on a good night, sexy revelers are packed in and pumping like you wouldn't believe. Two separate rooms each have a bar and DJ (music styles change weekly). An animal theme is prevalent throughout, with zebra stripes, jaguar spots, and other patterns visible from just about every angle. The influence is subtle, but don't be surprised if your inner beast bursts out. ⊠ *The Mirage, 3400 Las Vegas Blvd. S, Center Strip* ☎ *702/693–8300* ⊕ *1oaklasvegas.com* ⊗ *Closed Mon. and Wed.*

Bank. "Status is everything!" goes the motto at this white-hot, megadance club, which has replaced an old favorite known as Light. One of the biggest celeb-hangs in town, Bank sets itself apart with etched-glass walls, avant-garde chandeliers, and an entrance foyer lined floor to ceiling with illuminated Cristal bottles. The staff is every bit as classy and hot looking as at other Vegas nightspots. Weekends generally draw the biggest crowds, but other nights boast special parties, promo events, and live performances (by, say, Sean Paul or Common, among others). In fact, the only thing really wrong about Bank is its motto, because status isn't *everything*. Or is it? ⊠ *Bellagio, 3600 Las Vegas Blvd. S, Center Strip* ☎ *702/693–8300* ⊕ *thebanklasvegas.com* ⊗ *Thurs.–Sun.*

Chateau Nightclub and Gardens. A staircase leads revelers straight from the Paris casino floor up to this French-inspired nightclub. The space itself offers three distinct experiences: a main dance room, a bar, or the open-air terrace, which is flanked by exquisite gardens (hence the name). In the main room, house deejays spin from a booth atop a 10-foot-high fireplace, and go-go dancers in French maid costumes abound. If you're looking for something different, don't miss the chandeliers made of globes near the bar; with LED screens in every nightclub these days, the handmade fixtures are wonderfully unique. ⊠ *Paris Las Vegas, 3655 Las Vegas Blvd. S, South Strip* ☎ *702/776–7770* ⊕ *www. chateaunights.com* ⊗ *Wed.–Sat.*

Fodor'sChoice ★ **Hakkasan.** The 80,000-square-foot Vegas haunt is the one of the latest iterations of the nightclub brand that started in London. The space is one part nightclub, one part modern Cantonese restaurant—five floors

8

in all with three dedicated to nightlife. To fill this space, the venue has booked some of the biggest deejays in the world, including Calvin Harris Steve Aoki, and Tiësto. ⊠ *MGM Grand Hotel & Casino, 3799 Las Vegas Blvd. S, South Strip* ☎ *702/891–3838* ⊕ *www.hakkasanlv.com* ⊗ *Closed Mon.–Wed.*

Haze. Dioramas with living, breathing humans catch your attention the moment you walk into this oversexed nightclub inside Aria, and you know this place is different. Inside, suede walls and plush surfaces give way to a 20-foot wall of lights and a bunch of interactive projection screens. There are laser light shows, and a state-of-the-art sound system that is, essentially, surround sound on steroids. Did we mention that drinks and deejays here are top-notch, too? Perhaps the only downside to Haze is the line; because of its location on the ground floor of the resort, queuing can get messy, especially when folks are drunk. ⊠ *Aria, 3730 Las Vegas Blvd. S, Center Strip* ☎ *702/693–8300* ⊕ *www.aria. com/nightlife* ⊗ *Thurs.–Sat.*

Lavo. From the people who brought us the titanic Tao comes this restaurant–lounge–dance club with a vaguely—though attractive—Middle Eastern vibe. Ascend past cisterns and ceramics to the top floor's dome-roofed dance floor, complete with go-go dancers, chandeliers, boa-clad servers, eccentrically shaped bars, and a bendy-trendy crowd. ■TIP→ During the cooler months, Lavo hosts its Party Brunch, an excuse to drink and party by day, on Saturday. ⊠ *The Palazzo, 3355 Las Vegas Blvd. S, North Strip* ☎ *702/791–1818* ⊕ *www.lavolv.com* ⊗ *Closed Mon. & Thurs.*

LAX. At one point in recent Vegas history (circa 2007/08), this tremendous club was the hottest ticket in town. And while no single club in Vegas reigns supreme for too long, LAX still shines: crazy flashing lights, deafening music, and shaking sweaty bodies. Preferred spots to dance here are the anarchically crowded stage or the less frenetic wraparound balcony, which offers a delightful bird's-eye view of all the heaving, writhing behavior down below. Our favorite spot of all, though, doesn't really involve dancing: it's **Savile Row**, the elegant, tiny, and eminently chill private lounge-within-a-club downstairs. By private we mean private service—the bartender will ask you what your tastes are before bringing you an appropriate signature cocktail. It's the ultimate in VIP treatment. As such, it's only open Sunday and Monday nights. ⊠ *Luxor, 3900 Las Vegas Blvd. S, South Strip* ☎ *702/262–4529, 702/222–1500 Savile Row* ⊕ *angelmg.com* ⊗ *Wed.–Sat.*

Marquee. This cavernous joint boasts three different rooms spread across two levels, as well as 50-foot ceilings. In the main area, stadium-style seating surrounds the dance floor, while four-story LED screens and projection walls display light and image shows customized for every performer. For a more intimate experience, check out the "Boom Box," a smaller room (usually featuring something other than house music) with windows overlooking the Strip. On the top level, the Library provides a respite from the thumping downstairs with dark wood, books (actual books!), and billiard tables. In spring and summer, the hot spot opens Marquee Dayclub, which features two pools, several bars, a gaming area, and deejays all day long. ✉ *The Cosmopolitan, 3708 Las Vegas Blvd. S, South Strip* ☏ *702/698–7000* ⊕ *marqueelasvegas.com* ☾ *Mon. and Thurs.–Sat.*

Fodor'sChoice **Pure.** Although a few Vegas dance clubs are more provocative—and
★ thereby more tabloid-friendly— Pure still takes the cake for best all-around shake appeal. In addition to multiple rooms, the club has a secret weapon—an outdoor terrace, complete with private cabanas, dance floor, and an up-close view of the Center Strip. No wonder celebrities and celebrity deejays love coming here for big events. ✉ *Caesars Palace, 3570 Las Vegas Blvd. S, Center Strip* ☏ *702/731–7873* ⊕ *angelmg.com* ☾ *Tues. and Thurs.–Sun.*

Fodor'sChoice **Surrender.** Steve Wynn and nightclub impresario Sean Cristie came
★ together in 2010 to create an indoor/outdoor lounge unlike anything else on the Strip. The experience begins indoors, in a giant living room designed by Roger Thomas, the same aesthetic genius behind Encore itself. At the back, the space transitions into the Encore Beach Club, an intimate, open-air dayclub that is transformed into a nightclub after dark. Some of the private cabanas out here feature balconies that overlook Las Vegas Boulevard. There's also an open-air gaming pit. Perhaps the highlight of the entire facility is the 120-foot-long silver snake over the bar inside; this artwork, much like Surrender itself, glistens all night long. ✉ *Encore Las Vegas, 3131 Las Vegas Blvd. S, North Strip* ☏ *702/770–7300* ⊕ *www.surrendernightclub.com* ☾ *Wed.–Sat.*

Fodor'sChoice **Tao.** Nowhere else in Vegas furnishes you with the four Ds—dining,
★ drinking, dancing, and drooling—in quite as alluring a mix as this multilevel (and multimillion-dollar) playground. The ground floor and mezzanine levels are exquisite enough (you almost tumble into rosewater baths with women bathing inside before you're in the door), but once you get off the elevator at the top floor, where an army of dramatically lighted stone deities greets you, the party truly begins. Chinese antiques, crimson chandeliers, and a so-called Opium Room set the mood. It's still one of the best dance clubs in Vegas, with one of the most popular theme parties with its Thursday locals' "Worship" night. In spring and summer, Tao Beach opens with daytime pool parties. ✉ *Venetian, 3355 Las Vegas Blvd. S, North Strip* ☏ *702/388–8588* ⊕ *taolasvegas. com* ☾ *Thurs.–Sat.*

Fodor'sChoice **Tryst.** No other club in Vegas has its own 90-foot waterfall, a distinc-
★ tion that sets Tryst apart from competitiors right off the bat. Other touches worth digging: the eerie red lighting, the open-air dance floor, the gorgeous stairway at the entrance, and the discreetly curtained VIP section. Indeed, this club has firmly established itself as one of the best in the business. We're not the only ones who think so, either: Nightclub & Bar regularly names this one of the top nightclubs in town. Our only gripe: The queue, which stretches past Wynn hotel registration and sometimes back into the casino, but good things come to those who wait. ✉ *Wynn Las Vegas, 3131 Las Vegas Blvd. S, North Strip* ☏ *702/770–3375* ⊕ *www.trystlasvegas.com* ☾ *Thurs.–Sat.*

Fodor'sChoice **XS.** XS backs up onto a pool that converts into one of the most spacious
★ open-air dance floors in town. The club also features Wynn's signature

8

attention to detail with touches such as a chandelier that doubles as a psychedelic disco ball, light fixtures that turn into stripper poles, and walls imprinted with golden body casts (the waitresses modeled for them). At the pool are cabanas, another bar, and outdoor gaming, where the sexiest croupiers in town ply their trade. "Excess" is a pretty good word for all of this. ⊠ *Encore, 3131 Las Vegas Blvd. S, North Strip* ☎ *702/770–7000* ⊕ *www.xslasvegas.com* ⊗ *Fri.–Mon.*

LIVE MUSIC

Small, medium, or large? From bohemian indie-band showcases (the Beauty Bar) and kooky kitschy lounges (the Rocks Lounge) to big concert halls (the House of Blues, the Joint, and Pearl)—and *then* on to truly *gargantuan* venues like the new Smith Center for the Performing Arts and the MGM Grand Garden Arena—Vegas is a world capital of live music. The trick, as always with local nightlife, is to check current news listings for performers, showtimes, and locations. (Why locations? Because even certain hot spots not ordinarily given over to live music— Bank dance club, for example—will host concerts when you least expect it.) And, of course, the Vegas lounge act has come a long way. Nearly every big Strip resort features a high-energy dance band that expertly performs hits from the '60s to today's hottest tunes.

Cleopatra's Barge. This kitschy lounge, which features the replica of a floating boat that once carried Egyptian royalty down the Nile, has been transformed in recent years into The Gossy Room, home of throwback musician Matt Goss. When the fedora-wearing crooner isn't performing—which is to say, weeknights—the space is thumping with beats from one of the resident deejays. "The Barge," as it's known, isn't exactly cool or hip, but that's part of its appeal. Besides, where else can you dance around on a makeshift boat inside a casino with a manmade lake, all in the middle of the desert? ⊠ *Caesars Palace, 3570 Las Vegas Blvd. S, Center Strip* ☎ *702/731–7333* ⊕ *www.caesarspalace. com* ⊗ *Closed Mon.*

House of Blues. This nightclub–concert hall hybrid at Mandalay Bay was the seventh entry in this chain of successful, intimate music clubs. As if the electric roster of performers taking the stage almost nightly wasn't enough (past acts include Carlos Santana, Fall Out Boy, Slash, the Dropkick Murphys, and Seal), the decor is lusciously imaginative. (Our favorite decoration isn't inside, though—it's the Voodoo Mama statue greeting you outside.) The Gospel Brunch on Sunday has great live music and is worth a visit. ⊠ *Mandalay Bay, 3950 Las Vegas Blvd. S, South Strip* ☎ *702/632–7600* ⊕ *www.houseofblues.com.*

OFF THE STRIP AND DOWNTOWN

BARS AND LOUNGES

Fodor'sChoice ★ **The Artisan Lounge.** This not-yet-well-known favorite of ours is in the slightly out-of-the-way Artisan Hotel and is sort of an upscale version of the Peppermill. The vibe is relatively chill even on weekends, so it can serve as a tonic to the usual Vegas lunacy. The interior is filled with gilt-framed paintings (and sometimes frames without the paintings), which are even on the ceiling. Ordinarily, a crazy ceiling stunt like this one would seem silly, but the muted romantic ambience here (candlelight, soft music, dark wood, comfy leather couches) makes it work. On Friday and Saturday nights deejays spin electro, house, and techno from 10 pm until dawn. ⊠ *The Artisan Hotel, 1501 W. Sahara Ave., West Side* ☎ *800/554–4092* ⊕ *artisanhotel.com.*

Ghostbar. Perched atop the Palms, this apex of ultralounges has rock music, glamorous patrons, glowing lights, and a glassed-in view of the city that was remodeled in fuchsia, black, and white in 2013. Step outside and you'll find that the outdoor "Ghostdeck" is cantilevered over the side of the building, with a Plexiglas platform that allows revelers to look down 450 feet below. Because of the laughably complicated process to get in the door, some might find this spot frustrating (although, with the right blend of patience and good humor, getting inside can be highly entertaining). Still, for the views of the Strip skyline alone, it's worth the effort. During the cooler months, Ghostbar Dayclub takes over the venue with a rollicking party on Saturday. ⊠ *The Palms, 4321 W. Flamingo Rd., West Side* ☎ *702/942–6832* ⊕ *www.palms.com.*

Lucky Bar. This circular bar's casual, lively atmosphere, comfy couch-like seats, sexy staff, and giant chandelier make it one of the best in town, and worth the trip to the impressive Red Rock Resort complex. What's more, the bar is steps away from Rocks Lounge, another hip spot that features live performers (like Zowie Bowie!) most nights of the week. ⊠ *Red Rock Casino, Resort & Spa, 11011 W. Charleston Blvd., Summerlin* ☎ *702/797–7777* ⊕ *https://redrock.sclv.com.*

Paymon's Mediterranean Cafe and Hookah Lounge. The hookah is an elaborate Middle Eastern water pipe that is used to smoke exotic tobaccos (and yes, we just mean *tobacco*). It also happens to be a trend popular at Vegas lounges and clubs these days. Thanks to a helpful "Hookah Man" and some available samples, no prior experience with water pipes is required. But the hookah is only one part of the appeal here: designed by local entrepreneur Paymon Raouf for the ultimate chill-out experience, this red velvet–laden, exquisitely carpeted, incense-filled environment redefines Vegas plush, and its young, somewhat bohemian crowd and those sexy paintings on the wall don't hurt the romance, either. ⊠ *4717 S. Maryland Pkwy., University District* ☎ *702/731–6030* ⊕ *www.paymons.com.*

Scarlet. Don't judge a bar by its size. This 200-square-foot retreat bathed in red may only feature five seats at the bar, but a crazy number of infused drinks make the menu. Try one of the cocktails, served in trios,

8

such as the Pepper Blanco infused with various dried chile peppers and tequila blanco or Banana Bread with reposado tequila, dried banana chips, and allspice and sweetened with agave and simple syrup. This can be our own best-kept secret. ⊠ *Palms, 4321 W. Flamingo Rd., Center* ☎ *702/933–9900* ⊕ *www.palms.com/nightlife.*

VooDoo Rooftop Nightclub. Take in great views of the city at this indoor/outdoor club 51 floors atop the Rio. Deejays, great dance bands, and well-trained flair bartenders, serving concoctions such as the rum-packed Witch Doctor, keep things lively. Faux-primitive voodoo paintings on the walls of the dance rooms maintain a tenuous thematic connection. The crowd tends to be slightly older and less, shall we say, sophisticated than at similar clubs. The party starts at 9 pm daily. ⊠ *Rio, 3700 W. Flamingo Rd., West Side* ☎ *702/777–6875* ⊕ *www.riolasvegas.com.*

SPECIALTY BARS AND LOUNGES

IRISH PUBS

Brendan's Irish Pub. Drams taste more authentic at this slice of Ireland inside the Orleans Hotel. The pub imports bottled and draught beers, including Guinness, from the motherland, as well as ales and Irish whiskeys. Live music on weekends can be rollicking, though—curiously—not always Celtic in genre. ⊠ *Orleans Hotel & Casino, 4500 Tropicana Ave., West Side* ☎ *702/365–7111* ⊕ *www.orleanscasino.com.*

Quinns Irish Pub. At the Green Valley Ranch, this rollicking establishment mixes straight-from-Ireland whiskeys and beers, authentic Irish fare, and live Irish music (on most nights). The place offers great drink specials, too. ⊠ *Green Valley Ranch Resort & Spa, 2300 Paseo Verde Pkwy., Henderson* ☎ *702/617–7777* ⊕ *https://greenvalleyranch.sclv.com.*

WINE BAR

Fodor's Choice ★ **Hostile Grape.** Despite what the name implies, there's nothing hostile about this upscale wine bar in The M Resort downstairs, away from the casino floor. Instead, with 160 wines by the glass, the place offers visitors a welcoming and intimate environment in which to sample some new vino. The collection includes fine American, Italian, and French wines, as well as selections from Spain, South Africa, and Germany (to name a few). Visitors can taste as much as they like, thanks to the venue's innovative dispensing system that doles out prepaid tasting cards to allow guests to enjoy pours of one, three, or five ounces at a time. ⊠ *The M Resort, 12300 Las Vegas Blvd. S, Henderson* ☎ *702/797–1000* ⊕ *www.themresort.com* ☯ *Closed Sun.–Tues.*

DANCE CLUBS AND NIGHTCLUBS

Fodor's Choice ★ **Moon.** Packing in more futuristic technology than a space station, this vast megalopolis of cool occupies the top floor of the Palms' Fantasy Tower. The club has a retractable roof, multiple dance floors, two ample outdoor balconies, banquettes seating 20, stripper poles galore, and some of the best views in town (including a few without glass—it's just you and the vista). Occasionally, celebrities such as Questlove and DJ Jazzy Jeff seize control of the turntables. ⊠ *The Palms, 4321 W. Flamingo Rd., West Side* ☎ *702/942–6832* ⊕ *www.palms.com* ⊗ *Closed Sun.–Thurs.*

Stoney's Rockin' Country. What do you get when you fill a country-theme Texas saloon with slick dance-music-crazed nightclubbers? Madness— 10-gallon-hat madness. Behind the Texas-shaped neon sign, Stoney's (named after its owner) has all the glam hot-spot fixings: one of the largest dance floors in Nevada, private tables, a VIP lounge, bottle service, and music that can segue from Merle Haggard to Jay Z. With $15 all-you-can-drink draft beer specials on Thursday and free dance lessons daily, you can't beat the prices either. A new location in Town Square makes the club convenient to visit from casinos on the Strip. ⊠ *Town Square, 6611 Las Vegas Blvd. S, South Las Vegas* ☎ *702/435–2855* ⊕ *www.stoneysrockincountry.com.*

LOCAL HANGOUTS

Outside the realm of the big casinos, the Las Vegas bar scene is dominated by so-called video-poker taverns, named after the 15 video-poker machines they're legally allowed to have. Most other Vegas bars are generic, but there are exceptions—in some cases, glorious exceptions scattered about town, and clustered in the Downtown area. Despite the touristy "Fremont Street Experience," Downtown is the gritty birthplace of Las Vegas. It can be quite dangerous if you stray from the tourist circuit at night, but visiting its nightspots is essential if you want to claim you've truly experienced Vegas.

Beauty Bar. This charming little Downtown joint, spun off from a popular Manhattan watering hole, is laid out like an old-fashioned hair salon, complete with hair-dryer chairs acquired from a defunct New Jersey salon. It's a kitschy spot to listen to local bands (primarily rockers), get entranced by the curve of the pink walls, and ogle the hipster crowd. On warm nights, a spacious patio with a bar and stage for live music is opened out back. ⊠ *517 Fremont St., Downtown* ☎ *702/598–1965* ⊕ *www.thebeautybar.com.*

Blue Martini Lounge. It's in a shopping mall eight minutes from the Strip (by taxi), but we won't hold that against the Blue Martini, because it's still pretty cool. The cream of local bands plays here nightly, an attractive blue interior curves from room to room, and the cocktail menu is impressive (the signature martinis are served in the shaker). Also, there's a legendary happy hour from 4 to 8 pm daily. Best of all, hordes of the kind of people you'll want to meet (that is, sexy nontourists of both genders) keep pouring in. ⊠ *Town Square, 6593 Las Vegas Blvd. S, South Las Vegas* ☎ *702/949–2583* ⊕ *www.bluemartinilounge.com.*

Commonwealth. As urban renewal continues Downtown, the one-block stretch of Fremont east of Las Vegas Boulevard (dubbed "Fremont East") remains the hottest of the hot spots, and Commonwealth arguably is the epicenter. Inside, wrought-iron railings, chandeliers, and a tin ceiling create a feeling of old-school opulence without being excessive. Drink options range from handcrafted cocktails to microbrews; there's also good live music on most nights. For a change of scenery, venture upstairs to the rooftop bar, or try to secure an invite to the private Laundry Room speakeasy. ⊠ *525 Fremont St., Downtown* 🕾 *702/445–6400* ⊕ *www.commonwealthlv.com* ⊘ *Closed Mon. and Tues.*

Double Down Saloon. The grand poobah of Vegas dive bars, the Double D is a short walk from the Hard Rock Hotel and a long, long way from Paradise—although a sign above the door has proclaimed it to be "The Happiest Place on Earth." Delicious decadence prevails here; no wonder it's a fave of world traveler and chef Anthony Bourdain. For the boho crowd, this deliberately downscale bar has everything from great local bands to a satisfying jukebox with truly eclectic selections. Our advice: go late, wear black, and try the (fabled) Ass Juice cocktail. Also, don't miss the clever, mostly obscene graffiti; it'll have you guffawing in minutes. ⊠ *4640 Paradise Rd., Paradise Road* 🕾 *702/791–5775* ⊕ *www. doubledownsaloon.com.*

Downtown Cocktail Room. Hiding from your creditors? Seeking a good spot for a séance or a Spin-the-Bottle party? If so, then consider stepping—carefully—into the gorgeous gloom of this hipster hangout, which is just around the corner from the Griffin and the Beauty Bar. The modest-sized, minimalist lounge glows from candle-filled tables and thumps with simmering house music, making the vibe mysterious and romantic. Weeknight happy hour from 4 to 8 is popular among locals. ⊠ *111 Las Vegas Blvd., Downtown* 🕾 *702/880–3696* ⊕ *www. thedowntownlv.com.*

Frankie's Tiki Room. You want Polynesian tiki-bar culture, Vegas-style? You want grass huts, carved wooden furniture, and cocktails such as the Green Gasser, the Thurston Howl, the Lava Letch, and the Bearded Clam? You'll get it all here, and more. On Friday, if you wear a Hawaiian shirt, your first drink is half price from 4 to 8 pm. Better still: If you love your mug (and trust us, you will), there's a gift shop where you can buy one to bring the spirit of aloha home with you. ⊠ *1712 W. Charleston Blvd., West Side* 🕾 *702/385–3110* ⊕ *www.frankiestikiroom.com.*

Freakin' Frog. Prepare to get carded at this college bar with "1,000 beers in the cooler and 600 whiskeys in the attic." Although booze takes top billing, the two-story joint has a decent-sized stage, and attracts all sorts of live music acts from around the country. ⊠ *4700 S. Maryland Pkwy., University District* 🕾 *702/217–6794* ⊕ *www.freakinfrog.com.*

Fodor'sChoice ★ **The Lady Silvia.** Inspired by the library of Strahov Monastery in Prague, this lounge inside the SoHo Lofts features dazzling furniture on a black-and-white checkerboard floor, invoking an English-style library and cocktail bar ambience at the same time. The Silvia's cocktail list changes seasonally, and is perhaps best enjoyed on the joint's open-air patio. In summer, the party here regularly rages until 4 or 5 am. ⊠ *900 Las Vegas Blvd. S, Downtown* 🕾 *702/419–8333* ⊕ *www.theladysilvia.com.*

LIVE MUSIC

JAZZ AND CLASSICAL

Fodor's Choice ★ **The Smith Center for the Performing Arts.** Las Vegas got its very own ($150 million) world-class performing arts center in early 2012, and what a spot it is. The multi-building complex (complete with a bell tower) was designed to invoke 1930s-era art deco construction, the same motif you'll find at the Hoover Dam. Here, this elegance graces the main concert hall, which hosts everything from rock bands to musical theater and traveling orchestras. Caberet Jazz across the breezeway hosts live jazz every weekend. ⊠ *361 Symphony Park Ave., Downtown* ☎ *702/749–2000* ⊕ *www.thesmithcenter.com.*

ROCK

The Joint. From Tim McGraw to Bon Iver to Prince, this music venue inside the Hard Rock Hotel hosts some of the best touring acts in the nation. Not only does The Joint have some of the best acoustics in town, but short of the big arenas, it's also one of the largest venues around. Big-name acts take residency at the Joint, playing for monthlong and longer stretches. Past acts have included Guns N' Roses, Def Leppard, and Mötley Crüe. ⊠ *Hard Rock Hotel, 4455 Paradise Rd., Paradise Road* ☎ *702/693–5000* ⊕ *www.hardrockhotel.com.*

Fodor's Choice ★ **The Pearl.** Not only does the Palms have its own studio where the likes of Lady Gaga, Mary J. Blige, and The Killers recorded, it's got this gorgeous, state-of-the-art concert venue, which boasts a stream of big-name rock, country, and hip-hop acts year-round. Comedians such as Lisa Lampanelli and resident act Bill Maher also make regular appearances. ⊠ *Palms, 4321 W. Flamingo Rd., West Side* ☎ *702/942–7777* ⊕ *www.palms.com.*

Rocks Lounge. This venue became famous hosting Zowie Bowie, a guy-and-gal, too-blond-for-words act with music that sounds like Eminem and Frank Sinatra getting together to groove. Zowie Bowie still performs occasionally, and the intimate venue welcomes a variety of other entertainers, too. Not exactly worth a trip in and of itself from the Strip, but if you're already in Summerlin or at the Red Rock Resort it's a fun place to hang out. ⊠ *Red Rock Resort, 11011 W. Charleston Blvd., Summerlin* ☎ *702/797–7777* ⊕ *www.nightlifestation.com.*

GAY AND LESBIAN NIGHTLIFE

Las Vegas was never really known for gay tourism, but things have changed rapidly in the past few years. Now a number of bars and nightclubs cater to different segments of the community, and the gay-friendly **Blue Moon Resort** (⊕ *www.bluemoonlv.com*) has 45 rooms near Sahara Avenue and Interstate 15.

Most gay and lesbian nightlife is concentrated into two areas of town. The most prominent is the so-called "Fruit Loop"—which wins our award for best nickname for a North American gay neighborhood—which you enter near the intersection of Naples Drive and Paradise Road, just north of the airport and close to the Hard Rock. The other is the area in and around Commercial Center, one of the city's oldest

8

shopping centers, on East Sahara Avenue, just west of Maryland Parkway. If there are cover charges at all, expect them to be around $10 for dance clubs on weekends.

Unfortunately, there are no all-out lesbian bars in Vegas, although many of the gay bars (most prominently Freezone) host special nights for their sapphic sisters. These parties, like so much in Sin City, change frequently, so it's best to consult a copy of *Q Vegas*, the city's gay monthly, or visit its website ⊕ *www.qvegas.com.*

Badlands Saloon. Consider the "Badlands" a 24-hour haven for local gay cowboys. It's decorated with a mock-log-cabin façade and offers cubbyholes in which regulars can store their beer steins. There's also a jukebox crammed to the coin slot with country-and-western hits. Plus, the Nevada Gay Rodeo Association hosts its fundraisers here. Perhaps the only downside is the smoke. ⊠ *Commerical Center, 953 E. Sahara Ave., East Side* ☎ *702/792–9262.*

Flex. A small, neighborhood-oriented club for men, this 24-hour hot spot sometimes has floor shows, banana-eating contests, and entertainment (think male strippers, folks, sometimes in drag). Of course we like the strong and inexpensive drinks. ⊠ *4371 W. Charleston Ave., West Side* ☎ *702/385–3539* ⊕ *flexlasvegas.com.*

Fodor's Choice ★ **Freezone.** An egalitarian mix of (straight and gay) men and women congregates at this 24-hour bar with a dance floor, pool tables, karaoke, and video-poker machines. Each night brings a different theme: Ladies' Night is Sunday (lesbians, unite!), male go-gos "come out" on Thursday, and Drag Madness with lovely drag queens is held Friday and Saturday. ⊠ *610 E. Naples Dr., University District* ☎ *702/794–2300* ⊕ *www.freezonelv.com.*

Krave. Live entertainers and go-go dancers put a mixed crowd in motion at this club. An average night at Krave means lots and lots of men dancing around in skimpy thongs. Seasonal events are popular—Valentine's Day in particular tends to draw a colorful crowd. The club also has embraced social networking and sends out drink specials, free bottle service, and other promotions to followers of its Twitter handle, @KraveLasVegas. ⊠ *3765 Las Vegas Blvd. S, Center Strip* ☎ *702/677–1740* ⊕ *www.kravelasvegas.com* ⊗ *Fri. and Sat. only.*

Piranha Nightclub. Revelers pack this gorgeous spot very night of the week. While the dance floor at Piranha is legendary (*Seven* magazine voted it the best gay nightclub in town), the best spot in the house is the spacious, fireplace-ringed open-air patio out back. The club also runs promotions whereby patrons can receive free drinks by checking in on Facebook. ⊠ *4633 Paradise Rd., Paradise Road* ☎ *702/791–0100* ⊕ *www.piranhavegas.com.*

STRIP CLUBS

It's not called Sin City for nothing. "Exotic dancing" clubs are a major industry here, but they do have some quirks. Zoning laws restrict most clubs to industrial areas not far off the Strip. Fully nude clubs are available in Vegas but such venues can't carry liquor licenses. (The

Palomino Club, in North Las Vegas, is the one exception.) Joints with liquor licenses have the sharper designs, the bigger spaces, the more savory customers, and the more glamorous gals. Some, depending on how loosely you define the term, can be pretty classy.

Wherever you go, be prepared to shell out some serious cash. Most places have instituted cover charges of $20 or more, but that's just the beginning. The real money's made on the table dances continuously solicited inside, with most going for $20 per song (and four VIP dances often for a C-note).

Cheetah's. This gentleman's club is no stranger to headlines. It has been featured in that pinnacle of late-20th-century cinematic excellence, *Showgirls*, and also was a favorite hangout of famous Vegas casino scion and murder victim Ted Binion. The place ain't the Rhino, but it does have plenty of hotter-than-average dancers, plus a free shuttle from the Strip, cheap lap dances (two for $20) during daylight hours and free pizza and wings every day between noon and 5 pm. The club recently underwent a renovation to freshen up the place. ✉ *2112 Western Ave., West Side* ☎ *702/384–0074* ⊕ *www.cheetahslasvegas.com.*

Club Paradise. Club Paradise was one of the first local clubs to embrace the "gentlemen's club" boom of the 1990s. Be sure to ask about the facility's cigar menu. ✉ *4416 Paradise Rd., Paradise Road* ☎ *702/734–7990* ⊕ *www.clubparadise.net.*

Crazy Horse III. Rising from the ashes of two previous strip clubs (Sin and the Penthouse Club) on the same site is this mammoth tribute to flesh and hedonism. Unlike many other strip clubs in town, this one offers a number of promotions throughout the week, including free limo rides. Private cabanas off the main room require a one-drink minimum, one of the best "deals" in town. Posh Boutique Nightclub sits inside the strip club, open Friday and Saturday, as well as Wednesday. ✉ *3525 W. Russell Rd., West Side* ☎ *702/675–8033* ⊕ *www.crazyhorse3.com.*

OG. Yes, it's the granddaddy of Vegas strip clubs, and the first to install several smaller stages to take the place of the single stage found in older clubs. The cover charge is $30, but the fee is waived if you get there on your own before 6 pm (our advice: cab it to the Stratosphere, and walk the two blocks to the OG or use the complimentary limo service). Inside, a separate room has male revues for the ladies. ✉ *1531 Las Vegas Blvd. S, North Strip* ☎ *702/386–9200* ⊕ *www.ogvegas.com.*

Palomino Club. This is one of the oldest strip clubs in the area (the Rat Pack used to hang out here), as well as the most notorious; two separate owners have been accused of murders, and it was also owned briefly by a noted heart surgeon. Because the "Pal" was grandfathered into the North Las Vegas zoning codes, it's allowed to have both a full bar *and* full nudity. There's also a burlesque stage and an all-male revue dubbed Club Lacy's next door. ✉ *1848 Las Vegas Blvd. N, North Side* ☎ *877/399–2023* ⊕ *www.palominoclublv.com.*

Sapphire. The owners claim to have spent $26 million for the bragging rights of proclaiming their club the "largest adult entertainment complex in the world," which means that what it loses in intimacy it makes up for in excess. Formerly a gym, this place provides 70,000 square feet of topless dancing, complete with 10 second-floor "skyboxes" and a phalanx of dancers who rank among Vegas's most talented. Sapphire Pool & Dayclub opens during the warmer months on weekends with an $8 million, three-level party mecca with cabanas and daybeds. Kerry Simon's Sapphire Grill serves up the chef's dishes to both venues 24 hours a day. ⊠ *3025 S. Industrial Rd., West Side* ☎ *702/796–6000* ⊕ *www.sapphirelasvegas.com.*

Fodor's Choice **Spearmint Rhino.** At the "Rhino," as everyone calls it, you can expect
★ a veritable onslaught of gorgeous half-clad women: possibly the best-looking dancers west of the Mississippi. The place got a late start in Vegas, but it grew fast, expanding its original space to more than 20,000 square feet. It's also the rare topless club that offers lunch, including steak sandwiches, not to mention an adjoining shop for lingerie, sex toys, and various other implements of physical naughtiness. Of course it's always crowded, but tipping the staff lavishly will get you a table, not to mention anything else that's not too illegal, immoral, or fattening. (Further tipping might even snag you some of that immoral and fattening stuff.) Our only gripe: The lighting here is usually so low that you can't get a good enough gander at all the wonders worth gandering at. Still, that's a small price to pay for American beauty in all its grandeur. ⊠ *3340 S. Highland Dr., West Side* ☎ *702/796–3600* ⊕ *www.spearmintrhinolv.com.*

SIDE TRIPS FROM LAS VEGAS

WELCOME TO SIDE TRIPS FROM LAS VEGAS

TOP REASONS TO GO

★ **Experiencing geologic history:** The breathtaking 277-mile Grand Canyon was created by the Colorado River over the course of 6 million years, yet it never gets old.

★ **Enjoying the outdoors:** With expansive views and acres upon acres of open space, Mt. Charleston and the Lake Mead National Recreation Area are great places to reconnect with nature. Death Valley, although prohibitive in summer, is one of the most fascinating national parks in the United States.

★ **Celebrating engineering:** It's hard to find a monument to man's ingenuity more impressive than the 1,244-foot concrete span of Hoover Dam.

1 Mt. Charleston Area. The highest point in the Spring Mountain range is a favorite spot for Las Vegans to ski and hike. Take Route 157 to its end and enjoy the view (or a cocktail) at the Mt. Charleston Lodge.

2 Lake Mead Area. Lake Mead, the largest reservoir in the United States, and Hoover Dam are about 34 miles from Las Vegas. Nearby, Valley of Fire is a seemingly infinite landscape of sandstone outcroppings, petrified logs, and miles of hiking trails.

3 Grand Canyon. Only about four hours' drive from Las Vegas—less if you head to the West Rim—much of the Canyon is a national park. The South Rim is where all the action is, although the North Rim is more for the adventurous. The Skywalk, a relatively new attraction in the West Rim, provides jaw-dropping views straight down.

4 Death Valley. This is a vast, lonely, beautiful place with breathtaking vistas, blasting 120-degree heat, and mysterious moving rocks. The desert landscape is surrounded by majestic mountains, dry lake beds, spring wildflowers, and Wild West ghost towns.

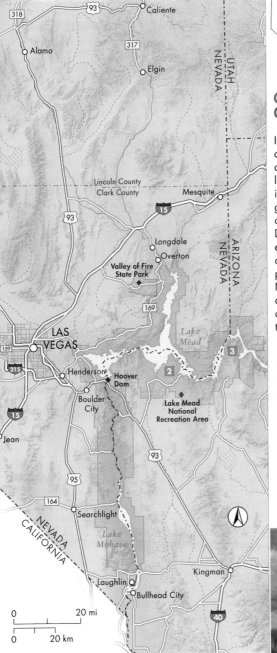

NEVADA

GETTING ORIENTED

In many ways, the expanse of Nevada to the west, south, and east of Las Vegas is a living museum. The breathtaking Grand Canyon offers a glimpse at 6 million years of erosion, while the Hoover Dam is an exhibit on modern engineering. Beyond these attractions, untrammeled places like Lake Mead National Recreation Area and Mt. Charleston provide a perfect counterpoint to the hubbub of Sin City.

9

Updated
by Mike
Weatherford

Nevada takes its name from a Spanish word meaning "snow-covered." So why, you might ask, is the southeastern corner of the state covered in scorching sands and desert landscapes that blend seamlessly with neighboring Arizona? Probably because prior to Nevada's becoming a state, most of the land in what's now Clark County belonged to Arizona's "lost county of Pah-Ute."

At that time Las Vegas was a tiny settlement situated at the crossroads of the Old Spanish Trail and the Mormon Road. The Mormon town of Callville, later drowned beneath the waters of Lake Mead, was the Pah-Ute county seat. A smattering of agricultural communities sat on the banks of the Colorado River, and steamboats plied the river's muddy waters. A lot has changed in the last 150 years.

Today the vast majority of the state's population resides in Clark County and the nearby lakes, state parks, and geological wonders entertain even the most jaded city dwellers. Those pressed for time can take a short drive from Vegas to go skiing at Mt. Charleston, hiking in the Humboldt–Toiyabe National Forest, or rock climbing in Red Rock Canyon. Those with a little more time can explore the wonderland of nearby waterways, stunning rock formations, and laid-back ranching communities. Water enthusiasts head to Lakes Mead, Mohave, and Havasu. Nature lovers find prime wildlife watching along the Colorado River. And those looking for the grandest spectacle in the region can take the longer drive to the Grand Canyon.

SIDE TRIPS PLANNER

WHEN TO GO

There's no bad time to visit the Grand Canyon, though summer and spring break are the busiest times. Visiting during these peak seasons, as well as holidays, requires patience and a tolerance for crowds. Weather changes on a whim in this exposed high-desert region. The more remote North Rim is off-limits for much of the winter. There are no services, and snow sometimes closes Highway 67 south of Jacob Lake.

The communities in southeastern Nevada and northwestern Arizona don't have distinct high and low seasons. The arid climate and clear winter skies attract retirees escaping harsh northern climes, and the hot, sunny summer months attract sports enthusiasts looking for water— despite 105°F temperatures. Things simmer down a bit during the spring and fall months.

As for Death Valley: it's aptly named for the summer months. Believe the hype; summer highs often average 115°F (a record 134°F was set in 2013).

MAKING THE MOST OF YOUR TIME

Plan ahead if you're going to explore Grand Canyon National Park. Reservations for everything fill up during the busy summer months; mule rides and lodging may be reserved up to 13 months in advance. Perhaps the easiest way to visit the West Rim from Vegas is with a tour. **Bighorn Wild West Tours** (☎ 702/385–4676 or 888/385–4676 ⊕ http:// bighornwildwesttours.com) will pick you up in a Hummer at your Vegas hotel for an all-day trip that includes the shuttle-bus package and lunch for $249.

Day-trippers heading to the Lake Mead National Recreation Area can stop at the Alan Bible Visitors Center near Boulder Beach (which has a new park film and exhibits after a $2.9-million renovation).

Death Valley can be reached by car in less than three hours. Leave early in the morning if you go late spring or early fall—midday temperatures can still reach triple digits during this time. In summer, count on temperatures in excess of 100 degrees.

WHAT TO DO AND WHERE TO DO IT

Looking to hook the big one? Head to Lake Mead for excellent year-round fishing. To explore ghost towns and the Old West, check out Oatman, Arizona, or the eastern reaches of Nevada en route to Death Valley. Nature buffs will find excellent birding and wildlife-watching at nature preserves along the Colorado River, but the grandest natural spectacle's just a short jaunt away at the Grand Canyon. The South and North rims offer outdoor adventure, multiple viewpoints, and rustic lodging for multiday excursions. The privately operated Grand Canyon West, easily accessible from Las Vegas by a quick flight or a relaxed bus tour, adds a Native American perspective to the world's grandest gorge with three developed viewpoints, horseback and Hummer rides to the rim, and the Skywalk—a glass U-shape bridge 4,000 feet above the Colorado River. Another geological marvel that's a short drive from Las Vegas is the dramatic red sandstone formations and stark views of the Mohave Desert at Valley of Fire State Park.

DRIVE TIMES

Approximate drive times from the Center Strip to areas of interest are as follows:

Grand Canyon South Rim: 4½ hours

Grand Canyon North Rim: 6 hours

Valley of Fire: 1 hour

Hoover Dam: 50 minutes

Mt. Charleston: 40 minutes

Death Valley: 2½ hours

SAFETY TIPS

Services can be few and far between in the more remote regions of southwestern Nevada and northeastern Arizona. Play it safe by packing an emergency car kit with basic automotive repairs, plenty of water, and overnight supplies. To avoid being stranded, let someone know where you're going and which route you plan to take. It's also a good idea to check road conditions (*Nevada:* ☎ 877/687–6237 ⊕ *www.nevadadot. com; Arizona:* ☎ 888/411–7623 ⊕ *www.azdot.gov; Utah:* ☎ 866/511– 8824 ⊕ www.udottraffic.utah.gov; Grand Canyon National Park:* ☎ 928/638–7888) before you set out.

ABOUT THE RESTAURANTS

Dining's generally relaxed and casual in southeastern Nevada. For the most part you'll find home-cooked American favorites and "South of the Border" specialties.

Dining options in Grand Canyon National Park are limited to the lodge restaurants working under contract with the government. However, you'll find everything from cafeteria food to casual café fare to elegant evening specials. On the Hualapai and Havasupai reservations in Havasu Canyon and at Grand Canyon West, options are limited to tribe-run restaurants.

ABOUT THE HOTELS

Of the 922 rooms, cabins, and suites in Grand Canyon National Park, only 203—all at the Grand Canyon Lodge—are at the North Rim. Outside of El Tovar Hotel, the canyon's architectural crown jewel, frills are hard to find. Rooms are basic but comfortable, and most guests would agree that the best in-room amenity is a view of the canyon. Reservations are a must, especially during the busy summer season.

Lodging options are even more limited on the West Rim. The Hualapai Lodge in Peach Springs and the Hualapai Ranch at Grand Canyon West are run by the Hualapai tribe. The Havasupai Lodge in Supai offers the only rooms in Havasu Canyon. At the South Rim, motel chains make up the most abundant and affordable options in Tusayan, just outside the park entrance (but about 15 minutes from the rim itself) and in Williams, about 50 minutes from the park entrance, and home of the historic railroad line into the park.

Hotel reviews have been shortened. For full information, visit Fodors. com.

WHAT IT COSTS				
	$	$$	$$$	$$$$
Restaurants	under $15	$16–$22	$23–$30	Over $30
Hotels	under $139	$140–$220	$221–$300	Over $300

Restaurant prices are the average cost of a main course at dinner or, if dinner is not served, at lunch. Hotel prices are the lowest cost of a standard double room in high season.

MT. CHARLESTON

45 miles northwest of Las Vegas.

GETTING HERE AND AROUND

Take U.S. 95 from Las Vegas. At the intersection of 95 and Route 157, turn left to Kyle Canyon, home of the township for year-round residents and the two lodge-restaurants. If you're in a hurry to ski, pass this turn and stay on the highway to the next left, Route 156, which takes you to Lee Canyon and the ski resort. But don't stress over the decision. If you take the Kyle road first, there's a scenic 25-minute drive midway up, connecting Kyle to Lee.

■**TIP→** Speed limits on the drive approaching and climbing Mt. Charleston vary and change quickly; it can be an easy ticket on weekends, when police are out in force. The descending drive especially can lead to speed violations. It's easy to exceed 55 mph without even realizing it, leading you right into the waiting arms of the law.

ESSENTIALS

Campground Information U.S. Forest Service ☎ 702/515–5400, 877/444–6777 *reservations* ⊕ *www.recreation.gov.*

Weather Reports Las Vegas Ski and Snowboard Resort ☎ 702/593–9500.

EXPLORING

FAMILY

Fodor'sChoice

★

Mt. Charleston. In winter Las Vegans drive about an hour to crowd the upper elevations of the Spring Mountains to throw snowballs, sled, cross-country ski, and even glide downhill at a little ski area. In summer they return to wander the high trails and escape the valley's 110°F heat (temperatures here can be 20°F–30°F cooler than in the city), and maybe even make the difficult hike to Mt. Charleston, the range's high point. Easier trails lead to seasonal waterfalls or rare, dripping springs where dainty columbine and stunted aspens spill down ravines and hummingbirds zoom. Or they might lead onto high, dry ridges where ancient bristlecone trees have become twisted and burnished with age. ⊠ *Kyle Canyon Rd., Outskirts, Las Vegas* ✛ *I–15 N to exit 42A, U.S.-95 N. Turn left onto Kyle-Canyon Rd.*

WHERE TO STAY

$

HOTEL

🏨 **Mount Charleston Lodge and Cabins.** At the end of Route 157 at 7,717 feet above sea level you find this lodge on the perch of Kyle Canyon, with a well-known restaurant and adjacent cabins (run by a separate operator than the restaurant). **Pros:** the seclusion and spectacular views; trails within walking distance. **Cons:** no cable TV (just DVD players), no phones, no Wi-Fi (although some might call these "pros"); can get crowded with hikers; restaurant goers on busy weekends. ⑤ *Rooms from: $110* ⊠ *5355 Kyle Canyon Rd., Outskirts, Las Vegas* ☎ *702/872–5408, 800/955–1314* ⊕ *www.mtcharlestonlodge.com* ⇌ *23 rooms* ❑ *No meals.*

$

HOTEL

🏨 **The Resort on Mt. Charleston.** This is the more upscale of the two lodging choices in Kyle Canyon, though the views aren't as good. **Pros:** mountain setting; special packages. **Cons:** not as high up the mountain as the other lodge, so the views aren't as spectacular and the summer temperatures not quite as cool; not much to do in immediate vicinity without getting back in a car. ⑤ *Rooms from: $100* ⊠ *2755 Kyle Canyon Rd., Las Vegas* ☎ *702/872–5500, 888/559–1888* ⊕ *www.mtcharlestonresort.com* ⇌ *61 rooms* ❑ *No meals.*

9

SPORTS AND THE OUTDOORS

HIKING

FAMILY

Fodor'sChoice

★

Mt. Charleston. In summer, hikers escape the heat by traveling 45 minutes up to the Spring Mountains National Recreation Area, known informally as Mt. Charleston, where the U.S. Forest Service maintains more than 50 miles of marked hiking trails for all abilities. Trails vary from the 0.7-mile (one-way) Robber's Roost loop trail to the 6.2-mile Bristlecone Loop trail to the extremely strenuous 10.3-mile (one-way) North Loop Trail, which reaches the Mt. Charleston summit at 11,918 feet; the elevation gain is 4,278 feet. There are also plenty of intermediate trails, along with marathon two-, three-, four-, and five-peak routes only for hikers who are highly advanced (and in peak physical condition). There are trails in the area open for horseback riding, and the Sawmill and Bristlecone trails are open for mountain-bike use. The Mt. Charleston Wilderness is part of the Humboldt–Toiyabe National Forest; for information, contact the U.S. Forest Service (☏ 702/515–5400 ⊕ www.fs.fed.us). ✉ Outskirts, Las Vegas ⊕ www.fs.fed.us.

SKIING AND SNOWBOARDING

FAMILY

Las Vegas Ski and Snowboard Resort. Southern Nevada's skiing headquarters is a mere 47 miles northwest of downtown Las Vegas. Depending on traffic and weather conditions, it can take less than two hours to go from a 70°F February afternoon on the Strip to the top of a chairlift at an elevation of 9,370 feet. "Ski Lee," as it's affectionately known (for its site in Lee Canyon), is equipped with four chairlifts—a double, surface or magic carpet, triple, and a quad—a ski school, a half pipe and terrain park, a ski shop, rental equipment, and a day lodge with a grab-and-go snack bar and lounge. Clothing rentals are available. There are 40 acres of groomed slopes: 20% of the trails are for beginners, 60% are intermediate, and 20% are advanced runs. The longest run is 3,000 feet, and there's a vertical drop of nearly 1,000 feet. You know you're at the closest ski resort to Las Vegas when you see the slope names: Blackjack, High Roller, Keno, the Strip, Bimbo 1 and 2, and Slot Alley. The lifts are open from about Thanksgiving to Easter for skiing. Lift tickets are approximately $50/weekdays and $60/weekends, but check the website for most current rates. A car service is available by reservation. A telephone call will get you snow conditions (☏ 702/593–9500); driving conditions can be had through the local road report (☏ 511 in NV, 877/687–6237 outside NV ⊕ www.nevadadot.com/traveler). ✉ 6725 Lee Canyon Rd., Mt. Charleston ✛ Take U.S. 95 north to the Lee Canyon exit (Hwy. 156), and head up the mountain ☏ 702/385–2754 ⊕ www.skilasvegas.com.

LAKE MEAD AREA

Southeast of Las Vegas sits Boulder City, which is prim, languid, and full of historic neighborhoods, small businesses, parks, and greenbelts—without a single casino. Over the hill from town, enormous Hoover Dam blocks the Colorado River as it enters Black Canyon. Backed up behind the dam is incongruous, deep-blue Lake Mead, the focal point of

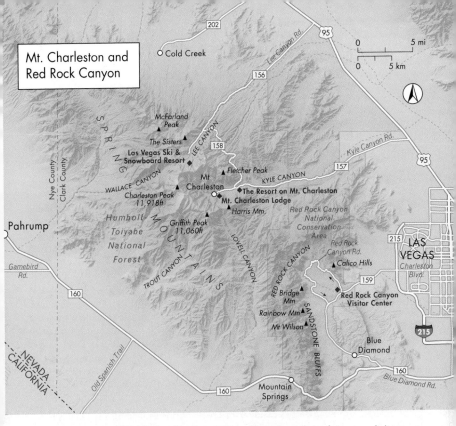

Mt. Charleston and
Red Rock Canyon

Cold Creek

Spring

McFarland
Peak

The Sisters

Las Vegas Ski &
Snowboard Resort

Wallace Canyon

Charleston Peak
11,918ft

Humbolt-

Toiyabe

National

Forest

Gamebird
Rd.

NEVADA
CALIFORNIA

Old Spanish Trail

Pahrump

Mt
Charleston

Griffith Peak
11,060ft

Lee Canyon Rd.

Nye County
Clark County

Lee Canyon

Fletcher Peak

KYLE CANYON

The Resort on Mt. Charleston
Mt. Charleston Lodge

Harris Mtn.

Kyle Canyon Rd.

Red Rock Canyon
National
Conservation
Area

Calico Hills

Red Rock
Canyon Rd.

Bridge
Mtn

Rainbow Mtn

Mt Wilson

Mountain
Springs

LOVELL CANYON

TROUT CANYON

RED ROCK CANYON

SANDSTONE BLUFFS

Red Rock Canyon
Visitor Center

Blue
Diamond

LAS
VEGAS

Charleston
Blvd.

Blue Diamond Rd.

0   5 mi
0   5 km

water-based recreation for southern Nevada and northwestern Arizona,
and the major water supplier to seven Southwestern states. The lake is
ringed by miles of rugged desert country. The breathtaking wonderland
known as Valley of Fire, with its red sandstone outcroppings, petrified
logs, petroglyphs, and hiking trails, is along the northern reach of the
lake. And all of this is an hour or less from Vegas.

BOULDER CITY

25 miles southeast of Las Vegas.

In the early 1930s Boulder City was built by the federal government to
house 5,000 construction workers on the Hoover Dam project. A strict
moral code was enforced to ensure timely completion of the dam, and to
this day the model city is the only community in Nevada in which gambling is illegal. (Note that the two casinos at either end of Boulder City
are just outside the city limits.) After the dam was completed, the town
shrank but was kept alive by the management and maintenance crews of
the dam and Lake Mead. Today it's a vibrant little Southwestern town.

GETTING HERE AND AROUND

It takes about 30 minutes via U.S. 93/Interstate 515 or Interstate 215/
Interstate 515 to get from the Las Vegas tourist corridor to Boulder City.

ESSENTIALS

Visitor Information Boulder City Chamber of Commerce ✉ *465 Nevada Way* ☎ *702/293–2034* ⊕ *www.bouldercitychamberofcommerce.com* ⊙ *Weekdays 9–5.*

EXPLORING

Boulder Dam Brewing Company. Across the street from the Boulder Dam Hotel, the Boulder Dam Brewing Company is a family-run brewery decorated with historic Hoover Dam photos and serving up beers with names such as High Scaler Pale Ale and Powder Monkey Pilsner. A patio garden offers live music on fair-weather weekends. ✉ *453 Nevada Hwy.* ☎ *702/243–2739* ⊕ *www.boulderdambrewing.com.*

Boulder Dam Hotel. Be sure to stop at the Dutch Colonial–style Boulder Dam Hotel, built in 1933. On the National Register of Historic Places, the 20-room bed-and-breakfast once was a favorite getaway for notables, including the man who became Pope Pius XII and actors Will Rogers, Bette Davis, and Shirley Temple. It's still a point of pride for Boulder City and the heart of Downtown. The guest rooms have been remodeled to stay competitive but retain a historic feel. ✉ *1305 Arizona St.* ☎ *702/293–3510* ⊕ *www.boulderdamhotel.com*

Boulder City/Hoover Dam Museum. For its size this small museum inside the Boulder Dam Hotel is well done. It includes hands-on exhibits, oral histories, artifacts from the building of Hoover Dam, and a glimpse at what it was like for Great Depression–era families to pull up roots and settle in the rock and dust of the harsh Mojave Desert. ✉ *1305 Arizona St.* ☎ *702/294–1988* ⊕ *www.bcmha.org* ☞ *$2* ⊙ *Mon.–Sat. 10–5.*

NEED A BREAK?

Grandma Daisy's Candy & Ice Cream Parlor. Grandma Daisy's Candy & Ice Cream Parlor makes its own fudge and peanut brittle within a nostalgic Main Street U.S.A. environment. ✉ *530 Nevada Hwy.* ☎ *702/294–6639* ⊕ *www.grandmadaisys.com.*

WHERE TO EAT

The old downtown area of Boulder City has become a fun zone for drinks, dining, and antiques shopping. The center of the action is the 500 block of Nevada Highway (aka Nevada Way).

$
DINER
✕ **The Coffee Cup.** The Coffee Cup is a breakfast-and-lunch diner that's been featured on the Food Network's Diners, Drive-Ins, and Dives. Tourists line up outside on weekends for the quintessential small-town diner experience, complete with newspaper-strewn counter seating and the owners' family photos and memorabilia on the walls. It delivers on the food front, too, with giant portions of vacation-breakfast favorites such as huevos rancheros, chile verde omelets, and skillet scrambles. ⑤ *Average main: $12* ✉ *512 Nevada Hwy.* ☎ *702/294–0517* ⊕ *www. worldfamouscoffeecup.com* ⊙ *No dinner.*

$
CAFÉ
✕ **Milo's Cellar.** Sure, you can sit inside, but what draws locals and tourists alike is the alfresco dining at Milo's, where you can sip a glass of wine and watch the world go by along historic Nevada Way, the quaint main street staunchly preserved by a city that loves its history.

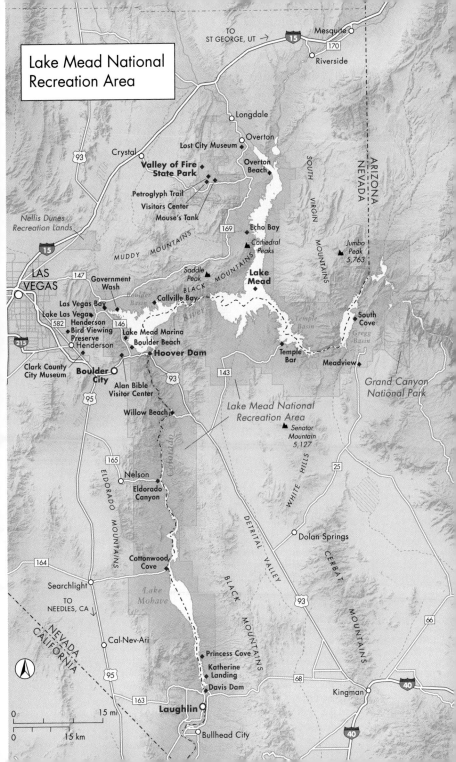

A well-considered menu offers gourmet sandwiches, soups and salads, platters for wine pairings, and a wide selection of both vino and beer by the glass. If it's too early for the grape, one corner of the place is a coffee and bakery nook. ⑤ *Average main: $12* ✉ *538 Nevada Hwy.* ☎ *702/293–9540* ⊕ *www.miloswinebar.com.*

HOOVER DAM

8 miles northeast from Boulder City.

GETTING HERE AND AROUND

Hoover Dam is about a 45-minute drive from Las Vegas via U.S. 93; it's about 15 minutes from Boulder City.

EXPLORING

FAMILY

Fodor's Choice

★

Hoover Dam. In 1928 Congress authorized $175 million for construction of a dam on the Colorado River to control destructive floods, provide a steady water supply to seven Colorado River basin states, and generate electricity. Considered one of the seven wonders of the industrial world, the art deco Hoover Dam is 726 feet high (the equivalent of a 70-story building) and 660 feet thick (more than the length of two football fields) at the base. Construction required 4.4 million cubic yards of concrete—enough to build a two-lane highway from San Francisco to New York. Originally referred to as Boulder Dam, the structure was later officially named Hoover Dam in recognition of President Herbert Hoover's role in the project. Look for artist Oskar Hansen's plaza sculptures, which include the 30-foot-tall *Winged Figures of the Republic* (the statues and terazzo floor patterns were copied at the new Smith Center for the Performing Arts in Downtown Las Vegas).

The tour itself is a tradition that dates back to 1937, and you can still see the old box office on top of the dam. But now the ticketed tours originate in the modern visitor center, with two choices of tour. The cheaper, most popular one is the **Powerplant Tour,** which starts every 15 minutes or so. It's a half-hour, guided tour that includes a short film and then a 537-foot elevator ride to two points of interest: a less-than-overwhelming view of a diversion tunnel, and the more impressive eight-story room housing still-functional power generators. Self-paced exhibits follow the guided portion, with good interactive museum exhibits and a great indoor/outdoor patio view of the dam from the river side. The more extensive **Hoover Dam Tour** includes everything on the Powerplant Tour but limits the group size to 20 and spends more time inside the dam, including a peek through the air vents. Tours run from 9 to 5 in the winter and 9 to 6 in the summer. Visitors for both tours submit to security screening comparable to an airport. January and February are the slowest months, and mornings generally are less busy. The top of the dam is open to pedestrians and vehicles, but you have to remain in your vehicle after sundown. The new bypass bridge is the way to and from Arizona. Those willing to pass a security checkpoint (with inspections at the discretion of officers) can still drive over the dam for sightseeing, but cannot continue into Arizona; you have to turn around and come back after the road dead-ends at a scenic lookout (with a snack bar and store) on the Arizona side. ■TIP→ The dam's High Scaler Café is fine for a cold drink or an ice-cream cone, and the outdoor café tables even have misters. But you can improve upon the $9 burger by having lunch in Boulder City instead. ⊠ *U.S. 93, east of Boulder City* ☎ *702/494–2517, 866/730–9097* ⊕ *www.usbr. gov/lc/hooverdam* 🖭 *Powerplant Tour $15, expanded Hoover Dam Tour $30, visitor center only $10; garage parking $10 (free parking on Arizona-side surface lots)* ☉ *Daily 9–5* ☞ *Security, road, and Hoover Dam crossing information: 888/248–1259.*

The Mike O'Callaghan–Pat Tillman bridge. The Hoover Dam now has sight-seer competition from the spectacular bridge that was built to bypass it. The Mike O'Callaghan–Pat Tillman bridge (named for the popular Nevada governor and the Arizona football star who was killed in Afghanistan) is the Western Hemisphere's longest single-span concrete arch bridge. It runs 1,905 feet long and towers nearly 900 feet above the river, and 280 feet above the Hoover Dam. You don't see much by driving over it—scarcely anything from a sedan—but walking it is quite a thrill. A pedestrian walkway is well separated from the driving lanes, the access path to the bridge has informational signage, and ramps offer an alternative to the steps. There are restrooms in the parking lot (labeled "Memorial Bridge Plaza"), where it can be hard to find a parking space on weekends. (If you can't get a spot, drive a few yards past the parking lot entrance and turn left into the lot for a trailhead on the other side of the road). Bring water and sunscreen for the walk and be prepared for broiling summer temperatures; there is no shade. ■**TIP**➔ Remember to take "Exit 2" if you want to go to the dam instead of the bypass bridge, or you will have to drive across it and turn back to visit the dam. ⊠ *U.S. 93* ⊕ *www.hooverdambypass.org.*

SPORTS AND THE OUTDOORS

RAFTING

Black Canyon, just below Hoover Dam, is the place for river running near Las Vegas. You can launch a raft here on the Colorado River year-round. On the Arizona side, the 11-mile run to Willow Beach, with its vertical canyon walls, bighorn sheep on the slopes, and feeder streams and waterfalls coming off the bluffs, is reminiscent of rafting the Grand Canyon. The water flows at roughly 5 miles per hour, but some rapids, eddies, and whirlpools can cause difficulties, as can headwinds, especially for inexperienced rafters.

If you want to go paddling in Black Canyon on your own, you need to make mandatory arrangements with one of the registered outfitters. They provide permits ($12) and the National Park Service entrance fee ($5) as well as launch and retrieval services (the road in and out is in a security zone for the dam). You can get a list of outfitters at ☎ 702/294–1414, or go to the paddle-craft and rafting-tours section on the Bureau of Land Management's website (⊕ *www.usbr.gov/lc/hooverdam*).

Black Canyon/Willow Beach River Adventures. If you're interested in seeing the canyon on large motor-assisted rafts, Black Canyon/Willow Beach River Adventures is a group excursion launching most mornings from the Hoover Dam Lodge (formerly Hacienda Casino and Hotel). You only get wet if you want to, and a picnic lunch on the riverbank is included. The trip is $92 for adults, or $35 for a half-hour "postcard" tour. ⊠ *Depart from Hoover Dam Lodge, U.S. 93* ☎ *800/455–3490* ⊕ *www.blackcanyonadventures.com.*

Desert Adventures. For a more hands-on approach, try a guided kayak trip through Black Canyon with Desert Adventures. Rates, which include permits, are $189 per person (plus a $17 permit fee). They'll pick you up at the Hoover Dam Lodge (formerly the Hacienda Hotel and Casino), or from your hotel on the Strip. ⊠ *1647 Nevada Hwy., Suite A* ☎ *702/293–5026* ⊕ *www.kayaklasvegas.com.*

LAKE MEAD

About 4 miles from Hoover Dam.

GETTING HERE AND AROUND

From Hoover Dam, travel west on U.S. 93 to the intersection with Lakeshore Drive to reach Alan Bible Visitors Center, which reopened in early 2013 with a new welcome film and exhibits after two years and nearly $3 million in renovations. It's open Wednesday to Sunday 9 to 4:30. Call ☎ 702/293–8990 for more information.

VISITOR INFORMATION

Alan Bible Visitors Center. The information center for Lake Mead had a 2013 face-lift, complete with a new hi-def film about the lake narrated by Stockard Channing. It's just past the Lake Mead turnoff from Highway 93, before you get to the pay booth for park entry. (A second visitor center in downtown Boulder City, 601 Nevada Way, is open weekdays, so there's one open every day of the week.) ☎ 702/293–8990 ⊕ *www.nps.gov/lake* ☉ *Wed.–Sun. 9–4:30.*

EXPLORING

Lake Mead. Lake Mead, which is actually the Colorado River backed up behind Hoover Dam, is the nation's largest man-made reservoir: it covers 225 square miles, is 110 miles long, and has an irregular shoreline that extends for 550 miles. You can get information about the lake's history, ecology, recreational opportunities, and the accommodations available along its shore at the Alan Bible Visitors Center. People come to Lake Mead primarily for boating, but a few areas or shoreline are cultivated for swimming: **Boulder Beach** is the closest to Las Vegas, only a mile or so from the visitor center.

Angling and house boating are favorite pastimes; marinas strung along the Nevada shore rent houseboats, personal watercraft, and ski boats. At least 1 million fish are harvested from the lake every year including the popular striped and largemouth bass. It's stocked with rainbow trout on a weekly basis from late October through March. You can fish here 24 hours a day, year-round (except for posted closings). You must have a fishing license from either Nevada or Arizona (details are on the National Park Service website), and if you plan to catch and keep trout, a separate trout stamp is required. Willow Beach is a favorite for anglers looking to catch rainbow trout; Cathedral Cove and Katherine are good for bass fishing. Divers can explore the murk beneath, including the remains of a B-29 Superfortress, which crashed into the Overton

Arm of the lake in 1948. Other activities abound, including waterskiing, sailboarding, canoeing, kayaking, and snorkeling. ⊠ *601 Nevada Way, Boulder City* ☎ *702/293–8990* ⊕ *www.nps.gov/lake* ⊠ *$10 per vehicle, good for 7 days; lake-use fees $16 1st vessel, good for 7 days. Annual pass is $30 per vehicle or per vessel.*

SPORTS AND THE OUTDOORS

BOATING

Lake Mead Marina. Lake Mead Marina, at Hemenway Harbor near Hoover Dam, has a general store, rentals, and a floating restaurant, the Harbor House Cafe. It's the closest marina to the public beach, Boulder Beach. The marina was moved in 2008 due to dropping water levels but has stayed put since. Boat rentals and personal watercraft are available through the **Las Vegas Boat Harbor** (☎ *702/293–1191 or 877/765–3745*). ⊠ *490 Horsepower Cove Rd., Boulder City* ☎ *702/293–1191* ⊕ *www.boatinglakemead.com.*

CRUISES

Lake Mead Cruises. At Lake Mead Cruises you can board the 300-passenger *Desert Princess,* an authentic Mississippi-style paddle wheeler that plies a portion of the lake, offering views of Hoover Dam and ancient rock formations such as an extinct volcano called Fortification Hill; brunch and dinner cruises are available seasonally. Ninety-minute sightseeing cruises occur year-round. ⊠ *Hemenway Boat Harbor near Boulder Beach* ☎ *702/293–6180* ⊕ *www.lakemeadcruises.com* ⊠ *Prices start at $26. Advance tickets available online.*

SCUBA DIVING AND SNORKELING

The creation of Lake Mead flooded a huge expanse of land, and, as a result, sights of the deep abound for scuba diving. Wishing Well Cove has steep canyon drop-offs, caves, and clear water. Castle Cliffs and Virgin Basin both have expansive views of white gypsum reefs and submerged sandstone formations. In summer Lake Mead is like a bathtub, reaching 85°F on the surface and staying at about 80°F down to 50 feet below the surface. Divers can actually wear bathing suits rather than wet suits to do some of the shallower dives. But visibility—which averages 30 feet to 35 feet overall—is much better in the winter months before the late-spring surface-algae bloom obscures some of the deeper attractions from snorkelers. Be aware that Lake Mead's level has dropped because of low snowfall in the Rockies. This has had some effect on diving conditions.

Outfitters Dive Into Fun ⊠ *50 N. Gibson Rd., Suite 170, Henderson* ☎ *702/479–7900* ⊕ *www.diveintofun.com.*

VALLEY OF FIRE

50 miles northeast of Las Vegas.

GETTING HERE AND AROUND

From Las Vegas, take Interstate 15 north about 35 miles to Exit 75–Route 169 and continue 15 miles. If you're coming from Lake Mead, look for the sign announcing the Valley of Fire a mile past Overton Beach. Turn left at the sign and go about 3 miles to reach the Valley of

DID YOU KNOW?

The inlaid design in Hoover Dam's terrazzo floor is a celestial map that provides the exact date that President Franklin D. Roosevelt dedicated the dam—September 30, 1935.

Fire Visitors Center. ■ **TIP➔** At this juncture it may also be possible to see some of the remnants of St. Thomas, a settlement that was washed away by the Colorado River after completion of the Hoover Dam, as drought conditions have lowered lake levels dramatically.

EXPLORING

FAMILY
Fodor's Choice
★

Valley of Fire State Park. The 56,000-acre Valley of Fire State Park was dedicated in 1935 as Nevada's first state park. Valley of Fire takes its name from its distinctive coloration, which ranges from lavender to tangerine to bright red, giving the vistas along the park road an otherworldly appearance. The jumbled rock formations are remnants of hardened sand dunes more than 150 million years old. You find petrified logs and the park's most photographed feature—Elephant Rock—just steps off the main road. Mysterious petroglyphs (carvings etched into the rocks) and pictographs (pictures drawn or painted on the rock's surface) are believed to be the work of the Basketmaker and ancestral Puebloan people who lived along the nearby Muddy River between 300 BC and AD 1150. The easy, essential trail is Mouse's Tank, named for an outlaw who hid out here and managed to find water; so will you in cooler months (but not for drinking). It's a short walk, shaded by steep canyon walls. Sci-fi fans also might recognize Fire Canyon as the alien planet in *Starship Troopers* and several other movies.

The **Valley of Fire Visitors Center** was remodeled in 2011 and has displays on the park's history, ecology, archaeology, and recreation, as well as slide shows and films, an art gallery, and information about the two campgrounds (73 campsites, 20 of them with power and water for RVs) within the park. Campsites at Atlatl Rock and Arch Rock Campgrounds are available on a first-come, first-served basis. The park is open year-round; the best times to visit, especially during the heat of summer, are sunrise and sunset, when the light is truly spectacular. ✉ *29450 Valley of Fire Rd., Overton ✛ I–15N to Exit 75. Turn right on Valley of Fire Hwy. Entrance to park is about 14 miles* ☎ *702/397–2088* ⊕ *www. parks.nv.gov or valley-of-fire.com* 💲 *$10 per vehicle ($2 discount for Nevada residents) or $20 per night plus $10 per vehicle for a campsite with hookups* ⊙ *Visitor center daily 8:30–4:30; park sunrise–sunset.*

OFF THE
BEATEN
PATH

Lost City Museum. The Moapa Valley has one of the finest collections of ancestral Puebloan artifacts in the American Southwest. Lost City, officially known as Pueblo Grande de Nevada, was a major outpost of the ancient culture. The museum's artifacts include baskets, weapons, a restored Basketmaker pit house, and black-and-white photographs of the 1924 excavation of Lost City. To get to the Lost City Museum from Valley of Fire, turn around on the park road and head back to the T intersection at the eastern entrance to the Valley of Fire. Turn left and drive roughly 8 miles into Overton. Turn left at the sign for the museum. Kids get in free. ✉ *721 S. Moapa Valley Blvd., Overton* ☎ *702/397–2193* 💲 *$5* ⊙ *Daily 8:30–4:30.*

9

GRAND CANYON

If you take only one side trip from Las Vegas, make it to the Grand Canyon. The Colorado River has carved through colorful and often contorted layers of rock, in some places more than 1 mile down, to expose a geologic profile spanning a time between 1.7 billion and 2.5 billion years ago—one-third of the planet's life. There's nothing like standing on the rim and looking down and across at layers of distance, color, and shifting light. Add the music of a canyon wren's merry, descending call echoing off the cliffs and spring water tinkling from the rocks along a trail, and you may sink into a reverie as deep and beautiful as the canyon.

GETTING HERE AND AROUND

There are two main access points to the canyon: the **South Rim** and the **North Rim,** both within the national park. The hordes of visitors converge mostly on the South Rim in summer, for good reason. Grand Canyon Village is here, with most of the lodging and camping, restaurants and stores, and museums in the park, along with the airport, railroad depot, rim roads, scenic overlooks, and trailheads into the canyon. The South Rim can be accessed either from the main entrance near Tusayan or by the East entrance near the Desert View Watchtower.

Directions to the South Rim: The South Rim is 278 miles southeast of Las Vegas (about a four-hour drive from Hoover Dam). Take Highway 93 south to Interstate 40. At Highway 64 drive 60 miles north to the park's southern entrance. ■TIP➜ In summer, roads are congested, so park your car and take the free shuttle. Traffic's lighter and parking easier October through April.

The North Rim, by contrast, stands 1,000 feet higher than the South Rim and has a more alpine climate, with twice as much annual precipitation. Here, in the deep forests of the Kaibab Plateau, the crowds are thinner, the facilities fewer, and the views even more spectacular.

Directions to the North Rim. The North Rim is 275 miles northeast of Vegas. Drive 128 miles north on Interstate 15 to Route 9 and then travel east 10 miles to Route 59/Route 389. Continue east 65 miles to the junction of U.S. 89A and then 30 miles east to Route 67, which dead-ends at the North Rim entrance.

If you don't have the time for the 5-hour drive to the North or South Rim, the **West Rim**—about 2½ hours from Las Vegas—is a more manageable excursion. A self-drive is possible, although it's a 14-mile road that's only partially paved so RVs and motorcycles, in particular, may find it a rough ride leading up to Grand Canyon West. As an alternative to driving, look into a helicopter, Hummer, or coach tour. Many tours will transport you to and from your Vegas hotel; park fees and lunch are usually part of the package. You can also take the shuttle from the Park and Ride Center in Meadview. At the West Rim, which isn't part of the Grand Canyon National Park and is run by the Hualapai tribe, you can view the canyon from the controversial Skywalk.

Directions to the West Rim: Grand Canyon West is 121 miles southeast of Las Vegas. Travel 72 miles south on Highway 93 to Pierce Ferry

Road (about 30 minutes from Hoover Dam) and travel north 28 miles to Diamond Bar Road. Drive 21 miles on Diamond Bar Road to the entrance at Grand Canyon West Airport, where a shuttle takes visitors to the West Rim.

SAFETY AND PRECAUTIONS

To report a security problem, contact the Park Police stationed at all visitor centers. There are no pharmacies at the North or South Rim. Prescriptions can be delivered daily to the South Rim Clinic from Flagstaff. A health center is staffed by physicians from 8 am to 6 pm, seven days a week (reduced hours in winter). Emergency medical services are available 24 hours a day.

Contacts **Emergency services** ☎ *911, 9–911 in park lodgings.* **North Country Grand Canyon Clinic** ✉ *Grand Canyon Village* ☎ *928/638–2551.* **Park Police** ☎ *928/638–7805.*

ADMISSION FEES AND PERMITS

A fee of $25 per vehicle or $12 per person for pedestrians and cyclists is good for one week's access at both rims.

The $50 Grand Canyon Pass gives unlimited access to the park for 12 months. The annual America the Beautiful **National Parks and Recreational Land Pass** (☎ *888/275–8747* ⊕ *store.usgs.gov/pass* ⊠ *$80*) provides unlimited access to all national parks and federal recreation areas for 12 months.

No permits are needed for day hikers; but **backcountry permits** (☎ *928/638–7875* ⊕ *www.nps.gov/grca* ⊠ *$10, plus $5 per person per night*) are necessary for overnight hikers. Permits are limited, so make your reservation as far in advance as possible—they're taken up to four months ahead of arrival. **Camping** in the park is restricted to designated campgrounds (☎ *877/444–6777* ⊕ *www.recreation.gov*).

TOURS

Air Tours. Ground tours to the Grand Canyon can be had from the Grand Canyon Tour Company, but if you're short on time (and can check your fear of heights at the bell desk), consider winging your way there in a small plane or helicopter. A host of air-tour companies will give you a bird's-eye view of the Strip, Hoover Dam, and Lake Mead on the way to the Grand Canyon rim and even down to the Colorado River bed itself on tours as brief as two hours and as inexpensive as $200 per person. Helicopter tours are usually more expensive than those in a small fixed-wing plane. All possible permutations of flight plans and amenities are available, from lunch to river rafting to overnight accommodations. Most tours include pickup and drop-off service from your hotel (sorry, Hotshot, you get picked up in a van or limo, not by a chopper). Weekday tours actually fill up faster than weekends; it can't hurt to book a few days in advance. The scenery is spectacular, but the ride can be bumpy and cold, even in summertime.

Air Tour Contacts **Grand Canyon Express** ☎ *702/655–6060, 800/222–6966* ⊕ *www.airvegas.com.* **Grand Canyon Tour Company** ☎ *702/655–6060, 800/222–6966* ⊕ *www.grandcanyontourcompany.com.* **HeliUSA** ☎ *702/736–8787, 800/359–8727* ⊕ *www.heliusa.com.* **Maverick Helicopter Tours**

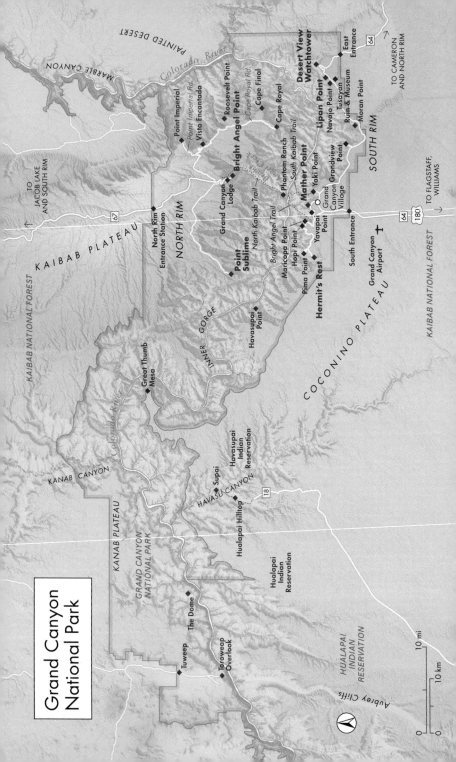

Grand Canyon National Park

PAINTED DESERT

MARBLE CANYON

Colorado River

TO CAMERON AND NORTH RIM

East Entrance

64

TO FLAGSTAFF, WILLIAMS

180

64

Desert View Watchtower

Lipan Point

Navajo Point

Tusayan Ruin & Museum

Moran Point

SOUTH RIM

Point Imperial

Roosevelt Point

Point Imperial Rd.

Vista Encantada

Cape Royal Rd.

Cape Final

Cape Royal

Bright Angel Point

Phantom Ranch

South Kaibab Trail

Yaki Point

Grandview Point

Grand Canyon Village

Grand Canyon Lodge

North Kaibab Trail

North Rim Entrance Station

NORTH RIM

67

TO JACOB LAKE AND SOUTH RIM

KAIBAB PLATEAU

KAIBAB NATIONAL FOREST

Point Sublime

Bright Angel Trail

Maricopa Point

Hopi Point

Pima Point

Yavapai Point

South Entrance

Grand Canyon Airport

COCONINO PLATEAU

Hermit's Rest

Havasupai Point

INNER GORGE

Great Thumb Mesa

Colorado River

KANAB CANYON

KANAB PLATEAU

Havasupai Indian Reservation

Supai

HAVASU CANYON

18

Hualapai Hilltop

Hualapai Indian Reservation

GRAND CANYON NATIONAL PARK

The Dome

Tuweep

Toroweap Overlook

HUALAPAI INDIAN RESERVATION

Aubrey Cliffs

KAIBAB NATIONAL FOREST

Mather Point

10 mi

10 km

0

WHEN TO GO TO THE GRAND CANYON

Time of Year	Advantages	Disadvantages
Mar.–May	Cool temperatures and more elbow room than in summer.	Weather is unpredictable. Be prepared for chilly climate changes.
June–Sept.	Highs in the low to mid-80s but mostly pleasant.	High humidity from frequent afternoon thunderstorms.
Oct.–Feb.	You'll experience the South Rim in a different light, literally and figuratively.	Winter conditions can be extreme. The road to the North Rim is closed from mid-October (or the first heavy winter snow) until mid-May.

WHERE TO GO: SOUTH RIM VS. NORTH RIM

Grand Canyon National Park is located in the northeastern corner of Arizona. The Grand Canyon and the Colorado River physically separate the park's two distinct halves into the North Rim and the South Rim. The average distance from the North Rim to the South Rim is 10 miles, but to travel from rim to rim by car requires a journey of 200 miles. The action's in the South Rim: Grand Canyon Village has year-round lodging, dining, shopping, museums, and shuttle stops. Higher in elevation by 1,000 feet, the North Rim offers more solitude and higher, grander views, but it's only open part of the year.

	SOUTH RIM	NORTH RIM
Distance from Vegas	278 mi.	275 mi.
Distance from Phoenix	231 mi.	351 mi.
The experience	Fast action and a hurried pace, with plenty to see and do.	A leisurely look at the remote rim of this famous national park.
Why?	More amenities than the North Rim.	Geared for outdoor activities
Elevation	7,000 feet	8,000 feet
Timing	It's best to spend at least one night here. One day is good to see the main sites; two days are best for a leisurely exploration.	With the added driving distance, most people spend two days exploring this far-away corner.
Rim drives	Self-guided Desert View Drive and Hermit Road, accessible by shuttle only from March through November.	Self-guided driving tours to developed overlooks on Cape Royal Road and Point Imperial Road.
Trails	9-mile rim hike from Mather Point to Hermits Rest. 8 trails including the popular inner canyon South Kaibab and Bright Angel Trails.	10 trails including the popular inner canyon North Kaibab Trail; an extensive network of rim hikes.
Overlooks	18 developed viewpoints	7 developed viewpoints, one accessible by foot from the Grand Canyon Lodge. Folks with 4WD can take the 17-mi. dirt route to Point Sublime.
Other activities	Train travel; tours; mule and horse rides; camping; fine dining; guided hikes; ranger programs; shopping.	Biking, horseback riding, picnicking, camping, and ranger programs.

9

☎ 702/261–0007, 888/261–4414 ⊕ www.maverickhelicopter.com. **Papillon** ☎ 702/736–7243, 888/635–7272 ⊕ www.papillon.com. **Scenic Airlines** ☎ 702/638–3300, 800/634–6801 ⊕ www.scenic.com. **Sundance Helicopters** ☎ 702/736–0606, 800/653–1881 ⊕ www.sundancehelicopters.com.

Hiking Tours. The Grand Canyon Field Institute leads a full program of educational guided hikes around the canyon year-round. Topics include everything from archaeology and backcountry medicine to photography and natural history. Reservations are essential and cost from $115 to $895. For a personalized tour of the Grand Canyon and surrounding sacred sites, contact Marvelous Marv, whose knowledge of the area is as extensive as his repertoire of local legends.

Contacts Grand Canyon Field Institute ☎ 928/638–2485, 866/471–4435 ⊕ www.grandcanyon.org/fieldinstitute. **Marvelous Marv** ☎ 928/707–0291 ⊕ www.marvelousmarv.com.

Jeep Tours. If you'd like to see parts of the park that are accessible only by dirt road, a jeep tour can be just the ticket. Rides can be rough; if you've had back injuries, check with your doctor before taking a jeep tour. Offerings include trips into the Kaibab Forest, sunset tours, Old West tours, inner canyon trips, and helicopter/jeep combos. Grand Canyon Store switched from jeeps to 13-passenger buses for visitors sensitive to dust and heat. Their day trips to the inner canyon on the Hualapai Reservation depart year-round from Williams and Flagstaff.

Contacts Grand Canyon Jeep Tours and Safaris ☎ 928/638–5337, 800/320–5337 ⊕ www.grandcanyonjeeptours.com. **The Grand Canyon Store** ☎ 928/638–2000, 800/716–9389 ⊕ www.grandcanyonjeeps.com.

Special-Interest Tours. The National Park Service sponsors all sorts of free Ranger Programs at both the South and North rims. These orientation activities include daily guided hikes and talks. The focus may be on any aspect of the canyon—from geology, flora, and fauna to history and early inhabitants. Programs change seasonally. For schedules, go to Grand Canyon Visitors Center on the South Rim or the Contact Station on the North Rim.

Several of the free programs are designed especially for children. Seasonally, there are also Junior Ranger Discovery Packs for children that include field guides, binoculars, magnifying glasses, and other exploration tools that can be checked out, but they go fast.

Contacts Ranger Programs ☎ 928/638–7888 ⊕ www.nps.gov/grca.

VISITOR INFORMATION

PARK CONTACT INFORMATION

Grand Canyon National Park. Before you go into the park, get the complimentary *Trip Planner,* updated regularly, from the Grand Canyon National Park. ☎ 928/638–7888 ⊕ *www.nps.gov/grca.*

VISITOR CENTERS

SOUTH RIM

Desert View Information Center. Near the watchtower, at Desert View Point, the nonprofit Grand Canyon Association store and information center has a nice selection of books, park pamphlets, gifts, and educational materials. All sales from the Association stores go to support the park programs. ⊠ *East entrance* ☎ *800/858–2808, 928/638–7888* ⊗ *Daily 9–5; hrs vary in winter.*

Grand Canyon Verkamp's Visitor Center. This small visitor center is named for the Verkamp family, who operated a curios shop on the South Rim for over a hundred years. The building serves as an official visitor center, ranger station (get your Junior Ranger badges here), bookstore, and museum, with compelling exhibits on the Verkamps and other pioneers in this region. ⊠ *Desert View Dr. across from El Tovar Hotel, Grand Canyon Village* ☎ *928/638–7146* ⊗ *Daily 8–7; ranger station 8–5.*

Grand Canyon Visitor Center. The park's main orientation center, known formerly as Canyon View Information Plaza, provides pamphlets and resources to help plan your visit. It also holds engaging interpretive exhibits on the park. Rangers are on hand to answer questions and aid in planning canyon excursions. A daily schedule of ranger-led hikes and evening lectures is posted on a bulletin board inside, and a 20-minute film about the history, geology, and wildlife of the canyon plays every 30 minutes in the theater. The bicycle rental office, a small café, and a huge gift store are also in this complex. There's ample parking by the information center; from here, it's a short walk out to Mather Point, or a short ride on the shuttle bus, which can take you into Grand Canyon Village, too. The visitor center is also accessible via a leisurely 1-mile walk on the Greenway Trail—a paved pathway that meanders through the forest. ⊠ *East side of Grand Canyon Village, 450 State Rte. 64* ☎ *928/638–7888* ⊕ *www.explorethecanyon.com* ⊗ *Daily 8–5; outdoor exhibits may be viewed anytime.*

Yavapai Geology Museum. Learn about the geology of the canyon at this museum and bookstore run by the Grand Canyon Association. You can also catch the park shuttle bus or pick up information for the Rim Trail here. The views of the canyon and Phantom Ranch from inside this historic building are stupendous. ⊠ *1 mile east of Market Plaza, Grand Canyon Village* ☎ *928/638–7888* ⊗ *Daily 8–8; hrs vary in winter.*

9

NORTH RIM

North Rim Visitor Center. View exhibits, peruse the bookstore, and pick up useful maps and brochures at this visitor center. Interpretive programs are often scheduled in summer. If you're craving coffee, it's a short walk from here to the Roughrider Saloon at the Grand Canyon Lodge. ⊠ *Near the parking lot on Bright Angel Peninsula* ☎ *928/638–7864* ⊕ *www.nps.gov/grca* ⊗ *Mid-May–mid-Oct., daily 8–6.*

SOUTH RIM

278 miles east of Las Vegas.

Visitors to the canyon converge mostly on the South Rim, and mostly during the summer. Grand Canyon Village is here, with most of the park's lodging and camping, trailheads, restaurants, stores, and museums, along with a nearby airport and railroad depot. Believe it or not, the average stay in the park is a mere four hours; this is not advised! You need to spend several days to truly appreciate this marvelous place, but at the very least, give it a full day. Hike down into the canyon or along the rim to get away from the crowds and experience nature at its finest.

GETTING HERE AND AROUND

By car, travel south on U.S. 93 to Kingman, Arizona; Interstate 40 east from Kingman to Williams; then Route 64 and U.S. 180 to the edge of the abyss. The South Rim is open to car traffic year-round, though access to many of the overlooks is limited to shuttle buses from March through November. Roads leading to the South Rim near Grand Canyon Village and the parking areas along the rim are congested in summer as well. If you visit from October through February, you can experience only light to moderate traffic and have no problem with parking.

When driving off major highways in low-lying areas, watch for rain clouds. Flash floods from sudden summer rains can be deadly.

There are also three free shuttle routes. Hermits Rest Route operates from March through November between Grand Canyon Village and Hermits Rest; it runs every 15 to 30 minutes from as early as 4:30 am until one hour after sunset, depending on the season. The Village Route operates year-round in the village area from one hour before sunrise until as late as 10 pm; it's the easiest access to the Grand Canyon Visitor Center. The Kaibab Trail Route travels from Grand Canyon Visitor Center to Yaki Point, including a stop at the South Kaibab Trailhead.

TOURS

Narrated motor-coach tours on the South Rim cover Hermits Rest Road and Desert View Drive. Other options include sunrise and sunset tours. Prices range from around $22 to $65 per person.

SCENIC DRIVES

Desert View Drive. This heavily traveled 23-mile stretch of road follows the rim from the East entrance to Grand Canyon Village. Starting from the less-congested entry near Desert View, road warriors can get their first glimpse of the canyon from the 70-foot-tall watchtower, the top of which provides the highest viewpoint on the South Rim. Eight overlooks, the remains of an ancestral Puebloan dwelling at the Tusayan Ruin and Museum, and the secluded and lovely Buggeln picnic area make for great stops along the South Rim. The Kaibab Trail Route shuttle bus travels a short section of Desert View Drive and takes 50 minutes to ride round-trip without getting off at any of the stops: Grand Canyon Visitor Center, South Kaibab Trailhead, Yaki Point, and Pipe Creek Vista, Mather Point, and Yavapai Geology Museum. ⊠ *Grand Canyon.*

Hermit Road. The Santa Fe Company built Hermit Road, formerly known as West Rim Drive, in 1912 as a scenic tour route. Nine overlooks dot this 7-mile stretch, each worth a visit. The road is filled with hairpin turns, so make sure you adhere to posted speed limits. A 1.5-mile Greenway trail offers easy access to cyclists looking to enjoy the original 1912 Hermit Rim Road. From March through November, Hermit Road is closed to private auto traffic because of congestion; during this period, a free shuttle bus carries visitors to all the overlooks. Riding the bus round-trip without getting off at any of the viewpoints takes

75 minutes; the return trip stops only at Pima, Mohave, and Powell points. ⊠ *Hermit Rd.*

HISTORIC SITES

Kolb Studio. Built over several years beginning in 1904 by the Kolb brothers as a photographic workshop and residence, this building provides a view of Indian Garden, where, in the days before a pipeline was installed, Emery Kolb descended 3,000 feet each day to get the water he needed to develop his prints. Kolb was doing something right; he operated the studio until he died in 1976 at age 95. The gallery here has changing exhibitions of paintings, photography, and crafts. There's also a small Grand Canyon Association store here. During the winter months, a ranger-led tour of the studio illustrates the role the Kolb brothers had on the development of the Grand Canyon. Call ahead to sign up for the tour. ⊠ *Grand Canyon Village near Bright Angel Lodge* ☎ *928/638–2771* ⊕ *www.grandcanyon.org/kolb* ⊠ *Free* ☉ *Apr.–mid-Oct., daily 8–7; mid-Oct.–Apr., daily 8–6.*

Tusayan Ruin and Museum. Completed in 1932, this museum offers a quick orientation to the lifestyles of the prehistoric and modern Indian populations associated with the Grand Canyon and the Colorado Plateau. Adjacent, an excavation of an 800-year-old dwelling gives a glimpse of the lives of some of the area's earliest residents. Of special interest are split-twig figurines dating back 2,000 to 4,000 years ago, a replica of a 10,000-year-old spear point, and other artifacts left behind by ancient cultures. Twice daily, a ranger leads an interpretive tour of the ancestral Puebloan village along a 0.1-mile, paved loop trail. ⊠ *About 20 miles east of Grand Canyon Village on E. Rim Dr.* ☎ *928/638–7888* ⊠ *Free* ☉ *Daily 9–5.*

SCENIC STOPS

The Abyss. At an elevation of 6,720 feet, the Abyss is one of the most awesome stops on Hermit Road, revealing a sheer drop of 3,000 feet to the Tonto Platform, a wide terrace of Tapeats sandstone about two-thirds of the way down the canyon. From the Abyss you'll also see several isolated sandstone columns, the largest of which is called the Monument. ⊠ *About 5 miles west of Hermit Rd. Junction on Hermit Rd.*

Desert View and Watchtower. From the top of the 70-foot stone-and-mortar watchtower, even the muted hues of the distant Painted Desert to the east and the Vermilion Cliffs rising from a high plateau near the Utah border are visible. In the chasm below, angling to the north toward Marble Canyon, an imposing stretch of the Colorado River reveals itself. Up several flights of stairs, the watchtower houses a glass-enclosed observatory with powerful telescopes. ⊠ *About 23 miles east of Grand Canyon Village on Desert View Dr.* ☎ *928/638–2736* ☉ *Daily 8–8; hrs vary in winter.*

Hermits Rest. This westernmost viewpoint and Hermit Trail, which descends from it, were named for "hermit" Louis Boucher, a 19th-century French-Canadian prospector who had a number of mining claims and a roughly built home down in the canyon. The trail served as the original mule ride down to Hermit Camp beginning in 1914. Views from here include Hermit Rapids and the towering cliffs of the

9

Continued on page 330

THE STORY OF THE
COLORADO RIVER
THE GRAND CANYON, HOOVER DAM

By Carrie Frasure

High in Colorado's Rocky Mountains, the Colorado River begins as a catch-all for the snowmelt off the mountains west of the Continental Divide. By the time it reaches the Grand Canyon it has become a raging river, red with silt as it sculpts spectacular landscapes. Even though it's partially tamed by a network of dams, the Colorado is still a mighty river.

D LAKE MEAD

As the primary artery of the Colorado River Basin, the Colorado River provides a vital lifeline to the arid southwest. Its natural course runs 1,450 miles from its origin in Colorado's La Poudre Pass Lake to its final destination in the Gulf of Colorado. Along the way it gathers strength and speed from a multitude of tributaries. In northern Arizona, it's known as the primary sculptor of the Grand Canyon, where it now flows 4,000 to 6,000 feet below the rim. The river takes a lazy turn at the Arizona–Nevada border, where Hoover Dam creates the reservoir at Lake Mead. The river continues at a relaxed pace along the Arizona–California border, bringing energy and irrigation to people in Arizona, California, and Nevada before flowing into northwestern Mexico.

CREATION OF THE GRAND CANYON

Considered one of the seven natural wonders of the world, the Grand Canyon stretches along 277 miles of the Colorado River, ranging in width from 4 to 18 miles. Nearly 2 billion years of geologic history is revealed in exposed layers cut up to a mile deep in the Colorado Plateau. As uplift raised the plateau, the river and its tributaries slowly cut into the canyon's layers. Under the sculpting power of wind and water, the shale layers eroded into slopes and the harder sandstone and limestone layers created terraced cliffs, resulting in the canyon profiles seen today.

ENVIRONMENTAL CONCERNS
When the Grand Canyon achieved national park status in 1919, only 44,173 people made the grueling overland trip to see it. Today, the park receives nearly 5 million visitors a year. The construction of Lake Powell's Glen Canyon Dam and the tremendous increase in visitation has greatly impacted the fragile ecosystems. Air pollution has affected visibility, non-native plants and animals threaten the extinction of several native species, wildfire suppression has led to the dangerous overgrowth of forest landscapes, and the constant buzz of aerial tours has disturbed the natural solitude. ■TIP→ Help ease the South Rim's congestion by taking the free shuttles, which have comprehensive routes along both Hermit Road and Desert View Drive as well as throughout Grand Canyon Village.

WHO LIVES HERE
Paleo-Indian artifacts show that humans have inhabited the Grand Canyon for more than 12,000 years. The plateau-dwelling Hualapai ("people of the tall pines") live on a million acres along 108 miles of the Colorado River in the West Rim. The Havasupai ("people of the blue green water") live deep within the walls of the 12-mile-long Havasu Canyon—a major side canyon connected to the Grand Canyon at the Colorado River—as they have for nearly 1,000 years.

Above, & Right views of Colorado River in Grand Canyon from Toroweap.

BEST CANYON VIEWS

■ Hopi Point, South Rim

■ Yavapai Point, South Rim

■ Lipan Point, South Rim

■ Grandview Point, South Rim

■ Bright Angel Point, North Rim

■ Cape Royal, North Rim

■ Point Sublime, North Rim

HOOVER DAM

HISTORY

Hoover Dam was built in 1935 and was the world's largest hydroelectric power plant and tallest dam. It has since lost these titles; however, it's still the tallest solid concrete arch-gravity dam in the western hemisphere. The dam was completed two full years ahead of the six year construction schedule during the Great Depression.

ENVIRONMENT VERSUS ECONOMY

Prior to the dam's construction, the river, swollen by snowmelt, flooded the lowlands along the California-Arizona border each spring before drying up so drastically that water levels were too low to divert for crops each summer. The dam tamed the mighty river and today provides a stable, year-round water supply for 18 million people and more than one million acres of farmland. However, the lack of flooding and the controlled waters have negatively affected the backwater riparian habitats bringing several native fish species to the brink of extinction.

WHAT'S IN A NAME?

Even though it was located in the Black Canyon, the Hoover Dam was originally referred to as the Boulder Dam Project. The dam was officially named

ARTISTIC LEANINGS

Hoover Dam is an engineering marvel *and* a work of art. The design features the flowing lines of Modernism and Art Deco used by architect Gordon B. Kaufmann, designer of the Los Angeles Times Building. Artist Allen True, whose murals are prominent in the Colorado State Capitol, used Native American geometric designs in the terrazzo floors. But it's the pair of 30-foot bronze statues—*Winged Figures of the Republic*—that dominate the dam. The striking figures were sculpted by Oskar J.W. Hansen, who also created the five bas-reliefs on the elevator towers and the bronze plaque memorial for the 96 workers who died during the construction.

after Herbert Hoover in 1931. When Hoover lost his bid for re-election to Franklin D. Roosevelt in 1932, Harold Ickes took the office of the Secretary of the Interior and immediately issued notice to the Bureau of Reclamation to refer to the structure as Boulder Dam. In 1947, Hoover was vindicated when the naming controversy was settled with a resolution signed by President Harry S. Truman, restoring the name to Hoover Dam—much to the retired Ickes' indignation.

Above, Hoover Dam and *Winged Figures of the Republic*. Opposite, Hoover Dam.

IN FOCUS THE STORY OF THE COLORADO RIVER

DID YOU KNOW?

Hoover Dam was the biggest man-made masonry marvel to surpass the Great Pyramid of Giza. The dam is made of more than 5 million barrels of cement and 4.5 million cubic yards of aggregate—enough to pave a standard 16-foot-wide highway stretching from San Francisco to New York City.

LAKE MEAD

HISTORY

Prior to the construction of Hoover Dam, the canyon lands and river valleys along this western section of the Colorado River were home to settlements including the towns of St. Thomas and Kaolin as well as hundreds of Native American archaeological sites. After the dam was built, these towns and sites became submerged by Lake Mead.

ENVIRONMENT

The lakes's cool waters are surrounded by the stark drama of the Mojave Desert—North America's hottest and driest. Nearly 96% of its water comes from snowmelt in Colorado, New Mexico, Utah, and Wyoming. This means the water level is at its highest in early spring and late fall. Levels drop in summer when agricultural demands are at their highest and the surrounding desert heats up.

TODAY

Construction of Hoover Dam created Lake Mead's 100-mile long reservoir, which was named after Bureau of Reclamation Commissioner Elwood Mead. This enormous reservoir became the United States' first National Recreation Area in 1964. Today, more than 9 million people visit this wonderland each year.

TOMORROW

Over the last few years, Lake Mead's water levels have dropped drastically. As one of the largest reservoirs in the world, it provides water to residents and farmers in Arizona, California, Nevada and northern Mexico. An extended drought and the increased demand for this critical resource have exceeded the amount of water deposited into the lake by the Colorado River. Already the dramatic drop in the lake's water level has led to the exposure of parts of St. Thomas, as well as a series of islands in Boulder Basin. A recent study by the Scripps Institution of Oceanography shows that if the current conditions continue, there's a 50% chance that Lake Mead may be dry by 2021.

Above, Lake Mead. Opposite, sailing on the lake.

SPORTS IN THE AREA

Water recreation dominates the placid waters of Lake Mead. The dramatic scenery of the surrounding Mojave Desert just adds to the year-round draw. Some of the favorite sporting activities at this far-reaching reservoir include:

■ fishing for striped bass and rainbow trout
■ relaxing on a houseboat
■ exploring hidden coves by canoe or kayak
■ swimming at Boulder Beach
■ hitting the wakes on water skis
■ scuba diving at North Boulder Beach's Dive Park

Ride the Rails

Grand Canyon Railway. There is no need to deal with all of the other drivers racing to the South Rim. Sit back and relax in the comfy train cars of the Grand Canyon Railway. Live music and storytelling enliven the trip as you journey past the landscape through prairie, ranch, and national park land to the log-cabin train station in Grand Canyon Village. You won't see the Grand Canyon from the train, but you can walk (0.25 mile) or catch the shuttle at the restored, historic Grand Canyon Railway Station. The vintage train departs from the Williams Depot every morning, and makes the 65-mile journey in 2¼ hours. You can do the round-trip in a single day; however, it's a more relaxing and enjoyable strategy to stay for a night or two at the South Rim before returning to Williams. ☎ 800/843–8724 ⊕ www.thetrain.com ✉ $70–$178 round-trip.

Supai and Redwall formations. In the stone building at Hermits Rest you can buy curios and snacks. ⊠ *About 8 miles west of Hermit Rd. Junction on Hermit Rd.*

Fodor'sChoice ★ **Hopi Point.** From this elevation of 6,800 feet, you can see a large section of the Colorado River; although it appears as a thin line, the river is nearly 350 feet wide below this overlook. The overlook extends farther into the canyon than any other point on Hermit Road. The unobstructed views make this a popular place to watch the sunset.

Across the canyon to the north is Shiva Temple, which remained an unexplored section of the Kaibab Plateau until 1937. That year, Harold Anthony of the American Museum of Natural History led an expedition to the rock formation in the belief that it supported life that had been cut off from the rest of the canyon. Imagine the expedition members' surprise when they found an empty Kodak film box on top of the temple—it had been left behind by Emery Kolb, who felt slighted for not having been invited to partake of Anthony's tour.

Directly below Hopi Point lies Dana Butte, named for a prominent 19th-century geologist. In 1919, an entrepreneur proposed connecting Hopi Point, Dana Butte, and the Tower of Set across the river with an aerial tramway, a technically feasible plan that fortunately has not been realized. ⊠ *About 4 miles west of Hermit Rd. Junction on Hermit Rd.*

Fodor'sChoice ★ **Mather Point.** You'll likely get your first glimpse of the canyon from this viewpoint, one of the most impressive and accessible (next to the main Visitor Center Plaza) on the South Rim. Named for the National Park Service's first director, Stephen Mather, this spot yields extraordinary views of the Grand Canyon, including deep into the inner gorge and numerous buttes: Wotans Throne, Brahma Temple, and Zoroaster Temple, among others. The Grand Canyon Lodge, on the North Rim, is almost directly north from Mather Point and only 10 miles away—yet you have to drive 215 miles to get from one spot to the other. ⊠ *Near Grand Canyon Visitor Center* ☎ *928/638–7888* ⊕ *www.nps.gov/grca.*

Fodor's Choice ★ **Yavapai Point.** This is also one of the best locations on the South Rim to watch the sunset. Dominated by the Yavapai Geology Museum and Observation Station, this point displays panoramic views of the mighty gorge through a wall of windows. Exhibits at the museum include videos of the canyon floor and the Colorado River, a scaled diorama of the canyon with national park boundaries, fossils and rock fragments used to re-create the complex layers of the canyon walls, and a display on the natural forces used to carve the chasm. Rangers dig even deeper into Grand Canyon geology with free ranger programs daily. Check ahead for special events, guided walks, and program schedules. There's also a bookstore. ⊠ *Adjacent to Grand Canyon Village* 🖼 *Free* ☉ *Daily 8–8; hrs vary in winter.*

HIKING

Although permits aren't required for day hikes, you must have a backcountry permit for overnight trips *(⇨ See Permits at start of this section).* Some of the more popular trails are here; more detailed information and maps can be obtained from the Backcountry Information Center. Also, rangers can help design a trip to suit your abilities.

Remember that the canyon has significant elevation changes and, in summer, extreme temperature ranges, which can pose problems for people who aren't in good shape or who have heart or respiratory problems. ■TIP➔ Carry plenty of water and energy foods. The majority of each year's 400 search-and-rescue incidents result from hikers underestimating the size of the canyon, hiking beyond their abilities, or not packing sufficient food and water.

⚠ It's not advised to attempt a day hike from the rim to the river and back. Canyon rangers will try to talk you out of the idea. It's legal, but only very fit, athletic people should attempt it. Remember that when it's 80°F on the South Rim, it's 105°F on the canyon floor. Allow two or more days if you want to hike rim to rim (it's easier to descend from the North Rim, as it's more than 1,000 feet higher than the South Rim). Hiking steep trails from rim to rim is a strenuous trek of at least 21 miles and should only be attempted by experienced canyon hikers.

9

EASY

Fodor's Choice ★ **Rim Trail.** The South Rim's most popular walking path is the 12-mile (one-way) Rim Trail, which runs along the edge of the canyon from Pipe Creek Vista (the first overlook on Desert View Drive) to Hermits Rest. This walk, which is paved to Maricopa Point and for the last 1.5 miles to Hermits Rest, visits several of the South Rim's historic landmarks. Allow anywhere from 15 minutes to a full day, depending on how much of the trail you want to cover; the Rim Trail is an ideal day hike, as it varies only a few hundred feet in elevation from Mather Point (7,120 feet) to the trailhead at Hermits Rest (6,650 feet). The trail also can be accessed from several spots in Grand Canyon Village and from the major viewpoints along Hermit Road, which are serviced by shuttle buses during the busy summer months. *Easy.* ■TIP➔ On the Rim Trail, water is only available in the Grand Canyon Village area and at Hermits Rest.

NEED A BREAK?

If you've been driving too long and want some exercise, along with great views of the canyon, it's an easy 1.25-mile-long hike from the Information Plaza to El Tovar Hotel. The Greenway path runs through a quiet wooded area for about half a mile, and then along the rim for another three-quarters of a mile.

MODERATE

Bright Angel Trail. This well-maintained trail is one of the most scenic hiking paths from the South Rim to the bottom of the canyon (9.6 miles each way). Rest houses are equipped with water at the 1.5- and 3-mile points from May through September and at Indian Garden (4 miles) year-round. Water is also available at Bright Angel Campground, 9.25 miles below the trailhead. Plateau Point, on a spur trail about 1.5 miles below Indian Garden, is as far as you should attempt to go on a day hike; the round-trip will take six to nine hours.

Bright Angel Trail is the easiest of all the footpaths into the canyon, but because the climb out from the bottom is an ascent of 5,510 feet, the trip should be attempted only by those in good physical condition and should be avoided in midsummer due to extreme heat. The top of the trail can be icy in winter. Originally a bighorn sheep path and later used by the Havasupai, the trail was widened late in the 19th century for prospectors and is now used for both mule and foot traffic. Also note that mule trains have the right-of-way—and sometimes leave unpleasant surprises in your path. *Moderate.* ⊠ *Trailhead: Kolb Studio, Hermits Rd.*

DIFFICULT

South Kaibab Trail. This trail starts near Yaki Point, 4 miles east of Grand Canyon Village, and is accessible via the free shuttle bus. Because the route is so steep (and sometimes icy in winter)—descending from the trailhead at 7,260 feet down to 2,480 feet at the Colorado River—and has no water, many hikers take this trail down, then ascend via the less-demanding Bright Angel Trail. Allow four to six hours to reach the Colorado River on this 6.4-mile trek. At the river, the trail crosses a suspension bridge and runs on to Phantom Ranch. Along the trail there is no water and little shade. There are no campgrounds, though there are portable toilets at Cedar Ridge (6,320 feet), 1.5 miles from the trailhead. An emergency phone is available at the Tipoff, 4.6 miles down the trail (3 miles past Cedar Ridge). The trail corkscrews down through some spectacular geology. Look for (but don't remove) fossils in the limestone when taking water breaks. ■TIP→ Even though an immense network of trails winds through the Grand Canyon, the popular corridor trails (Bright Angel and South Kaibab) are recommended for hikers new to the region. *Difficult.* ⊠ *Trailhead: Yaki Point, Desert View Dr.*

MULE RIDES

Mule rides provide an intimate glimpse into the canyon for those who have the time, but not the stamina, to see the canyon on foot. ■TIP→ Reservations are essential and are accepted up to 13 months in advance.

These trips have been conducted since the early 1900s. A comforting fact as you ride the narrow trail: no one's ever been killed while riding a mule that fell off a cliff. (Nevertheless, the treks aren't for the faint of heart or people in questionable health.)

OUTFITTERS

Fodor's Choice
★
Xanterra Parks & Resorts Mule Rides. These trips delve into the canyon from the South Rim to Phantom Ranch, or east along the canyon's edge (the Plateau Point rides were discontinued in 2009). Riders must be at least 55 inches tall, weigh less than 200 pounds (for the Phantom Ranch ride), and understand English. Children under 15 must be accompanied by an adult. Riders must be in fairly good physical condition, and pregnant women are advised not to take these trips.

The three-hour ride along the rim costs $114. An overnight with a stay at Phantom Ranch at the bottom of the canyon is $518 ($916 for two riders). Two nights at Phantom Ranch, an option available from November through March, will set you back $731 ($1,218 for two). Meals are included. Reservations (by phone), especially during the busy summer months, are a must, but you can check at the Bright Angel Transportation Desk to see if there's last-minute availability. ☎ 888/297–2757 ⊕ *www.grandcanyonlodges.com* ⌘ *Reservations essential* ☉ *Phantom Ranch rides daily; Rim rides mid-Mar.–Oct., twice daily; Nov.–mid-Mar., once daily.*

WHERE TO EAT

$$
STEAKHOUSE
✕ **Arizona Room.** The canyon views from this casual Southwestern-style steak house are the best of any restaurant at the South Rim. The menu includes such delicacies as chile-crusted pan-seared wild salmon, chipotle barbecue baby back ribs, and half-pound buffalo burgers with Gorgonzola aioli. For dessert, try the cheesecake with prickly pear syrup paired with one of the house's specialty coffee drinks. Seating is first-come, first served, so arrive early to avoid the crowds. ⑤ *Average main: $22* ⊠ *Bright Angel Lodge, Desert View Dr., Grand Canyon Village* ☎ 928/638–2631 ⊕ *www.grandcanyonlodges.com* ⌘ *Reservations not accepted* ☉ *Closed Jan. and Feb. No lunch Nov. and Dec.*

$
SOUTHWESTERN
✕ **Bright Angel Restaurant.** No-surprises, affordable dishes here will fill your belly at breakfast, lunch, or dinner. Entrées include such basics as salads, steaks, lasagna, burgers, fajitas, and fish tacos (sandwiches are options at lunch). Or you can step it up a notch and order some of the same selections straight from the Arizona Room menu, including prime rib, baby back ribs, and wild salmon. For dessert try the warm apple grunt cake topped with vanilla ice cream. Be prepared to wait for a table: the dining room bustles all day long. The plain decor is broken up with large-pane windows and original artwork. ⑤ *Average main: $12* ⊠ *Bright Angel Lodge, Desert View Dr., Grand Canyon Village* ☎ 928/638–2631 ⊕ *www.grandcanyonlodges.com* ⌘ *Reservations not accepted.*

$
AMERICAN
✕ **Canyon Café at Yavapai Lodge.** Open for breakfast, lunch, and dinner, this cafeteria in the Yavapai Lodge, across from Market Plaza, serves down-home staples like as chicken potpie, fried catfish, and fried chicken. Fast-food favorites include pastries, burgers, and pizza. There isn't a fancy bar, but you can order beer and wine with your meal.

Resembling an old-fashioned diner, the large cafeteria has easy-to-read signs that point the way to your favorite foods. $ *Average main: $7* ✉ *Yavapai Lodge, Desert View Dr., Grand Canyon Village* 🕾 *928/638–2631* ⊕ *www.grandcanyonlodges.com/canyon-cafe-423.html* ⚏ *Reservations not accepted* ☉ *Closed Nov.–Feb. (except during Thanksgiving weekend and Christmas wk).*

$$$
SOUTHWESTERN
Fodor'sChoice
★

✕ **El Tovar Dining Room.** No doubt about it—this is the best restaurant for miles. Modeled after a European hunting lodge, this rustic 19th-century dining room built of hand-hewn logs is worth a visit. The cuisine is modern Southwestern with an exotic flair. Start with the smoked salmon–and–goat cheese crostini or the acclaimed black bean soup. The dinner menu includes such hearty yet creative dishes as cherry-merlot-glazed duck with roasted poblano black bean rice, grilled New York strip steak with cornmeal-battered onion rings, and a wild-salmon tostada topped with organic greens and tequila vinaigrette. The dining room also has an extensive wine list. ■**TIP→** Dinner reservations can be made up to six months in advance with room reservations and 30 days in advance for all other visitors. If you can't get a dinner table, consider lunch or breakfast—the best in the region with dishes like polenta corncakes with prickly pear–pistachio butter, and blackened breakfast trout and eggs. $ *Average main: $27* ✉ *El Tovar Hotel, Desert View Dr., Grand Canyon Village* 🕾 *303/297–2757, 888/297–2757 reservations only* ⊕ *www.grandcanyonlodges.com/el-tovar-421.html* ⚏ *Reservations essential.*

$
AMERICAN

✕ **Maswik Cafeteria.** You can get a burger, hot sandwich, pasta, or Mexican fare at this food court, as well as pizza by the slice and wine and beer in the adjacent Maswik Pizza Pub. This casual eatery is 0.25 mile from the rim, and the Pizza Pub stays open until 11 pm (you can also order pizza to take out). Lines can be long during high-season lunch and dinner, but everything moves fairly quickly. $ *Average main: $7* ✉ *Maswik Lodge, Desert View Dr., Grand Canyon Village* ⊕ *www.grandcanyonlodges.com* ⚏ *Reservations not accepted.*

WHERE TO STAY

$
HOTEL
FAMILY

🛏 **Bright Angel Lodge.** Famed architect Mary Jane Colter designed this 1935 log-and-stone structure, which sits within a few yards of the canyon rim and blends superbly with the canyon walls. **Pros:** some rooms have canyon vistas; all are steps away from the rim; Internet kiosks and transportation desk for the mule ride check-in are in the lobby; good value for the amazing location. **Cons:** the popular lobby is always packed; parking is a bit of a hike. $ *Rooms from: $92* ✉ *Desert View Dr., Grand Canyon Village* 🕾 *888/297–2757 reservations only, 928/638–2631* ⊕ *www.grandcanyonlodges.com* ⇦ *37 rooms, 18 with bath; 50 cabins* ⧫⊙❙ *No meals.*

$$
HOTEL
Fodor'sChoice
★

🛏 **El Tovar Hotel.** The hotel's proximity to all of the canyon's facilities, European hunting-lodge atmosphere, attractively updated rooms and tile baths, and renowned dining room make it the best place to stay on the South Rim. **Pros:** historic lodging just steps from the South Rim; fabulous lounge with outdoor seating and canyon views; best in-park dining on-site. **Cons:** books up quickly. $ *Rooms from: $183* ✉ *Desert View Dr., Grand Canyon Village* 🕾 *888/297–2757 reservations* *only, 928/638–2631* ⊕ *www. grandcanyonlodges.com* ⤴ 66 *rooms, 12 suites* ⦿ *No meals.*

$$ ⛺ **Kachina Lodge.** The well-outfitted
HOTEL rooms at this motel-style lodge on
the south rim are a good bet for
families and are within easy walk-
ing distance of dining facilities at
nearby lodges. **Pros:** partial canyon
views in half the rooms; family-
friendly; steps from the best res-
taurants in the park. **Cons:** check-in
takes place at nearby El Tovar
Hotel; limited parking; pleasant but
bland furnishings. ⑤ *Rooms from:
$178* ✉ *Desert View Dr., Grand
Canyon Village* ☎ *888/297–2757
reservations only, 928/638–2631*
⊕ *www.grandcanyonlodges.com*
⤴ *49 rooms* ⦿ *No meals.*

ARRANGING TOURS

Transportation-services desks are
maintained at El Tovar, Bright
Angel, Maswik Lodge, and Yavapai
Lodge (closed in winter) in Grand
Canyon Village. The desks provide
information and handle bookings
for sightseeing tours, taxi and
bus services, mule and horseback
rides, and accommodations at
Phantom Ranch (at the bottom of
the Grand Canyon). The concierge
at El Tovar can also arrange most
tours, with the exception of mule
rides and lodging at Phantom
Ranch. On the North Rim, Grand
Canyon Lodge has general infor-
mation about local services.

$ ⛺ **Maswik Lodge.** Far from the noisy
HOTEL crowds, accommodations at this lodge are nestled in a shady ponder-
FAMILY osa pine forest, with options ranging from rustic cabins to more mod-
ern motel-style rooms. **Pros:** larger rooms here than in older lodgings;
good for families; affordable dining options. **Cons:** rooms lack historic
charm; tucked away from the rim in the forest. ⑤ *Rooms from: $90*
✉ *Grand Canyon Village* ☎ *888/297–2757 reservations only, 928/638–
2631* ⊕ *www.grandcanyonlodges.com* ⤴ *278 rooms* ⦿ *No meals.*

$ ⛺ **Phantom Ranch.** In a grove of cottonwood trees on the canyon floor,
B&B/INN Phantom Ranch is accessible only to hikers and mule trekkers; there are
40 dormitory beds and 14 beds in cabins, all with shared baths. **Pros:**
only inner-canyon lodging option; fabulous canyon views; remote access
limits crowds. **Cons:** accessible only by foot or mule; few amenities or
means of outside communication. ⑤ *Rooms from: $46* ✉ *On canyon
floor, at intersection of Bright Angel and Kaibab trails* ☎ *303/297–
2757, 888/297–2757* ⊕ *www.grandcanyonlodges.com* ⤴ *4 dormitories
and 9 cabins (some cabins with outside showers reserved for mule rid-
ers)* ⦿ *Some meals.*

$$ ⛺ **Thunderbird Lodge.** This motel with comfortable, simple rooms has all
HOTEL the modern amenities you'd expect at a typical mid-price chain hotel.
Pros: partial canyon views in some rooms; family-friendly. **Cons:** rooms
lack personality; check-in takes place at nearby Bright Angel Lodge;
limited parking nearby. ⑤ *Rooms from: $178* ✉ *Desert View Dr., Grand
Canyon Village* ☎ *888/297–2757 reservations only, 928/638–2631*
⊕ *www.grandcanyonlodges.com* ⤴ *55 rooms* ⦿ *No meals.*

$ ⛺ **Yavapai Lodge.** The largest motel-style lodge in the park is tucked
HOTEL in a piñon and juniper forest at the eastern end of Grand Canyon
Village, across from Market Plaza. **Pros:** transportation-activities desk
on-site in the lobby; walk to Market Plaza in Grand Canyon Village;
forested grounds. **Cons:** farthest in-park lodging from the rim (½

White-water rafting is just one of the many activities you can experience in the Grand Canyon.

mile). $ *Rooms from: $123* ✉ *10 Yavapai Lodge Rd., Grand Canyon Village* ☎ *888/297–2757 reservations only, 928/638–2961* ⊕ *www.grandcanyonlodges.com* ⇆ *358 rooms* ☾ *Closed Nov.–Feb., except during Thanksgiving weekend and Christmas wk* ⦿ *No meals.*

NORTH RIM

276 miles northeast of Las Vegas.

The North Rim stands 1,000 feet higher than the South Rim and has a more alpine climate, with twice as much annual precipitation. Here, in the deep forests of the Kaibab Plateau, the crowds are thinner, the facilities fewer, and the views even more spectacular. Due to snow, the North Rim is off-limits in winter. The park buildings are closed mid-October through mid-May. The road closes when the snow makes it impassable—usually by the end of November.

Lodgings are available but limited; the North Rim only offers one historic lodge and restaurant and a single campground. Dining options have opened up a little with the addition of the Grand Cookout, offered nightly with live entertainment under the stars. Your best bet may be to pack your camping gear and hiking boots and take several days to explore the lush Kaibab Forest. The canyon's highest, most dramatic rim views also can be enjoyed on two wheels (via primitive dirt access roads) and on four legs (courtesy of a trusty mule).

GETTING HERE AND AROUND

To get to the North Rim by car, take Interstate 15 east to Hurricane, Utah; Routes 59 and 389 to Fredonia; and U.S. 89 and Route 67 to the North Rim. The North Rim is closed to automobiles after the first heavy snowfall of the season (usually in late October or early November) through mid-May. All North Rim facilities close between October 15 and May 15, though the park itself stays open for day use from October 15 through December 1, if heavy snows don't close the roads before then.

Reaching elevations of 8,000 feet, the more remote North Rim has no services available from late October through mid-May. AZ 67 south of Jacob Lake is closed by the first heavy snowfall in November or December and remains closed until early to mid-May.

When driving off major highways in low-lying areas, watch for rain clouds. Flash floods from sudden summer rains can be deadly.

From mid-May to mid-October, the Trans-Canyon Shuttle leaves Bright Angel Lodge at 8 am and 1:30 pm and arrives at the North Rim's Grand Canyon Lodge at about 12:30 and 6 pm. The return trip leaves the North Rim each morning at 7 am and 2 pm, arriving at the South Rim at about 11:30 am and 6:30 pm. The one-way fare is $85 and the round-trip is $160; a 50% deposit is required, as are reservations. There's postseason shuttle service from October 16 to 31, but the schedule varies from the regular season.

PERMITS

The North Rim may be accessed in the winter by hiking, cross-country skiing, or snowshoeing. Winter visitors must obtain a backcountry permit for overnight use. Between the North Kaibab trailhead and Bright Angel Point, all overnight visitors are required to stay at the North Rim Campground. Winter campers can camp at large at all other areas between the northern boundary and the North Kaibab trailhead.

HISTORIC SITES

Grand Canyon Lodge. Built in 1937 by the Union Pacific Railroad (replacing the original 1928 building, which burned in a fire), the massive stone structure is listed on the National Register of Historic Places. Its huge sunroom has hardwood floors, high-beam ceilings, and a marvelous view of the canyon through plate-glass windows. On warm days, visitors sit in the sun and drink in the surrounding beauty on an outdoor viewing deck, where National Park Service employees deliver free lectures on geology and history. The dining room serves breakfast, lunch, and dinner; the Roughrider Saloon is a bar by night and a coffee shop in the morning. ✉ *Off Hwy. 67 near Bright Angel Point, 10 Albright St.* ☎ *928/638–2631* ⊕ *www.grandcanyonlodges.com.*

SCENIC DRIVE

Fodor's Choice ★ **Highway 67.** Open mid-May to roughly mid-November (or the first big snowfall), the two-lane paved road climbs 1,400 feet in elevation as it passes through the Kaibab National Forest. Also called the "North Rim Parkway," this scenic route crosses the limestone-capped Kaibab Plateau—passing broad meadows, sun-dappled forests, and small lakes and springs—before abruptly falling away at the abyss of the Grand

Perched on the North Rim's edge—1,000 feet higher than the South Rim—is the Grand Canyon Lodge.

Canyon. Wildlife abounds in the thick ponderosa pine forests and lush mountain meadows. It's common to see deer, turkeys, and coyotes as you drive through this remote region. Point Imperial and Cape Royal branch off this scenic drive, which runs from Jacob Lake to Bright Angel Point. ⊠ *Hwy. 67.*

SCENIC STOPS

Bright Angel Point. This trail, which leads to one of the most awe-inspiring overlooks on either rim, starts on the grounds of the Grand Canyon Lodge and runs along the crest of a point of rocks that juts into the canyon for several hundred yards. The walk is only 0.5 mile round-trip, but it's an exciting trek accented by sheer drops on each side of the trail. In a few spots where the route is extremely narrow, metal railings ensure visitors' safety. The temptation to clamber out to precarious perches to have your picture taken should be resisted at all costs. ⊠ *North Rim Dr.*

Cape Royal. A popular sunset destination, Cape Royal showcases the canyon's jagged landscape; you'll also get a glimpse of the Colorado River, framed by a natural stone arch called Angels Window. In autumn, the aspens turn a beautiful gold, adding even more color to an already magnificent scene of the forested surroundings. The easy and rewarding 1-mile round-trip hike along **Cliff Springs Trail** starts here; it takes you through a forested ravine and terminates at Cliff Springs, where the forest opens to another impressive view of the canyon walls. ⊠ *Cape Royal Scenic Dr., 23 miles southeast of Grand Canyon Lodge.*

Point Imperial. At 8,803 feet, Point Imperial has the highest vista point at either rim; it offers magnificent views of both the canyon and the distant country: the Vermilion Cliffs to the north, the 10,000-foot Navajo

WINTER ACTIVITIES

Due to heavy snow and extreme winter weather, the North Rim closes all of its services from mid-October through mid-May. However, Highway 67 stays open to the North Rim until snows force the closure of the road at Jacob Lake. After the road closes, the rim can be accessed by hiking, snowshoeing, and cross-country skiing. Winter visitors must obtain a backcountry permit for overnight use during the winter season (later October through mid-May). Between the North Kaibab trailhead and Bright Angel Point, all overnight visitors are required to stay at the North Rim Campground. Winter campers can camp at large at all other areas between the northern boundary and the North Kaibab trailhead.

Mountain to the northeast in Utah, the Painted Desert to the east, and the Little Colorado River canyon to the southeast. Other prominent points of interest include views of Mount Hayden, Saddle Mountain, and Marble Canyon. ⊠ *2.7 miles left off Cape Royal Rd. on Point Imperial Rd., 11 miles northeast of Grand Canyon Lodge.*

Fodor's Choice **Point Sublime.** You can camp within feet of the canyon's edge at this awe-
★ inspiring site. Sunrises and sunsets are spectacular. The winding road, through gorgeous high country, is only 17 miles, but it will take you at least two hours, one way. The road is intended only for vehicles with high-road clearance (pickups and four-wheel-drive vehicles). It is also necessary to be properly equipped for wilderness road travel. Check with a park ranger or at the information desk at Grand Canyon Lodge before taking this journey. You may camp here only with a permit from the Backcountry Information Center. ⊠ *North Rim Dr., Grand Canyon; about 20 miles west of North Rim Visitor Center.*

HIKING
EASY
FAMILY **Transept Trail.** This 3-mile (round-trip), 1½-hour trail begins near the Grand Canyon Lodge at 8,255 feet. Well maintained and well marked, it has little elevation change, sticking near the rim before reaching a dramatic view of a large stream through Bright Angel Canyon. The route leads to a side canyon called Transept Canyon, which geologist Clarence Dutton named in 1882, declaring it "far grander than Yosemite." Check the posted schedule to find a ranger talk along this trail; it's also a great place to view fall foliage. Flash floods can occur any time of the year, especially June through September when thunderstorms develop rapidly. *Easy.* ⊠ *Trailhead: near the Grand Canyon Lodge's east patio.*

MODERATE
⚠ Flash floods can occur any time of the year, especially from June through September, when thunderstorms develop rapidly. Check forecasts before heading into the canyon and use caution when hiking in narrow canyons and drainage systems.

Fodor's Choice
★
Widforss Trail. Round-trip, Widforss Trail is 9.8 miles, with an elevation change of only 200 feet. Allow five to six hours for the hike, which starts at 8,080 feet and passes through shady forests of pine, spruce, fir, and aspen on its way to Widforss Point, at 7,900 feet. Here you'll have good views of five temples: Zoroaster, Brahma, and Deva to the southeast, and Buddha and Manu to the southwest. You are likely to see wildflowers in summer, and this is a good trail for viewing fall foliage. It's named in honor of artist Gunnar M. Widforss, renowned for his paintings of national park landscapes. *Moderate.* ⊠ *Trailhead: Point Sublime Rd.*

DIFFICULT

North Kaibab Trail. At 8,241 feet, this trail leads into the canyon and down to Phantom Ranch. It is recommended for experienced hikers only, who should allow four days for the round-trip hike. The long, steep path drops 5,840 feet over a distance of 14.5 miles to Phantom Ranch and the Colorado River, so the National Park Service suggests that day hikers not go farther than Roaring Springs (5,020 feet) before turning to hike back up out of the canyon. After about 7 miles, Cottonwood Campground (4,080 feet) has drinking water in summer, restrooms, shade trees, and a ranger. *Difficult.* ■TIP→ A free shuttle takes hikers to the North Kaibab trailhead twice daily from Grand Canyon Lodge; reserve a spot the day before. ⊠ *Trailhead: 2 miles north of the Grand Canyon Lodge.*

OFF THE BEATEN PATH
Unpaved forested side roads branch off Highway 67 before the North Rim park entrance station, leading to several remote viewpoints not seen by the majority of Grand Canyon travelers. At Crazy Jug Point, you'll see the Colorado River as well as several canyon landmarks, including Powell Plateau, Great Thumb Mesa, and Tapeats Amphitheater. Timp Point features spectacular canyon views and a glimpse of Thunder River. Check with the Kaibab Forest Visitors Center in Jacob Lake for maps and road updates. The Forest Service maintains everything north of the rim, which is monitored by the National Park Service.

MULE RIDES

FAMILY **Canyon Trail Rides.** This company leads mule rides on the easier trails of the North Rim. A one-hour ride (minimum age seven) runs $40. Half-day trips on the rim or into the canyon (minimum age 10) cost $80. Weight limits are 200 pounds for canyon rides and 220 pounds for the rim rides. Available daily from May 15 to October 15, these excursions are popular, so make reservations in advance. ☎ *435/679–8665* ⊕ *www. canyonrides.com.*

WHERE TO EAT

$ ✕ **Deli in the Pines.** Dining choices are limited on the North Rim, but
AMERICAN this is your best bet for a meal on a budget. Selections include pizza, salads, deli sandwiches, hot dogs, homemade breakfast pastries and burritos, and soft-serve ice cream. Best of all, there is an outdoor seating area for dining alfresco. It's open for lunch and dinner. ⑤ *Average main: $6* ⊠ *Grand Canyon Lodge, Bright Angel Point, North Rim* ☎ *928/638–2611* ⊕ *www.grandcanyonforever.com* ⌕ *Reservations not accepted* ☻ *Closed mid-Oct.–mid-May.*

$$ ✗ **Grand Canyon Lodge Dining Room.** The historic lodge has a huge, high-ceilinged dining room with spectacular views and decent food, though the draw here is definitely the setting. You might find pecan-glazed pork chop, bison flank steak, and grilled ruby trout for dinner. The filling, simply prepared food here takes a flavorful turn with Southwestern spices and organic selections. It's also open for breakfast and lunch. A full-service bar and an impressive wine list add to the relaxed atmosphere of the only full-service, sit-down restaurant on the North Rim. Dinner reservations are essential in summer and on spring and fall weekends. ⑤ *Average main: $20 ⌧ Grand Canyon Lodge, Bright Angel Point, North Rim* 🕾 *928/638–2611* ⊕ *www.grandcanyonforever. com* ⊗ *Closed mid-Oct.–mid-May.*

AMERICAN

Fodor'sChoice

★

$$$ ✗ **Grand Cookout.** Dine under the stars and enjoy live entertainment at this chuck-wagon-style dining experience—a popular family-friendly choice among the North Rim's limited dining options. Fill up on Western favorites at the all-you-can-eat buffet, including barbecue beef brisket, roasted chicken, baked beans, and cowboy biscuits. The food is basic and tasty, but the real draw is the nightly performance of Western music and tall tales. Transportation from the Grand Canyon Lodge to the cookout (1 mile away) is included in the price. Be sure to call before 4 pm for dinner reservations. Advance reservations are taken by phone (during winter months) or at the Grand Canyon Lodge registration desk. ⑤ *Average main: $30 ⌧ Grand Canyon Lodge, North Rim* 🕾 *928/638–2611, 928/645–6865 (winter)* ⊕ *www.grandcanyonforever. com* ⌂ *Reservations essential* ⊗ *Closed Oct.–May. No lunch.*

AMERICAN

FAMILY

$ 🏨 **Grand Canyon Lodge.** This historic property, constructed mainly in the 1920s and '30s, is the premier lodging facility in the North Rim area. **Pros:** steps away from gorgeous North Rim views; close to several easy hiking trails. **Cons:** as the only in-park North Rim lodging option, this lodge fills up fast; few amenities and limited Internet access. ⑤ *Rooms from: $124 ⌧ Grand Canyon National Park, Hwy. 67, North Rim* 🕾 *877/386–4383, 928/638–2611 May–Oct., 928/645–6865 Nov.–Apr.* ⊕ *www.grandcanyonforever.com* ⟳ *40 rooms, 178 cabins* ⊗ *Closed mid-Oct.–mid-May* ⦿ *No meals.*

HOTEL

Fodor'sChoice

★

9

DEATH VALLEY

The desert is no Disneyland. With its scorching summer heat and vast, sparsely populated tracts of land, it's not often at the top of the list when most people plan their California vacations. But the natural riches of Death Valley—the largest national park outside Alaska—are overwhelming: rolling waves of sand dunes, black cinder cones thrusting up hundreds of feet from a blistered desert floor, riotous sheets of wildflowers, bizarrely shaped Joshua trees basking in the orange glow of a sunset, tiny pupfish that enthrall youngsters, and a silence that's both dramatic and startling.

WHEN TO GO

Most of the park's 1 million annual visitors come between late fall and early spring, taking advantage of moderate temperatures and the lack of rainfall. During these cooler months you'll need to book a room in

If you're driving to the Grand Canyon from Las Vegas, a detour in Kingman will lead you to Route 66—the longest remaining uninterrupted stretch of the "Main Street of America."

advance, but don't worry: the park never feels crowded. If you visit in summer, believe everything you've ever heard about desert heat—it can be brutal, with temperatures often topping 120°F (a record 134°F was set in 2013). The dry air wicks moisture from the body without causing a sweat, so drink plenty of water. Bring sunglasses, a hat, and sufficient clothing to block the sun's rays and the wind. Flash floods are fairly common; sections of roadway can be flooded or washed away. The wettest month is February, when the park receives an average of 0.3 inches of rain.

GETTING HERE AND AROUND

It can take more than three hours to cross from one side of the park to another, so it's important to choose an entrance point that makes sense for what you want to see. From Las Vegas, enter from the north at Beatty, Nevada, or via the central entrance at Death Valley Junction.

Distances can be deceiving within the park: what seems close can be very far away. Much of the park can be viewed on regularly scheduled bus tours, but these often don't allow time for hikes to sites not seen from the road, such as Salt Creek, Golden Canyon, and Natural Bridge. The best option is to drive to a number of the sites, get out of the car, and walk.

When driving in Death Valley, reliable maps are important, as signage is often limited or, in a few places, nonexistent. Other important accessories include a compass and phone (though don't rely on cell coverage in every remote area), and extra food and water (3 gallons per person per day is recommended, plus additional radiator water). If you're able to take a four-wheel-drive vehicle, bring it: many of Death Valley's most spectacular canyons are otherwise inaccessible. Be aware of possible winter closures or driving restrictions due to snow.

Driving Information California State Department of Transportation Hotline. Call this hotline for updates on Death Valley road conditions. ☏ 800/427–7623 ⊕ www.dot.ca.gov. **California Highway Patrol.** The California Highway Patrol offers the latest traffic incident information. ☏ 800/427–7623 recorded info, 760/872–5900 live dispatcher ⊕ www.chp.ca.gov.

VISITOR INFORMATION

PARK CONTACT INFORMATION
Death Valley National Park ☏ 760/786–3200 ⊕ www.nps.gov/deva.

PARK FEES AND PERMITS
The entrance fee is $20 per vehicle and $10 for those entering on foot, bus, bike, or motorcycle. The payment, valid for seven consecutive days, is collected at the park's entrance stations and at the visitor center at Furnace Creek. (If you enter the park on Highway 190, you won't find an entrance station; remember to stop by the visitor center to pay the fee.) Annual park passes, valid only at Death Valley, are $40.

PARK HOURS
Most facilities within the park remain open year-round, daily 8–5.

VISITOR CENTERS
Furnace Creek Visitor Center and Museum. The exhibits and artifacts here provide a broad overview of how Death Valley formed; you can pick up maps at the bookstore run by the Death Valley Natural History Association. This is also the place to learn about or sign up for ranger-led walks (available November through April) or check out a live presentation about the valley's cultural and natural history. The helpful center offers a 20-minute movie about the park every 30 minutes. Your children are likely to receive plenty of individual attention from the enthusiastic rangers. ⊠ *Hwy. 190, 30 miles northwest of Death Valley Junction* ☏ *760/786–3200* ⊕ *www.nps.gov/deva* ☉ *Daily 8–5.*

Scotty's Castle Visitor Center and Museum. During your visit to Death Valley, make sure you make the hour's drive north from Furnace Creek to Scotty's Castle. In addition to living-history tours, you'll find a nice display of exhibits, books, self-guided tour pamphlets, and displays about the castle's creators, Death Valley Scotty and Albert M. Johnson. Fuel up with sandwiches or souvenirs (there's no gasoline sold here anymore) before heading back out to the park. ⊠ *Rte. 267, 53 miles northwest of Furnace Creek and 45 miles northwest of Stovepipe Wells Village* ☏ *760/786–2392* ⊕ *www.nps.gov/deva* ☉ *Daily 9–4:15 (hrs vary seasonally).*

TOURS
Death Valley Tours. Choose from a variety of roughly 10-hour tours via all manner of vehicles: luxury motor-coach, SUV, even a Hummer. Tours of the park pass through its most famous landmarks, and include lunch and hotel pickup from designated Las Vegas–area hotels. ☏ *800/719–3768 Death Valley Tours* ⊕ *www.deathvalleytours.net* ▢ *From $204.*

Furnace Creek Visitor Center tours. This center has many tour options, including a weekly 2-mile Harmony Borax Walk and guided hikes to

Mosaic Canyon and Golden Canyon. Less strenuous options include wildflower, birding, and geology walks, and a Furnace Creek Inn historical tour. Visit the website for a complete list. The visitor center also shows a movie about the park every half hour daily from 8 to 5. ⊠ *Furnace Creek Visitor Center, Rte. 190, 30 miles northwest of Death Valley Junction* ☎ *760/786–2331* ⊕ *www.nps.gov/deva/planyourvisit/ tours.htm*

Pink Jeep Tours Las Vegas. Hop aboard a distinctive, pink four-wheel-drive vehicle with Pink Jeep Tours Las Vegas to visit places—the Charcola Kilns, the Racetrack, and Titus Canyon among them—that your own vehicle might not be able to handle. Pink Jeep tours are professionally narrated, and last 9 to 10 hours from Las Vegas (you also can board at Furnace Creek). ⊠ *3629 W. Hacienda Ave., Las Vegas, Nevada* ☎ *888/900–4480* ⊕ *pinkjeeptours.com* ✆ *From $244.*

EXPLORING

HISTORIC SITES

FAMILY **Scotty's Castle.** This Moorish-style mansion, begun in 1924 and never completed, takes its name from Walter Scott, better known as Death Valley Scotty. An ex-cowboy, prospector, and performer in Buffalo Bill's Wild West Show, Scotty always told people the castle was his, financed by gold from a secret mine. In reality, there was no mine, and the house belonged to a Chicago millionaire named Albert Johnson, whom Scott had finagled into investing in the fictitious mine. Despite the con, Johnson and Scott became great friends. The house functioned for a while as a hotel and still contains works of art, imported carpets, handmade European furniture, and a tremendous pipe organ. Costumed rangers, with varying degrees of enthusiasm, re-create life at the castle circa 1939. Check out the Underground Tour, which takes you through a ¼-mile tunnel in the castle basement. ⊠ *Scotty's Castle Rd. (Hwy. 267), 53 miles north of Salt Creek Interpretive Trail* ☎ *760/786–2392* ⊕ *www.nps.gov/deva* ✆ *$15* ☉ *Daily 8:30–4:15, tours daily 9–4 (hrs vary seasonally).*

SCENIC DRIVE

Artist's Drive. This 9-mile, one-way route skirts the foothills of the Black Mountains and provides intimate views of the changing landscape. Once inside the palette, the huge expanses of the valley are replaced by the small-scale natural beauty of pigments created by volcanic deposits or sedimentary layers. It's a quiet, lonely drive, and shouldn't be rushed. Reach Artist's Palette by heading south on Badwater Road from its intersection with Route 190. ⊠ *Death Valley National Park.*

SCENIC STOPS

Artist's Palette. So called for the contrasting colors of its volcanic deposits and sedimentary layers, this is one of signature sights of Death Valley. Artist's Drive, the approach to the area, is one way heading north off Badwater Road, so if you're visiting Badwater from Furnace Creek, come here on the way back. The drive winds through foothills of sedimentary and volcanic rocks. About 4 miles into the drive, a short side road veers right to a parking lot that's a few hundred feet before the

"On my drive into Death Valley I was rewarded at Zabriskie Point with this amazing view." —photo by Rodney Ee, Fodors.com member

"palette," whose natural colors include shades of green, gold, and pink. ✉ *Off Badwater Rd., 11 miles south of Furnace Creek.*

Badwater. At 282 feet below sea level, Badwater is the lowest spot on land in North America—and also one of the hottest. Stairs and wheelchair ramps descend from the parking lot to a wooden platform that overlooks a sodium chloride pool, a small but remarkably persistent reminder that the valley floor used to contain a lake. You can continue past the platform on a broad, white path that peters out after a half-mile or so. Badwater is one of the most popular and easily accessible sites within the park. From this lowest point, be sure to look across to Telescope Peak, which towers more than 2 miles above the valley floor. ✉ *Badwater Rd., 19 miles south of Furnace Creek.*

Fodor's Choice **Dante's View.** This lookout is more than 5,000 feet up in the Black ★ Mountains. In the dry desert air you can see across most of 160-mile-long Death Valley. The view is astounding. Take a 10-minute, mildly strenuous walk from the parking lot toward a series of rocky overlooks, where with binoculars you can spot some of Death Valley's signature sites. A few interpretive signs point out the highlights below in the valley and across, in the Sierra. Getting here from Furnace Creek takes about an hour—time well invested. ✉ *Dante's View Rd., off Hwy. 190, 35 miles from Badwater, 20 miles south of Twenty Mule Team Canyon.*

Devil's Golf Course. Thousands of miniature salt pinnacles carved into surreal shapes by the desert wind dot this wildly varied landscape. The salt was pushed up to the earth's surface by pressure created as underground salt- and water-bearing gravel crystallized. Get out of your vehicle and take a closer look; you'll see perfectly round holes

DEATH VALLEY IN ONE DAY

If you begin the day in Furnace Creek, you can see several sights without doing much driving. Bring plenty of water with you, and some food, too. Get up early and drive the 20 miles on Badwater Road to **Badwater**, which looks out on the lowest point in the Western Hemisphere and is a dramatic place to watch the sunrise. Returning north, stop at **Natural Bridge**, a medium-size conglomerate rock formation that has been hollowed at its base to form a span across the canyon, and then at the **Devil's Golf Course**, so named because of the large pinnacles of salt present here. Detour to the right onto **Artist's Drive**, a 9-mile one-way, northbound route that passes **Artist's Palette**. The reds, yellows, oranges, and greens come from minerals in the rocks and the earth. Four miles north of Artist's Drive you'll come to the **Golden Canyon Interpretive Trail**, a 2-mile round-trip that winds through a canyon with colorful rock walls. Just before Furnace Creek, take Highway 190 3 miles east to **Zabriskie Point**, overlooking dramatic, furrowed red-brown hills and the **Twenty Mule Team Canyon**. Return to Furnace Creek, where you can grab a meal and visit the museum at the Furnace Creek Visitor Center. Heading north from Furnace Creek, pull off the highway and take a look at the **Harmony Borax Works**.

descending into the ground. ⊠ *Badwater Rd., 13 miles south of Furnace Creek. Turn right onto dirt road and drive 1 mile.*

Racetrack. Getting here involves a 28-mile journey over a rough dirt road, but the reward is well worth the trip. Where else in the world do rocks move on their own? This phenomenon has baffled scientists for years and is perhaps one of the last great natural mysteries. No one has actually seen the rocks in motion, but theory has it that when it rains, the hard-packed lake bed becomes slippery enough that gusty winds push the rocks along—sometimes for several hundred yards. When the mud dries, a telltale trail remains. The trek to the Racetrack can be made in a sedan, but beware—sharp rocks can slash tires; a truck or SUV with thick tires, high clearance, and a spare tire are suggested. ⊠ *27 miles west of Ubehebe Crater via dirt road.*

Sand Dunes at Mesquite Flat. These dunes, made up of minute pieces of quartz and other rock, are ever-changing products of the wind-rippled hills, with curving crests and a sun-bleached hue. The dunes are the most photographed destination in the park, and you can see them at their best at sunrise and sunset. Keep your eyes open for animal tracks—you may even spot a coyote or fox. Bring plenty of water, and note where you parked your car: it's easy to become disoriented in this ocean of sand. If you lose your bearings, climb to the top of a dune and scan the horizon for the parking lot. ⊠ *19 miles north of Hwy. 190, northeast of Stovepipe Wells Village.*

Titus Canyon. This popular one-way, 27-mile drive starts at Nevada Highway 374 (Daylight Pass Road), 2 miles from the park's boundary. Along the way you'll see Leadville Ghost Town and spectacular limestone and dolomite narrows at the end of the canyon. Toward the end, a two-way-section of gravel road leads you into the mouth of the canyon from Scotty's Castle Road. High-clearance vehicles are strongly recommended. ⊠ *Access road off Nevada Hwy. 374, 6 miles west of Beatty, NV.*

Zabriskie Point. Although only about 710 feet in elevation, this is one of Death Valley National Park's most scenic spots, overlooking a striking panorama of wrinkled, multicolor hills. It's a great place to watch the sunrise, but it can be bustling any time of day. Pair it with a drive out to magnificent Dante's View. ⊠ *Hwy. 190, 5 miles south of Furnace Creek.*

WHERE TO EAT

$$
×**Forty-Niner Cafe.** This casual coffee shop serves basic American fare for
CAFÉ breakfast (except in the summer), lunch, and dinner. It's done up in a rus-
FAMILY tic mining style with whitewashed pine walls, vintage map-covered tables, and prospector-branded chairs. Past menus and old photographs decorate the walls. ⑤ *Average main: $20* ⊠ *Ranch at Furnace Creek, Hwy. 190, Furnace Creek* ☎ *760/786–2345* ⊕ *www.furnacecreekresort.com.*

$$$$
×**Inn at Furnace Creek Dining Room.** Fireplaces, beamed ceilings, and spec-
AMERICAN tacular views provide a visual feast to match the inn's ambitious menu.
Fodor's Choice Dishes may include such desert-theme items as High Sierra Nevada
★ pasta, and simpler fare such as salmon and free-range chicken and filet mignon pair well with the signature prickly pear margarita. There's a seasonal menu of vegetarian dishes, too. There's a minimal evening dress code (no T-shirts or shorts). Lunch is served, too, and you can always have afternoon tea in the lobby, an inn tradition since 1927. Breakfast and Sunday brunch are also served. Reservations are essential for dinner only. ⑤ *Average main: $35* ⊠ *Inn at Furnace Creek, Hwy. 190, Furnace Creek* ☎ *760/786–3385* ⊕ *www.furnacecreekresort.com* ⚑ *Reservations essential* ⊙ *Closed Mother's Day–mid-Oct.*

WHERE TO STAY

During the busy season (November through March) you should make reservations for lodgings within the park several months in advance.

$$$$
▦ **The Inn at Furnace Creek.** Built in 1927, this adobe-brick-and-stone
HOTEL lodge nestled in one of the park's greenest oases is Death Valley's most
Fodor's Choice luxurious accommodation, going so far as to have valet parking. **Pros:**
★ refined; comfortable; great views. **Cons:** a far cry from roughing it; expensive. ⑤ *Rooms from: $375* ⊠ *Furnace Creek Village, near intersection of Hwy. 190 and Badwater Rd.* ☎ *760/786–2345* ⊕ *www. furnacecreekresort.com* ⤳ *66 rooms* ⊙ *Closed Mother's Day–mid-Oct.* ⦿ *Breakfast.*

$$
▦ **Panamint Springs Resort.** Ten miles inside the west entrance of the park,
B&B/INN this low-key resort overlooks the sand dunes and peculiar geological formations of the Panamint Valley. **Pros:** slow-paced; friendly; there's a glorious amount of peace and quiet after sundown. **Cons:** far from the park's main attractions. ⑤ *Rooms from: $79* ⊠ *Hwy. 190, 28 miles*

9

west of Stovepipe Wells ☎ *775/482–7680* ⊕ *www.deathvalley.com/psr* ⇨ *14 rooms, 1 cabin* ❘⊙❘ *No meals.*

$ ⬚ **Stovepipe Wells Village.** If you prefer quiet nights and an unfettered
HOTEL view of the night sky and nearby sand dunes and Mosaic Canyon, this property is for you. **Pros:** intimate, relaxed; no big-time partying; authentic desert-community ambience. **Cons:** isolated; a bit dated. ⑤ *Rooms from: $118* ⊠ *Hwy. 190, Stovepipe Wells* ☎ *760/786–2387* ⊕ *www.escapetodeathvalley.com* ⇨ *83 rooms* ❘⊙❘ *No meals.*

TRAVEL SMART
LAS VEGAS

GETTING HERE AND AROUND

The modern, sprawling city of Las Vegas is fairly easy to get around by car, as it's laid out largely in a grid and crisscrossed by freeways. The only pitfall is traffic. Lots of it.

In fact, traffic along the Strip and intersecting roads, as well as on parallel Interstate 15, can be horrendous. It's especially challenging on weekend evenings and when there are conventions in town, but traffic jams can spring up virtually any time of day or night. Give yourself plenty of time when you're traveling to or from the Strip. And be sure to keep your cool.

Parking is free at virtually every resort on the Strip. (Although some Downtown garages and lots charge a fee, the rate is often free if you get your ticket stamped by the casino cashier.)

Outside the Strip, the city sprawls in all directions, and renting a car is the best way to get around, especially if you're staying in Lake Las Vegas, Summerlin, or similar area located more than a few miles away from the Strip. Las Vegas is served by public buses, but it's impractical for visitors to rely on them.

▌ AIR TRAVEL

Approximate flying times to Las Vegas: from New York, 5 hours; from Dallas, 2 hours; from Chicago, 4 hours; from Los Angeles, 1 hour; from San Francisco, 1½ hours.

If you're leaving Las Vegas on a Sunday, be sure to arrive at the airport at least three hours before your scheduled departure time. Though the TSA has improved its operation at McCarran International, security lines on busy days still seemingly stretch forever, and inevitably, travelers miss flights.

Airline Security Issues Transportation Security Administration ☎ 866/289-9673 ⊕ www.tsa.gov.

AIRPORTS

The gateway to Las Vegas is McCarran International Airport (LAS), 5 miles south of the business district and immediately east of the southern end of the Strip. The airport, just a few minutes' drive from the Strip, is well served by nonstop and direct flights from all around the country and a handful of international destinations. The airport is consistently rated among the most passenger-friendly airports in the United States. A 1.9-million-square-foot expansion of Terminal 3 was completed in 2012, opening an additional 14 gates for domestic and international service, an eight-story parking garage, and more than a dozen stores and restaurants.

Also, McCarran is close enough to the Strip that, if you ever find yourself with a few hours to kill, you can easily catch a 5- to 15-minute cab ride to the Hard Rock or one of the South Strip casinos (Mandalay Bay and Luxor are closest) to while away some time. Additionally, as you might expect, McCarran has scads of slot machines to keep you busy.

Airport Information McCarran International Airport (LAS) ⊠ Paradise Rd., Airport ☎ 702/261-5211 ⊕ www.mccarran.com.

GROUND TRANSPORTATION

By bus: If you're heading Downtown or to the south end of the Strip, the public bus is the cheapest, and often quickest, way from the airport. The Westcliff Airport Express (WAX) travels south- and eastbound from McCarran Airport and includes stops along the Strip at Tropicana Avenue, and Downtown at 4th and Carson, located about a two-minute walk from Freemont Street Experience. The service operates seven days a week from approximately 5:45 am and 11:15 pm, weekdays, and from 6 am to 11:45 pm on weekends. The bus runs approximately every half-hour during peak hours and every hour during nonpeak hours. Note: The bus is clean and comfortable, but contains no racks for luggage. ■TIP→ When boarding the bus, tell the driver where you're going before paying. When onboard, alert him or her to your approaching stop by ringing the buzzer.

The transit stop for WAX is located on Level Zero, below baggage claim, at the south end of the bus plaza. When departing McCarran Airport from Terminal 1, follow signs for Ground Transportation. Once outside, proceed across pedestrian crosswalk, turn right toward parking garage, and follow signs for the public bus stop. Exact change of $2 ($1 with a Medicare card) is the fare for a single ride. The ticket vending machine accepts credit or debit cards to purchase a 2- or 24-hour pass, $3 and $5, respectively. The ride from the airport to the Strip will take 10 to 20 minutes, depending on ridership and traffic; to Downtown about 30 to 55 minutes.

By shuttle van: ■TIP→ First check with your hotel, because several of them, such as Green Valley Ranch in Henderson and Red Rock Resort in Summerlin, offer customers free round-trip shuttle rides. This is one of the cheapest ways to get from McCarran to your hotel otherwise. Shuttle service is shared with other riders, and costs $6 to $8 per person to the Strip, $9 to $15 to Downtown, and $12 to $33 to outlying casinos (excluding tips). The vans wait for passengers outside the terminal in marked areas. Because the vans often make numerous stops at different hotels, it's not the best means of transportation if you're in a hurry. For round-trip service, save time and money by booking online and printing out your vouchers beforehand.

By taxi: The metered cabs awaiting your arrival at McCarran are one of the quickest ways to get to your destination (⇨ *Taxi Travel below for more information*).

By town car: These rides are a bit more expensive than the average taxicab and must be reserved ahead of time, but they are cleaner and more convenient. A tuxedoed chauffeur from Presidential, for example, will meet and greet you at baggage claim, assist with luggage, and whisk you away in a luxury sedan, with seating for three, for $55 an hour.

Contacts Bell Trans ☎ 800/274-7433 ⊕ *www.bell-trans.com.* **Gray Line** ☎ 800/472-9546, 303/394-6920 ⊕ *www.grayline.com.* **Presidential Limousine** ☎ 800/423-1420, 702/438-5466 ⊕ *www.presidentiallimolv. com.* **Westcliff Airport Express (WAX)** ☎ 702/228-7433 ⊕ *www.rtcsnv.com.*

FLIGHTS

The major airlines operate frequent service from their hub cities and, as a whole, offer one-stop connecting flights from virtually every city in the country. In addition to nonstop service from the usual hub cities (e.g., Atlanta, Chicago, Cincinnati, Dallas, Denver, Houston, Minneapolis, Newark, Phoenix, Salt Lake City, San Francisco), nonstop service is offered to many other destinations, sometimes by smaller airlines. Southwest remains a dominant airline, offering frequent flights to many cities in the South and West, including San Diego, Los Angeles, San Francisco, Oakland, Seattle, Salt Lake, Denver, Albuquerque, and Phoenix. Virgin America also has come on strong in recent years. Be sure to check the rates of the other airlines that serve Las Vegas, such as Delta, jetBlue, Frontier Airlines, United, and Alaska Airlines.

Airline Contacts Alaska Air ☎ 800/252-7522 ⊕ *www.alaskaair.com.* **American Airlines** ☎ 800/433-7300, 800/223-5436 ⊕ *www.aa.com.* **Delta Airlines** ☎ 800/221-1212 ⊕ *www.delta.com.* **Frontier Airlines** ☎ 800/432-1359 ⊕ *www.flyfrontier.com.* **jetBlue** ☎ 800/538-2583 ⊕ *www.jetblue. com.* **Southwest Airlines** ☎ 800/435-9792 ⊕ *www.southwest.com.* **United Airlines** ☎ 800/864-8331 ⊕ *www.united.com.* **Virgin America** ☎ 877/359-8474 ⊕ *www. virginamerica.com.*

BUS TRAVEL

GREYHOUND

Greyhound provides regular Las Vegas service; the bus terminal is Downtown. Visit the website for fare, schedule, and baggage-allowance information. Cash and credit cards are accepted, but reservations aren't. Seating is on a first-come, first-served basis. The most frequent route out of Las Vegas is the one to Los Angeles, with departures several times a day; the trip takes five to eight hours, depending on stops. Fares begin at around $60 one way, often with substantial discounts offered on the website. Arriving at the bus station 30 to 45 minutes before your bus departs nearly always ensures you a seat. On Sunday evening and Monday morning, arriving an hour or more before departure is recommended.

RTC

The county-operated Regional Transportation Commission of Southern Nevada (RTC) runs local buses throughout the city and to most corners of sprawling Las Vegas Valley. The overall quality of bus service along the main thoroughfares is good. Nonlocals typically only ride RTC buses up and down the Strip, between Mandalay Bay and the Stratosphere. Some continue on to the Downtown Transportation Center. If you're heading to outlying areas, you may need to change buses Downtown. Mornings and afternoons the buses are frequently crowded, with standing room only. The fare for residential RTC buses, with photo ID card, is $2.

THE DEUCE

The Deuce is a special double-decker RTC bus that rides the Strip for $6. All Deuce fares include transfers on residential CAT routes as well. The Deuce, which began service in 2005, certainly is a unique way to explore new and old Vegas alike. Buses stop on the street in front of all the major hotels about every 15 minutes (in a perfect world) between 7 am and 2:30 am and every 21 minutes between 2:30 am and 5:30 am. Because traffic is quite heavy along the Strip, delays are frequent. Also, because the bus route has become popular among tourists, 24-hour passes ($8) and 3-day passes ($20) are available.

Bus Information Greyhound ☎ 800/231–2222 ⊕ www.greyhound.com. **Regional Transportation Commission of Southern Nevada** ☎ 800/228–3911, 702/228–7433 ⊕ www.rtcsnv.com.

CAR TRAVEL

Though you can get around central Las Vegas adequately without a car, the best way to experience the city can be to drive it. A car gives you easy access to all the casinos and attractions; lets you make excursions to Lake Mead, Hoover Dam, and elsewhere at your leisure; and gives you the chance to cruise the Strip and bask in its neon glow. If you plan to spend most of your time on the Strip, a car may not be worth the trouble, but otherwise, especially given the relatively high costs of taxis, renting or bringing a car is a good idea.

Parking on and around the Strip, although free, can require a bit of work. You'll have to brave some rather immense parking structures. Valet parking is available but can take a while at busy times and requires that you tip the valets ($2 to $3). Still, it's usually less expensive to rent a car and drive around Vegas, or to use the monorail (or even—gasp!—to walk), than to cab it everywhere.

NAVIGATING THE CITY

The principal north–south artery is Las Vegas Boulevard (Interstate 15 runs roughly parallel to it, less than a mile to the west). A 4-mile stretch of Las Vegas Boulevard South is known as the Strip, where a majority of the city's hotels and casinos are clustered. Many major streets running east–west (Tropicana Avenue, Flamingo Road, Desert Inn Road, Sahara Avenue) are named for the casinos—past and present—built at their intersections with the Strip. Highway 215 and

Interstate 15 circumnavigate the city, and the Interstate 515 freeway connects Henderson to Las Vegas and then to Summerlin. Because the capacity of the streets of Las Vegas hasn't kept pace with the city's incredible growth, traffic can be slow at virtually any time, especially on the Strip, and particularly in the late afternoon, in the evening, and on weekends. At those times drive the streets parallel to Las Vegas Boulevard: Koval Lane and Paradise Road to the east; Frank Sinatra Drive and Industrial Road/Dean Martin Drive to the west. The Industrial Road shortcut (from Tropicana Avenue almost all the way to Downtown) can save you an enormous amount of time. You can enter the parking lots at Caesars Palace, the Mirage, Treasure Island, Fashion Show Mall, and Circus Circus from Industrial Road. Exit Frank Sinatra Drive off Interstate 15 North, and you can access the hotels from Mandalay Bay to Bellagio (including CityCenter).

■ TIP➔ Visitors from Southern California should at all costs try to avoid traveling to Las Vegas on a Friday afternoon and returning home on a Sunday afternoon. During these traditional weekend-visit hours, driving times (along Interstate 15) can be more than twice as long as during other, nonpeak periods.

GASOLINE

It's easy to find gas stations, most of which are open 24 hours, all over town. There aren't any gas stations along the main stretch of the Strip, but you'll find them within a mile of the Strip in either direction, along the main east–west cross streets. Gas is relatively expensive in Las Vegas, generally 30¢ to 40¢ per gallon above the national average. There's no one part of town with especially cheap or pricey gas, although the stations nearest the airport tend to charge a few cents more per gallon—it's prudent to fill up your car rental a few miles away from the airport before returning it.

PARKING

You can't park anywhere on the Strip itself, and Fremont Street in the casino district Downtown is a pedestrian mall closed to traffic. Street parking regulations are strictly enforced in Las Vegas, and meters are continuously monitored, so whenever possible it's a good idea to leave your car in a parking lot or garage. Free self-parking is available in the massive garages and lots of virtually every hotel, although you may have to hunt for a space and possibly wind up in the far reaches of immense facilities. You can avoid this challenge by opting for valet parking, which is generally free. Parking in the high-rise structures Downtown is also generally free or inexpensive, as long as you validate your parking ticket with the casino cashier.

RENTAL CARS

The airport's rental-car companies are off-site at McCarran Rent-a-Car Center, about 3 miles from the main airport complex, and visitors must take the Rental Car Shuttle buses from the center median, located just outside the baggage claim Ground Transportation exits from Level 1 (Terminal 1) and Level Zero (Terminal 3) to get there. The new facility reduces congestion in and around the airport, and offers visitors the opportunity to check bags for flights on some airlines without stepping foot in the main terminal. Still, the centralized location is far enough away from the airport that it can add anywhere from 15 to 25 minutes to your travel time. The bottom line: If you rent a car, be sure to leave yourself plenty of time to return the vehicle and catch your flight.

RENTAL CAR RATES

The Las Vegas average is anywhere from $20 to $70 a day for intermediate to full-size cars—usually you can find a car for less than $30 a day (and at very slow times for less than $20), but during very busy times expect sky-high rates, especially at the last minute. Las Vegas has among the highest car-rental taxes and surcharges in the country, however, so be sure to factor in the 8.1% (in Clark County) sales tax, a 2% county tax on rentals, 10% concession recovery fee, and a $1.90 per-day vehicle licensing fee. If you rent your car at the airport, an additional $3.75 per-day "customer facility charge" applies. Owing to the high demand for rental cars and significant competition, there are many deals to be had at the airport for car rentals. During special events and conventions, rates frequently go up as supply dwindles, but at other times you can find bargains. For the best deals, check with the various online services, or contact a representative of the hotel where you'll be staying, as many hotels have business relationships with car-rental companies.

Although there are several local car-rental companies along the Strip itself, they tend to be more expensive than those at the airport or elsewhere in the city.

RENTAL CAR REQUIREMENTS

In Nevada you must be 21 to rent a car, and some major car-rental agencies have a minimum age of 25. Those agencies that do rent to people under 25 often assess surcharges to those drivers. There's no upper age limit for renting a car. Non-U.S. residents will need a reservation voucher, a passport, a driver's license, and a travel policy that covers each driver when picking up a car.

Rental Center McCarran Airport Rent-A-Car Center ☎ 702/261–6001 ⊕ www.mccarran. com.

ROAD CONDITIONS

It might seem as if every road in Las Vegas is in a continuous state of expansion or repair. Orange highway cones, road-building equipment, and detours are ubiquitous. But once the roads are widened and repaved, they're efficient and comfortable. The city's traffic-light system is state of the art, and you can often drive for miles on major thoroughfares, hitting green lights all the way. Signage is excellent, both on surface arteries and on freeways. The local driving style is fast and

can be less than courteous. Watch out for unsignaled lane changes and turns.

There are rarely weather problems in Las Vegas, but flash flooding can wreak havoc. For information about weather conditions, highway construction, traffic incidents, and road closures, visit the website of the Nevada Department of Transportation, or call its Travel Info system by dialing ☎ 511 in Nevada or ☎ 877/687–6237 if calling outside Nevada.

ROADSIDE EMERGENCIES

Call 911 to reach police, fire, or ambulance assistance. Dial *647 to reach the Nevada Highway Patrol.

RULES OF THE ROAD

Right turns are permitted on red lights after coming to a full stop. Nevada requires seat-belt use in the front and back seats of vehicles. Chains are required on Mt. Charleston and in other mountainous regions when snow is fresh and heavy; signs indicate conditions.

CHILDREN

Always strap children under age six or less than 60 pounds into approved child-safety seats. In Nevada children must wear seat belts regardless of where they're seated.

DWI

The Las Vegas police are extremely aggressive about catching drunk drivers—you're considered legally impaired if your blood-alcohol level is 0.08% or higher (this is also the law in neighboring states).

SPEED LIMITS

The speed limit on residential streets is 25 mph. On major thoroughfares it's 45 mph. On the interstate and other divided highways within the city the speed limit is 65 mph; outside the city the speed limit is 70 or 75 mph. Police officers are highly vigilant about speeding laws within Las Vegas, especially in school zones, but enforcement in rural areas is rare.

Nevada Department of Transportation ☎ 775/888–7000 ⊕ www.nevadadot.com. **Nevada Highway Patrol** ☎ 702/486–4100, 775/687–5300 ⊕ www.nhp.nv.gov.

■ MONORAIL TRAVEL

The Las Vegas Monorail stretches from MGM Grand, in the south, to Sahara Avenue Station, to the north, with five stops in between, including the Las Vegas Convention Center. All told, the trains make the 4-mile trip in about 14 minutes. The monorail runs Monday 7 am–midnight; Tuesday–Thursday 7 am–2 am; and Friday–Sunday 7 am–3 am. Fares are $5 for a single-ride ticket, $12 for a one-day pass, $22 for a two-day pass, $28 for a three-day pass, and so forth. Unlimited Ride passes are also available. You can purchase tickets at station customer-service offices (daily 9 am–7 pm) and vending machines or in advance online, where special deals on passes are sometimes offered. Children age five or under ride free.

A number of west-side Strip properties also are connected by free trams that run roughly every 10 minutes. There's one that runs between Excalibur and Mandalay Bay, from 11 am to 10:30 pm, extending until 12:30 am on weekends; one that runs between the Mirage and Treasure Island, from 9 am to 1 am, extending until 3 am on Friday and Saturday; and one that stretches from Monte Carlo through CityCenter to Bellagio, from 8 am to 4 am.

Contact Las Vegas Monorail Company ☎ 702/699–8200 ⊕ www.lvmonorail.com.

■ TAXI TRAVEL

Cabs aren't allowed to pick up passengers on the street, so you can't hail a cab New York–style. You have to wait in a hotel taxi line or call a cab company. If you dine at a restaurant off the Strip, the restaurant will call a cab to take you home.

FARES

The fare is $3.30 on the meter when you get in and 20¢ for every 1/13th mile (there's also a $30 per-hour charge for waiting). Taxis are limited by law to carrying a maximum of four passengers, and there's no additional charge per person. No fees are assessed for luggage, but taxis leaving the airport are allowed to add an airport surcharge of $2.

The trip from the airport to most hotels on the south end of the Strip should cost about $13 to $16, to the north end of the Strip about $16 to $27, and to Downtown about $22 to $26.

TIPPING

Drivers should be tipped around 15% to 18% for good service (⇨ *Tipping in Essentials*). Some drivers can't accept credit cards (and those that do usually add a surcharge); all drivers carry only nominal change with them.

SUGGESTED ROUTES

■TIP→ Be sure to specify to your driver that you don't want to take Interstate 15 or the airport tunnel on your way to or from the airport. This is always the longer route distance-wise, which means it's the most expensive, but it can sometimes save you 5 to 10 minutes on the trip if traffic is heavy on the Strip. Drivers who take passengers through the airport tunnel without asking are committing an illegal practice known as "long-hauling." You have every right to ask your driver about the routes he or she is using; don't be afraid to speak up. If you have trouble with your cab driver, be sure to get his or her name and license number and call the Taxi Cab Authority to report the incident.

Contact Taxi Cab Authority ☎ 702/668–4000 ⊕ www.taxi.nv.gov.

Taxi Companies Desert Cab ☎ 702/386–9102 ⊕ www.desertcabinc.com. **Whittlesea Blue Cab** ☎ 702/384–6111. **Yellow Checker Star** ☎ 702/873–2000 ⊕ www.ycstrans.com.

ESSENTIALS

▌BUSINESS SERVICES AND FACILITIES

Las Vegas is one of the nation's leading convention destinations, and all the town's major hotels have comprehensive convention and meeting-planning space and services. The best business centers in town are run by the chain FedEx Office, which has several locations throughout the area. Two outposts on the Strip include the Cosmopolitan of Las Vegas (Level 3, West End Tower) and Mandalay Bay (Level 1, South Convention Center).

Contact FedEx Office Print & Ship Center ✉ 3708 Las Vegas Blvd. S ☎ 702/207–2724 ⊕ www.fedex.com ✉ 3950 Las Vegas Blvd. S ☎ 702/262–5320 ⊕ www.fedex.com.

▌DAY TOURS AND GUIDES

BOAT TOURS

The *Desert Princess*, a 275-passenger Mississippi River–style stern-wheeler, cruises Lake Mead. Tours include a 90-minute, narrated Mid-Day Sightseeing or seasonal Champagne Brunch cruise, and a seasonal two-hour Dinner cruise.

Tour Operator Lake Mead Cruises ✉ Lake Mead marina ☎ 702/293–6180 ⊕ www.lakemeadcruises.com.

BUS TOURS

Gray Line and several other companies offer Las Vegas city and neon-light tours; trips to Red Rock Canyon, Lake Mead, Colorado River (rafting), Hoover Dam, and Valley of Fire; and longer trips to different sections of the Grand Canyon.

Tour Operator All Las Vegas Tours ☎ 702/233–1627, 800/566–5868 ⊕ www.alllasvegastours.com.

HELICOPTER TOURS

Helicopters do two basic tours in and around Las Vegas: a brief flyover of the Strip and a several-hour trip out to the Grand Canyon and back.

GREAT READS

Some of the most memorable literary works that have featured Sin City include Larry McMurtry's *Desert Rose*, which relates the tale of a showgirl struggling to prevail in Vegas as her age catches up with her; and Hunter S. Thompson's vaunted classic, *Fear and Loathing in Las Vegas*, a gripping work of gonzo journalism that takes us through a drug-induced road trip to Las Vegas. *Fools Die* is one of mob-chronicler Mario Puzo's most entertaining novels about Vegas, offering an up-close glimpse of the city's infamous casino culture. Poker fans will love James McManus's *Positively Fifth Street*, about the rise of the now-famous World Series of Poker.

Tour Operators Maverick Helicopter Tours ✉ 6075 Las Vegas Blvd. S ☎ 702/261–0007, 888/261–4414 ⊕ www.maverickhelicopter. com. **Papillon Grand Canyon Helicopters** ☎ 702/736–7243, 888/635–7272 ⊕ www. papillon.com. **Sundance Helicopters** ✉ 5596 Haven St. ☎ 702/736–0606, 800/653–1881 ⊕ www.sundancehelicopters.com.

▌HEALTH

The dry desert air in Las Vegas means that your body will need extra fluids, especially during the punishing summer months. Always drink lots of water even if you're not outside very much. When you're outdoors, wear sunscreen and always carry water with you if you plan a long walk.

▌HOURS OF OPERATION

Las Vegas is a 24-hour city 365 days a year. Casinos, bars, supermarkets, almost all gas stations, even some health clubs and video stores cater to customers at all hours of the day and night (many people work odd hours here).

Most museums and attractions are open seven days a week.

Most pharmacies are open seven days a week from 9 to 7. Many, though, including local outposts of Walgreens, Rite Aid, and CVS pharmacy—several of them on the Las Vegas Strip—offer 24-hour and drive-through services.

Shopping hours vary greatly around town, but many stores are open weekdays and Saturday from 9 or 10 am until 9 or 10 pm and Sunday from 10 or 11 am until 5 or 6 pm. The souvenir shops on the Strip and Downtown often remain open until midnight, and some are open 24 hours. Quite a few grocery stores are open around the clock.

▌ MONEY

Prices in Las Vegas can be gratis or outrageous. For example, you can get a sandwich wrap at one of the rock-bottom casino snack bars (Riviera, Four Queens) for $3–$4, or you can spend upward of $20 for a pastrami sandwich at the Carnegie Deli in the Mirage. A cup of coffee in a casino coffee shop or Starbucks will set you back $2 to $5, while that same cup is free if you happen to be sitting at a nickel slot machine when the cocktail waitress comes by. A taxi from the airport to the MGM Grand can be as little as $13 if you tell the driver to take Tropicana Avenue and there's no traffic, or can run as high as $27 if you take the Airport Connector and there's a wreck on the freeway. The more you know about Las Vegas, the less it'll cost you.

ATMs are widely available in Las Vegas; they're at every bank and at virtually all casinos, hotels, convenience stores, and gas stations. Casino ATMs generally tack on a fee of up to $4 per transaction (this, of course, is on top of any fees your bank might charge). In addition, all casinos have cash-advance machines, which take credit cards. You just indicate how large a cash advance you want, and when the transaction is approved, you pick up the

cash at the casino cashier. But beware: You pay a service charge up for this "convenience"—up to 18% or more—in addition to the usual cash-advance charges and interest rate; in most cases, the credit-card company begins charging interest the moment the advance is taken, so you won't have the usual grace period to pay your balance in full before interest begins to accrue. To put it another way, don't obtain cash this way.

▌ PACKING

Ever since the original Frontier Casino opened on the Los Angeles Highway (now the Strip), visitors to Las Vegas have been invited to "come as you are." The warm weather and informal character of Las Vegas render casual clothing appropriate day and night. However, there are some exceptions. A small number of restaurants require jackets for men, and some of the city's increasingly exclusive and overhyped "ultralounges" and high-profile dance clubs have specific requirements, such as no sneakers or jeans, or that you must wear dark shoes or collared shirts. At a minimum, even if there's no set dress code, you're going to fit in with the scene if you make some effort to dress stylishly when heading out either to the hipper nightclubs or even trendier restaurants (i.e., those helmed by celeb chefs or with trendy followings and cool decor). Just as an example, where jeans and T-shirts might be technically allowed at some establishments, try to wear plain, fitted T-shirts versus those with logos and designs, and choose jeans that are appropriate for a venue (crisp and clean for a nice restaurant, designer labels for a top club). It's always good to pack a few stylish outfits for the evening, and when you're making dinner reservations at an upscale spot or considering a visit to a nightclub, ask for the dress-code specifics. Also, flip-flops are best kept to pool areas and men should avoid wearing sandals (of any kind) pretty much anywhere.

Although the desert sun keeps temperatures scorching outside in warmer months, the casinos are ice-cold. Your best insurance is to dress in layers. The blasting air-conditioning may feel good at first, but if you plan on spending some time inside, bring a light sweater or jacket in case you feel chilly.

Always wear comfortable shoes; no matter what your intentions, you cover a lot of ground on foot.

▌RESTROOMS

Free restrooms can be found in every casino; you don't have to be gambling in the casino to use them. Many restrooms have attendants who expect tips for fetching you everything from breath mints to hand towels. You're not obligated to tip.

▌SAFETY

The well-known areas of Las Vegas are among the safest places in the world for visitors. With so many people carrying so much cash, security is tight inside and out. The casinos have visitors under constant surveillance, and hotel security guards are never more than a few seconds away. Outside, police are highly visible, on foot and bicycles and in cruisers. But this doesn't mean you can throw all safety consciousness to the wind. You should take the same precautions you would in any city—be aware of what's going on around you, stick to well-lighted areas, and quickly move away from any situation or people that might be threatening—especially if you're carrying some gambling cash. When Downtown, it's wise not to stray too far off the three main streets: Fremont, Ogden, and Carson between Main and Las Vegas Boulevard.

Be especially careful with your purse around slot machines. Grab-and-run thieves are always looking for easy pickings, especially Downtown.

Apart from their everyday vulnerability to aggressive men, women should have few problems with unwanted attention in Las Vegas. If something does happen inside a casino, simply go to any pit and ask a boss to call security. The problem will disappear in seconds. Outside, crowds are almost always thick on the Strip and Downtown, and there's safety in numbers. Still, be aware of pickpockets.

Men in Las Vegas also need to be on guard against predatory women. "Trick roller" is the name of a particularly nasty breed of female con artist. These women are expert at meeting single men by "chance." After getting friendly in the casino, the woman joins the man in his hotel room, where she slips powerful knockout drugs into his drink and robs him blind. Some men don't wake up. Prostitution is illegal in Clark County.

▌TIP➔ Distribute your cash, credit cards, IDs, and other valuables between a deep front pocket, an inside jacket or vest pocket, and a hidden money pouch. Don't reach for the money pouch once you're in public.

▌TAXES

The Las Vegas and Reno-Tahoe international airports assess a $4.50 departure tax (which is usually included in the ticket price), or passenger facility charge. The hotel room tax is 12% in Las Vegas. Moreover, virtually all hotels located on the Strip—and many Downtown—will charge an additional "destination" or resort fee of $5–$28 per room per night. These fees are sometimes waived, however, for high-tier players-club members or deluxe-room bookings, so be sure to check.

The sales tax rates for the areas covered in this guide are: Las Vegas, 8.10%; Arizona, 6.6%; and California, 8% (though in the latter two cases, individual counties can and do add their own).

TIPPING GUIDELINES FOR LAS VEGAS	
Bartender	$1 to $5 per round of drinks, depending on the number of drinks
Bellhop	$1 to $5 per bag, depending on the level of the hotel
Coat Check Personnel	$1 to $2 per item checked; if there's a fee, nothing
Hotel Concierge	$5 or more, if he or she performs a service for you
Hotel Doorman	$1 to $2, if he helps you get a cab
Hotel Housekeeping	$2 to $5 a day (daily preferably, or at the end of your stay, in cash)
Hotel Room-Service Waiter	$2 to $3 per delivery, even if a service charge has been added
Porter at Airport or Train Station	$1 per bag
Restroom Attendants	$1 or small change
Skycap at Airport	$1 to $3 per bag checked
Taxi Driver or Chauffer	15% to 20%, but round up the fare to the next dollar
Valet Parking Attendant	$2 to $3, but only when you get your car
Waiter	16% to 20%, with 20% being the norm at high-end restaurants; nothing additional if a service charge is added to the bill

TIME

Nevada and California are in the Pacific time zone. Arizona is in the Mountain time zone and doesn't observe daylight saving time.

TIPPING

Just as in other U.S. destinations, workers in Las Vegas are paid a minimal wage and rely on tips to make up the primary part of their income. A $1 tip per drink is appropriate for cocktail waitresses, even when they bring you a free drink at a slot machine or casino table. On package tours, conductors and drivers usually get $10 per day from the group as a whole; check whether this has already been figured into your cost. For local sightseeing tours, you may individually tip the driver-guide $5 if he or she has been helpful or informative. Tip dealers with the equivalent of your average bet once or twice an hour if you're winning; slot-machine change personnel and keno runners are accustomed to a buck or two. Ushers in showrooms may be able to get you better seats for performances for a gratuity of $5 or more. Tip the concierge 10%–20% of the cost of a ticket to a hot show. Tip $5–$10 for making dinner reservations or arrangements for other attractions.

▌ VISITOR INFORMATION

Before you go, contact the city and state tourism offices for general information. When you get there, you might want to visit the Las Vegas Convention and Visitors Authority, next door to The LVH, for brochures and general information. Hotels and gift shops on the Strip have maps, brochures, pamphlets, and free-events magazines—*What's On, The Las Vegas Guide, Las Vegas Magazine,* and *Las Vegas Today*—that list shows and buffets and offer discounts to area attractions.

Anthony Curtis's *Las Vegas Advisor,* a monthly print newsletter and website, keeps track of the constantly changing Las Vegas landscapes of gambling, accommodations, dining, entertainment, Top Ten Values (a monthly listing of the city's best deals), complimentary offerings, coupons, and more, and is an indispensable resource for any Las Vegas visitor. Visit the website (⊕ *www.lasvegasadvisor.com*) for a free sample issue; annual online memberships begin at $37 per year.

FOR INTERNATIONAL TRAVELERS

CURRENCY

The dollar is the basic unit of U.S. currency. It has 100 cents. Coins are the penny (1¢), the nickel (5¢), dime (10¢), quarter (25¢), half-dollar (50¢), and the very rare golden $1 coin and even rarer silver $1. Bills are denominated $1, $5, $10, $20, $50, and $100, all mostly green and identical in size; designs and background tints vary. You may come across $2 bills every now and then, but they're rare.

CUSTOMS

Information U.S. Customs and Border Protection ✉ *McCarran International Airport, Terminal 3, 5757 Wayne Newton Blvd., Airport* ☎ *702/730–6071, 702/730–6100* ⊕ *www.cbp.gov.*

DRIVING

Driving in the United States is on the right. Speed limits are posted in miles per hour (usually between 55 mph and 70 mph). Watch for lower limits in small towns and on back roads (usually 30 mph to 40 mph). Most states require front-seat passengers to wear seat belts; most states require children to sit in the backseat and to wear seat belts; infants and toddlers require a DOT-approved safety or booster seat, with either rear- or forward-facing seat placement, depending on the child's age, weight, and height. In major cities, rush hour is between 7 and 10 am and 4 and 7 pm.

Highways are well paved. Interstates—limited-access, multilane highways designated with an "I–" before the number—are fastest. Interstates with three-digit numbers circle urban areas, which may also have other limited-access expressways, freeways, and parkways. Tolls may be levied on limited-access highways. U.S. and state highways aren't necessarily limited-access, but may have several lanes. If your car breaks down on an interstate, pull onto the shoulder and wait for help, or have your passengers wait while you walk to an emergency phone (available in most states). If you carry a cell phone, dial *55, noting your location on the small green roadside mileage marker.

ELECTRICITY

The U.S. standard is AC, 110 volts/60 cycles. Plugs have two flat pins set parallel to each other.

EMBASSIES

Contacts Canada ☎ *202/682–1740* ⊕ *www.canadianembassy.org.* **United Kingdom** ☎ *212/745–0200 New York, 310/789–0031 L.A.* ⊕ *ukinusa.fco.gov.uk/en.*

EMERGENCIES

For police, fire, or ambulance, dial 911 (0 in rural areas).

HOLIDAYS

New Year's Day (Jan. 1); Martin Luther King Day (3rd Mon. in Jan.); Presidents' Day (3rd Mon. in Feb.); Memorial Day (last Mon. in May); Independence Day (July 4); Labor Day (1st Mon. in Sept.); Columbus Day (2nd Mon. in Oct.); Thanksgiving Day (4th Thurs. in Nov.); Christmas Eve and Christmas Day (Dec. 24 and 25); and New Year's Eve (Dec. 31).

MAIL

You can buy stamps and send letters and parcels in post offices. Most hotels sell stamps as well. You may find stamp-dispensing machines in airports, bus and train stations, office buildings, drugstores, and convenience stores.

U.S. mailboxes are stout, dark-blue steel bins; pickup schedules are posted inside the bin (pull down the handle to see them). Parcels weighing more than 13 ounces, bearing only stamps as postage, must be mailed at a post office or at a private mailing center.

Within the United States a first-class letter weighing 1 ounce or less costs 49¢; each additional ounce costs 21¢. Postcards cost 34¢. An airmail letter to most foreign countries starts as low as $1.15.

Most hotels will collect and send mail, but there are post offices throughout Las Vegas. The closest Strip one: 4632 South Maryland Parkway. The closest Downtown one: 201 Las Vegas Boulevard South. Most branches are open 8:30 until 5 on weekdays, and some are open Saturday (but with shorter hours). There are drop boxes for overnight delivery services all over town as well as at UPS Stores in most strip malls.

Contacts DHL Express ☏ *800/225-5345* ⊕ *www.dhl.com*. **United States Postal Service** ☏ *800/275-8777* ⊕ *www.usps.com* ☉ *Sun. and holidays*. **UPS** ☏ *800/742-5877* ⊕ *www.ups.com*.

PASSPORTS AND VISAS

Visitor visas generally aren't necessary for citizens of Canada and Bermuda coming for tourism and staying for fewer than 90 days and 180 days, respectively. International visitors from Australia, Japan, the United Kingdom, and most citizens of European Union countries who plan to travel to the United States on a plane or ship for tourism and stay for 90 days or less, are required to apply for authorization online via ESTA (Electronic System for Travel Authorization); the cost is $14. If you require a visa, the cost is $160 and waiting time can be substantial, depending on where you live. Apply for a visa at the U.S. consulate in your place of residence; check the U.S. State Department's special Visa website for further information.

Visa Information U.S. Department of State ☏ *202/485-7600* ⊕ *travel.state.gov/ visa/visa_1750.html*. **Electronic System for Travel Authorization (ESTA)** ☏ *202/325-8000* ⊕ *www.cbp.gov*.

PHONES

Numbers consist of a three-digit area code (702 in the Las Vegas region) and a seven-digit local number. Within many local calling areas you dial only the 7 digits; in others you dial "1" first and all 10 digits—just as you would for calls between area-code regions.

The same is true for calls to numbers prefixed by "800," "888," "866," and "877"—all toll-free. For calls to numbers prefixed by "900" you must pay—usually dearly.

For international calls, dial "011" followed by the country code and the local number. For help, dial "0" and ask for an overseas operator. Most phone books list country codes and U.S. area codes. The country code for Australia is 61, for New Zealand 64, for the United Kingdom 44. Calling Canada is the same as calling within the United States, whose country code, by the way, is 1.

For operator assistance, dial "0." For directory assistance, call 555-1212 or occasionally 411 (free at many public phones). You can reverse long-distance charges by calling "collect"; dial "0" instead of "1" before the 10-digit number.

Instructions are generally posted on pay phones (though with the rise of cell phones, there are fewer of these). Usually you insert coins in a slot (typically 25¢–50¢ for local calls) and wait for a steady tone before dialing. For long-distance calls the operator tells you how much to insert; prepaid phone cards, widely available in various denominations, can be used from any phone.

CELL PHONES

The United States has several GSM (Global System for Mobile Communications) networks, so multiband mobiles from most countries work here. It's also becoming more commonplace to find pay-as-you-go mobile SIM cards in the United States, which allow you to avoid roaming charges without having to buy a phone. That said, cell phones with pay-as-you-go plans are available for well under $100. The cheapest with decent national coverage are the GoPhone from AT&T and payLo from Virgin Mobile, which offers pay-as-you-go service.

Contacts AT&T ☏ *800/222-0300* ⊕ *www. att.com*. **Virgin Mobile** ☏ *888/322-1122* ⊕ *www.virginmobileusa.com*.

Another great resource: the Internet site, VegasChatter.

Contacts Las Vegas Advisor ☎ 702/252–0655, 800/244–2224 ⊕ *www.lasvegasadvisor. com.* **Las Vegas Convention and Visitors Authority** ✉ *3150 Paradise Rd., Paradise Road* ☎ *702/892–0711, 877/847–4858* ⊕ *www. lvcva.com.* **Nevada Commission on Tourism** ☎ *775/687–4322, 800/638–2328* ⊕ *www. travelnevada.com.* **VegasChatter** ⊕ *www. vegaschatter.com.*

ONLINE TRAVEL TOOLS
ALL ABOUT LAS VEGAS
VEGAS.com advertises, To Do Vegas Right, It's Who You Know. Part of the Greenspun Media Group, which also publishes the *Las Vegas Sun,* VEGAS.com offers information and instant-booking capabilities for everything from air and hotel packages to shows and tours. About.com has an excellent online "Las Vegas Travel" guide, which includes dozens of original articles and reviews as well as links to many other Vegas resources, as does the "Visitor Guide" page on the website of the Las Vegas Review-Journal.

One of the oldest sites is the Las Vegas Leisure Guide, which is full of hotel, restaurant, and nightlife info. Las Vegas Online Entertainment Guide has listings for hotels and an online reservations system, plus local history, restaurants, a business directory, and even some gambling instruction. LasVegas.com, the official Las Vegas tourism website, has a little bit of everything going on in Sin City. Find out about events, book hotels, get special deals, and find out other vital travel info; the Las Vegas Convention and Visitors Authority, which runs the site, also broadcasts great deals and updates on Twitter (⊕ *www.twitter.com/vegas*). The City of Las Vegas has its own website, which is a great resource for service-related information, including how to pay a ticket or citation. Remember, what happens in Vegas, stays in Vegas.

MARRIAGE LICENSES
If you plan on getting hitched during your Vegas stay, you might want to check out the Clark County website for necessary marriage license information.

Contacts About.com ⊕ *govegas.about. com.* **City of Las Vegas** ☎ *702/229–6011* ⊕ *www.lasvegasnevada.gov.* **Clark County** ☎ *702/455–0000* ⊕ *www.clarkcountynv.gov.* **Las Vegas Leisure Guide** ⊕ *www.lasvegas-nv. com.* **Las Vegas Online Entertainment Guide** ⊕ *www.lvol.com.* **Las Vegas Review-Journal** ⊕ *www.reviewjournal.com.* **Vegas.com** ⊕ *www.vegas.com.* **LasVegas.com** ⊕ *www. lasvegas.com.*

INDEX

PHOTO CREDITS

Front cover: Rudy Sulgan/Corbis [Description: Limousine on Las Vegas Boulevard]. 1, MGM Mirage. 2, Travel Pix Collection/age fotostock. 5, Michelle Chaplow/Alamy. Chapter 1: Experience Las Vegas: 8-9 Travel Pix Collection/age fotostock. 12 (top right), Liane Cary/age fotostock. 12 (top left), Hank Delespinasse/age fotostock. 12 (bottom right), LVCVB. 12 (bottom left), Ian Dagnall/Alamy. 14, Buzz Pictures/Alamy. 15 (left), Las Vegas News Bureau/LVCVA. 15 (right), Corbis. 16 (left), Tomasz Rossa. 16 (top center), MGM Mirage. 16 (top right), Las Vegas Ski & Snowboard Resort. 16 (bottom right), Hervè Donnezan/age fotostock. 17 (left), CityCenter Las Vegas. 17 (top center), Brent Bergherm/ age fotostock. 17, (bottom center), Kobby Dagan/Shutterstock. 17 (right), MGM Mirage. 18, Darius Koehli/ age fotostock. 19, Pictorial Press Ltd/Alamy. 20 (left and right), Library of Congress Prints & Photographs Division. 20 (center), wikipedia.org. 21 (top left), Harrah's Entertainment. 21 (bottom left), CSU Archive / age fotostock. 21 (right), Pictorial Press Ltd/Alamy. 22 (left), wikipedia.org. 22 (bottom center), Content Mine International/Alamy. 22 (right), Pictorial Press Ltd/Alamy. 23 (top left), Allstar Picture Library / Alamy. 23 (bottom left), By Carol M. Highsmith [Public domain], via Wikimedia Commons. 23 (right), LOOK Die Bildagentur der Fotografen GmbH/Alamy. 24, david sanger photography/ Alamy. 25, Ron Niebrugge/Alamy. 26, Konstantin Sutyagin/Shutterstock. Chapter 2: Exploring Las Vegas: 27, Gavin Hellier / Alamy. 28, Hard Rock Hotel & Casino. 30, MGM Mirage. 33, Scott Frances. 38, Las Vegas Sands Corp. 42, LVCVB. 48, by Marcin Wichary www.fl ickr.com/photos/ mwichary/4972813369/ Attribution-NonCommercial License. 52, lake las vegas by Ed Schipul www. fl ickr.com/photos/eschipul/5761020172/ Attribution-NonCommercial-ShareAlike License. 53, Green Valley Ranch. 56, Judy Crawford/Shutterstock. 58, © trekandshoot l Dreamstime.com. 59, Chee-Onn Leong/Shutterstock.Chapter 3: Where to Stay: 61, Wynn Resorts Holdings- LLC. 62, Harrah's Entertainment, Inc. 63 (top), MGM Mirage. 63 (bottom), Hard Rock Hotel & Casino. 64, Harrah's Entertainment, Inc. 65, LVCVB. 67-69, Thomas Hart Shelby. 72, Brad Mitchell / Alamy. 73, Mike Briner/ Alamy. 75, SuperStock /age fotostock. 77, Greg Anderson Photography/MGM Mirage. 79, © Rabbit75 l Dreamstime.com. 81, © Icefields l Dreamstime.com. 82, Marla Lampert / Alamy. 83, MGM Mirage. 85, CityCenter Las Vegas. 87, MGM Mirage. 89, Stuart Pearce/World Pictures/age fotostock. 91, Thomas Hart Shelby. 93, Mandarin Oriental Hotel Group. 95, Jerry Sharp/Shutterstock. 97, Emmanuel Coupe / Alamy. 99, Scott Frances. 100, LVCVB. 101, Rubens Abboud / Alamy. 103, Wynn Resorts. 105, Courtesy of The Palazzo. 107, © Minyun9260 l Dreamstime.com. 109, Wynn Resorts Holdings-LLC. 113, CityCenter Las Vegas. Chapter 4: Gamble: 117, The Venetian. 118, Lise Gagne/ iStockphoto. 126, Greg Vaughn/Alamy. 132, Lee Foster/Alamy. 134, Photo Network / Alamy. 142, Javier Larrea/age fotostock. 144, Danita Delimont / Alamy. 145, Mark Harmel / Alamy. 148, cloki/ Shutterstock. 152, www.imagesource.com. 158, Lee Foster/Alamy. 159, Harrah's Entertainment, Inc. 163, Jeff Thrower (WebThrower)/Shutterstock. 164, M. Timothy O'Keefe / Alamy. 168, Gayvoronskaya_Yana/ Shutterstock. 171, Thomas Hart Shelby. Chapter 5: Where to Eat: 177, MGM Mirage. 178, Station Casinos. 179, (top) Wynn Las Vegas. 179, (bottom) Marie-Louise Avery/Alamy. 180, Harrah's Entertainment. Chapter 6: Shopping: 225, Harrah's Entertainment. 228-29, Grand Canal Shoppes. Chapter 7: Shows: 253, Ricardo Funari/age fotostock. 258, Tomasz Rossa. 260, David Hawe/©BMP. 264 (top and bottom), Harrah's Entertainment. 270, Gerard Schachmes. 273, MGM Mirage. Chapter 8: Nightlife: 275, Douglas Peebles Photography/Alamy. 280, O'Gara/Bissell Photography/Mirage. Chapter 9: Side Trips from Las Vegas: 297, LVCVB. 298-99, NPS. 312, Kerrick James. 322-23, Christophe Testi/Shutterstock. 324, Anton Foltin/Shutterstock. 325, Geir Olav Lyngfjell/Shutterstock. 326 (left), Wendy Holden/iStockphoto. 326 (right), Kerrick James. 327, Alexander Hafemann/iStockphoto. 328, Paul B. Moore/Shutterstock. 329, Kerrick James. 336, MARK LELLOUCH, NPS. 338, Las Vegas Ski & Snowboard Resort. 342, Rolf Hicker Photography/Alamy. 345, Rodney Ee, Fodors.com member. Back cover (from left to right): Charles Zachritz/Shutterstock; DNY59/iStockphoto; Richard Cummins. Spine: Galushko Sergey/Shutterstock.

About Our Writers: All photos are courtesy of the writers.

NOTES

NOTES

NOTES

NOTES

NOTES

NOTES

NOTES

NOTES

NOTES

NOTES

NOTES

NOTES

NOTES

ABOUT OUR WRITERS

Dante Drago has more than 13 years of experience dealing table games in Atlantic City. His specialty is baccarat and blackjack, but he also deals many other games. When he is not working, he puts his collective experience and knowledge to use as a recreational gambler in Atlantic City and Las Vegas, which he has frequented many times. He can also be found doling out gambling advice and rarely known "tips" to his inquisitive friends on Facebook, who are curious about the inner workings of the casino and desire the perspective of an insider who has stood on both sides of the gaming table. He updated the Gambling chapter of this book.

 Francesca Drago is a publishing professional with more than a decade of industry experience, from arenas both corporate and commissioned. She lives in New Jersey but resided in Las Vegas for several years, where she operated her business, PerfectEdit Editorial Services, and served as managing editor for national gambling-lifestyle magazine *Casino Player*. Francesca has contributed editorial and photography to a variety of websites, newspapers, magazines, and books.

Heidi Knapp Rinella has been a restaurant critic since 1980 in Florida and Nevada, and a staff writer and restaurant critic with the *Las Vegas Review-Journal* since 1999. An award-winning journalist, she is the author of seven books. She and her family live in Henderson, Nevada.

 Susan Stapleton is a writer and editor based in Las Vegas. She edits *Eater Vegas* and *Racked Vegas*, making her an expert on all things food, drink, fashion, and beauty in the city. She's also a regular contributor to *Las Vegas Magazine* as well as *USA Today*. When she's not exploring all this city has to offer, she spends her time in the pool she worked so hard to get in her backyard or gardening

 Matt Villano is a writer and editor based in Healdsburg, California. He contributes to *Time* magazine, *The Wall Street Journal, The New York Times, Sunset,* and *Entrepreneur.* He serves as senior editor of the Expedia Viewfinder blog from Expedia. When he's not researching stories or working this guide's Where to Stay chapter (among others), he's playing with his daughters.

 Mike Weatherford came to well prepared for the task revising the Shows and S Trips chapters of this book He's lived in Las Vegas since 1987, is the author of *Cult Vegas—The Weirdest! The Wildest! The Swingin'e Town on Earth,* and, as the entertainment reporter for the *Las Vegas Review-Journal,* sees all the shows.